Instructional Practices That Maximize Student Achievement: For Teachers, By Teachers

William Ribas

Jenny Deane

Scott Seider

Published and distributed by Ribas Publications
9 Shermans Way
Westwood, MA 02090
Website: ribasassociates.com
Phone: 781-551-9120

ISBN 0-9715089-3-3

Dedicated to

Tom Ribas, a loving and devoted son, brother, uncle and godfather. He's always there when you need him
—Bill Ribas

those who have significantly helped me along the way

- my parents, for always believing in me and helping me achieve my fullest potential
- Alan, my husband and best friend, for his unwavering support and his help putting things into perspective
- My sisters, for the lifelong lessons they continue to teach me
- Dr. Lillie Albert, my friend and mentor, for always encouraging me to take things one step further

—Jenny Deane

Bonnie, Ross, Wendy, Selma and Jessica for their support of—and pride in—my passion for teaching.
—Scott Seider

Acknowledgements

The authors would like to thank the following educators for their contributions to this book. They are listed in alphabetical order.

Dr. Lillie Albert, Professor, Boston College, Lynch Graduate School of Education, for her contributions to Chapter 6.

Ms. Jeannette Bastien, Middle School Teacher, Westfield, Massachusetts, for her contributions to Chapter 4.

Ms. Jeanelle Bradshaw, Elementary School Teacher, Boston, Massachusetts, for serving as a reader.

Mary Burchenal, high school teacher, Brookline, MA for her contribution to chapter nine.

Mr. Wayne Chatterton, High School Teacher, Westwood, Massachusetts, for his contributions to Chapter 2.

Ms. Andrea Fowler, Elementary School Teacher, Marblehead, Massachusetts, for her contributions to Chapter 9.

Ms. Lisa Freedman, Special Education Teacher, Westwood, Massachusetts, for her contributions to Chapter 2.

Richard Higgins, High School Teacher, Weymouth, Massachusetts, for his contributions to Chapter 3.

Mr. Roger Grande, High School Teacher, Brookline, Massachusetts, for his contributions to Chapter 1.

Mr. Brian Greenberg, Principal, Leadership Public Schools, Richmond, California, for his contributions to Chapter 2.

Ms. Laurie Levin, Elementary Mathematics Curriculum Leader, Needham, Massachusetts, for her contributions to Chapter 6.

Mr. Michael Mao, High School Teacher, Westwood, Massachusetts, for his contributions to Chapter 5.

Dr. Gail Mayotte, Faculty of Supervision and Instruction, University of Notre Dame, for her contributions to Chapter 6.

Ms. Debbie Mercer, Teacher of the Gifted and Talented and a Literacy Specialist, Brookline, Massachusetts, for her contributions to Chapters 4 and 11.

Ms. Marge Modena, Technology Specialist, Needham, Massachusetts, for her contributions to Chapter 6.

The Needham Public Schools for its contributions to chapter 6

Ms. Emily Parks, Assistant Principal, Westwood, Massachusetts, for her contributions to Chapters 2 and 5.

Ms. Susan Plati, High School Teacher, Brookline, Massachusetts, for her contributions to Chapter 9.

Ms. Carol Rosengarten, Special Education Teacher, Westwood, Massachusetts, for serving as a reader.

Rhonda Ruegar, Principal, Oneida, New York, for serving as a reader.

Mitzi Sales, Middle School Teacher, Westwood, MA for her contributions to chapter 3.

Ms. Joyce Silberman, Elementary Teacher, Needham, Massachusetts, for her contributions to Chapter 4.

Dr. Sheila Cutler Sohn, Educational Consultant for Elementary and Middle School Students in Mathematics, Science, Organizational/Study Skills and Time Management, for her contributions to Chapter 6.

Mr. Matthew Underwood, Teacher, Francis Parker Charter School, Devens, Massachusetts, for his contributions to Chapter 8.

Dr. Chris Whitbeck, Principal, Acton, Massachusetts, for his contributions to Chapter 1.

Mr. Amir Zarrimpar, MD, Ph.D. Candidate, University of California at San Diego, for his contributions to Chapter 8.

About the Authors

William B. Ribas, Ph.D.

Bill Ribas has 26 years experience in Pre-K-12 education. Bill has written two other books, *Maximizing Teaching Success: A Book for Novice Teachers, Their Mentors, and Their Supervisors* and *Teacher Evaluation That Works!!* Bill taught elementary grades 2-5 and middle school grades 6-8. He also has been a curriculum coordinator, a vice principal, a principal, a director of pupil personnel services, and he has served as the assistant superintendent for personnel for the Brookline, Massachusetts, Public Schools.

Currently, Bill is the president of Ribas Associates, a consulting, training and publishing company dedicated to the growth and development of teachers and administrators in ways that

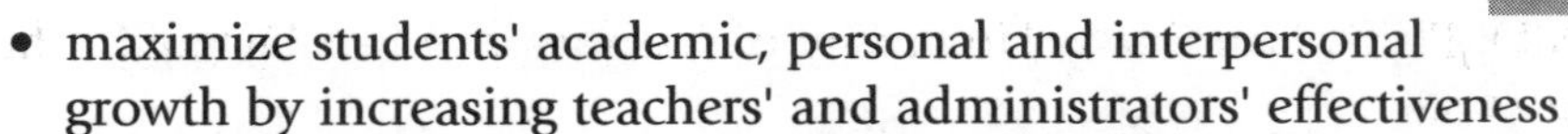

- maximize students' academic, personal and interpersonal growth by increasing teachers' and administrators' effectiveness
- increase teachers' and administrators' job satisfaction by helping educators improve their performance and better meet the needs of all students

Jennifer Antos Deane, Ph.D.

Jenny Deane holds a doctorate from Boston College in curriculum and instruction with an emphasis on math and literacy education in the elementary and middle school classrooms. While working in Braintree, Massachusetts, she was chosen as Teacher of the Year. She also was a classroom teacher in the North Reading and Needham, Massachusetts, Public Schools. She presently works as a mathematics resource teacher in the Needham Public Schools. Jenny has been influential in developing materials and training teachers to extend and remediate mathematics and literacy teaching. She also assists teachers with integrating mathematics and literacy across the curriculum. She authored the article "Daily Journals Connect Mathematics to Real Life" which appeared in the *Journal of Mathematics Teaching in the Middle School*.

Scott Seider, M.Ed.

After graduating from Harvard College with a degree in English and American language and literature, Scott worked as an English and service-learning teacher in the Westwood, Massachusetts, Public Schools. He also served as a summer director of programs for the Phillips Brooks House Association, Harvard University's undergraduate public service organization. Scott is currently working as a part-time administrator at Fenway High School, a Pilot school in the Boston, Massachusetts, Public Schools, while pursuing a doctorate at the Harvard Graduate School of Education where he received the prestigious Presidential Fellowship. Scott's doctoral research focuses on service-learning and how schools can support students in becoming socially responsible citizens.

Table of Contents

Introduction

Objectives for the Introduction

After reading this introduction, the reader will be able to

a. explain the intended purpose of the authors in writing this book
b. explain to a colleague the reason for the move, both nationally and internationally, to standards-based (mastery-based) teaching
c. explain the advantages to students of standards-based (mastery-based) teaching
d. explain the advantages to teachers of standards-based (mastery-based) teaching
e. explain the disadvantages to students when standards-based (mastery-based) teaching is not carefully implemented by schools and school districts
f. find content-specific instructional methods within the various chapters

Purpose of the Book

The decision to write this book stemmed from the frustration expressed to us by many of our teaching and administrative colleagues. Those educators described the difficulty they encountered in finding a book that incorporated into a single reference the current practice and research about instructional strategies that lead to the highest levels of student achievement. For many of these educators, the time needed to read the literally dozens of relevant books on topics such as the brain and learning, differentiated instruction, questioning techniques, assessing student learning, planning, professional development, working with parents, classroom management and the nature of intelligence would require a year's leave of absence just for professional reading. Few educators have such an opportunity. It was our objective to write a book that will do three things for educators:

1. Provide a single, comprehensive book that contains teacher-friendly information on the most current effective instructional strategies;
2. Provide numerous examples of effective classroom strategies already in use by teachers;
3. Include in each chapter a reference list of sources that educators may use to study the topics in each chapter in greater depth.

Choosing the Authors for This Book

We were chosen to write this book in order to ensure expertise in a broad range of student grade levels and academic content areas. We have taught all elementary grades from two through five, middle school grades from six through eight and high school grades from nine through twelve. Our content-specific teaching experience includes reading, writing, mathematics, science and social studies. We also have experience in teaching in urban, suburban and rural schools. In order to ensure that each chapter has relevance to elementary, middle and high school teachers, all three of us have co-written each of the chapters. Because we were aware that even our wide range of practical knowledge was not sufficient, we enlisted a number of other teachers with experience in teaching all grades and disciplines from kindergarten through grade 12 to contribute classroom practices and to comment on drafts of the book.

Content Specific Instructional Methods, Generic Instructional Methods and Grade Level Specific Instructional Methods

We believe that it is important for teachers to know the generic instructional methods that work in multiple disciplines and across grade levels. We further believe that it is important for teachers to know the content-specific instructional methods designed primarily for their specific disciplines and specific grade levels. In this book, we devote a chapter to each of the major areas of effective instruction. Within many of the chapters, we have embedded explanations and examples of many content-specific instructional methods for a variety of grade levels. For example, the chapter on mastery planning contains a sample lesson plan for high school social studies that demonstrates methods that are effective for that grade and discipline. Chapter 1 includes a sample unit plan for middle school science that contains content-specific methods for that grade and discipline. The chapter on assessment contains several examples of content-specific instruction in the area of writing as well as information on student self-assessment in the areas of mathematics and science. It also contains examples for various grade levels from elementary through high school. The chapter on intelligence presents content-specific methods for the teaching of mathematics and reading with examples for grade levels from elementary to high school. To find content-specific and/or grade-specific methods, we encourage you to use the following table.

Table I-1

Chapter	*Page*	*Content Area (e.g. English/Language Arts, Math etc.)*	*Level (ES, MS, HS)*
Introduction			
Chapter 1	pp. 18-23	Social Studies	HS
	pp. 24-28	Science	MS
Chapter 2	p. 50	Physical Education	MS, HS
	p. 50	English and Reading	ES
	p. 43	Science (chemical reaction KWL)	MS, HS
	p. 51	Mathematics (review problem at top of worksheet)	ES
	pp. 36-37	English/Language Arts (adjectives)	ES
	pp. 40-41	Social Studies (Civil War)	MS, HS
	p. 49	Science (Chemistry)	HS
	pp. 49-50	English/Language Arts (old man and sea, punctuation)	HS
	p. 51	Social Studies (Cold war)	HS
	p. 51	Math (multiplication)	ES
	pp. 52-54	English/Language Arts (paragraph writing)	HS
	pp. 57-58	English/Language Arts (DEAR time)	ES
	p. 58	English/Language Arts (short stories)	HS
	pp. 58-59	English/Language Arts (odyssey)	HS
	p. 61	English/Language Arts (poetry)	HS
	p. 61	Math (math journals)	ES
	pp. 61-62	English/Language Arts (odyssey, children's stories)	HS
	p. 62	English/Language Arts (vocabulary)	HS
	p. 62	English/Language Arts (vocabulary)	ES
	p. 62	Math (architect)	ES, MS
	p. 63	Social Studies (labor unions)	HS
	p. 63	Social Studies (newswatch)	ES
	p. 64	English/Language Arts (Shakespeare/Hawthorne)	HS
Chapter 3	p. 84	Science	MS
	p. 85	English/Language Arts	HS
	pp. 88-91	Science	MS
Chapter 4	p. 117	Math	ES
	pp. 118-120	Math	ES
	pp. 121-128	Math	ES
	pp. 129-130	Science	ES
	p. 131	Science	ES
	p. 135	English/Language Arts	ES
	pp. 135-136	Math	ES
	p.138	Math	ES
	p. 139	Science	ES
	pp. 142-145	Science	ES
	p. 146	English/Language Arts	MS
	pp. 147-148	Math	ES
	pp. 149-150	English/Language Arts	MS
	p. 150	Math	MS
	p. 162	Social Studies	MS
Chapter 5	pp. 166-168	English/Language Arts (Raisin in the Sun)	HS
	p. 169	English/Language Arts (parts of speech)	MS
	p. 170	Social Studies (Salem with trials)	HS

	pp. 171-172	Graphic Arts (Do Now)	HS
	pp. 172-173	English/Language Arts (John Donne)	HS
	pp. 173-174	Social Studies (Civil War)	MS, HS
	p. 176	Science (labs)	MS, HS
	pp. 177-178	Social Studies (Civil rights)	HS
	p. 180	Social Studies (Boston tea party)	HS
	p. 181	Math (equations)	HS
	pp. 181-182	English/Language Arts (odyssey, poetry)	HS
	p. 182	Math (fractions)	HS
	p. 182	Social Studies (Boston tea party)	HS
	p. 183	English/Language Arts (Romeo and Juliet)	HS
	pp. 184-185	Social Studies (atomic bomb)	HS
	p. 190	Social Studies (Cold war)	HS
	p. 190	Social Studies (atomic bomb)	HS
	p. 192	Social Studies (WWI)	HS
	p. 193	English/Language Arts (Romeo and Juliet)	HS
	p. 196	English/Language Arts (Of Mice and Men)	HS
Chapter 6	pp. 207-209	English/Language Arts	ES
	pp. 212-213	Math	MS
	pp. 215-216	Math	MS
	p. 220	English/Language Arts	ES, MS
	p. 221	Math	ES, MS
	pp. 224-225	Math	ES, MS
	p. 226	Writing	ES
	p. 231	Math	MS, HS
	p. 232	English/Language Arts	ES, MS
	p.235	English/Language Arts	ES
	pp. 236-239	English/Language Arts	HS
	pp. 239-240	Science	HS
Chapter 7	pp. 261-262	English/Language Arts	ES,MS,HS
	pp. 268-274	English/Language Arts	ES,MS
	pp. 274-277	English/Language Arts	MS,HS
	pp. 278-280	Mathematics	ES, MS
	pp. 280-281	Mathematics	ES,MS,HS
Chapter 8	pp. 290-291	English/Language Arts	ES, MS, HS
	pp. 291-293	Mathematics	ES, MS, HS
	p. 335	Music (left brain, right brain)	ES, MS, HS
Chapter 9	pp. 337-343	Science	HS
Chapter 10	pp. 357-361	English/Language Arts	ES, MS
	pp. 361-367	Math	ES, MS, HS
Chapter 11	pp. 390-391	Math (problem of the day)	ES, MS
	pp. 393-394	English/Language Arts	ES
	pp. 396-397	Science	ES

Special Education

We purposely did not include a specific chapter on special education. The special education teachers who assisted with the writing of this book indicated that most of the information and skills described in Chapters 1 through 8 are directly relevant to the teaching of special needs students in the regular education classroom. Throughout the book, however, we have highlighted some of the strategies identified by special educators as most important for special needs students.

A Definition of Standards-Based (Mastery-Based) Teaching

In the last decade, a movement toward standards- or mastery-based teaching has become quite popular. This trend has generated a great deal of discussion about the definition of standards- or mastery-based teaching. There has also been considerable controversy about the advantages and disadvantages of standards-based teaching. Disagreements are often fueled by the lack of a common understanding of the meaning of the words and phrases *high expectations, teaching the standards, teaching to mastery* and others. The next part of this introduction explains our definitions of these words and phrases.

The terms **standards-based teaching** and **mastery-based teaching** are often used interchangeably in the literature. In this book, we continue to use the terms interchangeably only as the title for the collective group of teaching methods that have been proven to ensure the highest level of student acquisition of usable information and skills. Using this definition, you might argue that teachers have always taught for mastery. It would be hard to find an era in the history of education when it wasn't a teacher's wish to impart to students usable information and skills, however, what we may have lacked is well structured, specifically articulated and coordinated standards (among and within disciplines) for curriculum and instruction.

We define **standard** as the list of information and skills that have been identified as important for students to acquire. Standards are usually established by the federal government, the state (or provincial) government or local school districts. Although these government entities customarily include teachers on the committees that develop the standards, the average classroom teacher gives little or no input into what standards are identified as important for students to learn. From the perspective of most teachers, standards are established externally.

The **curriculum standards** are the learning and behaviors students are expected to know and use. The curriculum standards typically contain the body of information and skills that must be mastered. They articulate the level of quality and quantity that must be demonstrated to show mastery. **Behavior standards** include behavior in the classroom (e.g., independent, group or partner work) and in other school locations and events (e.g., walking to lunch, working in the library attending a school sporting event).

Mastery is the level to which our students have acquired the information and skills identified in the standards. Mastery comes at six levels: The first level is **Introduction** (a.k.a. exposure). A student is at the introduction level immediately after the information and/or skill in the standard has been presented to the student for the first time. At this level, there is no expectation that the student will be able to demonstrate mastery of the standard. The second level is **Guided practice**. At this level we expect that the student can demonstrate the knowledge or skill only with prompting from the teacher or another person who has mastered the standard. The third level is **Immediate mastery**. At this level the student can demonstrate the information or skill of the standard independently shortly after the teacher has presented the information or skill of the standard. **Immediate application mastery** is when the student is able to use the information and skill in an unfamiliar setting shortly after the presentation of the concept. **Mastery** is when the student can demonstrate the information or skill after a period of time has passed since the standard was taught. **Application mastery**[1] is when the student can demonstrate mastery after a period of time and in an unfamiliar situation.

Figure I-1, shows the typical progression students follow as they learn new information and skills. It is important to note two of the factors that make teaching so complex.

1. All students *do not* follow the same path to application mastery.
2. All students *do not* move through these steps at the same pace.

Chapter 4 discusses the strategies that teachers may use to differentiate their instruction to accommodate these variations among students.

Figure I-1

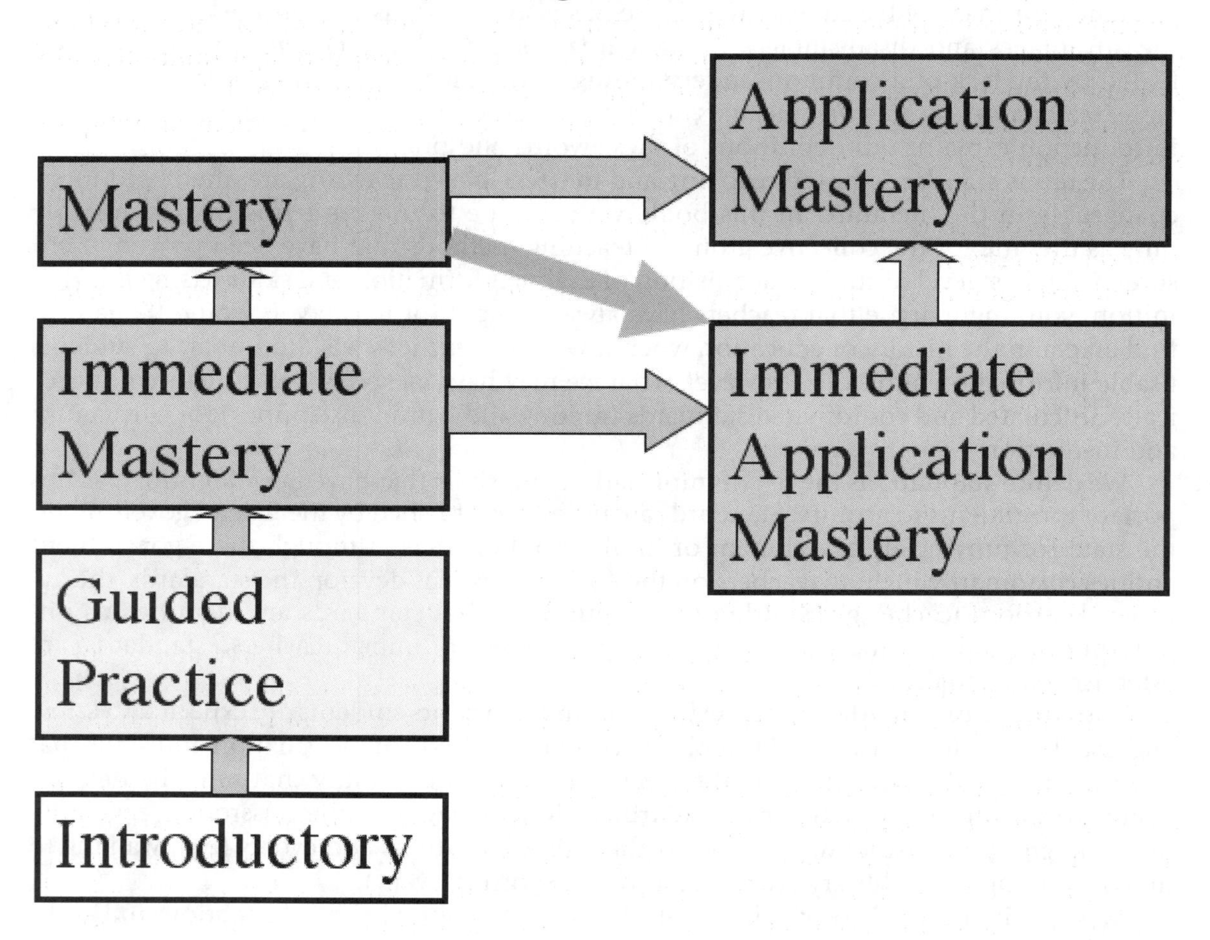

[1] In chapter 4, you will learn about Bloom's taxonomy which identifies a hierarchy of categories about the application level.

To better understand the six levels of mastery, let's look at the example of teaching the following standard.

> "By the end of the period, students will be able to successfully complete a two-digit multiplication problem using clusters."

Students in the class are at the introduction level, the point at which the teacher has first presented all the steps to completing a two-digit multiplication example. Often the next step in teaching this concept is to have the students complete one or more examples in class. Those students who can correctly complete the example with only one or more prompts from the teacher or with the assistance of a peer are at the guided practice level. Those students who can correctly complete the example independently are at the immediate mastery level. Those students who can complete the assigned problem and the two-digit multiplication story problem given for extension are at immediate application mastery level. Those students who can complete a two-digit multiplication algorithm two weeks[2] later are at the mastery level. Those students who can write and solve their own two-digit multiplication story problem two weeks later are probably at the application mastery level.

An **expectation** is the level of mastery that the teacher believes a student or group of students can reach on a given standard. Setting high expectations is a two-step process. A teacher's first step is having the belief that the students can master the standard at the highest level. His or her second step is employing those teaching methods that result in the highest level of mastery.

The level of mastery that students reach is impacted primarily by the following five factors:

1. The teacher's instructional skill level;
2. The level of student motivation,
   a. those areas the teacher can impact
   b. those areas the teacher cannot impact;
3. The level of previous learning the students bring to the class (from home, school or other environments);
4. The resources that the teacher has available to use in teaching the standards;
5. Students' physical, cognitive or emotional disabilities.

The first item, teacher's instructional skill level, is completely within our control as teachers. We can always become more skillful at our teaching as a result of self-reflection, peer-reflection, participation in workshops, books and other forms of professional development.

The second item, student motivation, is partly within our control and partly influenced by factors outside of our control (e.g., home, peers, content to be learned). We have the ability to teach in ways that increase the level of student motivation. We can work with parents in ways that make them more effective participants in motivating students to work hard. And we can work within our classroom environment to increase the level of peer encouragement of hard work and high achievement. We can increase our skills in all of these areas with appropriate professional development.[3]

We recognize that this still leaves important components out of the teacher's control, however, we believe that whatever the status of those factors not in our control, we can increase the level of student mastery in our classroom by increasing our effectiveness in those

---

[2] We use two weeks only for the purpose of this example. Research will indicate that differing periods of time may be more appropriate for various information and skills.

[3] We define professional development as workshops, courses, peer reflection and discussion (e.g., peer observing or lesson study), self reflection (e.g., reflection journals and other forms of classroom research), reading and other techniques for improving our teaching skills.

areas that *are* in our control. For example, let's look briefly at the *resource* of class size. The size of classes in most schools is driven more by the availability of money for the school budget than by other factors. We believe that students will reach higher levels of mastery in a class of fifteen than in a class of thirty-five if items 1, 2 and 3 above are equal. We also believe that whether the class has fifteen or thirty-five students, there are skills the teacher can use to increase the students' levels of mastery. The more skilled the teacher is, the higher is the level of mastery that students can reach. This book is designed to help teachers increase their teaching skill levels and thereby increase their students' levels of mastery of the standards.

Since the days of Aristotle, we have believed that skilled teachers cause students to achieve at higher levels than less skilled teachers. It is only in the last decade that the work in value-added testing has given us quantitative proof that the skill of the teacher correlates with the level of student achievement. Value-added testing programs are another area about which there is a great deal of discussion and debate. We don't advocate for or against the use of such testing programs, however, we do wish to share with you the following statistical evidence that value-added research has provided us about the impact of good teaching on student achievement. The following paragraphs from Stronge and Tucker (2000, p.2) describe some of this evidence.

> "When children, beginning in third grade, were placed with three high performing teachers in a row, they scored, on average at the 96th percentile on Tennessee's statewide mathematics assessment at the end of fifth grade.
>
> When children with comparable achievement histories starting in third grade were placed with three low performing teachers in a row, their average score on the same mathematics assessment was at the 44th percentile."[4]

We are in an era of educational accountability which is increasingly governed by state laws and federal legislation (such as the No Child Left Behind Act) that requires quantitative proof of student achievement against set standards such as the proof noted above.

Advantages of Teaching for Mastery as Defined Above

Prior to writing this book, we worked with thousands of teachers in dozens of school districts. We have found that teachers who work in districts that have well constructed curriculum standards and in which all the teachers have been trained in the generic and content-specific instructional methods that increase student mastery report the following positive outcomes:

1. Students arrive at the start of the school year having been taught the same information and skills regardless of who their teachers were in previous years.
2. Students arrive at the start of the year with higher levels of information and skills acquired in their prior years of schooling. Not all the students are at the application mastery or mastery levels on all the knowledge and skills. Some students may even be only at the introductory level, however, overall, the level of knowledge and skills is higher than it would otherwise have been.
3. Students have been taught learning strategies that enable them to learn more efficiently and effectively.
4. Students are more motivated to learn new information and skills.
5. When standards are set at appropriate levels, teachers know what students are expected to master by the end of the year. Teachers may then focus on teaching that body of information and skills. The teacher is no longer held accountable for poorly

[4] These findings first appeared in Sanders, W. and Rivers, J. (1996).

defined and limitless amounts of information and skills. It is stressful for teachers when the expectation is that they will teach everyone everything!

6. Students achieve at higher levels on teacher, district and state assessments.
7. Teachers experience greater levels of success and higher job satisfaction.

Districts may perform certain functions to assist teachers in ensuring that students reach the highest levels of mastery. Firstly, curriculum mapping[5] maximizes the effectiveness and efficiency of teaching the standards at all levels. Secondly, appropriate levels of funding for staff enable districts to provide favorable class sizes and support and enrichment programs. Thirdly, high quality professional development ensures that teachers have the highest instructional skill levels. Curriculum mapping, funding levels and district-wide professional development structures are left for discussion in other books. We have written this book to provide each teacher with the generic and content-specific instructional strategies that ensure the highest level of mastery for all of the students in his or her class.

References

Jacobs, H. H. (1997). *Mapping the big picture: Integrating curriculum and assessment K–12.* Alexandria, VA: Association for Supervision and Curriculum Development (ASCD).

Sanders, W. L., & Rivers, J. C. (1996). *Cumulative and residual effects of teachers on future student academic achievement.* Knoxville, TN: University of Tennessee Value-Added Research and Assessment Center.

Stronge, J. H., & Tucker, P. (2000). *Teacher evaluation and student achievement* (p. 2). Washington, DC: National Education Association. (see Sanders)

[5] Curriculum mapping is a process made popular by Heidi Hayes Jacobs. It enables districts to "map" their curriculum to ensure that information and skills are taught as often as needed thus avoiding overteaching or gaps in teaching specific information and/or skills (Jacobs, 1997).

CHAPTER 1

Lesson and Unit Planning That Maximizes Student Growth and Achievement

Objectives for the Chapter

After reading this chapter, the reader will be able to

a. write objectives for a lesson and unit in language that describes what the students will know and be able to do after the teaching is finished
b. write objectives for a lesson and unit in language that enables him or her to readily assess whether or not the objectives have been mastered
c. choose assessments that measure student mastery of the objectives
d. choose activities that maximize student mastery of the objectives

The way in which we do our planning is a window into our thinking about teaching. Many of us were trained to plan in a way that started with focusing on the activities we wanted to do with the students, a process called **activity-based planning.** For example, in activity-based planning, we start by asking ourselves questions such as the following:

1. What can I do to make my teaching interesting for the students?
2. Will I lecture to my students or do some cooperative activity?
3. If I do a cooperative activity, will I have the students in pairs or in groups?
4. If I put the students in groups, how many should be in each group?
5. How will I decide who will be in each group?

The questions above are an important part of any planning process, however, they should come at the end of our planning process rather than at the beginning. Before we decide how we are going to teach, we need to be very clear as to what we want students to know and be able to do by the end of the lesson or unit. Our next step is to choose assessments that tell us during and at the end of the lesson or unit what information and skills each student has mastered. It is only then that we should turn our focus to structuring the activities for teaching the information and skills. For many of us, planning in a way that focuses on student outcomes first, rather than classroom activities first, requires a change in our thinking about teaching. We have been so programmed to start with the activities that we must consciously push ourselves to invert this process each time we plan. Eventually, this shift in thinking will become natural and automatic, but old habits die hard, and even the best veteran teachers must operate on an introductory level when first making this transition in their planning.

Before we decide how we are going to teach, we need to be very clear as to what we want students to know and be able to do by the end of the lesson or unit.

Mastery-based planning, or what Wiggins and McTighe (1998) call **backward design planning,** is one area in which some new teachers are initially at an advantage. We are now seeing more teachers entering the profession with training in mastery planning during their pre-service education. For these teachers, it is their first training in the techniques of effective planning and, therefore, there is no need to unlearn and relearn, however, the planning challenges for new teachers are still greater than those for veteran teachers for three reasons. First, they do not have the experience to make the fast and effective judgments about the activity-based questions listed previously once they have determined what they want students to know and to be able to do. Second, new teachers usually lack the repertoire of assessment techniques readily available to more veteran teachers. Third, a challenge shared by new teachers, experienced teachers new to a district and teachers who change grade or subject level is knowledge of the specific curriculum standards for the district at their teaching level. For experienced teachers, the challenge is to invert their thinking and begin the planning process with the question, "What do I want the students to know and be able to do by the end of this lesson or unit?"

The Four Basic Steps

Step 1—Be certain that the concepts we are teaching are indeed in our district's curriculum standards.

Step 2—Be specific in your own mind about which standards you want the students to master by the end of the teaching time for which you are planning, and plan teaching that will lead to mastery of these standards.

Step 3—Plan assessments that effectively assess, both formatively and summatively, student mastery of the concepts in your district's standards.

Step 4—Plan activities that maximize student mastery of the concepts and promote high student engagement.

There are many models for mastery planning. Each of these models asks the teacher to use four steps when planning. The first step is for the teacher to teach what is in the school's or district's curriculum standards. To do this, the teacher needs to have the standards readily available when planning. This step may sound rudimentary; however, in busy schools, the curriculum standards often become something we believe we are teaching but find in fact that we are not.

Step 1—Be certain that the concepts we are teaching are indeed in our district's curriculum standards. I have often seen a similar dynamic related to districts' curriculum development and implementation that leads to poor student performance on assessments of students' mastery of the standards. In these districts, the curriculum standards are carefully and painstakingly developed by a committee of teachers and administrators. Upon completion, the standards are given to all of the staff. Some districts do this with great fanfare and other districts send the standards to each teacher with little or no publicity. Some districts conduct considerable professional development programs about these standards and thereby ensure that all the teachers know and are able to use the standards. Others do nothing more than distribute the documents to the teachers. Few districts go back to check the teachers' understanding and use of the specific curriculum standards in the subsequent years after they are released. The documents are often put in a "safe place" by teachers, rarely to be opened again after their initial introduction. The teaching of these standards, by teachers other than the teachers on the development committee, often drifts to topics and information other than that in the standards. This tendency is not due to anyone's deliberate decision not to use the standards. Rather, it is due to the hectic pace of a teacher's day and year which offers little time for reflection on the curriculum documents.

The gap between the district curriculum standards and what is actually taught often becomes more pronounced as new staff members are hired. The newly hired teachers often receive little or no training in the effective implementation of the standards. These teachers are handed the documents and expected to implement them with little or no training. The training given to the entire staff at the implementation stage of the standards, when they were introduced, was designed to deepen teachers' understanding of the context in which the standards were developed and to demonstrate the effective implementation of the standards. Teachers hired after this implementation stage may never receive this training. The lack of comprehensive training and understanding, such as that given upon the implementation of the standards, leads to the teaching of concepts that are not in the standards or to the teaching of concepts in the standards without adequate depth. As a result, students perform poorly when those standards are assessed.

The first step we must take in our planning is to look at the district curriculum and choose the information and skills we will teach from those standards.

Step 2—Be specific in your own mind about which standards you want the students to master by the end of the teaching time for which you are planning and plan teaching that will lead to mastery of these standards. The second step is for the teacher to be clear about the specific information and skills in those standards he or she wants the students to know and be able to do at the end of the teaching time. As we visit schools, we see a lot of great instruction preceded by hours of planning that, unfortunately, either does not teach all the information and skills that are in the curriculum or only introduces the information and skills and does not teach them to mastery. This problem may be avoided by reviewing the curriculum standards documents, deciding what information and skills are most important for students to master at the highest levels and focusing our planning on a clear vision of what we want students to know and be able to do by the end of the teaching time.

Step 3—Plan assessments that effectively assess, both formatively and summatively,[1] student mastery of the concepts in your district's standards. The third step is to plan

[1] Chapter 6 contains a comprehensive explanation of strategies for effective assessment.

assessments that enable the teacher to determine what students know and are able to do as related to the material that has been determined as important in steps 1 and 2 above. The assessment should be both formative and summative. **Formative assessments** are the ways in which the teacher assesses student progress toward mastery during the teaching. **Summative assessments** are those assessments teachers use to assess the students' learning after the teaching is completed. Before we can assess a topic effectively we must be clear in our own mind about our desired outcomes. It is only then that we will be able to effectively assess what we want students to know and be able to do.

An example of this step is that of two teachers we worked with who were teaching the same curriculum standards in the same district. The mastery objectives in the curriculum were the following.

By the end of this unit, the students will be able to

a. given a diagram of a human skeleton, label at least fifteen bones in the human body
b. explain the function of hinge, ball and socket and glide joints in the human body
c. given a diagram of a human skeleton, identify at least one hinge, one ball and socket and one glide joint.

One teacher prepared an elaborate summative assessment that required students to first draw the skeleton. They then needed to cut pieces of paper to sizes that matched the labels they wished to write on those pieces of paper. They were asked to paste labels for the parts noted in a, b and c on the appropriate parts of the skeleton.

The second teacher gave the students a choice of how best to label the parts noted above. They could either use the skeleton diagram she gave them or, for students who wished to draw, they could draw their own skeletons and label the parts. The teacher was careful to *guide* those students who would struggle with the act of drawing their own skeletons toward using the pre-drawn skeleton diagram.

After the assessment was given, both teachers brought the student work to a group of colleagues to discuss their assessment activities. The first teacher indicated that students spent a great deal of time trying to accurately draw the skeleton. Many of the drawings were of poor quality, and this made it difficult for the students to label the parts. Other students found it difficult to cut labels to the correct size, so they spent a great deal of time cutting the labels. It was difficult for the teacher to assess what the students knew of the standards stated above because their performance was hindered by their ability to draw, cut and paste.

Upon discussion, it became apparent to the first teacher that her assessment more accurately assessed the students' ability to

a. draw a human skeleton,
b. cut paper shapes to a size that matched the text for the appropriate label, and
c. paste the labels neatly on the diagram.

The students completing the first teacher's assessment did have a lot of fun and were actively engaged in the assessment, however, the activity did not effectively assess what students knew about the bones and joints of the human body. The second teacher's assessment gave an accurate representation of what the students knew or did not yet know about the concepts noted above.

Step 4—Plan activities that maximize student mastery of the concepts and promote high student engagement. Chapters 2 through 8 contain numerous examples of classroom strategies that maximize student mastery and engagement. We have distilled the recommended steps into the five-question template described below. There are many variations of this template in mastery or backward design planning; however, all contain the same basic concepts.

> 1. *What do I want the students to know and be able to do by the end of the lesson (my mastery objectives)?*
>
> 2. *What is the district curriculum standard or framework from which these concepts are derived?*
>
> 3. *How will I formatively and summatively assess the students' level of mastery of these concepts?*
>
> 4. *Describe the sequence of events in the lesson.*
>
> 5. *If a colleague were observing my class to give me ideas for improving the teaching of this lesson, what would I want the colleague to focus on during the observation?*

1. What do I want the students to know and be able to do by the end of the lesson (my mastery objectives)? Mastery objectives list the content of the curriculum in language describing student products and performances that can be observed and, therefore, assessed. Words such as *know, think about* and *understand*[2] are not observable and, so, are difficult to assess. Words with observable outcomes such as *describe, memorize, select, list, define, label, state, locate, identify, recite, match, rewrite, illustrate, apply, sow, paint, sketch* and *name* allow the teacher to observe whether or not the student has reached mastery and, therefore, can be assessed formatively and summatively. Some words that may be used to articulate objectives related to higher level thinking skills are *organize, summarize, dramatize, distinguish, interpret, appraise, judge, classify,* and *hypothesize.* For more information on developing higher levels of thinking, see Chapter 5.

Well written curriculum typically contains objectives written in mastery form. Later in this chapter, you will see a page from an eighth-grade curriculum in which the objectives are written in mastery form.

Mastery objectives should be given to the students at the start of the lesson or unit. Telling the students what they will be expected to know and be able to do by the end of the teaching will give them a context within which to understand the concepts as they are presented. Chapter 2 explains the positive impact on student achievement when we give students the mastery objectives at the start of the lesson and unit.

Since we tell the students the mastery objectives at the outset of the lesson, mastery objectives should be written in language that is easily understood by the students. Most curricula are written for adults, as they should be. The mastery objectives may, therefore, contain multiple concepts or language too complex for the students to understand. In those circumstances, we will need to divide the objectives into smaller parts that the students can understand. Later in this chapter is a lesson plan from a unit on the Renaissance. You will see that the teacher has written several mastery objectives to teach about Machiavelli, a piece of the multiple component standard that was written in the curriculum document.

The mastery objectives in the curriculum also may be written in language too difficult for the students to comprehend. The language of the curriculum objectives for high school students may be used as it appears in the curriculum, however, the language in elementary curricula is often too difficult for those students to understand. In those cases, the language will need to be translated into words the students can understand.

---

[2] In their book, *Understanding by Design*, which we highly recommend, authors Jay McTighe and Grant Wiggin suggest using the word *understand* in objectives. We prefer that teachers instead use words that indicate observable performance such as those noted in this section.

Sample Mastery Objectives

Kindergarten

1. By the end of the lesson, students will be able to retell a short story and identify the beginning, middle and end parts (language arts).
2. By the end of the lesson, students will be able to count, sort and classify objects (math).
3. By the end of the lesson, students will be able to describe details and state similarities and differences among objects (science).
4. By the end of the lesson, students will be able to identify water and land on a globe (social studies).

Language the students can understand (number 1)

By the end of the lesson, you will be able to tell a story after I have told (or read) it to you. You will be able to tell me what part is the beginning, what part is the middle and what part is the end of the story (language arts).

Grade 2

1. By the end of the lesson, students will be able to explain their reasons for an opinion about a story or an idea (language arts).
2. By the end of the lesson, students will be able to locate information on a simple bar graph (math).
3. By the end of the lesson, students will be able to handle whiffle ball equipment safely (physical education).
4. By the end of the lesson, students will be able to explain a conclusion they reached based on their observations of a demonstrated experiment (science).

Language the students can understand (number 1)

By the end of the lesson, you will be able to tell me *why* you like or don't like a story I read to you (language arts).

Grade 5

1. By the end of the lesson, students will be able to draw outlines or graphic organizers (on paper or electronically) to organize their ideas (language arts).
2. By the end of the lesson, students will be able to write addition, subtraction, multiplication and division problems from information in the science and/or social studies curriculum (math).
3. By the end of the lesson, students will be able to perform an eight-measure solo on the recorder on pitch, in rhythm and with correct posture and hand technique (music).
4. By the end of the lesson, students will be able to use graphic organizer software to visually represent collected data (science/computers).

Language the students can understand (number 2)

By the end of the lesson, you will be able to write addition, subtraction, multiplication and division problems from the data in the social studies unit on immigration (math).

Grade 7

1. By the end of the class, you will be able to search a database and extract specific information (computers).
2. By the end of the class, you will be able to create timelines using the designated timeline software (social studies/computers).
3. By the end of the class, you will be able to mix and use neutral colors with tempera paint (art).
4. By the end of the unit, you will be able to demonstrate the laboratory safety and emergency procedures for the use of hot plates, eye safety goggles, chemicals, laboratory glassware and lab specimens (science).

Grade 9

1. By the end of the class, you will be able to translate a McDonald's menu and correctly pronounce all the items (foreign language).
2. By the end of the unit, you will be able to write a convincing argument and support its claims with detailed evidence (language arts).
3. By the end of the class, you will be able to calculate the percent increase or decrease in different situations (math).
4. By the end of the class. you will be able to explain the major goals of the New Deal programs as they related to industry, workers and farmers (social studies).

2. What is the district's curriculum standard or framework from which these concepts are derived? As stated earlier, this often appears to be a rudimentary step, however, teachers' planning often strays from the actual curriculum standards as time passes since the adoption of those standards. In the following lesson plan and unit plan,you will see the improvement in the quality of the lesson plan when the teacher refocuses on the curriculum standards. Students are not going to do well on assessments if we are not teaching the curriculum objectives which the assessments are designed to assess.

3. How will I formatively and summatively assess the students' level of mastery of these concepts? Effective assessment includes techniques for both formative assessment and summative assessment. Formative assessments are the ways in which the teacher assesses student progress toward mastery during the teaching. In chapter five, we discuss the use of questioning techniques to assess student knowledge and mastery.

Summative assessments are those assessments teachers use to assess the students' learning after the teaching is completed. Thess types of assessments involve judging final products or performances. In recent years, we have significantly improved our ability to assess student products and performances. Of particular note is the wider implementation of rubrics. In chapter six, we explain effective and time-efficient strategies for the development and use of rubrics and other assessments.

4. Describe the sequence of events in the lesson. It is at this point that we decide upon the best activities for teaching the concepts we have identified. Our choice of the best activities should be driven by the desired outcomes.

5. If a colleague were observing my class to give me ideas for improving the teaching of this lesson, what would I want him or her to focus on during the observation? Professional developers have increasingly become aware of the importance of teacher self-reflection and coaching in the development of new and veteran teachers. The importance of self-reflection and peer coaching was recently affirmed in the 1999 Milken Family Foundation Report, "A Matter of Quality." It quotes the National Center for Education Information's, "Profiles of Teachers in the U. S. Survey" (1996), in which educators identified the five most valuable factors in developing competency to teach as follows:[3]

• Own teaching experience	92%
• Courses in the subject taught	73%
• Other teachers	72%
• Studying on one's own	43%
• Education methods courses	37%

[3] Teachers rated eight different professional development options as *very valuable, somewhat valuable, not very valuable, not at all valuable* or *not applicable.* Teachers were permitted to give any of the ratings to more than one professional development option.

It is for this reason that we include question 5 in the planning process. This question pushes us to analyze what we are teaching through the lens of another person. Even when no other professional is in our room to observe (which is usually 95% to 99% of the time when we are teaching), asking ourselves this question helps to stimulate our self-reflection and improve our planning and teaching. Chapters 10 and 11 contain information on professional development structures in which teachers assess their practice individually or with peers.

Three Lesson Plans That Illustrate the Transformation From Activity-Based Planning to Mastery-Based Planning

Most of us learned in our pre-service training that all teaching requires lesson plans and unit plans. We learned that the definition of a lesson plan was a teaching activity that could be conducted in one class period in middle school and high school or in a single contiguous time block in elementary school. Lesson plans are not restricted to this definition, however; a single lesson plan may take several periods or larger blocks of time. In some cases, lesson plans interconnect in a way that makes it difficult to clearly determine when one lesson ends and another begins. Thinking about our teaching in lessons and units is helpful for effective planning, however, the time it takes to teach these lessons should be determined by the concepts in the curriculum we need to teach rather than by the period of time the schedule allows for one class period.

The time it takes to teach these lessons should be determined by the concepts in the curriculum we need to teach rather than by the period of time the schedule allows for one class period.

To illustrate the difference between activity-based lesson planning and mastery-based lesson planning, we have included three plans for the same lesson. Each of these plans is a lesson in ninth grade social studies that addresses the following standard:

> Ninth-Grade History Curriculum Framework Page 54:
> Students will be able to describe the origins and development of the Renaissance including the influence and accomplishments of Machiavelli, Michelangelo, Leonardo da Vinci, Raphael, Shakespeare and Johannes Gutenberg. Students will be able to explain how these concepts relate to current events.

Lesson Plan 1 is written with an activity focus rather than a mastery focus. You will note that the bulk of the lesson plan talks about what the teacher and students will do. There is no specific identification of the information or skills the students are expected to acquire as a result of this lesson.

Lesson Plan 1

Objective: In groups, students will discuss a passage from Machiavelli's *The Prince*.

Steps to the Lesson

1. Sitting in groups, students will take a very brief self-assessment[4] (Machiavellian language simplified and disguised). In groups, students will discuss their responses to the questions. Highlight one response from each group and allow for full class exchange.
2. In groups, students will read a selection from *The Prince* aloud.

[4] The self-assessment given to the students and the passage from *The Prince* they were asked to read can be found after the sample lesson plans.

3. Students will answer the following questions (according to Machiavelli) in their groups.
   - Why should a prince be concerned with warfare?
   - Should a prince be cruel? Why or why not?
   - How should a prince utilize fear? Why?
   - How should a prince regard property?
   - Why did Machiavelli write *The Prince*?
4. As a whole group, students will discuss the question, "Does the end justify the means?"
5. The teacher will present a contemporary example for discussion.
6. Return to self-assessment. Connect questions to Machiavelli.

Lesson plan 2 is the same lesson. This lesson differs from lesson plan 1 because the teacher used the five-question template as the structure for the lesson plan. The result is that the first part of the lesson talks about the learning that should take place rather than the activities. The wording of the objectives for learning, however, uses words such as *comprehend* and *strengthen* which are difficult to observe. You will also notice that the assessment question is answered with only a summative assessment. There is no indication of how the teacher will formatively assess during the teaching so he or she may make instructional decisions.

Lesson Plan 2

Niccolo Machiavelli and Political Theory During the Renaissance

Unit: The Renaissance and Reformation

The students will know and be able to

- comprehend the key ideas of Machiavelli (from *The Prince*)
- strengthen primary source reading skills
- self-assess and critically analyze his or her own political theory and strengthen skills in defending a position
- make Machiavelli relevant to today

What district curriculum standard does this lesson address?
Renaissance, Machiavelli, political theory, forming opinions

How will I formatively and summatively assess the students' level of mastery of these concepts?
Students are presently working on essays and will not be given homework on today's lesson. Students will be asked to reflect, at end of the lesson, on their personal political theories as they relate to Machiavelli's.

List the activities that will take place during the lesson.

1. Sitting in groups, students will take a very brief self-assesment (with Machiavellian language simplified and disguised). In groups, students will discuss responses. They will highlight one response from each group and allow for full class exchange.
2. In groups, students will read selections from *The Prince* aloud.

3. Students will answer the following questions. According to Machiavelli,
   a. Why should a prince be concerned with warfare?
   b. Should a prince be cruel? Why or why not?
   c. How should a prince utilize fear? Why?
   d. How should a prince regard property?
   e. Why did Machiavelli write *The Prince*?
4. Discuss as whole group. Present the question, "Does the end justify the means?" Present a contemporary example.
5. Return to self-assessment. Connect questions to Machiavelli.

What information about your teaching or the students would be most helpful to you in self-assessing your teaching in this lesson?

1. Did lesson extend well (from personal to Machiavelli to contemporary)?
2. Was time managed well?
3. Was there enough time to manage content and understanding?

Lesson plan 3 was written after the teacher received a day of training in mastery planning.

Lesson Plan 3

Niccolo Machiavelli and Political Theory During the Renaissance

Unit: The Renaissance and Reformation

What do I want the students to know and be able to do?
By the end of this class the students will be able to

- demonstrate comprehension of the following key ideas of Machiavelli (from *The Prince*)
  a. the end does not justify the means
  b. using authority unjustly is not acceptable
- strengthen the following primary source reading skills
  a. identify a specific effect or acquire specific information from a primary source passage
  b. articulate the realization that the author's ideas may not immediately reveal themselves
  c. state the belief that their struggle to understand the author's ideas is worth it because the knowledge that is acquired is important
  d. describe how the passage relates to their own lives
- describe their self-assessment and critical analysis of their own political theories
- demonstrate skills in defending a position
- explain how Machiavelli's lessons are relevant to today's political events

What district curriculum standard does this lesson address?

Ninth-Grade History Curriculum Framework Page 54:
Describe the origins and development of the Renaissance, including the influence and accomplishments of Machiavelli, Michelangelo, Leonardo da Vinci, Raphael,

Shakespeare and Johannes Gutenberg. Students will be able to explain how these concepts relate to current events.

How will I formatively and summatively[5] assess the students' level of mastery of these concepts?

1. During the group discussions, I will circulate around the room and listen to the discussions.
2. The verbal class reports from the groups will help me assess the level of student understanding.
3. Students will be asked to reflect, at end of the lesson, on their personal political theories as they relate to Machiavelli's ideas.

List the activities that will take place during the lesson.

1. Students will sit in the same groups they have been working with on their research papers.
2. I will do a brief check-in with the groups on the progress of their research papers.
3. Students will take a very brief self-assessment using Machiavellian language that has been simplified and disguised. See attached self-assessment.
4. In the groups, they will discuss their responses.
5. Discuss one response from each group and allow for full class exchange.
6. In groups, read selected paragraphs from *The Prince* aloud (see attached paragraphs).
7. Answer the following questions in each group, according to how Machiavelli would answer the questions.
   a. Why should a prince be concerned with warfare?
   b. Should a prince be cruel? Why or why not?
   c. How should a prince utilize fear? Why?
   d. How should a prince regard property?
   e. Why did Machiavelli write *The Prince*?
8. Discuss as a whole class. Present the question, "Does the end justify the means?" for discussion in the groups.
9. Discuss the answers to this question with the whole class.
10. Present contemporary examples of political situations and discuss how they apply to Machiavelli.
11. Return to the self-assessment. Connect the questions and comments from the assessment and the contemporary examples to Machiavelli.
12. In their groups, students will reflect on how their personal political theories relate to Machiavelli. These personal theories will be shared at the end of class or in the next class depending on the time that is available

What information about your teaching or the students would be most helpful to you in self-assessing your teaching in this lesson?

- Did the lesson perform well in connecting their personal political theories to Machiavelli's ideas and to contemporary political events?
- Was the time managed well?
- Was there enough time to teach the content and ensure student understanding?

[5] Chapter 6 contains a comprehensive explanation about assessing student work. It provides a definition of formative assessment and summative assessment. Each definition is followed by a list of assessments in each category.

Pre-Modern World History, Mr. Grande
Unit VII: The Renaissance and Reformation

Political Theory Self-Assessment

Mark a score of 1–5 for each statement.
1=never true/strongly disagree
2=rarely true, disagree
3=somewhat true, generally agree
4=frequently true, usually agree
5=always true, strongly agree

1. ______ Nice people always get ahead eventually. Being kind will always earn someone's respect.

2. ______ It's better for people to fear you somewhat than to simply love you. People who love you may easily take advantage of you.

3. ______ The President should demonstrate that he is human too—that he may cry when people are hurt and that he may not always know the answer. Such a president will be loved by his fellow citizens.

4. ______ A good leader needs to be strong and respected, even if it means that the leader is feared by her people. No one will hate a leader who is feared.

5. ______ Peace is not worth it if you have to kill or act unjustly to obtain it.

6. ______ It is important to get what you need in life—more important than how you get it.

7. ______ Although it may be difficult sometimes, people should put their families first during difficult times.

8. ______ People should value their property above all else, as this will result in a secure society, even if it means having some conflict with people around you.

______ Total

Excerpts from *The Prince* by Niccolo Machiavelli
Niccolo Machiavelli (1469–1527) was born in Florence, the son of a struggling lawyer. As a young boy he received a solid humanist education and excelled in his studies. At age 25, he served the Republic of Florence, an Italian state, as a diplomat and political advisor. Although he mingled with many powerful people, his career was cut short when the

Republic was overthrown in 1512. Machiavelli was jailed, tortured and finally exiled. The following year, he wrote *The Prince,* which is Machiavelli's theory on the art of governance and, specifically, on the role of a prince. He wrote it to gain favor among rulers and be restored to a prominent political role.

Source: Machiavelli, N. *The prince.* (W. K. Marriott, Trans.). Retrieved: March 29, 2004 from http://www.constitution.org/mac/prince00.htm (Original work published 1505)

CHAPTER XIV: That Which Concerns A Prince On The Subject Of The Art Of War
A prince ought to have no other aim or thought, nor select anything else for his study, than war and its rules and discipline; for this is the sole art that belongs to him who rules, and it is of such force that it not only upholds those who are born princes, but it often enables men to rise from a private station to that rank. And, on the contrary, it is seen that when princes have thought more of ease than of arms they have lost their states....For among other evils which being unarmed brings you, it causes you to be despised, and this is one of those ignominies against which a prince ought to guard himself....And therefore a prince who does not understand the art of war, over and above the other misfortunes already mentioned, cannot be respected by his soldiers, nor can he rely on them. He ought never, therefore, to have out of his thoughts this subject of war, and in peace he should addict himself more to its exercise than in war; this he can do in two ways, the one by action, the other by study.

CHAPTER XVII: Concerning Cruelty And Clemency, And Whether It Is Better To Be Loved Than Feared
Coming now to the other qualities mentioned above, I say that every prince ought to desire to be considered clement and not cruel. Nevertheless he ought to take care not to misuse this clemency. Cesare Borgia was considered cruel; notwithstanding, his cruelty reconciled the Romagna, unified it, and restored it to peace and loyalty....Therefore a prince, so long as he keeps his subjects united and loyal, ought not to mind the reproach of cruelty; because with a few examples he will be more merciful than those who, through too much mercy, allow disorders to arise, from which follow murders or robberies....And of all princes, it is impossible for the new prince to avoid the imputation of cruelty, owing to new states being full of dangers....

Upon this a question arises: whether it be better to be loved than feared or feared than loved? It may be answered that one should wish to be both, but, because it is difficult to unite them in one person, is much safer to be feared than loved, when, of the two, either must be dispensed with...and as long as you succeed they are yours entirely; they will offer you their blood, property, life and children....For love is preserved by the link of obligation which, owing to the baseness of men, is broken at every opportunity for their advantage; but fear preserves you by a dread of punishment which never fails.

Nevertheless a prince ought to inspire fear in such a way that, if he does not win love, he avoids hatred; because he can endure very well being feared whilst he is not hated, which will always be as long as he abstains from the property of his citizens and subjects and from their women. But when it is necessary for him to proceed against the life of someone, he must do it on proper justification and for manifest cause, but above all things he must keep his hands off the property of others, because men more quickly forget the death of their father than the loss of their patrimony.

Unit Planning

Mastery unit plans can be structured in a similar manner to the lesson plans. Unit plans tend to be made up of a series of lessons designed to teach much larger concepts. The following is a page taken from a district curriculum document. The items in italics are addressed in the unit below. Following this page are two examples of unit plans written to address a number of the concepts described in the curriculum document. In the first example, the teacher was asked to use the five-question template but did not receive any training in mastery planning. In the second example, the teacher received a day of training in mastery planning prior to writing the plan.

Sample School District
Science Learning Expectations
Grade Eight

I. Science Skills

During eighth grade, students will be able to demonstrate a variety of science skills. *These skills have been introduced in grade seven and will continue in grade eight. In grade eight, students will develop the ability to transfer these skills to other areas.* For example, students will be able to identify the roles of variables in a specific class lesson, as well as in self-directed experiments and problem-solving activities.

A. Students will demonstrate the ability to design, perform and analyze scientific experiments.

They will be able to

- *formulate questions that lead to experimentation and recognize questions that may be answered without experimentation*
- *demonstrate independent use of the scientific method (stating an objective, forming a hypothesis, creating an experiment and collecting and analyzing data to form a conclusion)*
- *identify the roles of trials, constants, dependent and independent variables in experiments designed and performed by students*
- *construct and interpret data tables and flowcharts to present and understand collected data*
- *describe trends in data even when patterns are not exact*
- *use collected data to create a well reasoned conclusion and generate questions and alternate procedures for further study based on experimental outcomes*
- *use the scientific method to create solutions to technological problems and realize that there is often more than one solution to such problems*

B. Students will demonstrate the ability to work safely and thoughtfully in the laboratory.

They will be able to

- *describe and follow laboratory safety and emergency procedures regarding the use of heat sources, safety goggles, chemicals, glassware*
- *demonstrate organizational skills including managing a science notebook, taking notes from a variety of resources and creating charts for data collection*

Unit planning should be done with the same five-question template used in lesson planning. We recommend that the unit plan be completed prior to starting lesson planning. The objectives in the unit plan should drive the decision as to what standards should be taught in each lesson plan. During the course of planning the lessons, however, the teacher may need to revisit the unit plan. This may occur when the amount of time needed to complete the lessons in the unit is more than the teaching time that is available for the unit. In these circumstances, the teacher should review the objectives in the unit plan and determine which objectives are the highest priorities for the students to master, which objectives are lower priorities and which objectives are interesting material that is connected to the topic but not priorities or high priorities. The highest priority information and skills are those that will result in the highest level of a) student achievement on local, state and national assessments and b) future school, career and personal success. The objectives deemed to be high priorities or lower priorities are ones on which we should focus most of our time and activities.

Unit Plan 1

As you read unit plan 1, you will notice the following:

a. The answer to question 1 is answered with activities rather than with descriptions of the knowledge and skills that the students will acquire.
b. The answer to question 2 has given only a general statement referring to the expectations document.
c. The answer to question 3 contains only summative assessments.
d. The answer to question 5 is too general to allow the teacher to effectively self-assess the student's behavior.

Duration of the Unit: This unit plan will take approximately nine class periods to complete.

1. What do I want the students to know and be able to do by the end of the unit (my mastery objectives)?

a. Build a working water wheel.
b. Explain how a waterwheel can be used as a tool.
c. Explain the characteristics of a waterwheel that efficiently lifts the most weight.
d. Explain the characteristics of a waterwheel that efficiently lifts a set amount of weight in the least amount of time.

2. What is the district curriculum standard or framework from which these concepts are derived? Eighth grade science curriculum expectations

3. How will I formatively and summatively assess the students' levels of mastery of these concepts?

a. Correct and grade the end-of-unit test.
b. Grade the completed waterwheels.

4. Describe the sequence of events in the lesson.

a. Activate students' present knowledge about waterwheels.
b. Set up the lab groups.
c. Demonstrate a working waterwheel using the materials the students will use to build their waterwheels.
d. Explain the materials that each lab group will be given to complete the experiment.

e. Give each group a set of lab materials.
f. Assign half the groups to build a waterwheel that works quickly. Assign the other half of the groups to build a waterwheel that lifts the most nails.
g. Have the students build the waterwheels in groups.
h. Have the students write about their waterwheels in their journals.
i. Have each group demonstrate its waterwheel.

5. **If a colleague were observing my teaching of this unit to give me ideas for improving the teaching of the unit, what would I want the colleague to focus on during their observations?**
   Student behavior

Unit plan 2 was written by the teacher after he received instruction in mastery planning. The teacher was also given the page from the district curriculum standards shown above and was asked to review those concepts prior to answering the questions.

Mastery-Based Unit Plan 2

1. **What do I want the students to know and be able to do by the end of the lesson (my mastery objectives)?**
   a. Use scientific method when presented with a research question (stating an objective, forming a hypothesis, creating an experiment by collecting and analyzing data to form a conclusion).
   b. Identify the roles of trials, constants and dependent and independent variables in experiments designed and performed by students.
   c. Use scientific method to create solutions to technological problems.
   d. Demonstrate that there is often more than one solution to such problems.
   e. Demonstrate the organizational skill of taking notes on the salient information obtained from an experiment in a science notebook.[6]

2. **What is the district curriculum standard or framework from which these concepts are derived?**

   The concepts in the Sample District eighth grade science curriculum learning expectations IA and B that coincide with the objectives noted in 1

3. **How will I determine if the students have mastered the concepts noted in 1 (my plan for assessment of student learning)?**
   a. Observe their group work against the criteria for effective group work found in the rubric for lab group work.
   b. Review the student reflection journals against the criteria stated in the journal rubric.
   c. Correct the end-of-unit test.

4. **Describe the sequence of events in the lesson.**
   a. Activate students' present knowledge about waterwheels.
   b. Transition the students into teacher-determined mixed ability lab groups.
   c. Explain and demonstrate where needed the materials that each lab group will be given to complete the experiment.

[6] The criteria sheet used to teach the students the correct format for lab notebooks follows this plan.

   d. Demonstrate a rudimentary waterwheel made from the same materials the groups have been given and answer any questions the students have about constructing their own waterwheels.
   e. Assign half the lab groups the task of devising a waterwheel that will enable them to explain the characteristics of a waterwheel that efficiently lifts the most weight.
   f. Assign the other half of the lab groups the task of devising a waterwheel that will enable them to explain the characteristics of a waterwheel that efficiently lifts a set amount of weight in the least amount of time.
   g. Assign students to write in their journals what they learned at each step of the construction of the waterwheel and their conclusions.

5. **If a colleague were observing my class to give me ideas for improving the teaching of these standards, what would I want the colleague to focus on during the observation?**

   I would like my colleague to focus on the extent to which all students contribute equally to the project. I would like ideas for getting the uninvolved students to be more involved.

Lab Book Criteria Sheet

The following page contains the criteria sheet used to assess the students' entries into their lab journals. Chapter 6 contains information on developing rubrics and criteria sheets for lessons and units.

WATERWHEELS: LAB BOOK CRITERIA

As you work on the water wheel project, you will keep a detailed journal of your experience. The journal will have different types of entries in it: lab write-ups, drawings, plans and reactions. Please use the information below to guide your work.

My Lab Book entry is a
lab write-up—go to A.
drawing—go to B.
plan or reaction or
observation—go to C.

A. LAB WRITE-UP

- Does my lab have a title, question, hypothesis, materials list, procedure, data chart, data analysis and conclusion?
- Is the Hypothesis based on evidence or experience?
- Does my procedure clearly test my hypothesis?
- Is my procedure in step-by-step format?
- Is my data chart clearly labeled, and have I consistently used the proper units of measurement?
- Are my data analysis and conclusion both written in paragraph form?
- Does my data analysis report what happened and where errors might have been made?
- Does my conclusion answer my question and explain how the data supports or does not support my hypothesis?

B. DRAWING

- Is my drawing large enough to clearly show the detail that I want?
- Have I added written descriptions to make my drawing easier to understand?
- Do I need to show my drawing from different points of view to show what is happening in many places?
- Is my drawing detailed enough so that people can understand what I tried to show?

C. PLAN, REACTION OR OBSERVATION

- Have I chosen the correct format? Is this an informal reaction or should my writing be part of a formal lab?
- Are these notes to myself? If they are, will I understand them later and have I labeled them so that my teacher knows what they are?
- Are these brief reactions to a class question or homework thinking problem? Have I labeled them and included the original question?

Activity for Mastery-Based Lesson Plans

1. Read mastery-based plans 1 and 3.
2. Describe the differences between the plans below.

3. In what way does the planning in mastery plan number 3 better enable the teacher to ensure student mastery of the curriculum standards?

Mastery Lesson and Unit Planning Template

What do I want the students to know and be able to do by the end of the lesson/unit (my mastery objectives)?

What is the district's curriculum standard or framework from which these concepts are derived?

How will I formatively and summatively assess the students' levels of mastery of these concepts?

Describe the sequence of events in the lesson/unit.

If a colleague were observing my class to give me ideas for improving the teaching of this lesson/unit, what would I want the colleague to focus on during the observation?

Conclusion

Teaching for mastery begins with planning for mastery. We need to first be clear about which information and skills in the curriculum are the highest priorities. Second, we need to be clear in our own minds and when communicating to the students about what students will know and be able to do at the end of the teaching. Third, we need to plan formative and summative assessments that enable us to determine each student's level of mastery. Finally, the activities we choose should focus student time on learning the highest priority information and skills.

References

Machiavelli, N. *The prince.* (W. K. Marriott, Trans.). Retrieved: March 29, 2004 from http://www.constitution.org/mac/prince00.htm (Original work published 1505).

Milken, Lowell. (1999). *A matter of quality: a strategy for assuring the high caliber of America's teachers.* Milken Family Foundation.

Ribas, W. (2002). *Teacher evaluation that works!!* Westwood, MA: Ribas Publications.

Saphier, J. & Gower, R. (1997). *The skillful teacher.* Carlisle, MA: Research for Better Teaching.

Whitbeck, C. *Waterwheels: Lab book criteria.* Unpublished manuscript.

Wiggins, G. (1998). *Educative assessment: designing assessments to inform and improve student performance.* San Francisco: Jossey-Bass.

Wiggins, G. & McTighe, J. (1998). *Understanding by design.* Alexandria, VA: Association of Supervision and Curriculum Development.

C H A P T E R

2

Creating a Context for the Learning to Increase Student Understanding, Retention and Motivation

Objectives for the Chapter

After reading the chapter, the reader will be able to

a. use mastery objectives to create a context that leads to deeper understanding and longer retention of independent facts as they appear in the lesson
b. use an agenda to tell students what they will do during the lesson
c. use activators to show students how the information and skills taught in the lesson connect to their previous learning
d. use summarizers to increase student mastery and retention of the information and skills taught in the lesson
e. create increased motivation and retention by explaining to students why the knowledge and skills taught in the lesson are relevant to them

"Well begun is half done."
Benjamin Franklin from *Poor Richard's Almanac*

Introduction

While Chapter 1 focused on the preparation and planning that we as educators need to do in order to begin the school day ready to serve as effective *teachers,* we will turn now in Chapter 2 to the steps we can take to help our students begin a class period, unit or activity in the mindset of effective *learners.* Specifically, we will focus on the pedagogical strategies supported by research that we have used in our own classrooms to help our students more fully understand and then remember the information and skills they learn in class. These strategies fall into two categories: 1) strategies related to how we *present* information to our students or 2) strategies related to how we *prepare* our students to understand and process this information. Behind each one of these strategies is an explanation, from a cognitive perspective, of how each particular strategy supports student learning and retention. Some of these explanations we will discuss in great detail in this chapter; others we will touch upon briefly but withhold a full explanation until Chapter 8, "The Brain and Student Learning."

> *We will turn now in Chapter 2 to the steps we can take to help our students begin a class period, unit or activity in the mindset of effective learners.*

Strategies for Presenting Content

Sharing Mastery Objectives

In Chapter 1, we discussed the use of mastery objectives in lesson and unit planning. To review briefly, **mastery objectives** list the information and skills of a given curriculum in language that describes student products and performances. You will notice that each chapter in this book begins with the mastery objectives for the learning we expect to occur upon reading that chapter. What is the value of beginning each chapter in this way? The answer to this question varies for each reader. Some readers, upon acquiring this book, are willing to dive straight into each chapter with only the chapter's title for guidance. Other readers are more discerning. Before investing the time and energy to read a particular chapter in this book, they want to know precisely what they will get out of it. One reason we have included the mastery objectives at the outset of each chapter is for this second type of reader.

A second reason we have included mastery objectives at the outset of each chapter is to support *all* of our readers in learning and retaining the information presented in these chapters. How do mastery objectives provide this support? In *Accessing the General Curriculum,* Victor Nolet and Margaret McLaughlin (2000, pp. 40–41) explain that "teachers can help their students employ more expert storage strategies when they are clear about the kind of information they want their students to learn and the manner in which students will be asked to use the information." In other words, students are better able to learn and retain information when their teacher explains at the outset of the lesson what students will be expected *to do* with this information. Likewise, our readers are better able to learn and retain the information in each chapter of this book when we include mastery objectives at the outset of each chapter. These mastery objectives provide a context for our readers' learning. While we will discuss learning and memory in greater detail in Chapter 8, we provide this explanation here to show, from a cognitive perspective, why sharing mastery objectives with students (and readers) is an important pedagogical strategy.

> *Students are better able to learn and retain information when their teacher explains at the outset of the lesson what students will be expected to do with this information.*

In reading the earlier description of this book's two types of readers, it may have occurred to you that our students typically fall into these same two categories as well. Some students, upon entering our classrooms, are uninterested in discovering what the upcoming class period will hold. Whether out of a belief that *anything* we teach them will be useful or, in some cases, the opposite belief, some of our students feel no need for a preview of the learning that lies ahead. As is the case with readers of this book, however, there is a second group of students that feels differently. These are the students that, upon entering the classroom, immediately demand to know "what are we doing today?" They might also fire questions at us like the following:

"Are we doing something fun?"
"Are we watching a video?"
"Can we go outside?"
"Are you collecting the homework?"
"Are we going over the homework?"
"Will there be time to review for the test tomorrow?"

The list of these types of questions could go on and on. For these students, the mastery objectives help to answer these questions. And for *all* students, the mastery objectives create a context for the information and skills they are about to learn. As mentioned above, such a context increases the likelihood of students retaining this new learning in their long term memories.

For middle school and high school teachers, our students are often advanced enough that we can simply share our mastery objectives with the class as they exist in our lesson plans. For elementary school teachers, we will likely need to translate the mastery objectives in our lesson plans into language more comprehensible to younger learners. Examples of such translations can be found in Chapter 1.

In what form should we share these mastery objectives? Different teachers utilize different strategies. Some teachers prefer to type up their mastery objectives for a particular unit and then distribute them to students as a handout upon beginning the unit. Students are expected to keep this handout in the front of their binders for the duration of the unit. This technique seems particularly suited to middle and high school teachers for whom a unit may last several weeks. One high school science teacher we know actually has her students slip their mastery objectives handouts into the transparent storage pocket on the front cover of their binders. She wants her students to notice these mastery objectives every time they open their binders, whether at the start of class or when doing their nightly homework.

Other teachers prefer to write the mastery objectives on a large sheet of flipchart paper, and then hang these mastery objectives on the front wall of the classroom in a location where students will notice them. Such a technique has several advantages. First, when students enter the classroom or take their seats, they will immediately notice the mastery objectives for the particular unit or lesson on which they will be focusing. Those students who like to ask "What are we doing today?" will have the answer directly in front of them. A second advantage to posting these mastery objectives at the front of the classroom is explained by Eric Jensen in *Teaching with the Brain in Mind.* Jensen (1998) reports on several research studies that have found that classrooms decorated with educational posters, student work, affirmations, daily agendas, etc. can have a positive impact on learning. He explains that these stimuli serve to "feed the brain" by providing students with an opportunity to continue processing relevant information during the moments when their attention temporarily drifts away from their teacher's direct instruction. More information about students' attention spans can be found in Chapter 8.

Sharing Daily Agendas

For those students who enter class needing to know "what are we going to do today?" the mastery objectives provide only half of the answer. The mastery objectives essentially describe the finished product; they list the content that students in the class will hold and the skills they will be able to perform at the conclusion of the unit or lesson. The **agenda,** in contrast, describes the steps that the class will take to achieve these outcomes. An example of a class's agenda might be the following:

Figure 2-1

Agenda for February 6th, Period 3
1. Collect and answer questions about last night's homework. 2. Record the definition of *adjective* in the "Grammar Terms" section of our notebooks. 3. Do the paper bag activity with partners. 4. Practice finding adjectives in the sentences on the overhead projector. 5. If there is time, get started on the night's homework.

As is the case with mastery objectives, middle and high school teachers will often be able to transcribe the agendas they share with their students word-for-word from their daily lesson plans. In contrast, the agendas that elementary school teachers share with their students may have to be "translated" into language more comprehensible to young learners.

Also similar to mastery objectives is our recommendation that teachers write their daily agendas on the blackboard or on pieces of flipchart paper and then post these papers in easily visible spots on the front wall of their classrooms. Such a practice is in keeping with Nolet and McLaughlin's (2000, p. 34) recommendation that teachers "establish and keep schedules of classroom activities and events, and provide systematic reminders for students of the sequence in which activities will occur." What is the value of keeping students informed about the sequence of activities within a given lesson or class period? First, in situations both inside and outside of school, most of us appreciate knowing what a particular meeting or engagement will involve. We generally expect our principals to provide us with an agenda at the start of faculty meetings and we expect the same from our department heads prior to department meetings. If we don't know how many items are on the agenda or what topic is coming next, we may find it difficult to concentrate on the current topic of discussion. Instead, our mind is preoccupied with whether the meeting will end in time for us to make it to the dry cleaners or whether we are finally going to get to discuss new book orders for next year. Without an agenda, our students can become similarly preoccupied and unable to focus on the instruction that is taking place.

A second way in which an agenda supports student learning relates to Nolet and McLaughlin's mention of keeping students informed about the sequence of activities within a given class period. If you glance back at the sample agenda in Figure 2-1, you can see how providing students with an agenda better enables them to understand how the various pieces of a lesson fit together. In this sample lesson on adjectives, for example, the agenda reveals a logical sequence for learning. Students first learn and write down the definition of adjectives and then do the paper bag activity with partners, an activity in which students must reach into a lunch bag without looking and come up with five words that describe the object hidden inside. Such an activity allows students to connect the definition of *adjective* that they have written in the "Grammar Terms" section of their notebooks with the describing words they come up with during the paper bag activity. Finally, students will work as a class to identify the adjectives in sentences projected onto the front board. Such a lesson moves students from a *definition* to making a *connection* and finally to an *application.* Informing students of this sequence through a posted agenda allows them to better understand the way in which each of these separate activities fits into the teacher's larger goals, the mastery objectives. A teacher who posts his or her daily agenda then is less likely to hear student comments such as, "What's the point of reaching into this paper bag?" or "How does this relate to anything?" If such questions do arise, the teacher can use the agenda as a visual prompt to explain the rationale behind the different parts of the lesson.

Of course, fending off potential complaints is not the primary benefit of allowing students to understand how the various pieces of a lesson connect to each other and to the unit's mastery objectives. As we will discuss in more detail both later in this chapter and then again in Chapter 8, students are better able to transfer information into their long-term memory when teachers help them to recognize "patterns that may exist in soon-to-be-learned information" (Nolet & McLaughlin, 2000, p. 44). In other words, students are better able to commit information to their long-term memory when they understand how a particular piece of information relates to other information they have learned about that same topic as well as to the overarching goals (mastery objectives) for the unit. Posting both an agenda and mastery objectives, then, can provide students with the context they need to transfer the content they are learning into their long-term memory.

Posting both an agenda and mastery objectives, then, can provide students with the context they need to transfer the content they are learning into their long-term memory.

Perhaps just as important for students as understanding the way in which different activities within a class period connect to each other is knowing the different *types* of activities that lie ahead. For example, in the lesson on adjectives, students begin the class with some fairly standard "seat work." They are working independently to transcribe the definition of adjectives into the "Grammar Terms" section of their notebooks. For students who are kinesthetic learners or who are dying to interact with their friends, such an activity can feel like a tedious one. By virtue of posting an agenda, however, those students itching for a more hands-on activity or the opportunity to work with a partner can see that such an activity is just a few moments away. As a result, these students will be better able to concentrate on the task at hand. Were the agenda not posted and these students not provided with information about what the rest of the period holds, they would be more likely to become distracted, begin chatting with neighbors, stand up to sharpen pencils or ask permission to go to the bathroom. And for that student who even with an agenda claims to need to go to the bathroom at some point during every class, we have found that an agenda allows us to say, "You can go as soon as we finish the paper bag activity" or "Can you wait until we are working on sentences on the overhead projector?" Students find such a response far more satisfactory than a vague promise of "I'll let you go later."

One example of a teacher utilizing the agenda to inform his or her students about the different types of activities ahead involves a young colleague of ours with a particularly chatty class of students. In essence, he had difficulty keeping them quiet long enough to provide any direct instruction himself. As a means of solving this problem, our colleague began writing in parentheses after each item on the daily agenda either "teacher talks" or "students talk." His goal in this modification was to help his students understand before the daily lesson had even begun that there would be some points in the lesson at which they would need to listen to his direct instruction and other points in the lesson at which he would solicit their thoughts and insights. While this young colleague of ours has since grown more adept at integrating his direct instruction and students' contributions, this slight modification to the agenda went a long way towards a more orderly environment during his class periods. His chatty students were better able to listen to what their teacher had to say when they could see on the agenda that several opportunities lay ahead for them to contribute to the class discussion.

Finally, posting an agenda also has the positive effect of keeping both us and our students on track over the course of a lesson or class period. The agenda effectively represents what we believe the class should accomplish over the course of the period. Though as teachers we sometimes need to make adjustments to take advantage of a particularly astute question or to explain a particularly difficult concept, the agenda can also remind us not to linger unnecessarily on defining the term *adjective* at the expense of the paper bag activity. And, ironically, we have found that posting an agenda can often lead to our students keeping *us* on track. While it is easy to forget to consult the lesson plan we have created for the day's lesson, posting the agenda involves our students in ensuring that we get through all of the necessary content for that particular class period. Somewhat to our surprise, students really do tend to keep us honest in regard to getting through the activities posted on the agenda. Whether it is because they know that they will need to complete all of these activities in order to successfully complete their nightly homework assignment or because they enjoy the opportunity to good-naturedly chastise their teacher, a good number of our students really do pay attention to the posted agenda and take steps to move the class along if they fear that we are in danger of not getting through the listed activities.

Posting an agenda also has the positive effect of keeping both us and our students on track over the course of a lesson or class period.

Assigning Homework

In the previous section, we shared the point that students are more likely to store the content we are teaching them in their long-term memory when they are informed at the outset of the lesson of 1) what kind of information they will be learning and 2) what they will be expected to do with this information. Providing students with a lesson's mastery objectives allows them to see what kind of information they are about to learn as well as the various skills they will acquire. Providing students with the night's homework assignment *at the outset of the lesson* addresses the second point; such a strategy informs students of what they will be expected to do with the information or skills they acquire.[1]

Providing students with their homework assignment at the beginning of a lesson is likely the opposite of what you recall from your own days as a student. Most of us remember our teachers announcing the homework assignment in the final moments of class or even as the bell signifying the end of the period was ringing. The advantage of such a strategy is that the teacher could adjust that evening's homework assignment based on how much content he or she had covered during the class period. However, educators now recognize that students become more focused, attentive learners throughout the class period when they understand precisely what they will be expected to do that night for homework. Such a benefit seems to outweigh the greater flexibility that comes with announcing the night's homework at the end of the class period or lesson. Of course, on those occasional days when we find we have covered either far more or far less than we expected, we certainly feel free to adjust the homework assignment accordingly at the conclusion of the period. Interestingly, there may be some hidden value in such adjustments. When we announce to our students at the end of the course period that we have decided to adjust the night's

Students become more focused, attentive learners throughout the class period when they understand precisely what they will be expected to do that night for homework.

[1] For students with some disabilities, the teacher will need to check to ensure that the assignment is written correctly. These students may be more likely not to write the assignment down or to transcribe it incorrectly. Special education teachers also note that when special needs students get their homework assignments correctly written, the special educators are better able to assist those students with the assignments.

homework assignment, we are conveying to them the message that the homework we assign them is directly based on the content we cover in class, not some tangential means of making their lives busier! Occasionally adjusting the night's homework assignment then serves to underscore the message that homework represents what students are expected *to do* with the information we teach them, a message that increases the likelihood of our students transferring the content they learn in class to their long-term memory.

It should be noted that several of our elementary school colleagues have noted to us that assigning homework at the outset of a lesson may be a strategy better suited to middle and high school teachers than to elementary school teachers. Their reasoning is that younger children may find it alarming to be assigned homework for which they have not yet learned the information or skills necessary to complete it successfully. Our colleagues' point is well taken. Other elementary school teachers find the strategy of assigning homework at the outset of a lesson quite successful as long as the assignment is accompanied by a clear, reassuring explanation to students that they are about to learn the skills *right now* that are necessary to complete the evening's homework assignment.

In this section, we have discussed *when* in the course of a lesson or class period homework should be assigned. A final point about assigning homework concerns *where* the assignment itself should be written. As is the case with mastery objectives, different teachers have different strategies concerning this topic. Some teachers prefer to provide students on Monday morning with a handout listing the homework assignments for the entire week (or longer). Such a practice gives eager students the opportunity to work ahead if they so choose. Even for teachers who follow such a practice, however, we recommend listing the night's homework assignment on either a corner of the blackboard or on a second piece of flipchart paper hanging in the front of the classroom. The reasoning is the same as that behind posting the mastery objectives and agenda for a given class period; posting homework assignments, inspirational quotations, student work, etc. around the classroom serves as a stimulus that "feeds the brain." Posting the nightly homework assignment might be particularly useful in that a student who "spaces out" for a moment and finds himself or herself glancing at that evening's homework assignment will be reminded of the content or skills necessary to complete that assignment. Such a reminder will serve as a motivator for this student to refocus on the lesson at hand!

Activators

Activators are activities utilized at the beginning of a lesson or class period that provide either a brief review of the previous day's work or that activate students' present knowledge of the topic to be taught in the upcoming lesson or class period. The most effective activators are those that accomplish both of these goals, effectively serving as a bridge that links the previous day's lesson to the lesson ahead. Activators also serve to give us a sense of how much information our students already know or remember about a particular topic.

> ***Activators** are activities utilized at the beginning of a lesson or class period that provide either a brief review of the previous day's work or that activate students' present knowledge of the topic to be taught in the upcoming lesson or class period.*

An example of an activator we often use is called "Give-One-Get-One." In this activity, our students receive a sheet of paper with six to twelve boxes (see the following sample), and they are asked to write in *one* of the boxes a fact about the topic of the upcoming lesson that they already know. We then instruct students to circulate around the room for approximately five minutes, sharing their piece of information with other students in the class and collecting information from their peers in return. They are to place the information they learn from their peers in the empty boxes contained on their handout. At the end of this activity, students have filled in as many boxes as possible with information about the topic of the day's lesson. The following are examples of this activity used in various ways.

Example of a Give-One-Get-One

As noted in our mastery objectives, today we will learn about the causes of the Civil War. Write one fact you know about the causes of the Civil War in the box in the upper left-hand corner. When the teacher says "Circulate," approach a classmate and give your fact to that classmate. Then write that classmate's fact in another box (if it is different than the one you have). Continue to trade information with classmates until you either fill up your boxes or the teacher asks you to stop.

Example of a Give-One-Get-One

As noted in our mastery objectives, today we will learn about the causes of the Civil War. Write one fact you know about the causes of the Civil War in the box in the upper left-hand corner. When the teacher says "Circulate," approach a classmate and give your fact to that classmate. Then write that classmate's fact in another box (if it is different than the one you have). Continue to trade information with classmates until you either fill up your boxes or the teacher asks you to stop.

Below is an example of the sheet after the activity is completed.

The disagreement between the north and south about the abolition of slavery	The south favored stronger states rights. The north favored a stronger central government.
The south wanted the northerners to aggressively enforce laws that required escaped slaves to be returned to their masters. Many northerners openly disobeyed these laws.	The south had an agrarian society and the north had an industrial society. This lead to disagreements about laws regulating and/or taxing trade.
The south had an active trade with England. England bought much of the cotton, tobacco and other crops raised by southern farmers. Since the south had very little industry they wanted to purchase English manufactured goods without added costs due to tariffs.	

Other examples of a Give-One-Get-One are the following:

1. In the box in the upper left-hand corner, write one piece of information you remember from yesterday's class. When the teacher says "Circulate," approach a student and give your fact to that student and then write that student's fact in another box (if it is different than the one you have). Continue to do this with other students until you either fill up your boxes or the teacher asks you to stop.
2. In the box in the upper left hand corner, write one of the common applications of physics we see in our everyday lives. When the teacher says "Circulate," approach a student and give your fact to that student and then write that student's fact in another box (if it is different than the one you have). Continue to do this with students until you either fill up your boxes or the teacher asks you to stop.

K-W Activator

Another commonly used activator is referred to as a **K-W Activator.** The K-W stands for *Know* and *Want to Know*. This activity involves asking students to chart what they already know or think they know about a topic to be studied and the questions they have about the topic. This activator can be completed individually, in pairs, in small groups or as a full class brainstorming activity. The following is an example of a K-W Activator.

K-W Activator	
What I know about chemical reactions.	What I want to know about chemical reactions.

In the following section of this chapter when summarizers are described, we will discuss variations of the K-W Activator known as the **K-W-L Activator/Summarizer** (*Know, Want to Know* and *Learned*) and the **K-W-L-U Activator/Summarizer** (*Know, Want to Know, Learned* and ***Used***).

What is the value of activators? First, activators serve to connect new learning to students' previously held knowledge. This connection is crucial for helping students to commit this new information to their long-term memory. In the following passage, Nolet and McLaughlin (2000, p. 36) explain the manner in which the human mind processes information:

> [Newly received] information is held in working memory temporarily while it is compared with information already stored in long-term memory. If the new information is related to some prior knowledge, it is moved out of working memory and stored along with that related information in long-term memory...If the new information cannot be connected to prior knowledge, it is less likely to be moved into long-term memory.

While the topics of working and long-term memory will be discussed in greater depth in Chapter 8, it is clear from this explanation by Nolet and McLaughlin that the work of activators to connect new learning to previously held knowledge is a crucial ingredient in the act of learning.

A second way in which activators facilitate teaching and learning is by informing the teacher of any misconceptions about the previous day's content that a student or students may possess. It is important to discover these misconceptions as quickly as possible for two reasons. First, students who connect their new learning to these prior misconceptions may come away with even *more* confusion about the particular topic of study. Second, as will be discussed in greater detail in Chapter 8, it can be difficult for a student's brain to "unlearn" a misconception if this misconception is not quickly corrected. Imagine your own experiences in listening to music. Once you hear a song lyric incorrectly, it can feel nearly impossible to stop singing the song with that incorrect lyric inserted. The neurological reasoning behind this difficulty in "unlearning" information will be discussed in Chapter 8, but it is enough here to note that activators are an important tool for quickly catching and correcting students' misconceptions.

The Do Now Activator

The **Do Now** is a particular type of activator developed by Dr. Lorraine Monroe, the nationally recognized founding principal of the Frederick Douglass Academy in Central Harlem. The Do Now is a 3–4 minute activator that is already written on the blackboard or flipchart paper when students enter the classroom at the beginning of a class period. It is called a Do Now because students are expected to begin working on this activator immediately upon entering the classroom and taking their seats. The Do Now is collected and graded each day— perhaps with a check, check plus or check minus grading system. Each of the examples of activators provided in this chapter could serve as effective Do Now's as long as students are able to begin working on them upon entering the classroom.

One benefit of the Do Now is that it effectively serves as what Madeline Hunter once called a sponge activity. A **sponge activity** is an activity designed to soak up valuable class time that might otherwise be wasted. The Do Now can serve as an effective sponge activity because students are expected to begin working on their Do Now upon entering the classroom. This means that the teacher does not have to wait to start class until every student is present, and students have no excuse for standing around chatting as they wait for class to begin. Rather, each student in the class is expected to begin working immediately upon entering the classroom. As Lorraine Monroe notes, the Do Now allows for "bell-to-bell" teaching and learning. While the ability of a Do Now to utilize 2–3 minutes of otherwise wasted class time may initially strike educators as "small potatoes," it is unquestionably the case that making good use of an additional 2–3 minutes a day, five days a week over the course of an entire school year can actually have a dramatic impact upon a class's learning. Moreover, as is discussed in more detail in Chapter 8, the first 10–15 minutes of a class period represent the prime period for student learning in the entire class period (Erlauer, 2003). This research reveals the opening minutes of class to be all the more valuable for student learning and makes the Do Now that much more important a strategy for teachers to utilize.

It should also briefly be noted that the Do Now has the capability of saving even more class time within a given period. One of the routines that we establish with our students is that they should put the previous night's homework on their desks prior to starting on the Do Now. Then, as students are working on their Do Now's, we move about the room taking attendance and checking off in our grade books which students have and have not completed the previous night's homework assignment. Such a practice allows us to avoid wasting instructional time later in the lesson taking attendance and checking on students' homework completion. More information about classroom routines and practices can be found in Chapter 3.

Some tips for using Do Now's from teachers who use them regularly are the following:

1. The first time you use a specific Do Now activity that is not familiar to the students, be sure to explain the directions carefully the day before. Do Now's need to be activities the students can do without teacher explanation.
2. The Do Now's should be factored into your grading system. This will help eliminate the problem of some students lingering in the hallway to avoid doing them.
3. Ensure that some of your Do Now's can be done with partners or groups. This also serves as a motivator to students.
4. Be certain that your Do Now's are important learning activities and not busy work.

Summarizers

As might be guessed from its name, a summarizer serves the opposite function from that of an activator. While activators are intended to activate and gauge students' prior knowledge of a topic before studying it, **summarizers** are typically utilized at the *conclusion* of a lesson or unit to accomplish a number of different goals.

First, summarizers can be an opportunity for students to describe their learning *in their own words*. We mentioned in the previous section that a common activator is the K-W Activator. Many educators utilize this activity as both an activator and summarizer by adding either one or two columns to the teaching tool. A K-W-L Activator/Summarizer (*Know, Want to Know* and *Learned*) has an extra column for students to fill in at the conclusion of the unit. The additional column is labeled "What I Learned"

Summarizers can be an opportunity for students to describe their learning in their own words.

and represents an opportunity for students to describe what they learned over the course of the unit or lesson.

Some teachers instruct students to fill in the "What I Learned" column as they proceed through the unit. Other educators utilize this column as a reflection activity to be completed at the unit's conclusion. Both strategies allow students the opportunity to express for themselves the learning that has taken place.

A teacher might also use the K-W-L as a summarizer by asking students to read over and reflect upon the thoughts and ideas they expressed at the unit's outset. Did everything they thought they knew about the topic turn out to be true? Did all of their "want to knows" get addressed? If not, we can reserve some class time for addressing any of these lingering "want to knows." Demonstrating this commitment to the issues and questions that particularly interest students heightens their motivation and effort-level to understand the larger lesson or unit.

In *The Brain Compatible Classroom*, Laura Erlauer (2003) recommends adding a fourth column to the K-W-L activity, creating the K-W-L-U Activator/Summarizer (***Know**, **Want to Know**, **Learned*** and ***Used***). The following two pages are examples of K-W-L and the K-W-L-U Activators/Summarizers.

K-W-L Activator/Summarizer

What I know.	What I want to know.	What I learned.

K-W-L-U Activator/Summarizer

Chemical Reactions

What I know.	What I want to know.	What I learned.	How I will use this learning.

As you can see in the K-W-L-U example, the fourth column asks students to reflect upon how they will utilize the content or skills they have acquired over the course of the unit. Asking students to reflect upon this question of application increases the likelihood of students transferring their learning into their long-term memory systems. Why? In *Transformations: Leadership for Brain-Compatible Learning,* Jane McGeehan (1999) notes that the brain wants to know that the information it is learning will be useful in the future. In *How People Learn,* Bransford, Brown and Cocking (1999, p. 7) report that "learners of all ages are more motivated when they can see the usefulness of what they are learning." In short, Erlauer's suggestion to add the "Usefulness" column to this activator/summarizer increases the likelihood that students will process and remember the learning they have engaged in throughout the lesson or unit.

In the same way that activators can be valuable in alerting us to our students' misconceptions or misunderstandings of a particular topic, a summarizer can also be useful in alerting us to content or skills that our students have not yet acquired or mastered. For example, if none of our students reference diatomic molecules in the column under what they learned about chemical reactions, we might take this data as a clue that we did not cover this topic as thoroughly as originally intended. This information might lead us to extend the chemical equations unit an additional day to readdress the topic of diatomic molecules, or perhaps we will simply add in our notes for next year that this topic should be addressed more rigorously.

Finally, in this chapter's sections on activators and agendas, we have explained that students are better able to transfer information into their long-term memory when they understand how a particular piece of information relates to other information they have already learned about that same topic. Using a summarizer, then, to reflect upon their learning gives students the opportunity to consider how new information they have acquired connects to previously held knowledge and also helps them to identify patterns and categories that provide structure to this newly acquired content. Both of these acts—linking new information to previous learning and categorizing new information—are crucial steps in transferring this newly learned content into students' long-term memory.

Using a summarizer, then, to reflect upon their learning gives students the opportunity to consider how new information they have acquired connects to previously held knowledge and also helps them to identify patterns and categories that provide structure to this newly acquired content.

Preparing Lessons That Flow Logically From One Activity to the Next

Earlier in this chapter, we discussed how posting an agenda can help students to understand the flow of a lesson from one activity to the next and how the various components of the lesson fit together. However, this is only the case when we as educators have thought carefully about structuring our lesson plan so that each aspect of a lesson logically follows the activity or direct instruction that precedes it. In other words, a lesson plan that jumps from a mini-lesson on writing thesis statements to an unrelated discussion of *The Old Man and the Sea* to an activity involving semicolons will make it more difficult for students to transfer the information conveyed in any of those activities to their long-term memory. The activities are simply too disconnected from one another. Instead, Nolet & McLaughlin (2000, p. 44) suggest that teachers can support student learning by "arranging information into logical categories prior to instruction, by modeling and leading students through a process of categorizing information and by pointing out patterns that may exist in the soon-to-be-learned information." This strategy suggested by Nolet and McLaughlin stems from their understanding that our students' brains are better able to learn and commit to memory information that is conveyed in logical, recognizable patterns rather than in unconnected pieces. To return to the previously described lesson, then, a teacher might better serve his or her students by choosing one of those topics—say, semicolons—to focus on, and then taking the time to explicitly connect this lesson on semicolons to the previous day's lesson on dashes and the similarities and differences in the uses of these two types of punctuation.

Issue Directions One Step at a Time[2]

In our discussion of activators and summarizers earlier in this chapter, we explained the process by which our students' brains commit new information to memory. To review briefly, newly received information is first held in our students' working memory and compared to information already stored in their long-term memory. If the new information can be connected to existing knowledge, this new information is much more easily transferred to our students' long-term memory than if no such connection can be made. In *Accessing the General Curriculum,* Nolet and McLaughlin (2000) explain that the capacity of our students' *working memories* is quite limited. Approximately seven units of information can be stored in the working memory at one time, and only for about ten to twenty seconds. For this reason, we as educators need to be strategic when providing our students with directions for accomplishing a particular activity or task.

For example, imagine a high school physical education teacher is instructing his or her students on the proper technique for shooting a foul shot in basketball. There are several different components that go into a successful foul shot: keeping one's knees bent, keeping one's eyes on the hoop, aiming for the back of the rim, properly positioning one's hands on the basketball, etc. A physical education teacher who simply describes each of these different components at once and then tells his or her students to "go to it" will almost certainly be disappointed when students begin practicing foul shots. In contrast, a physical education teacher who lists each of these different components on a blackboard, models each component and has students practice each component in isolation before putting the entire routine together will likely meet with more successful results.

How would such a strategy work in an English classroom? Imagine we are teaching an activity involving a worksheet on semicolons in which we would like students to read the sentences on the worksheet, decide whether or not a semicolon belongs in the sentence, add the semicolon if one is necessary and, if not, expand the sentence in a manner that requires a semicolon. Rather than issuing all of those instructions at once and then trusting our students' working memories to keep all of that information straight, we are better served to divide our instructions into two or even three parts. First, we might ask our students to read through the sentences and circle those that require semicolons. When students have completed this task, we might ask them to pencil in the semicolon in the appropriate place for those sentences that are circled. Finally, we might instruct them to reread the sentences that they did not circle and add to them in such a way that they utilize a semicolon. Perhaps after issuing each step of these directions, we then write that particular step on the blackboard. This teaching strategy acknowledges that students can only hold a limited amount of information in their working memory at one time.

Strategies for Preparing Students to Understand and Process Information

Actively Connect New Learning to Prior Knowledge

Earlier in this chapter, we discussed the importance of utilizing activators as a tool to connect new learning to prior knowledge. Such a connection, of course, is crucial to helping students transfer new learning into their long-term memory. We raise the point here that teachers can continue to help students create these connections between new learning and

[2] Special education teachers indicate this can be particularly important for special needs students.

prior knowledge *throughout* a lesson or activity. For example, a teacher might begin a unit on the Cold War in the following way:

> "At the very end of our unit on World War II last week, we talked about the ways in which, as the War was ending, Russia and the United States began to see the possibility that they could become competitors instead of allies. In that way, the very end of World War II was also the start of the Cold War."

By explicitly connecting the new unit on the Cold War to the information on World War II that students have already committed to their long-term memory, this teacher is greatly increasing the likelihood that his or her students will transfer this new information about the Cold War into their long-term memory as well. This instructional technique is called **elaboration**—"when the learner thinks about new information to be learned and prior knowledge to which it is to be linked at the same time" (Nolet & McLaughlin, 2000, p. 43). Nolet and McLaughlin (2000) recommend that educators keep the principles of elaboration in mind when creating instructional materials as well. For example, an elementary school math teacher creating a worksheet on borrowing numbers might include on the top half of the sheet a brief summary and sample problem from the previous day's lesson on carrying numbers. Helping students to see that both processes call for cross-column interaction within a multi-digit number enables these students to link their new knowledge of borrowing to their previously held knowledge of carrying, greatly increasing the likelihood that the new lesson on borrowing will "stick" (i.e. transfer to their long-term memory).

Chunking

The instructional strategies described in the preceding sections work to take advantage of the fact that students are more likely to transfer newly-learned information into long-term memory if this new information can be connected to previously-held knowledge. Nolet and McLaughlin (2000, p. 36) explain that "it also is possible to increase the amount of information that can be processed in working memory [and transferred to long-term memory] by **chunking** smaller bits of information into larger units." For example, many third grade students learning their multiplication tables find it difficult to answer the question, "What is 7 × 4?" If asked to recite the 7's tables, however, these same students might be able to do so: "7, 14, 21, 28, 35, etc." In fact, such a child might choose to answer the initial question ("7 × 4") by simply reciting the 7's tables until arriving at the correct answer ("28"). How can elementary school students find it harder to remember the solution to "7 × 4" than all of the 7's tables chunked together? Nolet and McLaughlin (2000, p. 37) explain that "chunking has the effect of simplifying the cognitive load by imposing meaning on otherwise disconnected bits of information." Understanding this aspect of learning and memory has important implications for structuring student learning.

Graphic Organizers:

Graphic organizers can support student learning by helping students to chunk newly learned information. A **graphic organizer** is any kind of diagram or outline which assists students in visually arranging information in such a way that the information becomes more accessible. Graphic organizers are also sometimes referred to as *knowledge maps, concept maps, story maps, cognitive organizers, advance organizers* or *concept diagrams* (Hall & Strangman, 2003). Graphic organizers are referred to as ***advance organizers*** when provided to students prior to introducing the new information for which they will be responsible and ***post organizers*** when provided to students following their introduction to the information to be learned (Hall & Strangman, 2003). In Figure 2-2, an example is shown of a graphic organizer we use with middle school students learning to write a body paragraph.

Figure 2-2

Name: English 8

Body Paragraph Toolkit

Components of a Body Paragraph:

1. ____________________
2. ____________________
3. Quote from Text
4. ____________________
5. ____________________
6. ____________________

Title of Short Story to Be Analyzed: ______________

Author of Short Story: ______________

Claim You Will Make in This Body Paragraph:

____

____

Topic Sentence:

____

____

Quote from Text:

____

____

____

(________________) ***citation***

The value of a graphic organizer is that the information for which students are responsible to learn is conveyed not as unconnected pieces of information but rather in coherent chunks. With the graphic organizer in Figure 2-2, for example, we first work with our students to fill in the different components of a body paragraph to ensure that they remember the correct structure. We then ask our students to write down the claim they will make in this body paragraph and a topic sentence that conveys this claim. Finally, we ask our students to search through the short story being analyzed for a quotation that can serve as evidence of their claim. Having utilized a graphic organizer to collect this information, students can then write the actual body paragraph for homework. The graphic organizer has allowed them to collect the "tools" necessary to complete this assignment on their own. A filled-in example of the graphic organizer in Figure 2-2 might look like Figure 2-3.

The value of a graphic organizer is that the information for which students are responsible to learn is conveyed not as unconnected pieces of information but rather in coherent chunks.

Figure 2-3

Name: English 8

Body Paragraph Toolkit

Components of a Body Paragraph:

1. Topic sentence (includes claim)
2. Information reader needs to understand the quote
3. Quote from Text
4. Cite the quote
5. Explain how quote supports claim
6. Concluding sentence

Title of Short Story to Be Analyzed: "Brother Jerome"

Author of Short Story: Gloria Naylor

Claim You Will Make in This Body Paragraph:

People who are bad at one thing can sometimes be really good at something else

Topic Sentence:

Gloria Naylor shows in her story "Brother Jerome" that people who are bad at one thing can some times be really good at something else.

Quote from Text:

"At seventeen, he couldn't write his own name, couldn't count money or go to the store, but he could make that piano tell any story that he wanted."

(Naylor, p32) ***citation***

How effective are graphic organizers in supporting student learning? Moore and Readence (1984) analyzed twenty-three different research studies on the effectiveness of graphic organizers and concluded that the use of graphic organizers yielded a consistently positive effect on students' comprehension of new information. They also found that graphic organizers were particularly suited to helping students improve their vocabulary knowledge.

It must be noted, however, that several research studies on graphic organizers have suggested that organizers do not support student learning unless teachers provide explicit instruction in how to use them (Carnes et al. 1987; Clements-Davis & Ley, 1991). In other words, simply handing out the graphic organizer shown in Figure 2-2 without an accompanying lesson on how to utilize the graphic organizer is unlikely to be useful to students. Instead, we must use the graphic organizer to explicitly demonstrate to students how 1) new information can be connected to previously-held knowledge and 2) how the organizer serves to chunk the information into clusters or categories. The graphic organizer, then, serves as a tool for helping students to recognize the relationships that exist in the information and skills they are learning. More information about incorporating graphic organizers into practice can be found in Chapter 4.

Less Is More

In this chapter, we have suggested a number of strategies for supporting student learning that take advantage of recent advances in our understanding of memory. A final suggestion we have in regards to students, memory and learning is one over which we as classroom teachers often do not have as much control as we would like: namely, the decision to favor a more in-depth study of a few topics over a more cursory study of many topics. Such an emphasis is more likely to result in students' understanding *and retaining* what they learn because of the greater ease with which students can transfer information into long-term memory when they can connect this information to previously-held knowledge. One can see then how students are more likely to remember the content included in an in-depth study of one historical time period than a more cursory study of three historical periods. As Robert Fried (2001, p. 240) explains in *The Passionate Teacher*, "Students cannot dig deeply when they are rushing to get through quantities of stuff." Unfortunately, our autonomy as educators to determine the depth versus the breadth of the curriculum we cover is sometimes limited by high stakes testing and state frameworks. To the extent possible, however, we try to design our curriculum and units with an emphasis on depth over breadth. In *The Passionate Teacher,* Fried (2001, p. 242) asks teachers to consider the following question: "If the school board decreed that the final exam for any course had to be given a year after the course was completed, would that change how you teach?" For many of us, such a "late" final exam system would dramatically impact our teaching. We know that too many of our students spend the few nights before the final exam cramming information into their working memory, only to forget this information a few days later. And, yet, if our goal is for students to truly understand and retain the content of our courses beyond the final exam, then we should already be designing our curriculum in such a way that allows our students to dig deeply into the content we are teaching them and hold on to what they uncover.

One way we can control the quality versus quantity struggle is to review the curriculum with an eye for identifying the skills and information that are most important for our students to learn. In any curriculum, there are typically information and skills that we consider to be of the highest priority, those that are a lower priority and those that are connected but are not a priority.

One way we can control the quality versus quantity struggle is to review the curriculum with an eye for identifying the skills and information that are most important for our students to learn.

We determine the level of importance of a particular skill or piece of information by asking ourselves a) what information and skills will result in the highest level of student achievement on the district, state and national assessments? and b) what information and skills will result in future school, career and personal success?

Once we have determined how the various units and lessons within our curriculum fit onto the continuum shown in Figure 2-4, we can then work to allocate our available instructional time accordingly. As can be seen in Figure 2-4, our "High Priority" lessons and units should receive the greatest allocation of instructional time and those units or lessons that fall under "Connected but Not a Priority" should receive the least instructional time.

Figure 2-4

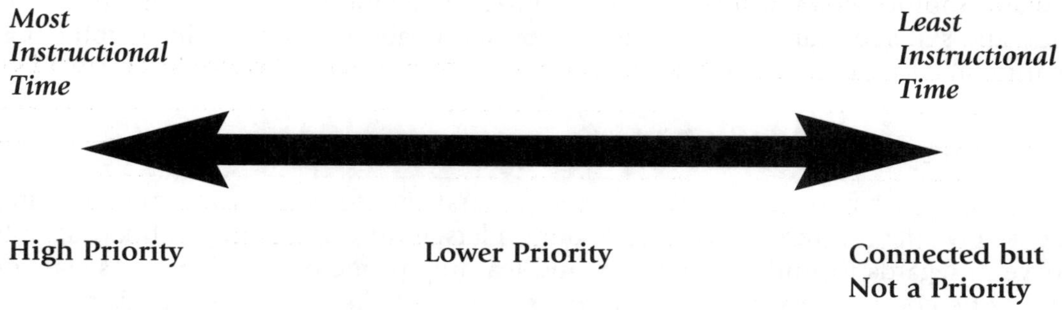

Most Instructional Time ⟷ *Least Instructional Time*

High Priority — **Lower Priority** — **Connected but Not a Priority**

Goal-Setting

Marzano, Pickering and Pollock write in *Classroom Instruction that Works* that "**goal-setting** is the process of establishing a direction for learning"(Marzano et al, 2001, p. 93, emphasis added). A goal-setting activity that we have utilized in our classrooms with great success during the first week of the school year is a variation on a classic visioning exercise for non-profit organizations called **"The Cover Story"** (COOL and Idealist Civic Engagement Curriculum, 2003). For this activity, we ask our students to imagine that it is the end of the school year and the local newspaper is planning to devote an entire issue to our class. What would our students like the front page of this newspaper to look like? More specifically, what would they like the titles of the four or five front-page articles to say? Often, our first homework assignment of the school year is for each student to come up with four or five possible article titles to bring with them to class the next day. We then divide our students into groups of four or five, provide pieces of flipchart paper and magic markers, and ask each group to take fifteen minutes to pool their ideas into a single front page. In an eleventh-grade English class, a final product might look something like the following example.

September 7, 2004	The Newbury Gazette	$1.00

Students Ace SAT's with Expert Vocabulary!

Students Craft Brilliant Research Papers

Entire Class Understands Hamlet

Students Avoid Grammar Mistakes: Receive A's on Final Exams

Given additional time, students might choose to draw in a front-page photograph or to write the opening sentence or two of each "story." Upon completing their front page, each group takes a turn presenting its flipchart paper to the class. We then hang up each group's front page on a classroom wall visible to our students from their seats where they remain for the rest of the school year.

For the rest of the year, when introducing a unit or activity, we try to connect this unit or activity with the learning goals that our students established for themselves during the first week of school. We literally walk over to the front pages on the wall and point out the goal that we believe this upcoming lesson addresses. What is the value of such a practice? Psychologist Mihalyi Csikszentmihalyi (1990, p. 40) explains that "when information that keeps coming into awareness is congruent with personal goals, thought flows effortlessly... Attention can be freely invested to achieve a person's goals because there is no disorder to straighten out, no threat for the self to defend against." In other words, students are more focused, effective learners when they understand how a particular unit or lesson relates to their own goals.

An Incentive to Aim For: Another reason for using mastery objectives and agendas

Another type of goal-setting that we have used to motivate students involves jointly deciding upon the mastery objectives for which the class will strive and a reward the class will earn upon achieving these goals. In developing appropriate objectives and incentives, we as a class literally draw up a contract for both students and teachers to sign. For example, one of our elementary school colleagues drew up a contract with her class to motivate their reading during DEAR (Drop Everything and Read) time. One half hour a week was devoted to DEAR time; literally every member of the school community was expected to drop everything and read for thirty minutes. Our colleague and her students jointly decided that when the class had accumulated thirty-thousand minutes of total reading time, the entire class would earn a pizza party. The class created a chart that they posted on a side bulletin board to record their progress toward this goal and would adjust this chart accordingly at the conclusion of each weekly DEAR session. Students who finished their work early during other parts of the week and chose to use their "free" time reading could earn additional minutes for the class. Our colleague brilliantly utilized this chart in some of the class's mathematics lessons as well. The pizza party took place in early June. Over the years, we have heard of many different goals and incentives that teachers and students have come up with to motivate student learning. Perhaps the strangest was another elementary school colleague of ours who agreed to shave his head if every member of the class diligently completed their homework assignments for a certain number of days in a row. While we don't necessarily advise such appearance-altering bargains, working jointly with students to develop mastery objectives and an incentive for achieving these objectives can be an effective motivator for student engagement and learning.

Giving the Final Assignment First

Earlier in this chapter, we discussed the importance of sharing mastery objectives with students at the outset of a lesson or unit. Similar to this practice is beginning a unit by handing out the assignment for the essay, project or performance that students will be expected to complete as the final assessment of the unit. For example, prior to beginning a unit on short stories, we might hand out to students the final assignment of the unit: to write a 4–7 page short story and then to write an analytic essay identifying three literary elements within the story. What is the value of providing this final assignment at the outset of the unit? Remember Nolet and McLaughlin's (2000, p. 41) explanation that "teachers can help their students employ more expert storage strategies when they are clear about the kind of information they want their students to learn and the manner in which students will be asked to use that information." In other words, letting students know ahead of time that, by the end of the unit, they will be expected to write a short story and then identify and analyze the literary elements within that story will better enable them to understand and retain the content about short stories and literary elements that the unit seeks to convey. During each lesson within the unit—whether on setting, tone or internal conflict—students will understand precisely how the information they are learning will be useful to them in completing the unit's final assignment.

Essential Questions

In *Understanding by Design*, Grant Wiggins and Jay McTighe (1998, p. 30, emphasis added) explain that "**essential questions** are those that go to the heart of the discipline, recur naturally throughout one's learning and in the history of a field, [and] raise other important questions." Teachers utilize essential questions to guide students' investigations of a particular topic of study. Therefore, these questions must be complex enough to serve as an appropriate frame for the topic of study and engaging enough to pique and hold students' interest. For example, in a ninth-grade English class embarking upon a study of *The Odyssey*, the essential questions laid out at the start of the unit might be the following:

1. What is a hero?
2. Is Odysseus a hero?
3. Are there differences between the Ancient Greeks' definition of a hero and ours today?

we read and discuss *The Odyssey* with our students, we keep these questions in mind
rch for aspects of the plot and themes that contribute to our understanding of these

questions. What is the value of such questions? According to Wiggins and McTighe, these questions "get at matters of deep and enduring understanding" (Wiggins and McTighe, 1998, p. 28). In short, then, essential questions support our students' learning by providing several complex, important questions upon which to focus as they make their way through a particular literary work, unit or content area. An entire course can also utilize an essential question or questions. For example, another English teacher we know taught a humanities class in which the overarching essential question was "What does it mean to be human?" In providing a consistent lens for inquiry, such questions can be a powerful tool in maintaining students' interest and engagement in a work as lengthy as *The Odyssey* or even in an entire course examining various works of literature.

A natural question that arises for many teachers is how essential questions differ from mastery objectives. These pedagogical tools are similar but not identical; they strive to achieve the same purpose but through different means. In our previous section on mastery objectives, we explained that providing students at the outset of a unit with our expectations for what they will know and be able to do at the end of the unit leads them to be more focused, attentive learners and better able to transfer new information into their long-term memory. For example, a student who has been alerted at the start of a unit on *The Odyssey* that one of the class's mastery objectives is *understanding and identifying Homeric meter* will be better able to transfer this information into his or her long-term memory when the teacher points out examples of Homeric meter within the epic poem. Essential questions also work to increase the likelihood that students will transfer new information into their long-term memory, however, essential questions support students in achieving this goal by providing a framework that connects all of the different pieces of a unit of study into a coherent whole. For example, the essential question for *The Odyssey*— "What is a hero?"—provides a structure through which a student can reflect upon the many different plotlines and themes running through *The Odyssey*: Odysseus making his way home over eighteen long years, Penelope fending off the suitors, Telemachus setting out in search of his father. The essential question, "What is a hero?", provides a framework for students to use in reflecting upon each of these plotlines and increases the likelihood that students will transfer each to their long-term memory. As we may recall from Nolet and McLaughlin's explanations of the brain and memory, information that is chunked together is more easily transferred to long-term memory than individual bits of information. While mastery objectives and essential questions both aim to support students in transferring skills and content to their long-term memory, they help students to accomplish this goal in different ways.

Exhibitions, Projects, Performances

Earlier in this chapter, we suggested providing students with a unit's final assignment at the *start* of the unit as a means of increasing students' motivation for understanding the unit's information. Supporting students in *retaining* this information, however, is very much dependent on the nature of the final assignment itself. While we recognize that time constraints prohibit concluding each unit of study with a performance assessment, we do believe that such assessments can be deeply effective in allowing students to retain the knowledge they have acquired. According to Marilee Sprenger (1999, p. 83, emphasis added), "A **performance assessment** describes any assessment in which students may demonstrate knowledge and understanding through various means." Examples of performance assessments include the following:

1. reciting a passage from one of Shakespeare's plays
2. demonstrating how a particular math problem was solved
3. carrying on a conversation in Spanish with a classmate

4. completing a science lab and explaining the conclusions that result
5. constructing a timeline of the Civil Rights Era

More information on performance assessments can be found in Chapter 6. What is the value of such types of assessment? Robert Fried (2001, p. 33) notes in *A Passionate Teacher* that "years after students have performed these projects, the experience and the pride remain for all involved. These are experiences that shape careers or engender a lifelong interest in an area of study." In other words, Fried believes these types of assessments "stick" with students far longer than traditional tests, quizzes or essays. Moreover, when students know that their work will be viewed not only by their classroom teacher but by peers, friends and family members as well, their motivation to learn and understand the skills and concepts necessary to create high-quality products is impacted dramatically. As Lauren Resnick (1995, p. 481), director of the University of Pittsburgh's Learning and Research Development Center, observes, "School community nights can become occasions for displaying work, organizing exhibitions, and putting on performances . . . It is critical that these celebrations include people who matter to the students, and that what is celebrated is work that matters." Resnick recognizes that students are motivated to produce high-quality work when they know their work will be viewed by people they respect. It is for this reason then that final assignments that push students to demonstrate their learning through exhibitions, projects and performances can effectively motivate students to *want* to learn and understand the content necessary to produce high-quality products. In Chapter 8, we will examine the different learning systems within the human brain and discuss in detail the ability of a students' *social* and *emotional* learning systems to derail their more *academic* learning systems (cognitive and reflective). While we will wait until Chapter 8 to delve into these terms in detail, it is enough to note here that heightening students' motivation by involving family and friends in viewing and celebrating their work is an example of educators' utilizing students' social and emotional learning systems to *support* and *enhance* their academic learning systems.

Students are motivated to produce high-quality work when they know their work will be viewed by people they respect.

Connecting Learning to the "Real World"

One of the forefathers of American education, John Dewey (1897, pp. 230–231), wrote, "I believe that the school must represent present life—life as real and vital to the child as that which he carries on in the home, in the neighborhood, or on the playground." In other words, Dewey believed that motivating students to be engaged, attentive learners involves convincing them that their learning is connected to the goings-on of the *"real world."* Here we suggest several strategies for helping students to see that connection. In each of these examples of connecting learning to the "real world," we describe teachers who are capitalizing upon the point made by Jane McGeehan (1999) that the brain wants to know that new information or skills it is learning will be useful in the future. In other words, our students' brains are actually better able to learn and remember content that strikes them as important and relevant. The following activities and strategies are those that we and other educators have found to strike such a chord with our students.

Motivating students to be engaged, attentive learners involves convincing them that their learning is connected to the goings-on of the "real world."

Beginning Units by Explicitly Connecting Learning to the "Real World"

A colleague of ours who teaches at the high school level explained to us that, on the first day of school, he promises his students that he will always take the time to answer the question, "When are we ever going to use this?" And the lesson won't continue until he can answer that question to the class's satisfaction. Other teachers we know are even more proactive. One math teacher begins each unit by describing the different jobs that utilize the mathematical concepts found in the upcoming chapter. An English teacher we know begins a unit on poetry by citing Supreme Court justice John Stephens' contention that the best preparation for law school may be the study of poetry. After quizzing his students on possible connections between poetry and the law, he quotes English professor and attorney George Gopen, who says that "no other discipline so closely replicates the central question asked in the study of legal thinking: here is a text; in how many ways can it have meaning?"(Kennedy, 1990, p. 6). These teachers recognize that engaging students in the content they are learning requires helping them to understand how this content is actually utilized in the "real world."

Concluding Lessons by Explicitly Connecting Learning to the "Real World"

One way in which an elementary mathematics teacher connects learning to the "real world" is through having students write in a daily math journal. One night each student brings home a notebook and writes about how he or she used mathematics beyond the classroom that day. In addition, the student is also required to create a mathematical problem based upon how he or she used math that day. The following day, the students share their journal entries and problems with the rest of the class. Then the entire class works together to solve each problem. As Albert and Deane (2000, p. 527) explain, "In this activity, students not only are given the opportunity to express and communicate their mathematical knowledge and creativity but are also exposed to collaborative learning situations in which they can experience multiple ways to solve a problem." By pushing students to reflect upon the "real world" application of skills they have just learned, this elementary school math teacher greatly increases the likelihood that her students will retain the information and skills they have acquired.

Developing "Real World" Assignments

Students are also motivated by assignments that they regard as real. For example, earlier in this chapter, we described a final assignment for a unit on short stories in which students wrote their own short stories and then completed an analysis of the literary elements within the short story. One year, as a means of "shaking things up" a bit, we assigned our students to write and illustrate *children's* stories and then to write their analysis of the literary elements found within their respective children's stories. Moreover, we explained to our students that, upon completion of the assignment, we planned to donate their stories to a first grade class at one of the local elementary schools. The reaction of our students was extremely positive. They loved the idea of local children actually benefiting from their assignment, and, though the process of writing, illustrating and binding a children's story involved far more effort than the more basic story-writing assignment of previous years, we heard far less complaining from our students. They were willing to do more work because they saw the work as real.

That same class of students regarded another assignment as real in a different way. Upon completing *The Odyssey*, we typically assign our students to write an essay addressing the question, "Was Odysseus a hero?" In order to "shake things up" again, however, we changed our assignment slightly. More specifically, we decided to put Odysseus on trial for the deaths of every member of his crew. The question became, "Is Odysseus guilty of murder?"

We divided our students into two sides—one side prosecuting Odysseus for murder and the other side defending him—and assigned our students to write either an opening or closing statement that supported the side of the case to which they had been assigned. Though the form of the writing assignment and its topic were somewhat different than in previous years, the expectations for quality remained the same. Students were expected to find textual evidence to support their arguments and utilize all of the mechanics of good writing in making their case. As in previous years, a rubric was provided to ensure that students understood what was expected of them. Rather than simply turning in the assignment, however, we took an additional two class periods to put Odysseus on trial. Each team assigned students to play either witnesses (characters from the story) or lawyers, and the entire team worked together to develop questions that they could pose to these witnesses to prove their side's claim about Odysseus's actions. On the day of the trial, several students for each side read their opening and closing statements, and, in between, witnesses from both sides were called. At the conclusion of the trial, the legal studies teacher who had been recruited to serve as the judge rendered his verdict. Perhaps not surprisingly, in end-of-the-year course evaluations, students listed this activity as one of their favorite of the year. At its core, the writing assignment they completed was essentially the same as in previous years; however, placing that assignment within the context of a trial lent an authenticity to the project that motivated our students to focus more deeply on the content they were learning and, as a result, more successfully commit this content to their long-term memory.

Using Primary Source Materials

Another "real world" connection that motivates student learning is the use of primary source (i.e. "real world") materials. For example, rather than assigning students to learn a vocabulary list photocopied from a textbook, we might bring in a recent article from the *New York Times* and ask students to read the article carefully, circling any words they don't immediately recognize. We can then put together our own vocabulary list from the circled words. What is the benefit of assembling a vocabulary list in this manner? Students can see firsthand that these words are utilized out in the "real world" as opposed to simply being in a vocabulary textbook. Likewise, in a math class, students are far more motivated to understand concepts such as perimeter and area when their teacher brings in an actual blueprint for them to examine instead of relying upon the diagram within their textbooks. In both of these examples, substituting a "real world" artifact for a textbook excerpt allows students to see for themselves how the skill or concept they are learning plays out in the "real world". See Chapter 1 for a specific example of a lesson that shows how a high school teacher used primary source material from the book *The Prince* by Machiavelli.

Newspaper articles as primary source materials can be valuable teaching tools at the elementary school level as well. One of our elementary school colleagues uses newspaper articles in her mathematics class to help students develop number sense in a "real world" context. This particular teacher chooses several appropriate sentences containing numbers. She then rewrites the sentences without the numbers and creates a "Number Bank" at the top of the sheet with the numbers that have been taken out. The students must fill in the missing blanks with the appropriate numbers. At the conclusion of the lesson, the teacher shows her students the original newspaper article and allows them to check their answers against the original sentences. In this way, her students can see how their number sense is developing as well as the way in which numbers are utilized in everyday reading materials such as newspapers.

Guest Speakers

Even better than bringing in a "real world" artifact is bringing in a "real world" human being. For that same unit on area and perimeter, for example, perhaps a friend of yours, the spouse of a teacher in your school or the parent of a student in your class is an architect. While our initial impulse might be to assume that such an architect would be too busy to visit our class for half an hour to explain his or her work, we have found that, quite the contrary, the various professionals we have invited into our classrooms are excited and honored by the invitation to talk to a class full of students about the work that they do. Of course, there is virtually nothing more motivating for students than the opportunity to hear firsthand about the ways in which the skills they are learning are actually applied in the "real world."

We find that this strategy is most effective when the speaker is given information related to the purpose of the visit. For example, telling the architect the topics we teach that are reflected in architecture and asking the speaker to make these connections for the students will lead to a very productive experience.

Role-Plays and Simulations

A final way in which we try to engage our students is through role-plays and simulations. A colleague of ours who teaches high school social studies uses a fantastic simulation to help students understand the Homestead Strike of 1892 in which factory workers at Andrew Carnegie's steel factory in Pittsburgh struck over the right to unionize, receive better pay and have improved working conditions. In the simulation, approximately one-third of the class takes the role of management, one-third takes the role of skilled workers employed by Carnegie and one-third takes the role of unskilled workers employed by Carnegie. The simulation allows students to truly come to understand the competing goals, motivations and concerns of these different groups and then to compare the resolution of their simulation to the violence and tragedy that actually ensued in 1892. Simulations such as this one engage students deeply in their learning.

One of our elementary school colleagues uses a particular type of simulation throughout the school year. He divides his students into news teams, and they are expected each week to deliver a ten minute news program to their classmates, utilizing the current events articles they have found for homework. By role-playing the work of newscasters, this teacher has discovered a particularly engaging way to teach his students (and have his students teach each other) about both current events and public speaking.

Conveying Passion and Enthusiasm

In the second half of this chapter, we have described several strategies that teachers use to increase their students' engagement and motivation for the content they are learning. Perhaps more obvious than some of the strategies already described, but unquestionably as important, is our own passion and enthusiasm for the content we are teaching. If we truly feel that our subject area—be it literature, physical education, chemistry or photography—is utterly fascinating and worth knowing, our students will pick up on that enthusiasm and more willingly devote their energy and attention to understanding this subject matter. How does this work on a cognitive level? Showing our passion for our subject matter to our students is another example of utilizing our students' *emotional* learning system to support their more *academic* learning systems. While we will hold off until Chapter 8 on describing these different learning systems in detail, we can note

If we truly feel that our subject area—be it literature, physical education, chemistry or photography—is utterly fascinating and worth knowing, our students will pick up on that enthusiasm and more willingly devote their energy and attention to understanding this subject matter.

here that students who are privy to their teachers' positive emotional response to a particular subject matter are better able to focus their cognitive learning system on learning and understanding this subject matter. For this reason, we recommend that teachers explicitly share their enthusiasm for their subject matter with students as well as *what* they believe makes this subject matter so exciting. One of our colleagues who is a high school English teacher admitted to us that his students begin teasing him midway through the year for claiming at the start of each unit or book, "This is my favorite one to teach. I think you're going to like this one best." Despite their good-natured teasing, our colleague's students are motivated by their teacher's enthusiasm to give authors such as Shakespeare and Hawthorne a fair chance, instead of preemptively declaring these authors to be boring. His passion for these authors then plays a crucial role in his students' learning.

Conclusion

The various strategies described in this chapter draw upon our understanding of learning, memory and motivation to support student learning. More specifically, these strategies seek to create a context within our classrooms that maximize our students' ability to understand and retain the information and skills that we teach them. For many years, the education world considered student learning to be solely a function of each student's effort and intelligence. If students succeeded, it was because they were smart, studious or both. If students were not succeeding, it was because they lacked either innate intelligence or the diligence to succeed. While innate intelligence to some extent and students' effort to a much larger extent do play a role in student achievement, we have also learned in recent years of the ways in which we as teachers can utilize structures, strategies and activities to support student learning. While the ability of our students to learn the information and skills we are teaching them is unquestionably impacted by the effort they expend, there are also steps that we can take as educators to increase the likelihood that information and skills—when effort is expanded—will "stick."

References

Albert, L. & Deane, J. (2000). Daily journals connect mathematics to real life. *Mathematics Teaching in the Middle School.* pp526-531.

Bransford, J., Brown, A. & Cocking, R. (1999). *How people learn: Brain, mind and experience at school.* Washington DC: National Academy Press.

Carnes, E. R., Lindbeck, J. S., & Griffin, C. F. (1987). Effects of group size and advance organizers on learning parameters when using microcomputer tutorials in kinematics. *Journal of Research in Science Teaching, 24*(9), 781–789.

Clements-Davis, G. L., & Ley, T. C. (1991). Thematic preorganizers and the reading comprehension of tenth-grade world literature students. *Reading Research & Instruction, 31*(1), 43–53.

Checkley, K. (2004, April). A is for audacity: Lessons in leadership from Lorraine Monroe. *Educational Leadership*, 70–72.

COOL and Idealist Civic Engagement Curriculum. Accessed July 21, 2004. "The cover story: A shared visioning activity." *www.cool2serve.org/tools/pdf/Cover-Story.pdf*

Csikszentmihalyi, M. (1990). *Flow: The psychology of optimal experience.* New York: Harper & Row.

Dewey, J. (1897). My pedagogic creed. In L. Hickman and T. Alexander (Eds.), *The essential Dewey* (pp. 229–235). IN: Indiana University Press.

Erlauer, L. (2003). *The brain-compatible classroom.* Alexandria, VA: Association for Supervision and Curriculum Design (ASCD).

Fried, R. (2001). *The passionate teacher.* Boston, MA: Beacon Press.

Hall, T. & Strangman, N. Graphic organizers. Accessed July 20, 2004 . *National Center on Accessing the General Curriculum.* www.cast.org/ncac/index.cfm?i=3015

Jones, F. (2001). *Tools for teaching.* Santa Cruz, California: Jones Publications.

Kennedy, X. J. (1990). *An introduction to poetry.* United States: HarperCollins Publishers.

Marzano, R., Pickering, D., & Pollock, J. (2001). *Classroom instruction that works: Research-based strategies for increasing student achievement.* Alexandria, VA: Association for Supervision and Curriculum Development (ASCD).

McGeehan, J. (1999). *Transformations: Leadership for brain-compatible learning.* Kent, WA: Books for Educators, Inc.

Monroe, L. (2003). *The Monroe doctrine.* New York: Public Affairs, Inc.

Monroe, L. Leadership for excellence. Presented March 28-April 1, 2000. *2000 SPANZ Conference Report.*

Moore, D. W., & Readence, J. E. (1984). A quantitative and qualitative review of graphic organizer research. *Journal of Educational Research, 78*(1), 11–17.

Naylor, G. (1995). *The men of Brewster Place.* NY: Hyperion.

Nolet, V. & McLaughlin, M. (2000). *Accessing the general curriculum: Including students with disabilities in standards-based reform.* Thousand Oaks, CA: Corwin Press, Inc.

Resnick, Lauren. (1995). From aptitude to effort: A new foundation for our schools. *Daedalus, 124* (4) 55–62.

Sprenger, M. (1999). *Learning and memory: The brain in action.* Alexandria, VA: Association for Supervision and Curriculum Development (ASCD).

Wiggins, G. and McTighe, J. (1998). *Understanding by design.* Virginia: Association for Supervision and Curriculum Development (ASCD).

CHAPTER

3

Classroom Management: With a Section on the Effective Use of Homework

Objectives for the Chapter

After reading the chapter, the reader will be able to

a. develop classroom rules/standards, routines and expectations that maximize the level of respectful, on-task behavior
b. develop an effective homework routine with students and parents
c. develop a classroom management plan that includes a system of rewards and consequences for reinforcing respectful, on-task behavior
d. obtain students' attention at the start of the lesson, after group and partner activities, after interruptions and after student attention has deteriorated

A recent article by Walker, Ramsey and Gresham (2004) states that a survey of teachers who are members of the American Federation of Teachers indicates that:

> Seventeen (17) percent said they lost four or more hours of teaching time per week thanks to disruptive student behavior; another nineteen (19) percent said they lost two or three hours. In urban areas, fully twenty-one (21) percent said they lost four or more hours per week. And in urban secondary schools the percentage (who report losing four or more hours of instruction) is twenty-four (24) percent.

For the typical teacher who has between twenty and thirty hours a week of contact with students, this is a significant loss of instructional time over the course of the year. Even if we take the lower figure (two hours) and multiply that by thirty-eight weeks in a school year, we see a loss of seventy-six hours of instructional time. That is equal to over three weeks of school!

Teachers have long been aware that effective and engaging instruction is an excellent means of avoiding classroom management issues, however, we also know that even the most engaging teacher will have classroom management issues unless he or she has an effective plan for classroom management.

There are many in-service programs designed to teach classroom management. Most provide a great deal of success for some teachers, some success for others and miserable failure for still others. Classroom management is one of the more difficult skills to teach teachers because it is so situational in nature. There are many variables and social structures that must be considered when developing a classroom management plan. In this chapter, we will look at the various social structures that must be considered when developing a classroom management plan. We will then look at specific steps we take when establishing such a plan. In the last part of the chapter, we will look at what we do with individual students who still disrupt even when we have a well constructed and consistently implemented classroom management plan.

Variables to Consider When Constructing a Classroom Management Plan

One of the variables to consider when constructing a classroom management plan is our (the teacher's) belief system. One set of beliefs we have is about what constitutes appropriate student behavior. A second set of beliefs is about the best way to shape students' behavior. A third variable is the belief system of the students. Students come to us from a broad range of parenting structures and previous classroom management structures. Each student has taken those varied experiences and integrated them into his or her personality. The result is an individual interpretation of various interpersonal interactions. The fourth variable is our teaching team. Students see many teachers in the course of a day. Even in elementary grades, students often interact with teachers in specialty areas such as art, music, physical education and other classroom teachers from our grade level at lunch or recess. The fifth variable is the school culture. Schools operate on different overt and covert cultural norms related to students. The sixth variable is the parenting beliefs in the school community. Parents' education levels, socio-economic strata, religious beliefs, personal beliefs and cultural norms all have an impact on the effectiveness of any classroom management plan. With all of these variables at play, it is little wonder that behavior management may be such a difficult area for teachers to master each and every year.

Teachers' Beliefs

Each of us operates with a belief system on two levels. The first is our cognitive level. This is what we learned in our pre-service training, our in-service training and through our experiences in working with students. The second level is our subconscious beliefs. This is how we react to students' behavior when we don't have the time to clearly reflect on a problem situation, weigh alternatives and choose the best alternative based on our cognitive belief system. Our subconscious beliefs are the result of how we were parented, the classroom management we experienced as students and a host of other factors (e.g., religion, culture, previous trauma). In the stress of the classroom, our subconscious beliefs may control our classroom management decisions as much or more than our cognitive beliefs.

In the stress of the classroom, our subconscious beliefs may control our classroom management decisions as much or more than our cognitive beliefs.

There is a physiological reason for the domination of our subconscious beliefs. Our brain is made up of three primary parts: the *brain stem*, the *paleocortex* and the *neocortex*. Dr. Frederic Jones, in his book, *Tools for Teaching* (2000, pp. 168–173), talks about the impact on our brain when we are confronted with a classroom discipline issue. Student misbehavior is stressful for teachers because it detracts from the learning the teacher is trying to achieve. Each student's misbehavior distracts the teacher and detracts from the teacher's learning goals. Not achieving our goals is a stress producer for all people. Confronted with this stressful situation, we ideally want to be able to calmly and rationally assess the situation, draw on our acquired knowledge, generate alternatives, assess each alternative and select the alternative that is best suited for the situation at hand. To do this, we need to be operating in the higher level of our brain, the **neocortex.** Unfortunately, when confronted with a stressful situation, the brain's physiological response is to prepare for either flight or fight. This response has been conditioned in us through millions of years of evolution. The blood leaves the neocortex and the paleocortex and moves to the brain stem. This move prepares us well to flee or to fight. It serves us poorly with solving complex problems such as discipline situations. We respond by avoiding, becoming aggressive or resorting to conditioned responses, rather than using our cognitive belief system and problem-solving skills to deal with the situation.

Students' Beliefs

Prior conditioning at home and at school, coupled with students' innate emotional intelligence, results in each student responding differently to different situations. We often see patterns in student behavior, however, two students exhibiting the same behavior may be doing so for different reasons. That means that the teacher's response that extinguishes the behavior in one student may not have the desired result in another student. Take, for example, two boys who may be constantly talking to each other in class.[1] One may come from a home in which the children hold equal or higher status with the adults. He may be permitted to interrupt adults and choose to ignore adults when they are speaking. This student's belief is that talking to his neighbor during class is an entirely appropriate activity. The other student may come from a home in which he is required to listen to adults, not allowed to disagree or contradict adults and certainly not allowed to interrupt an adult. Talking to his neighbor is a form of "pushing the envelope" and "walking on the wild side." For the second student, a firm look (or what we refer to later in the chapter as the *hairy eyeball*) may be sufficient to stop the behavior. For the other student, the look may only cause confusion.

Teaching Team's Beliefs

Classroom management plans work best when they are consistent among the teachers in a team (and the school, which we will talk about next). By *teams*, we are referring to those teachers who have contact with the same students with whom we have contact. In elementary schools with self-contained classrooms, the team includes the music, art and physical education teachers. It includes teachers who may have lunch or recess duty when our students are in these activities. In middle schools, teams of teachers often share the same students, with each person teaching a different subject area. In high school, the team is often the teachers in the same department. Over the course of a high school career, a student will have four to six teachers from each department. A high level of consistency with classroom

Classroom management plans work best when they are consistent among the teachers in a team.

[1] Dr. Jones's research indicates that 80% of the student misbehavior in classrooms (Jones, 2000, p. 154) is students talking to their neighbors. Think how much easier classroom management would be if we could do away with this one behavior!

behavior expectations (and academic expectations) will make classroom management more effective for everyone. Later in this chapter, we will see a plan for teaching the expectations for cleaning up after a science lab. It would be significantly easier for teachers to convey these expectations if all the science teachers established, taught and consistently required the same ones.

Students have spent many years figuring out the adults in their lives. By kindergarten, they have had six years of practice. By their senior year in high school, they have had seventeen or eighteen years of practice. They become very good at knowing what they can do with whom. This knowledge is evidenced by the ability that students have developed to assess each teacher's behavior limits and "push the envelope" to those limits. One elementary principal with whom we worked could observe lines of students waiting for the bus from his office window without the students' seeing him. Even though the school had written behavior expectations for the bus lines, teachers would implement these expectations with varying consistency. Student behavior would vary, based on who was on duty. A middle school assistant principal with whom we worked who was the building "disciplinarian" was often in the position of monitoring the behavior of the repeat offenders from the various classes. He found marked improvement in the behavior of the students in all classes when the teachers began responding to inappropriate behaviors in a consistent fashion. He described with excitement the way in which a plan of common techniques for responding to inappropriate behavior, designed to address the behaviors of one or two students, resulted in improved behavior for all the students. In general, the more consistent the expectations and implementation of them among the teaching team, the more effective each teacher will be in managing the classroom. Classroom management is one of those areas where the consistent whole is more effective than the sum of the parts.

School Culture

Each school has its own culture. In that culture, we should work to develop common expectations for student behavior, however, this is not always easy to do. There are many teachers in a school with many different sets of conscious and subconscious beliefs. The result is that even the best school-wide behavior plan will have gaps as a result of varying implementation. The goal of the school is to have common expectations and consistent implementation among the staff. This is one of those goals that schools never fully reach, however, constant effort from all staff toward this goal will result in more effective classroom management for all teachers.

An example of the value of school-wide behavior routines and expectations was observed in an urban district in a school located in the poorest neighborhood in the city. The governor of the state had come to present a successful achievement award to the school, which had previously been identified as underperforming and was placed under state monitoring. Over 1000 students from grades K–8 and their teachers were gathered into the school gymnasium to hear the governor speak. The whispering, shuffling and talking of over 1000 people added up to a significant level of noise. The superintendent stepped forward and raised his hand high over his head without speaking a word, and the entire gymnasium fell silent. The raised hand had become the signal for quiet in every classroom, in the entire school and in the entire district!

We want to have a plan that the administration supports and is reasonably consistent with other teachers' plans.

It is important that we consider the culture in our school when crafting our classroom management plans. We want to have a plan that the administration supports and is reasonably consistent with other teachers' plans. One author taught a workshop on classroom management to a group of teachers from several neighboring districts. In the workshop was a novice elementary music teacher who taught in two schools. The trainer could see the teacher's frustration each time he spoke about team consistency and school culture. At the break, the trainer asked the teacher what was frustrating him. He shared with him that in his district the four elementary schools were built in a cluster on the same site. Each school had a different philosophy. Parents in that community could choose the school they wished their children to attend. He happened to be assigned to two schools with very different cultures related to student behavior. One school was "traditional." Most of the classrooms were arranged with students in rows. Students all passed through the halls in lines. The other school was an open concept school. There were large teaching spaces that several classes shared. Students flowed through the halls from one place to another without walking in lines. The students called the teachers and the principal by their first names. The music teacher had tried to develop a classroom management plan that worked in both schools, but he ended up with one that did not work well in either school. The trainer spent some time with the teacher, modifying his single plan by turning it into two plans, with one for each school. The teacher reported significant improvement when his classroom management plans matched the culture in each school.

Fortunately, most of us don't have to work in more than one school culture at a time, however, this story does emphasize the importance of understanding the school culture and crafting a plan that is not inconsistent with that culture.

Parents' Beliefs

Parents' beliefs, as a group, often correlate fairly closely with the school culture. The exception to this is when a school has been deemed in need of a significant change in its culture. In those cases, the school's stated culture and its operating culture will be separated by a fairly large gap. In these circumstances, it is important to be aware of both cultures and adjust our classroom plans as the culture of the building changes. The parents' culture might reflect the stated school culture, the operating school culture or a completely different culture.

Within the parent group, there are significant numbers of parents who have a belief system that is outside of the group's. This is less the case in schools such as the ones described above, in which the parents get to match their belief system with the school's culture. Most school enrollments, however, are determined by geography. This leaves a greater likelihood that there will be parents with beliefs outside of the group belief system. This difference may be even more pronounced in cities and counties in which students are bused across neighborhood and community lines. In those cases, the socio-economic, religious and cultural differences tend to be greater than in schools that draw from a specific geographic neighborhood. We worked with an assistant superintendent in an urban/suburban district with eight neighborhood schools. One school had a parent education level that was in the top 1% in the state. The parent income level was in the top 2% in the state. Across the district was another school in which over 30% of the students were on free and reduced lunch and many lived in public housing. In a third school, 20% of the student population was first- and second-generation Japanese–American. In still another school, the population was 40% Jewish and 40% white Anglo-Saxon protestant. Another school had a very large concentration of Chinese and Latino students who were predominantly Catholic and also a growing Muslim community. These were all neighborhood schools with their own school cultures and some similarity in family beliefs about student behavior. All eight schools with their different cultures sent their ninth graders to a single high school. One may just imagine the multitude of parent belief systems and school cultures faced by the teachers of these ninth graders.

Rules/Standards, Routines and Expectations

In thinking about classroom management, we focus on three levels of behaviors. The first is our **rules or standards.** These tend to be only a few and also are generally worded. We try to write rules/standards in terminology that is positive rather than focusing on the negative. Samples of rules/standards include the following:

1. We will treat everyone in the class with respect.
2. We will treat all school and personal materials and supplies in an appropriate manner.
3. We will support the learning and growth of all members of the class.
4. We will arrive to class on time with our materials, and we will complete our work in a timely manner.

Rules/standards are often established on a school-wide basis. If not, then it is important that we start our work in developing our classroom management plans by creating the rules/standards. These should be posted in a prominent place in the classroom.

In order to help students better understand and appreciate the rules, some teachers have the students brainstorm a list of rules they think would be important to have in their classrooms. Students usually contribute a long list of fairly specific rules. As a class, rules are categorized into one of four or five general rules. For example, the following rules could all be categorized under *we will treat everyone with respect.*

1. I will listen when the teacher or another student is talking.
2. we I will raise my hand when I have something to say in class.
3. we I will ask permission if I would like to use another students' materials.
4. we I will keep quiet when we are doing independent work.
5. I will make sure everyone is included when we are at lunch and recess.

After the class agrees upon approximately five general rules, the students create a poster showing the rules and students are asked to sign their names to the poster. In essence, they are signing a contract. There is a common understanding that if a student breaks a rule, he or she will face consequences which are also known and discussed ahead of time.

After rules/standards, the second level of our classroom management planning is **routines.** These are specific tasks students must successfully complete to meet the standard. Later in this chapter, you will see the expectations developed by one teacher for her classroom routine.

The third level is the **expectations.** These are the observable descriptions of the behaviors a student must exhibit to demonstrate successful implementation of the routine.

Teachers often start the year poorly with their classroom management because they fail to devote adequate time to teaching students the routines and expectations that *operationalize* the rules/standards. Many teachers state and post their rules/standards at the start of the year and never go beyond that point. The problem with this is that words may mean different things to different students, based on their beliefs. The definition of *respect* may vary in different homes and in the classrooms of the various teachers the students had during prior years. The definition also changes for people as they enter different stages of their lives. Treating a person with *respect* means one thing to us when we are five, another when we are ten, another when we are fifteen, another when we are twenty and still another when we are forty-five. This is why it is important that we clearly state the routines and our expectations for the behaviors that lead to success in each routine.

> *Teachers often start the year poorly with their classroom management because they fail to devote adequate time to teaching students the routines and expectations that operationalize the rules/standards.*

Before a teacher can teach routines to students, he or she must have a clear and specific understanding of the expectations for each routine. For example, we were teaching a group of second-year high school teachers about developing routines. Several had expressed concern that the flow of the class was often interrupted by student requests to go to the bathroom. We asked each teacher to write down his or her expectations for bathroom use and the time he or she spent telling and/or teaching[2] the routines to students. Several gave a one-sentence explanation of routines such as, "You must ask permission to use the bathroom in my class." All indicated they spent a minute or less telling students the bathroom expectations at the start of the school year. A series of questions was asked of one of the teachers who had given a single sentence as his bathroom expectation and we uncovered that the teacher in fact had fifteen expectations that made up the classroom bathroom routine. The conversation went like this.

Author: What are your expectations for students using the bathroom in your class?
Teacher: They may not use the bathroom.
Author: When during the school day can they go to the bathroom?
Teacher: Before school, between classes, during lunch, after school.
Author: What if a student has a medical problem that requires frequent bathroom use?
Teacher: I had one student like that last year. I let her go whenever she needed to go.
Author: How did you know she had a medical issue?
Teacher: She told me after class. I checked it with the guidance counselor and it was true.
Author: How did the other students respond to her being the only one who was able to use the bathroom?
Teacher: I actually did allow students to use the bathroom. I told the students they could go if it is an emergency. I am mostly concerned that they don't abuse the privilege and don't go during the first ten minutes or the last ten minutes of class.
Author: Why are the first ten minutes and the last ten minutes so important?
Teacher: The first ten minutes is when I'm giving directions. After that students are often doing group or individual work. If they miss the first ten minutes, they miss the information they need to work productively throughout the lesson. During the last ten minutes, I summarize what we did for the day and give out the homework. The summary is important because it pulls together the entire lesson. If they miss the homework explanation they won't be able to do the homework.
Author: Do you let students know why the first ten minutes and the last ten minutes are so important?
Teacher: No
Author: Do the students who have an emergency need to tell you they need to use the bathroom or can they just go?
Teacher: They raise their hands.
Author: What do you do?
Teacher: I ask if it is an emergency.
Author: Did you tell them your expectation is that they should only ask to go to the bathroom if it is not the first ten minutes or the last ten minutes and only if it is an emergency?
Teacher: I don't remember.

[2] The authors differentiate between the words telling and teaching in the following way. "Telling" is an activity done solely by the teacher. Tellers give out the requisite information but do not assess and ensure the students' level of understanding or mastery of the information. "Teaching" transfers a body of information in a way that maximizes understanding and retention. It includes an assessment of the students' understanding of the information and their mastery of any behavior required in the learning.

Author: How long can they be out of the room?
Teacher: Less than five minutes.
Author: When did you tell them that?
Teacher: During the second week of school, I was getting frustrated. Students were going to the bathroom and coming back ten, fifteen and even twenty minutes later. I finally got angry at one class and took away their bathroom privileges. I eventually calmed down and gave them back the privilege about a week later, but I required a five-minute maximum time out of the classroom.
Author: How do you keep track of how long students are out?
Teacher: At first I tried to monitor the clock myself, however, when I got back into working with the students after a student left for the bathroom, I would forget when he or she left. I was talking with a colleague about the problem, and she suggested I have the students sign out, writing the time they leave and then sign back in, writing the time they return. That has worked well.
Author: When leaving the class, can they stop to talk to a friend?
Teacher: No, they must go straight to the sign out list and to the bathroom without talking.
Author: Can they take anything with them?
Teacher: No.
Author: How do you want them to return to their seats?
Teacher: I want them to sign in and go directly to their seats without talking to anyone or touching anyone.
Author: Have you told them this?
Teacher: Not yet, but I will.
Author: What happens if they don't follow these expectations?
Teacher: They lose the right to go to the bathroom.
Author: For how long?
Teacher: I don't know.
Author: What do you think is the right amount of time?
Teacher: I guess a week.
Author: What if, after the week, they don't follow the expectations again?
Teacher: I had one student who did that last year, and I took his bathroom privileges away for a month.
Author: It sounds like you've changed the consequence from denying bathroom privileges to all students to just withholding them from those who do not follow your expectations.
Teacher: Oh, yeah. You're right.
Author: Ok, let's go over your expectations.

1. No asking to go to the bathroom unless it is an emergency.
2. If you have a doctor-confirmed medical reason indicating you need to use the bathroom frequently, you should speak to me privately.
3. Emergency use is restricted to after the first ten minutes and before the last ten minutes of class.
4. You must raise your hand and ask permission.
5. You must sign out and include the time you leave.
6. You must walk directly to the door without detours and without talking to or touching anyone or anything.
7. You must go directly to the bathroom and directly back without disturbing any other classes along the way.
8. You may not take anything with you.
9. You must return in five minutes or less.

10. You must sign in and include the time you return.
11. You must walk directly to your seat without detours and without talking to or touching anyone or anything.
12. You must quietly check with a neighbor to see what you missed.
13. The first failure to follow these expectations means you lose bathroom privileges in this class for a week.
14. The second failure to do so means you lose bathroom privileges in this class for a month.
15. The third failure to do so means you will receive a discipline referral to the assistant principal.

Author: How will you check to see if the students understand your expectations?
Teacher: I will ask a student to repeat them back to the class.
Author: How will you teach these expectations?
Teacher: I'll tell them the expectations and why they exist. I'll demonstrate how *not* to walk to and from the door by imitating the way many of them do this (e.g., stopping at a friend's desk, poking other students, etc.). I do role-play sometimes when teaching and they find it funny. It usually helps them remember what I'm teaching.
Author: Many teachers have different expectations. How will you ensure they remember your bathroom expectations?
Teacher: I'll write the expectations on a chart and hang it on the wall.
Author: How long do you think it will take you to teach the expectations and check for understanding?
Teacher: Probably about fifteen to twenty minutes.
Author: How will you know when you need to reteach the expectations?
Teacher: I will review the expectations at the start of each class for the first week. After that, I will reteach them if students stop following the expectations.

Below is a list of the specific routines that need to be thoroughly considered. Put a check next to each routine for which you have already created specific expectations for your students. As you read through this list, you may write down any notes you wish to remember about any of the listed routines.

Beginning Class Routines and Expectations **Notes**

____ Roll call, attendance (including procedures for tardiness)
____ Seat work requirements when students first enter the class
____ Distribution of materials
____ Class opening
____ Sitting in assigned seats
____ Procedure for turning in homework
____ Procedure for students absent the previous day to collect missed handouts and assignments
____ Writing down that night's homework assignment

General Classroom Routines and Expectations

____ Materials students are expected to have in class each day
____ Shared materials
____ Teacher's desk
____ Food and drinks (water)
____ Gum
____ Bathroom
____ Pencil sharpener
____ Student storage, lockers, cubbies
____ Dismissing class
____ Lining up for assemblies, trips to library or computer lab

Routines and Expectations for Behavior During Independent and Group Work

____ Do you permit talk among students?
____ If so, when and how?
____ Identification of resources such as Internet and dictionaries and how they may be accessed during the work time
____ Passing out of books, supplies
____ Interim checkpoints
____ Signals for students' attention (See the section later in this chapter on obtaining and regaining student attention.)
____ Signals for teacher's attention
____ Activities to do when work is done
____ Student participation
____ Turning in work
____ Handing back assignments

Notes

____ Getting back assignments after signed by parents or other reasons we need them returned
____ Missed work
____ Laboratory procedures
____ Movement in and out of small groups
____ Bringing materials to school
____ Expected behavior in group[3]
____ What to do if you finish early
____ Homework expectations and procedures
____ Putting away supplies, equipment
____ Cleaning up
____ Organizing class materials

Expectations for Appropriately Completed Work

____ Heading papers
____ Use of pen, pencil or word processor
____ Writing on the back of papers
____ Neatness, legibility
____ Incomplete work
____ Late work
____ Use of manuscript, cursive, typing
____ Margins, font, single- or double-spaced type
____ Cutting "fringes" off paper taken from spiral notebook

Grading Policies and Procedures

____ Determining grades
____ Recording grades
____ Grading long assignments
____ Extra credit work
____ Keeping papers, grades, assignments
____ Grading criteria
____ Contracting for grades
____ Rewrites and retests
____ Make-up work policy (if absent)
____ Late homework penalty system

Other Routines and Expectations

____ Fire drills
____ Lunch procedures
____ Student helpers
____ Safety procedures
____ Out-of-seat policies
____ Consequences for misbehavior
____ Behavior in the computer lab, library, auditorium

[3] Monitoring the level of conversation during small group work that is on-task and off-task may be difficult when we are helping individual groups with their work. One technique we have used to teach the expectations for appropriate group discussions and at times to monitor that expectation is to record on audiotape the work of some groups. In the next section of this chapter is an explanation of how this may be done.

Teaching Routines and Expectations

The time spent teaching routines and expectations is time well spent. Over the course of the year, a teacher will save a great deal of instructional time if he or she devotes adequate time at the start of the year to teaching routines and expectations.

Over the course of the year, a teacher will save a great deal of instructional time if he or she devotes adequate time at the start of the year to teaching routines and expectations.

In his book, *Tools for Teaching* (2000, p.125), Fred Jones states,

> Research has repeatedly shown that the teachers with the best-run classrooms spend most of the first two weeks of the semester teaching their procedures and routines. Teachers who do not make this investment deal with the same behavior problems over and over all semester long. It is a case of: Pay me now, or pay me later. Do it right, or do it all year long.

Teaching Classroom Routines

Step one in effectively teaching routines is to be clear about what it looks like when a student successfully completes the expectations for the routine and what it looks like when a student does not follow the expectations correctly. Wording the expectations in language that is observable will help you teach the expectation clearly.

Step two is to test the reality of the expectations for the routine. The teacher in the earlier example originally wanted no one to go to the bathroom. Upon reflection, he realized this was not a viable routine.

Step three is to ensure that the routine you have planned is consistent with the expectations for the school and team.

Step four is to create a plan for teaching the routine.

It will be helpful to model and/or role-play routines as part of teaching the routine. For example, if one of your expectations as an elementary educator is that students should make an effort to include others they see are being excluded during recess time, it would be helpful to have a few students role-play this scenario while the other students observe. After role-playing, the class might discuss other means by which to make sure everyone is included.

One high school teacher role-plays leaving the classroom to go to the bathroom, assigning himself the role of the student. The first time he shows the students how *not* to leave the class. He takes on the persona of the student by getting out of his chair and swaggering on a circuitous route around the room, before eventually getting to the door. On his way around, he pauses at the desks of a couple of his friends to make a comment or flip their books shut. This role-play always results in laughs from the students as many of them can see themselves in his behaviors. He then role-plays the appropriate way one leaves the room to use the bathroom after receiving permission from the teacher.

Once a routine is taught, we need to expect students to consistently use it and we should assess students' success in carrying it out. We should look for opportunities to consistently reinforce successful performance of the routine. We should also be ready to reteach the routine if we see student performance regressing. One of the most important parts of establishing and maintaining good routines is consistent enforcement and reinforcement!

Although there are too many classroom routines to post them all, it may be helpful to post those routines that are particularly important. For example, you may want to make a poster listing activities for students to complete when work is finished. You may also want to post a list of expectations for students engaged in collaborative work.

Using an Audiotape as a Management Technique

One technique we have found to be particularly helpful in teaching and managing expectations of group work is the use of an audiotape. (A recording is also useful for observing and analyzing student learning and for self-reflection.)

Implementing This Tool

First, begin by introducing the audiotape and explaining to the students that this tool will be used to help you better understand where they are in their learning, to monitor their progress and to listen to their conversations that you were unable to hear when you are working with another group. Explain to them that they will also have an opportunity to listen to their conversations.

Before actually using the audiotape to record conversations, have a discussion with the students about how the recording device works and how students might feel the first couple of times they are being recorded. Give students time to "play around" with the audiotape for a few minutes and allow them to practice using it. We found that this practice eliminates some of the silliness and uneasiness that sometimes goes along with being recorded.

Next, select a group to record for a collaborative activity. (We usually recorded only one group at a time.) Make sure the students understand that they need to speak clearly and into the microphone (if there is one). Be present until they get situated. Once they begin the activity, you will have more time to spend with the other groups, as you will be able to go back to the taped group and analyze their work at a later time.

Analyzing the Conversations

Try to listen to the audiotape as soon as possible. In this way, you may quickly address any learning misunderstandings or inappropriate group work behaviors immediately. For example, one teacher was able to uncover and consequently address an ongoing problem one literature circle group was experiencing. The audiotape allowed her to listen to this group's entire conversation and analyze what was happening with regard to group dynamics. Without being able to do so, it is unlikely she would have uncovered what was happening in this particular group. In this case, one student dominated the conversation, and, because he was so outspoken, all group members listened to him, agreed with him and even changed their views. Because the teacher only listened to small pieces of the group's conversation during the class, she assumed that the vocal student understood the text and was able to clarify any confusion his group members had. Unfortunately, this student communicated his *misunderstandings* of the text to the other students. Because the teacher was able to take a deeper look at this group via the audiotape, she was able to address these issues the following day.

The teacher also had these students listen to their conversation and asked them to reflect on the dynamics of their group. The outspoken student immediately realized he had dominated the conversation and commented, "I never realized how much I talked. I guess I should work on giving other students a chance to talk, too." This group came up with a plan to help one another take turns talking and, consequently, had much more interactive, effective discussions in the future.

Unexpected Outcome

The students also remarked that the audiotape had the effect of keeping them on task as they knew the teacher was going to be listening to their entire conversation at some point. The teacher found that she had to spend less time dealing with discipline issues with the group that was using the audiotape. The students seemed to like using the audiotape, as they felt that it helped them to stay more focused and eliminated some of the off-task behaviors groups experienced when a teacher wasn't working with them.

Sample plan for teaching homework routines to upper elementary students

Homework seems to be an issue with which teachers and students at all grade levels struggle from time to time. When students do not complete homework assignments, they are often not adequately prepared for class. There is much teachers can do proactively at the beginning of the year, however, to increase students' success with homework. Teaching children the routine of effectively completing homework during first three weeks of school will help make the homework experience a positive one for both parents and children. The amount of time needed to teach the routine may vary, depending on grade level.

A. Objective

Students will complete their homework assignments on time, with correct paper setup, with appropriate parent support and to the best of their ability.

B. Criteria for Success

1. 100% of the homework will be completed by the start of the class. Any student with extenuating circumstances that caused the homework not to be finished will have a note from his or her parent explaining the situation.
2. Papers will be set up as noted in the criteria posted on the wall.
3. Homework should be completed independently by the student, and parents should assist only as a last resort. Students will solicit parent support only upon the following conditions:
   a. attempted the assignment independently without success
   b. reviewed the classroom notes and/or textbook pages explaining the concepts required in the homework
   c. attempted the assignment independently at least one additional time without success
4. The student's homework will be completed to the best of his or her ability. The homework will demonstrate a level of quality similar to that completed in class and accepted by the teacher as the student's best work.
5. Students will copy the assignment each day, exactly as written on the white board, in their homework notebook.
6. Students will bring their homework notebook and all necessary materials home each night.

C. Teaching Steps

1. The expectations noted above in the criteria for success section will be taught during the first week of school.
2. The students will be given copies of exemplars saved from previous years.
3. The homework expectations will be posted on the wall. (See the following sample.)
4. Students will complete all homework assignments in class during the first three weeks of school. The teacher will closely monitor students' adherence to the expectations to ensure that all students understand and successfully follow the expectations.
5. A homework packet containing a letter describing the homework procedures, homework expectations and ideas for setting up an area conducive for doing homework will be sent to parents the first week of school. (See the following sample.)
6. The homework expectations (particularly the one about help from parents as "last resort") will be explained on parents' night.

7. Students' homework during the first three weeks of school will be to bring home the homework assignments they completed in school for parent review and signature. Parents should be encouraged to write back with any questions they have about the homework procedure. Homework is the one routine that requires training the parents as well as the students!

The following pages contain sample letters and checklists that might be sent home to parents. It includes a specific list of the homework expectations referred to previously.

Sample Letter Explaining Homework for the First Two Weeks of School

September 4, 2002
Dear Parents and/or Guardians,

As we work to become more responsive to the needs of our students, I have developed a new approach to "teaching" homework. For the first three weeks of school, time will be devoted each day to clearly define my expectations of good work and to teach students how to successfully complete homework. Among many other things, we will discuss the following: how to become an organized student; how to prioritize assignments; how to get started on homework assignments; what to do when an assignment is difficult; how to set up a space at home conducive to fostering good study habits, etc. All written work will be completed in class for the first three weeks of school.

During this time, your child's homework will be to bring home and share and explain these assignments to you. This task will reinforce the learning that took place during the school day. In addition, all students are expected to read for at least fifteen minutes each night. I will give specific directions in class regarding at-home reading assignments.

In a couple of weeks, I will be sending home another letter that clearly outlines my policy on homework. If you have any questions, please contact me.

Please sign this letter below and have your child return it to me.

Sincerely,

Mrs. Deane

Parent/Guardian Signature: ______________________________

Sample Letter Explaining Homework Policies and Procedures

Dear Parents and/or Guardians,

I believe homework is important because it is a valuable aid in helping students make the most of their experience in school. Homework is given because it is useful in reinforcing what has been learned in class, prepares students for upcoming lessons, extends and generalizes concepts, teaches responsibility and helps students develop positive study habits.

Fifth graders will be given homework Monday through Thursday nights. Homework should take students no longer than 45–60 minutes each night, not including studying for tests and working on long-term projects. A mathematical problem of the week will be given each Monday, and students are expected to turn this assignment in on Friday. Spelling units will also be given each Monday and will be due on Thursday. A spelling test will be given each Friday. Students will be given at least one week's notice to study for most tests.

Students are expected to do their best on homework. Since homework reflects what one has learned, it should be done independently. If your child has difficulty with an assignment, he or she should ask for help after giving his or her best effort. Please contact me if your child consistently needs help with homework.

All homework assignments will be checked and sometimes they will be graded. I will not always announce when I will be grading homework. Therefore, it is important for each child to be well prepared.

If students consistently choose not to complete their homework, I will ask that parents begin checking and signing their child's assignment notebook each night. If students still choose not to complete their work, they also choose to lose certain privileges, such as recess. If students choose to make up their homework the next day, their homework will be accepted. If they choose not to make up missed assignments, students will receive a zero for those assignments.

Please be assured that if there is a legitimate reason why a student is not able to finish homework, I will make exceptions. Please send a note to me on the day the assignment is due.

I feel that parents play an important role in making homework a positive experience for children. Therefore, I ask parents to make homework a priority. You may do this by providing necessary supplies and a quiet work environment, setting a daily homework time, providing support and encouragement and not allowing children to avoid homework. I encourage you to contact me if there is a problem or concern.

Please read and discuss this policy with your child and sign and return the bottom portion of this letter to me. Thank you for your cooperation. I look forward to working with you and your child.

Sincerely,
Mrs. Deane

I have read the homework policy and discussed it with my child,________________

Comments:____

____

Parent Signature:____

Homework Expectations

- All homework should have your name and date and the subject on the top of the page.
- All math homework should be completed in pencil.
- All other written homework should be completed in one color of pen.
- All work should be done in your neatest handwriting or word-processed if appropriate.
- All work should be carefully proofread and edited.
- No cross-outs.
- Paper should not be torn from a spiral notebook and should not have jagged edges.
- Homework should be clean and unwrinkled.
- Homework should be turned in on time.
- Remember to always do your best.

Helpful Homework Hints

Work Area:

- Clean area
- Quiet area
- All supplies available

Time:

Make a plan for

- Homework time
- Break/Snack time

Supplies:

- Pens, pencils
- Erasers
- Crayons, markers
- Glue
- Lined paper
- Scissors
- Ruler
- Dictionary
- Thesaurus

Prioritize your assignments. Assignments that are due the next day should be completed first. Map out a schedule for long-term assignments so that they are not left until the last minute.

When implementing this homework policy, teachers found this strategy to be well-received by the parents and students alike. Parents commented that it really taught the students good study habits and gave them an opportunity to practice them with guidance. It also concretized what good study habits look like and how to develop them. Teachers found that it reduced the number of missing and incomplete homework assignments as the expectations were laid out and practiced at the beginning of the year before bad habits were established. Although this strategy does take time during the first few weeks of school, we feel it is an invaluable process and ultimately saves time over the course of the year.

Sample plan for teaching classroom routines to middle school students
Below is a plan created to teach middle school science students the routine for cleaning up after a lab.

1. **Objective:** The students will clean up their lab areas, have all equipment returned to its proper location and have their lab areas ready for the next class within five minutes of being given the direction to clean up.
2. **Criteria for success**
    a. Partner one will wipe all fluids from the microscope, dry the microscope thoroughly and place the microscope on the shelf that corresponds with the number on the microscope.
    b. Partner two will return the specimens to their containers and to the appropriate shelf and then wipe down the lab area and discard all disposable materials.
    c. Each partner will check the other's work to ensure it meets the criteria.
    d. The lab area will show no sign that there was a lab.
3. **Teaching Steps**
    a. I will explain this routine and explain why it is important at the end of the next science class, prior to the next lab.
    b. At the start of the next class, I will explain the steps for correctly cleaning up and post the steps on a chart paper.
    c. I will set up a lab area and have a pair of students demonstrate the procedure.
    d. At the end of the next lab period, I will have the group that finishes first walk through the steps while I describe them to the class.
    e. I will structure the lesson so there is more than the typical time at the end for cleanup. I will plan my time so I am free to monitor and coach the groups during the cleanup.

Independent Practice: In the next lab period, I will review the steps and keep myself free to coach, but I will require the independent completion of the cleanup in ten minutes. In each subsequent lab, I will slightly decrease the cleanup time until the targeted time is achieved.

Sample plan for teaching classroom routines to high school students
Below is a plan created to teach high school students in an English class the routine for peer-editing drafts of each other's essays.

1. **Objective:** The students will utilize already-created rubrics to peer-edit the rough drafts of four to five other students in the class.
2. **Criteria for success**
   a. Students must place their own rough drafts on their desk along with a blank rubric.
   b. Students will all stand up and find a new seat where they will read and edit the rough draft of another student in the class.
   c. Students will offer detailed comments on the blank rubric form.
   d. Upon completing this task, students will go to the front of the classroom to pick up a second blank rubric form.
   e. Students will then choose a second peer's rough draft to edit and peer-review using the blank rubric.
   f. Students will repeat this process until they have read and edited the drafts of four to five of their peers.
3. **Teaching steps**
   a. I will first explain this routine in general terms when initially discussing the due date of students' rough drafts in order to emphasize the importance of having one's draft in school on the day on which feedback will be solicited from peers.
   b. I will explain that the purpose is to support each other in producing high-quality final drafts and to practice catching spelling and grammatical errors.
   c. I will explain the steps of this routine in detail at the beginning of the class period in which students bring their drafts to be peer-edited.
   d. I will ask the students to read and edit four to five of their peers' rough drafts by doing the following:
      - I will first ask students to clear their desks of all materials except for their rough draft and a rubric.
      - Next, I will ask students to stand up and find a new seat within the classroom.
      - Next, I will read through the various components of the rubric with my students.
      - Next, I will describe to students the procedure for acquiring a new rubric and finding a new rough draft to edit upon completing their edits of the rough draft currently in front of them.
      - Finally, I will remind students of the expectation that they edit four to five of their peers' rough drafts within the specified time.
   e. I will float around the classroom, guiding students on the next steps to take as they complete their edits of the first manuscript, namely, acquiring a new rubric and finding a new peer's rough draft to edit and review.

   Independent Practice: By the second time that students bring in their rough drafts to be read and edited by peers, they will have grown accustomed to the routines that accompany a workshop period.

Student Self-Assessment of the Expectations for Routines Using Rubrics and Criteria Sheets

In the academic disciplines we have learned that rubrics and criteria sheets are an excellent means of assessing student performance on various skills. Chapter 6 contains information on assessing student work. We are increasingly asking students to use rubrics and criteria sheets as a means of self-assessing their progress throughout the period of time they are learning new tasks. We do this so students may objectively measure their progress with the goal of determining how far they have come and how far they have left to go to be successful. It also serves as a concrete reminder of the expectations for successful completion of the task. The same is true for student behavior. Once we have determined observable expectations for a routine and have taught those expectations to the class, we are in a position to have the students periodically self-assess their performance. Following are two samples of student self-assessments used by a high school teacher and a middle school teacher, respectively.

The sheet in the first sample is given to students at the start of each week. At the end of the class, students are given a minute to assess their performance on each of the areas. They put a check in the box for each criterion they successfully met. The comments section is for writing any information they want to tell the teacher. For example, a student may wish to tell the teacher that he or she was late as a result of being called to the office at the end of the previous class. At the end of the week, the students count up the number of checks and place the number (1 to 20) in the box at the bottom of the last column. The sheets are passed in to the teacher on Fridays. The teacher records the students' "grades" for the week. If the teacher believes the form has not been accurately filled out by a student, he will change the final grade on the form to match his observation. At the start of the year, there are usually a couple of students who test the teacher by rating themselves higher than their actual achievement. Correcting the form and speaking to those students eliminates the behavior in the first two weeks.

Some teachers incorporate the student's performance on these sheets into the grade. For example, the teacher will add up the points every five weeks and use that total as a quiz grade. Other teachers don't incorporate it into grades but do provide other incentives.

Some teachers choose to be more specific with the expectations for the categories. For example, the category, *do not make any disruptions,* might include the following criteria:

- show respect for others by including no back talk
- use only appropriate language
- do not diss others
- sharpen pencils only when others are not speaking
- keep hands and feet to oneself

Name: ______________________________ Period: __________

CHECKLIST FOR SUCCESS IN A HIGH SCHOOL CLASSROOM

Did I . . .	come to class on time.	come to class prepared. (This includes binder, writing utensil and h.w.)	finish my class work.	participate positively at least once.	not make any disruptions.	Comments
Monday						
Tuesday						
Wednesday						
Thursday						
Friday						
						Total =

Reprinted with permission from Richard Higgins of the Weymouth, MA, Public Schools

Mid-Quarter 1: Self-Assessment
Middle School Science

Now that you have had a chance to review your progress report, here is an opportunity to think about your actions, increase self-understanding and take responsibility for your choices. The following worksheet includes questions on academic performance, class behavior, organizational skills, use of your agenda book, preparation for class, responsibility with homework and ability to work in groups. After answering these questions, you will then design a plan to address your deficiencies and define steps you need to take to be successful in science class. This information will be the center of our discussion during student–teacher conferences, which will take place in the coming weeks.

Rate yourself according to the scale below. Be honest. This self-assessment does not factor into your final grade for the quarter; it is only a tool to help you succeed.

		1 Needs a Lot of Work	2 Needs Some Work	3 Achieved Near-Mastery	4 Achieved Mastery
Homework	My homework assignments are completed on time.				
	I check my work before I decide my homework is done.				
	If I'm absent I go directly to the absent homework folder for my block.				
	I always have my agenda book for every class.				
	I have my HW assignments written down before Ms. Sales reminds the class to. I understand what I wrote in my agenda book when I get home.				
Class Behavior	The first thing I do when I come into class is look at the white board.				
	I always come to class with a pencil and pen/marker.				
	My Science Journal (binder) is organized. I am not missing anything that I should have.				
	I am always ready to start class when Ms. Sales is.				
	I do my best in every task.				
	I always raise my hand when I would like to speak.				
	I actively listen to what my classmates say during class discussion.				

		1 Needs a Lot of Work	2 Needs Some Work	3 Achieved Near-Mastery	4 Achieved Mastery
Class Behavior (continued)	I don't talk out of turn.				
	When Ms. Sales makes transitions between class activities I don't take that opportunity to talk.				
	When other students try to distract me, I ignore them or tell them to stop.				
	I don't distract other students from being successful in class.				
	I effectively communicate my ideas during class discussion.				
Group Work	When working in a lab team, I respect the ideas of my classmates.				
	During lab activities, I am on task.				
	During lab activities, I follow directions correctly.				
	During lab activities, I communicate effectively with my partners.				
	During lab activities, I share tasks equitably.				
	During lab activities, I handle equipment safely and appropriately.				
	I check my work before handing in a lab.				
Academic Performance	I actively seek help from Ms. Sales when I need it.				
	I check my work before handing in a quiz/test.				
	For TTEs, I write for the entire time and use all the lines I'm supposed to.				
	I feel prepared for quizzes/tests because I know what to study.				
	I do my best on quizzes/tests.				

Do lab activities help you better understand what is read in your textbook and talked about in class? Why or why not?

Does your lab grade correctly reflect your effort? Why?

What is your best work so far in this class? Why do you take pride in it?

Does your homework grade correctly reflect your effort? Why?

Does your quiz/test grade correctly reflect your understanding of the material? Why?

At this point in time, what areas do you feel are your deficiencies? (What areas do you need to work on?)

List three things you may do to improve upon your deficiencies.

1.

2.

3.

What do you need to be successful in science class?

What can Ms. Sales do to help in executing your plan for success?

Reprinted with the permission of Mitzi Sales of the Westwood, MA, Public Schools

Obtaining, Maintaining and Regaining Student Attention

Teachers use a wide variety of strategies for signaling to students that it is time to be quiet. An article in the *Responsive Classroom Newsletter* (McErlane, 2002) categorizes these as visual strategies and auditory strategies. Visual strategies include hand signals, specific teacher posture (e.g., hands on hips), closing our eyes and other teacher behaviors the students know mean it is time to be quiet. The second category of signals discussed in the article is auditory strategies. Auditory strategies include chimes, a bell, playing notes on a musical instrument and other sounds that signal to the students that it is time to be quiet. In the book, *The Skillful Teacher* (Saphier and Gower, 1997), the authors identify fifty-three different attention moves they have observed in various classrooms. It is important for teachers to have a large repertoire of strategies to gain student attention. If our voice is the only strategy we use to gain student attention, students soon learn to tune it out.

The following steps for establishing the effective use of signals for getting students to be quiet are based on the steps identified in the *Responsive Classroom Newsletter* (2002) by Mark Farnsworth, a high school physical education teacher.

1. Choose signals that are easily noticed.
2. Teach and practice the signals with the students before expecting students to use them.
3. Always use the designated signals to achieve quiet.
4. Expect everyone, even adults who enter your room, to adhere to the signal.
5. Don't begin talking until you have everyone's attention.
6. If some children aren't paying attention, stop and practice the signal again.
7. Use frequent and specific, positive praise with the class and with individuals who demonstrate timely adherence to the signal.
8. Have clearly defined warnings and consequences for those students who do not respond.
9. Remember that the goal of the signal is to gain the children's attention. If everyone is paying attention it is okay to start talking.

Auditory Strategies for Gaining Attention

1. bell
2. whistle—often used by coaches and by teachers in large group situations
   Mr. Farnsworth uses different numbers of whistles to indicate different behaviors in his physical education classes. For example, a single loud whistle can mean everyone freeze and be quiet. *Two short whistles can mean* continue with the activity but stop talking and listen for instructions.
3. speaking softly
4. piano notes (or other instrument notes)
5. chime
6. alarm or buzzer from a timer when it reaches the set end time of a group or partner discussion activity
7. humorous comment
   Please note that educators make a distinction between humor and sarcasm. Humor is something that is funny (appropriately so) that does not make one of the students the target of the humor. Sarcasm, though at times seen as funny by many in the room, may have a derogatory impact on the self-image of the target student and/or generate fear among other students that they may be the next target student.
8. clapping hands to a familiar rhythm
9. humming or singing a specific tune
10. asking students to stop talking

11. singing a tune
12. playing a music CD
13. counting down (5, 4, 3, 2 ...) or counting up (1, 2, 3, 4 ...)
14. telling students they may have or do something they all would like only when everyone is listening
    This strategy places peer pressure on those still not listening.
15. saying "Excuse me" in a firm but calm voice and repeating "Excuse me" in a softer and softer voice until room is silent
16. beginning to speak in a quiet voice—students stop talking to hear
17. saying "Excuse me, Mark" to a particular student who is speaking
18. making instructional statements that raise the students' curiosity
    For example, one high school social studies teacher starts his classes by singing a humorous song that was popular with adolescents during the period they are studying.

Visual Strategies

1. flash the lights
   This strategy may cause problems for some autistic students.
2. hand signal
   a. hands on head
   b. hand in the air
      A variation of this used by some teachers when students are working in pairs or groups is to allow the students to put up one finger to request an additional minute to finish their conversation.)
   c. hold up two fingers as a peace sign
3. close eyes
4. point to or hold up a *quiet please* sign
5. teacher places a single finger over her lips
6. humorous activity
   One teacher stood on his head at the front of the room to get the students' attention.
7. wave one's arms dramatically and humorously to signal for attention
8. stand quietly in the front of the room until all students are quiet
9. use a "Yacker Tracker"
   This is a device that looks like a stoplight with green, yellow and red-lights and is sensitive to noise levels in the room. When the noise is at an appropriate level, the green light is on. If the noise nears the maximum appropriate level, the yellow light goes on. If the noise exceeds the appropriate level, the red light goes on.
10. signal for quiet and then hold up a stopwatch to gauge how many seconds it takes for the room to fall completely silent
    Compliment students on a job well done or note the need for improvement if a quiet classroom took too much time to achieve.
11. For example, one middle school social studies teacher frequently greets students in an outfit from the period they are learning

Some high school and middle school teachers who use inanimate objects, such as the chime, music and/or flashing lights, report that students who are displeased with the need to be quiet associate their displeasure with the object rather than the teacher.

Some high school and middle school teachers who use inanimate objects, such as the chime, music and/or flashing lights, report that students who are displeased with the need to be quiet associate their displeasure with the object rather than the teacher. They report statements from students such as "that darn chime," rather than indicating displeasure with the teacher. Although we can find no research that supports or refutes this, these teachers report that it helps them maintain their positive relationships with the students.

Strategies for Getting the Attention of Those Students Who Don't Respond to the Group Signal

1. using the ***hairy eyeball***
   This is a stern look and stare teachers give to those students who are not yet adhering to the signal for quiet.
2. turning squarely to face student, making eye contact and saying that student's name in a calm but firm voice
3. moving next to the student or students who are still talking
4. praising those students who are quiet
5. rewarding the students who are quiet
   For example, you may allow these students to present their ideas first or leave for lunch first, etc.
6. asking those students who are talking to stop
7. putting the name of the student who is talking on the board as a warning that there will be a consequence as the next step
8. giving the student a *warning card*
   The warning card indicates to the student that if the talking does not stop immediately he or she will get a consequence.
9. giving the student a *consequence card*
10. startling the students with a loud noise or surprise behavior

Deciding to Use Negative or Positive Strategies

The strategies above may also be categorized on a continuum of negative, neutral and positive reinforcers. Those that directly identify or provide a consequence for students not exhibiting the desired behavior are **negative reinforcers.** Those that affirm or reward appropriate behavior are **positive reinforcers.** Still others, such as a chime, are **neutral.** We identify attention strategies in this way to highlight the impact of relationships on classroom management. A consideration every teacher must include in his or her decision to choose a specific strategy to gain student attention is the impact it has on the self-image of individual students, the relationship between the teacher and the students and the relationship among the students. As discussed above, sarcasm may effectively obtain student attention; however, most educators believe the negative impact on student self-image outweighs its value in gaining attention. Another example of an impact on students' self-image is the constant use of peer pressure after the teacher finds that certain students are always the ones who cause the class to miss some opportunity (e.g., go to recess late in elementary school or go to the pep rally late in high school). The impact this may have of undermining the classroom community or making the student angry with the teacher, thereby motivating additional acting-out behavior, might lead the teacher to use this strategy less often than some of the more positive strategies (e.g., those who are ready get to go first or complimenting those who are ready). Later in this chapter, we will talk more about the impact of the student–teacher relationship on classroom management and appropriate ways to use peer pressure during classroom management.

As discussed above, sarcasm may effectively obtain student attention; however, most educators believe the negative impact on student self-image outweighs its value in gaining attention.

Almost all strategies discussed previously may be appropriate in certain situations. It is important to be aware, however, that disproportionate use of negative strategies as opposed to positive strategies may undermine some of the teacher's long-term goals, such as raising students' self-image, building a supportive classroom community among the students and building trusting and supportive relationships between the teacher and the students.

Cooperative Learning Jobs Grid

The easiest way to regain students' attention is never to lose it. Transitions between activities are a time when many teachers lose students' attention. Well planned transitions help maintain student attention as we shift from one activity to the next. One technique for ensuring quick transitions from teacher-directed work to student group work is the *cooperative learning jobs grid*. Figure 3-1 is an example of a cooperative learning jobs grid for working in groups of four students.

Each student may only have one job at a time. Beginning with the top box, the students get into their groups and figure out who best fits the description in each description column box. Once the leader is established he or she is out of the running for the scribe position in the second description box. Once the scribe is set, the final two members of the group vie for the recorder position. The last person without a job is the materials person.

Each job has specific responsibilities. The leader's job is to ensure that the job gets done correctly in the time allowed. The leader must ensure that everyone contributes to accomplishing the task. This means that the leader must encourage the reticent to speak and contain any member who tries to disproportionately dominate the discussion. The scribe keeps notes as a record of the group's work. The notes must be legible enough so that the reporter can read them to give the group report or so others can copy the notes if that is required. The reporter gives the oral report of the group's work to the entire class. The materials person is the one who gets any materials the group needs. He or she is the one who fetches the dictionary from the bookcase, goes to the library if a research material is needed or goes to the cabinet for the science lab equipment. All members of the group are responsible for monitoring themselves and others with following the basic group work expectations such as voice volume, good listening, courtesy, etc.

Once the grid is set, the teacher has the jobs ready for four different activities. Since the students rotate through the jobs, there is little concern about fairness. Students typically find the initial placement in jobs by the randomly set descriptions more fair than when the teacher assigns the jobs. In circumstances, however, when the teacher thinks it is best, the teacher may certainly assign the first set of jobs and then let the students rotate through the jobs during the next three activities. The cooperative learning jobs grid significantly reduces the time it takes to assign jobs each time there is a new activity and eliminates the bickering that may occur over who will do which job.

Figure 3-1

Description Column	Activity 1	Activity 2	Activity 3	Activity 4
Wearing the most red	Leader	Materials	Reporter	Scribe
Traveled to the farthest place on summer vacation	Scribe	Leader	Materials	Reporter
Most unusual pet at home	Reporter	Scribe	Leader	Materials
Whoever is left	Materials	Reporter	Scribe	Leader

Reinforcement of Appropriate Behavior and Consequences for Inappropriate Behavior

The best way to maximize the effectiveness of our classroom management plan is to maximize the use of positive reinforcement when students are carrying out our expectations. A psychologist named Hernstein (1961 and 1974) wrote about his research related to what is known as the *"matching law."* Walker, Ramsey and Gresham (2004, p. 2) describe the matching law as follows:

> The rate of any given behavior matches the rate of reinforcement for that behavior. For example, if aggressive behavior is reinforced once every three times it occurs (e.g., by a parent giving in to a temper tantrum) and pro-social behavior is reinforced once every fifteen times it occurs (e.g., by praising a polite request) then the Matching Law would predict that, on average, aggressive behavior will be chosen five times more frequently than pro-social behavior.

Subsequent research (Snyder, 2002) has shown that behavior does, in fact, closely follow the matching law.

Walker, Ramsey and Gresham (2004, p. 4) describe effective praise as being genuine, immediate, frequent, enthusiastic, descriptive, varied and involving eye contact. They suggest that teachers use praise at least four times as often as criticism and more often, if possible. They also found that teachers do tend to praise their regular students for good behavior, but they tend not to seize opportunities to praise the more disruptive students when they are behaving well. This may create a cycle of behavior in which "the rich get richer and the poor get poorer."

Teachers do tend to praise their regular students for good behavior, but they tend not to seize opportunities to praise the more disruptive students when they are behaving well.

In addition to praise, teachers often use other rewards to reinforce appropriate behavior. In some instances, these are individual rewards and, in others, they are group rewards. An example of an individual reward in an elementary school is to provide those students who exhibit appropriate behavior over a period of time with the opportunity to go to recess a few minutes early. In middle and high schools, an individual reward might be the privilege to go to the library during study hall or to leave class first for the bus, so the student may acquire that coveted back seat. A note home or phone call to a parent commending the student's good behavior has been found to be an effective reward for students on all levels.

A classroom management plan with clearly taught and consistently enforced expectations coupled with ample positive reinforcement and a system of rewards will eliminate most disruptive behavior, however, there will be times when we need to give students consequences for not following our expectations.

Robert Marzano, in his book *Classroom Management that Works* (2003, pp. 28–32), tells us that the most effective plan for classroom management contains consequences as well as rewards. Consequences are not the same as punishment. In their book *Rules in School* (2003, p. 89), Brady, Forton, Porter and Wood draw a clear distinction between consequences and punishments. Some of the characteristics of **punishment** are that it has an angry tone, is not related to the behavior, leaves the child feeling he or she is the problem rather than his or her behavior, uses fear as an external motivator for stopping the behavior and leaves the child feeling shamed. **Consequences**, on the other hand, are assigned using a calm and matter-of-fact voice, are a logical outcome of the behavior, help the child understand the negative impact of the behavior on themselves and others, leave the child believing the behavior is the problem (not him or her) and build an intrinsic desire to use more appropriate behaviors.

Group Rewards and Consequences

Walker, Ramsey and Gresham (2004, p. 9–10) explain the appropriate and inappropriate use of group rewards and consequences for classroom management. **Group reinforcement** (Walker, Ramsey and Gresham refer to it as *group reinforcement contingencies*) involves the group receiving a reward as the result of meeting a measurable behavior goal. It is important that the group reward we choose is one that we, our teammates and the building administration feel is appropriate. For example, if a lab group completes science lab cleanup in the time allotted, they can earn a point toward leaving for lunch five minutes early one day. In elementary school, students can earn points toward extra recess time. Some teachers and/or administrators disagree with "free time" incentives. In those cases, reward points may be used toward time when the class will play an educational game like Jeopardy or for an extra point on a quiz. Group reinforcements have been found to be quite successful when used as part of the overall behavior plan, however, it is important to note that Walker, Ramsey and Gresham warn that the group contingency should never be a group consequence. The distinction here is that the failure to obtain an additional benefit (such as extra recess) is appropriate, however, a group consequence, such as the class losing five minutes of recess should never be applied to the group because of the behavior of some or even most of the students. Consequences should be applied only to those individuals who fail to meet the behavior requirements.

Students Who Do Not Respond to Our Classroom Management Plan

Up to this point, we have looked at the various components that make up a successful classroom management plan. Even the best classroom management plan may fail to cause some students to conform to our rules and routines. These students typically have anti-social behaviors that are the result of influences beyond the school. We may have students in our class who have experienced the trauma of a parent's death or who are the victims of verbal, physical or sexual abuse. We may have students in our class who have been the victims of repression in their native countries, are experiencing the contentious divorce of their parents or use drugs or alcohol. We have students who have chemical or brain abnormalities that are unrelated to their environment but do cause anti-social behavior. According to Walker, Ramsey and Gresham (2004, p. 4) research indicates that troubled students may actually be between 2% and 16% of the general population, yet only about 1% of the school population is identified with emotional disorders through the special education process.

Most troubled students can be accommodated by a well constructed classroom management plan, however, for one to five percent of the classroom population, our classroom management plan will not be sufficient to make these students conform to classroom rules and expectations. For these students, we will need to have individual contingencies within our classroom management plan. The goal of these individual contingencies is to decrease the negative behaviors and limit their impact on the learning environment. It is hoped that the individual contingencies will bridge the gap between what these students need to be productive members of the class and the routines and expectations in our classroom management plans.

Individual contingencies are most effective when the student, teacher, parent and a third party in the school (assistant principal, special education teacher, etc.) are in agreement about the plan. Individual contingencies should include both incentives and consequences. Effective incentives may vary from student to student, so it is important that you choose incentives that truly are valued by the students. They may be incentives given by the school or incentives given by the parent(s) (provided the parent(s) will follow through consistently with the incentive). Some school-given incentives include

a. a note home to the parent
b. a phone call home to the parent
c. lunch with the teacher
d. a gift certificate to a favorite ice cream shop or fast food restaurant (our apologies to the department of education and their efforts to limit obesity)
e. a pass to a school dance or sporting event
f. homework passes
g. the privilege of listening to music
h. a magazine on a topic of interest to the student (cars, sports, wrestling, fashion)
i. candy/food
j. baseball cards
k. the privilege of borrowing a CD

Some parent-given incentives include

a. additional TV time
b. staying up an extra half hour
c. a play date or sleepover with a special friend
d. extra phone or computer privileges
e. a trip to a sporting or other enjoyable event
f. extra time to play the guitar
g. a trip to the mall

Some teachers have asked the following logical questions related to school incentives: "Is it fair to the other students that these students get a reward for doing the same thing the other students must do without a reward?" or "Won't it be upsetting to the other students that they don't get a reward when they show the same behavior?" We would note here that students are often relieved if a system is implemented that reduces the disturbance within the classroom caused by a disruptive student.

In response to these questions, we suggest that teachers respond by defining the concept of *fairness* in their classrooms as meaning that *people get what they need. Fairness* should *not* mean that everyone gets the same. Most students understand this concept, however, some students may still raise the questions. Typically, those students understand that *fairness* is getting what you need as it relates to academics. In those cases, we suggest pointing out privately to any student complaining of unfairness that people get to ask all the questions they need to ask or get all the help they need to succeed with academics, thereby showing them that the definition for *fairness* is consistently applied, as it relates to behavior.

Many teachers find they have the ability to keep individual contingency reward plans a private matter between the adults in the students' lives and the particular students involved. The students involved often prefer this arrangement.

Rewards can be a very powerful motivator of appropriate behavior, however, they do not always achieve the desired results. In these cases, consequences (as defined earlier) will be needed. Some logical school consequences are

a. losing recess to make up the time a student did not pay attention in class
b. notifying parents of the misbehavior
c. losing points that are accumulating toward an incentive
d. spending time after class or after school to make up the time a student did not pay attention
e. changing a student's seat

f. sending a student from the class to a prearranged time-out area (office, in school suspension room, etc.)[4] in extreme cases when the previous interventions do not work
g. keeping a student after class to discuss the disruptive behavior
h. asking a student to take a walk for five minutes and to come back when he or she is ready to work
i. sending a student into another teacher's classroom with work to complete silently
j. not allowing a student to attend an extracurricular practice, game or event
k. calling in parents for a conference to discuss the disruptive behavior

Teacher–Student Relationships and Classroom Management

A good relationship between the student and the teacher is a strong motivator for positive behavior. All of us can think back to some teacher or adult in our lives who we genuinely respected so much that it was important to us to please this person and gain his or her respect. This adult motivated us to work harder at our academics, at a sport, in our job and/or in the appropriateness of our behavior. This person motivated us to try hard in any or all of these areas because we truly wanted his or her approval and respect. Being motivated by a good relationship is very different from being motivated by fear of consequences or punishment.

> A *good relationship between the student and the teacher is a strong motivator for positive behavior.*

Marzano, Marzano and Pickering (2003, p. 29) reviewed 100 studies related to classroom management. In this meta-analysis, they found that "teachers who had high-quality relationships with their students had 31 percent fewer discipline problems, rule violations, and related problems over a year's time than did teachers who did not have high-quality relationships with their students."

The following is a list of techniques for building relationships with students. We collected these ideas from our own teaching and from that of our colleagues.

1. talking informally with students
2. greeting students outside of school
3. greeting students at the door when they enter class
4. singling out students for conversations in the lunchroom
5. commenting on important events in the students' lives
6. complimenting students on important achievements outside of school
7. making eye contact with individual students when talking to the group
8. attending students' sporting events and performances
9. being clear about expectations and enforcing rules consistently and fairly
10. making it clear to students that we are committed to helping them succeed
11. making it clear to students that we enjoy our jobs and getting to work with them
12. taking their insights and ideas seriously
13. being willing to work with struggling students before and after school
14. being passionate and enthusiastic about what we are teaching
15. writing notes to students for good work done in or out of class
16. making phone calls home to inform parents of good news!
17. greeting students when we pass them in the hallway

---

[4] It is important to note that students should not be sent without supervision unless the teacher is absolutely certain that the student will report to the designated area. The designated area should be supervised. This consequence is most productive if students can be sent with class work or another productive activity, however, this may not be possible given the students' emotional state at the time he or she is sent from class.

18. occasionally sharing stories from our own experiences as a student
19. taking a few moments of Monday class time to ask students about their weekends
20. following the grading formula of *three compliments for every word of constructive criticism*
21. making an effort to stand physically close to all students at different points in the class
22. providing appropriate wait time so more students may successfully participate in class discussions
23. being flexible about deadlines in genuine emergencies
24. never using sarcasm to embarrass a student in front of the class
25. whenever possible, handling disciplinary conversations in private
26. sharing with individual students common interests you both share (e.g., soccer, jazz, NASCAR racing, gardening)

Think again about that person who motivated you to work harder or behave better. How many of the above behaviors did that person exhibit?

Student-to-Student Relationships Within the Classroom

It is also important to establish a community of trust and care in our classrooms, as this goes hand-in-hand with building relationships with our students. Students need to know and understand that both their teacher and their classmates are going to do their best to take care of them throughout the year. Providing opportunities for both us and our students to get to know one another, celebrating the successes of others and helping students get through difficult times are all critical components to creating a trusting and caring community.

Student Ownership for the Class

We also encourage teachers to follow the advice, *don't do anything for students that they can do for themselves.* Instead, follow the lead of an elementary school colleague of ours who each year creates a job wheel that lists approximately twenty-five classroom responsibilities. At the beginning of each week, she utilizes the job wheel to assign a responsibility to each member of the class. These jobs range from taking attendance to collecting homework to hanging up student work. How does assigning students responsibilities within a classroom relate to creating an effective context for teaching and learning? In short, creating a classroom structure in which students play a role in the effective operation of the classroom sends the explicit message to students that they are active participants in what goes on inside the classroom. They are not there to sit passively and let the teacher do all of the work, but, rather, they have a role to play in making the classroom one in which effective teaching and learning can occur. Such a message may have a powerful impact not only on the jobs that students are assigned, but also in helping them as well to see their learning as a process in which they must take an active role rather than a passive one.

Getting Started

The following questions may be used as a guide to get teachers started on setting up a classroom management plan.

1. Can I clearly articulate to another adult all of the routines noted earlier in this chapter? If not, what do I need to do or with whom do I need to talk to reach this goal?
   a. Can I clearly articulate and teach these routines to my students?
   b. When and how will I teach the routines to my students, using the steps noted earlier in this chapter?

   c. Have I decided on group rewards that will be an incentive to the class but do not violate my beliefs, those of my team and/or those of the school culture?
   d. Have I developed a consistent system (e.g., a point system) by which the students may earn the rewards?
   e. Do I have individual consequences set for those students who do not follow the routines but are not on an individual contingency plan such as that noted in number 3?

2. Have I decided on the strategies I will use to obtain and maintain student attention?
   a. Have I taught these to the students?
   b. Do I have group reinforcements set that are consistent with number 1?
   c. Do I have individual consequences set that are consistent with number 1?

3. Do I know which students need an individual contingency plan?
   a. Who, beside the student and me, should be a party to the plan?
   b. Do I have a reward for the student that will act as an incentive and that does not violate my beliefs, those of my team and/or those of the school culture?
   c. Have I set a system in place to ensure I notice and reinforce this student whenever he or she is exhibiting the appropriate behavior?

Sample Elementary Classroom Management Plan

I. Opening Days

A. I will spend a good part of the first two weeks of school teaching my students the rules, norms and expectations in my classroom as well as establishing a community of trust and concern for others.

1. Creating classroom rules (Note: This process may take several sessions to complete.)
    a. Have class brainstorm a list of ideas that students feel are important to helping them learn best as well as achieve their desired goals.
    b. Have the class create approximately five general categories based upon the list of ideas. (Categories may include rules about how we treat each other, rules about how we take care of things, rules about how we do our work and rules about safety issues.)
    c. From these general categories, create four to five rules to be posted in the classroom.
    d. Discuss, model and role-play (where appropriate) what adherence to each of these rules looks like.
    e. Have students sign the poster with the list of rules.
2. Over the next two weeks, I will discuss, model and practice classroom procedures. For example, we will practice morning routines, beginning with unpacking book bags, placing book bags and coats in lockers, making lunch choices, reading the morning message and following the directions given in the morning message. We will also practice quietly lining up and walking down the halls, transitioning from one subject to another and effectively completing homework as well as many other procedures. *(learning class norms)*
3. Students will sit in clusters of four students assigned by me. Name tags will inform students of their seats. *(setting classroom norms—working in teams)*
4. Students will complete several Getting to Know You activities and projects. Activities will be completed independently and shared with the class at a later time, completed in pairs, completed in teams or completed as a class. I will also participate in many of these activities. These activities will be incorporated into different subject areas and will provide some review of the curriculum for students.
5. Before students share their completed work, I will teach them how to share work as well as how to respond when others share work. I will ask for student volunteers to model this process for the class.
6. The first night's homework assignment will include a questionnaire asking parents to answer a variety of questions about their children. *(acknowledging importance of parental involvement and communication)*–Students will also be asked to complete a reflection sheet about their first day of school which will provide me with more information about each student.
7. I will explain how I would like students to organize their desks, notebooks and binders. This process will be completed as a class and input from the students will be encouraged. *(learning class norms)*

8. I will introduce and explain each of the centers, reading, math and writing, in my classroom. We will talk about how to use each center appropriately. Students will be given opportunities to practice using each of these centers.
9. I will explain the portfolio system that students will use throughout the year. As a class, we will decide what types of things should be placed in a portfolio.

II. Building Relationships

A. Effective behavior management is dependent upon positive teacher–student relationships and a classroom in which students care about one another.

1. I will write a morning message specific to the class every day to acknowledge successes of the class, offer encouragement when it is needed and ask students to complete a task relevant to the curriculum.
2. We will begin each morning with a meeting which we will begin with a greeting. In this way, everyone is greeted first thing each day. Our meeting will also include going over the message together, reviewing the academic task and asking a few students to share something important to them. We will end our meeting with a brief team-building activity. (Note: This process will be discussed, modeled and practiced by the students.) Each component of the meeting, including the greeting, academic task, sharing and team-building activity, will be introduced and practiced separately.
3. I will greet students as they come into the classroom each morning as well as in hallways and in the lunchroom.
4. I will make an effort to learn about each child's interests and ask questions regarding these interests.
5. I will make myself available to work with struggling students both before and after school.
6. I will attend my students' sporting events and performances when appropriate.
7. I will maintain consistent contact with parents through weekly newsletters, phone calls, in-class volunteers and monthly breakfasts to share projects students have completed in class.

III. Consistent Expectations

A. I will consistently enforce all rules and expectations with clear and logical consequences. The consequences of breaking rules will be known and discussed in advance.

1. Consequences related to the infraction (a.k.a. **logical consequences**), for example:
   a. If a student hurts another child's feelings, he or she may "fix" them by writing an apology letter or asking that child to play a special game at recess.
   b. If a student repeatedly chooses not to complete homework, he or she also chooses to lose recess in order to complete the assigned homework.
   c. If a student has become particularly disruptive during group work, a time out may be necessary. In this situation, I would ask the student to remove himself or herself from the group and work independently on the task at hand.

2. Time out
   For example, if the student previously discussed in c continues to be disruptive, I may ask him or her to work in the back of my colleague's classroom. (Author's Note: This arrangement needs to be discussed in advance. We have found this change of scenery to be helpful for some students.) As a last resort, I would send the student to the resource/behavioral room. In schools where no such room exists, this may be the point at which the student is sent to the office. Again, this arrangement needs to be worked out in advance. If the student appears to be out of control, it may be necessary to escort him or her or to call the resource teacher for additional assistance.
3. Loss of privilege
   In this instance, the student loses an opportunity he or she might otherwise have had. For example, a student who is consistently talking to a neighbor in class may lose a part of his or her recess time. (Author's Note: This consequence differs from the loss of recess for the purpose of completing homework noted above because the talking behavior and the consequence are not directly related. We use loss of privilege in those circumstances in which there is not a readily usable related consequence).

Sample Individual Contingency Plan

For the student who may have difficulty following the norms of the classroom, it may be necessary to develop an individual behavioral/academic plan. The following steps may be used to create a plan for a student experiencing difficulty in meeting expectations.

a. Identify areas of weakness
   i. Is the student disruptive during whole-class instruction?
   ii. Is the student disruptive during independent work?
   iii. Does the student have difficulty working collaboratively?
   iv. Does the student have difficulty completing class and/or home assignments?
   v. Does the student have difficulty during lunch and/or recess?
   vi. Is the student disrespectful to other students and/or adults?
b. Once the areas of weakness have been identified, set up a chart in which each weakness is stated positively. When a student is able to meet each expectation, he or she will earn a point. See the table below as an example.

	Monday	Tuesday	Wednesday	Thursday	Friday
I worked well independently.	AM: PM:	AM: PM:	AM: PM:	AM: PM:	AM: PM:
I worked well during group work.	AM: PM:	AM: PM:	AM: PM:	AM: PM:	AM: PM:
I completed my class assignments.	AM: PM:	AM: PM:	AM: PM:	AM: PM:	AM: PM:
I completed home assignments.	AM: PM:	AM: PM:	AM: PM:	AM: PM:	AM: PM:
Total Points:					

c. Determine and explain to the student how points will be earned. I have found it to be extremely important to separate the school day into a morning session and an afternoon session. In this way, the student who is having a difficult morning has an opportunity to start over in the afternoon.
d. Determine with the student what will happen when the student earns a certain number of points. It is important that the incentive is something that is meaningful for the student.
d. Be sure to involve the parents as well as any other adult who will be working closely with this student.
f. Contact previous teachers to get information regarding which techniques worked well and which were not particularly helpful for this student.
g. Determine a specific time at which you and the student will go over the chart together.

IV. Group Incentive System

A. I will utilize a group incentive system to reward my students for good work and behavior. As a class, students need to earn a total of fifteen points to earn the chosen incentive.

1. The incentive will be decided upon by both the students and me. In the past, the following incentives have been chosen:
    a. fifteen minutes of extra recess at the end of the day
    b. fifteen minutes of a team-building activity
    d. fifteen minutes of an educational game
    d. a special snack
    e. a pizza party during lunch time
2. We will brainstorm and discuss how the class may earn points. In the past, the following behaviors were awarded points:
    a. doing something extra to help another class or student
    b. reducing lost class time through efficient transitions from one subject to another
    c. achieving a class goal
    d. doing exemplary collaborative work during literature circles or problem solving
    e. working exceptionally well for another teacher or specialist
    (Note: We also discuss that there are certain behaviors and rules students are expected to follow at all times. The class cannot earn points for such expectations.)
3. I will keep track of the point total in a corner on the white board. In addition, it is not possible for the class to lose points.

Sample High School Behavior Management Plan

I. Opening Days

A. I will spend the bulk of the first few days of class teaching my students the rules, norms and expectations in my classroom.

1. Three to four clear and specific rules will be clearly posted on a classroom wall.
   a. Use professional language at all times.
   b. One person speaks at a time.
   c. Ask permission before leaving your seat.
   d. Treat everyone in the classroom with respect.
   (setting classroom expectations)
2. Students will sit in assigned seats (alphabetically) to enable me to learn their names more quickly. *(setting classroom norms)*
3. Students will fill out index cards with information about themselves and their parents for my records. *(sending message about my willingness to communicate with parents)*
4. I will not only tell my students about classroom procedures, but we will practice them. For example, we will practice coming into the classroom, immediately sitting down and getting started on the Do Now activity on the blackboard. *(learning class norms)*
5. The first night's homework assignment will include students setting up their binders and notebooks in the specified manner. *(learning class norms)*
6. I will ask my students to sign a contract signifying their understanding of the classroom expectations. I will photocopy these contracts and keep them on file. Students will be expected to keep their original copies in the front of their binders. *(learning class norms)*
7. I will explain the Choose Your Own Activity incentive system we will use throughout the year. (explained below)
8. I will ask students to tell me a bit about themselves, their likes and dislikes either orally or in writing. I will share a bit about myself and why I decided to become a teacher. *(relationship building)*

II. Building Relationships

A. Effective behavior management is dependent upon positive teacher–student relationships.

1. I will always make it clear, both orally and in writing, that I am committed to my students' success.
2. I will greet students in hallways and in the lunchroom.
3. I will always make positive comments (and not only constructive criticism) on students' graded work.
4. I will make myself available to work with struggling students.
5. I will attend my students' sporting events and performances.

6. I will try to make phone calls home to parents for positive results (and not only negative results).

III. Consistent Expectations

A. From day one, I will consistently praise behavior that supports the rules and immediately cease instruction to deal with any violation of the classroom rules listed above. *(learning class norms)*

1. If a student is disruptive in any way, I will immediately cease instruction, turn to squarely face that student and say that student's name in a calm but firm voice. If the student returns to work, I will say "thank you" in a pleasant voice and return to my instruction.
2. If the student continues to be disruptive, I will calmly approach that student's desk and repeat the procedure above (but from a closer proximity).
3. If the student continues to be disruptive, I have several options.
   a. I might ask to speak to that student out in the hallway.
   b. I might return to my instruction but find a moment to move to my desk, find the index card filled out by that student at the beginning of the school year and *subtly* place the card on the student's desk (with a *whispered* warning that I am considering making a phone call home).
   c. I might ask the student to take a brief walk around the school and return when he or she is ready to learn again.
   d. I might ask the student to leave the classroom, go to the library and return at the end of the period to speak to me in private.
4. If (as happens in rare cases) the student refuses to leave, I have several options.
   a. I might call the school security guard or police officer (if they exist) to take the student away.
   b. I might tell the student, "Well, if you won't leave, please just sit quietly while I teach the rest of the class, and we'll talk about this at the end of class."
   c. If I know of an empty classroom nearby, I might actually instruct the rest of my class to come with me to another classroom and continue my instruction from there. (Author's Note: This option is dependent upon having a strong relationship with the majority of the students.)

IV. Group Incentive System

A. I will utilize a group incentive system to reward my students for good work and behavior.

1. The incentive will be an educational game (of my students' choosing) to be played on Friday.
   a. The length of time that the game is played is dependent upon my students' behavior during the week.
   b. For each day that every student (present in school) is in his or her seat when the bell signifying the start of class rings, I will give the class two minutes toward a game on Friday.

c. For each day that every student (present in school) has his or her binder, notebook and a pen or pencil with him or her at the start of class, I will give the class two minutes toward a game on Friday.
d. I will also offer the opportunity to gain minutes through efficient, successful completion of various in-class assignments and group work.
e. I will keep track of my students' accumulated minutes on a corner of the blackboard.
f. If the students can accumulate some particular number of minutes (say, fifteen minutes) I will bring in candy for them to enjoy during the educational game on Friday.

V. Individual Contingency Plans

Occasionally, there will be a student for whom the group incentive system does not serve as a successful motivator. Typically, this student will negatively affect the impact of the group incentive system on the rest of the class. A student like this needs an individual contingency plan. At the high school level, individual contingency plans are developed by counselors, special education teachers or assistant principals with input from the classroom teachers.

To start, we disassociate this student from the group incentive system. This student's behavior will not inhibit the class's ability to earn the incentive. Instead, we meet with the student to determine an individual incentive system for that student. Perhaps he or she would be motivated by time on Friday to read a sports, car or fashion magazine of his or her choosing. Whenever possible, we recommend conferencing with that student and his or her parents to determine an incentive for successful behavior that the parents would then deliver at home (an extra computer or more phone time, more frequent opportunities to borrow the car). The ultimate goal is for the teacher to develop a relationship with this student that ultimately results in a joint decision by the teacher and the student to rejoin the group incentive system. Below is a sample of an individual contingency plan for a high school senior.

Robert Condon Individual Behavior Plan

Robert has difficulty staying seated, remaining still and paying attention. He also has a tendency to distract other students. In order to keep Robert on track for a successful senior year, the following behavior plan has been agreed to by Robert, his mother and all of his teachers.

The expectations

- Robert should not ask to leave class, short of a medical emergency.
- Robert is required to have a pass if he is scheduled to see the school psychologist, nurse, guidance counselor or another teacher (for extra help). He should not wander the hallways.
- He should use the nurse's bathroom before homeroom, between classes (specifically, during the 9:22–9:28 AM break) and during his lunchtime.
- He should not be in the cafeteria (except for his lunch).

- If Robert does need to leave class, his pass will include a five-minute time limit to get to where he is going and back to class. (Robert may be allowed to leave his study hall only once per period and only for five minutes, unless scheduled to be somewhere else and holding a pass to that location.)
- Robert will not touch anyone (hugging, patting, hitting, etc.). If he does, the staff member who observes him doing so will warn him about this behavior. (Please document this, as Mr. Sanchez will be checking in regularly to determine the amount of warnings Robert has received. Further action may be necessary.)

If Robert is disruptive in a class (i.e., makes inappropriate comments, interrupts lesson, gets up without asking, etc.), the teacher should use the following language with him.

First warning: "Robert, you are interfering with my teaching."

Second warning: "Robert, this is the second time today that I've told you that you're interfering with my teaching."

Third time: "Please go to Mr. Sanchez' office." He will then receive a detention which he will serve on that same day.

If Robert is demonstrating a need to go to the nurse or psychologist, and a teacher gives him permission to go, the teacher should call the nurse or psychologist to let him or her know Robert is on his way.

Some suggestions for success:

1. Robert may be helpful with classroom chores that involve movement (writing on the board, collecting papers, etc.), however, these are privileges that may be revoked if not successful or distracting to other students.
2. Help Robert to reflect about why he made a bad decision and what to do for next time. Use calm, clear and consistent language to communicate desirable and undesirable behaviors.
3. Be positive and compliment appropriate and on-task behaviors.
4. Make consequences clear and consistent. Good communication among staff is important. Please see Mr. Sanchez immediately with any problems or concerns.

Incentive: Robert will receive one point for each class in which he is able to remain in the room for the entire period. He will receive two points for any class in which he does not receive any warnings. Mr. Sanchez will e-mail Mrs. Condon each Friday with a report on the number of points Robert earned during that week. Robert may use his points to "purchase" time using Mrs. Condon's car. Robert will be permitted to use the car for one hour for every ten points he earns.

We agree to the following behavior plan.

________________________ Robert Condon

________________________ Mr. Sanchez

________________________ Mrs. Condon

Conclusion

Developing good relationships with students, engaging students in teaching and carefully teaching students routines and expectations will significantly assist with classroom management. Coupling these factors with a plan that includes group incentives and individual consequences will result in a plan that will ensure that the time in your class devoted to student learning is maximized. The most important component for success in classroom management, however, is our consistent follow-through in carrying out the previously described components.

References

Anonymous. (1998, Summer). Punishment vs. logical consequences: What's the difference? *Responsive Classroom Newsletter, 10*(3).

Brady, K., Forton, M., Porter, D., & Wood, C. (2003). *Rules in school.* Greenfield, MA: Northeast Foundation for Children.

Denton, P., & Kriete, R. (2000). *The first six weeks of school.* Greenfield, MA: Northeast Foundation for Children.

Farnsworth, M., & McErlane, J. (2002, Summer). Signals for quiet. *The Responsive Classroom Newsletter, 14* (3), pp. 1–4.

Hernstein, R. (1961). Relative and absolute strength of response as a function of frequency of reinforcement. *Journal of the Experimental Analysis of Behavior, 4*, pp. 267–272.

Hernstein, R. (1974). Formal properties of the matching laws. *Journal of the Experimental Analysis of Behavior, 21*, pp. 486–495.

Jones, F. (2000). *Tools for teaching (p. 125).* Santa Cruz, CA: Frederick H. Jones and Associates, Inc.

Marzano, R. (2003). *Classroom management that works,* Alexandria, VA: Association for Supervision and Curriculum Development (ASCD).

Marzano, R., & Marzano, J. (2003, September). The key to classroom management. *Educational Leadership, 61*(1), pp. 6–13.

Snyder, J. (2002). Reinforcement and coercive mechanisms in the development of antisocial behavior: Peer relationships. In J. Reid, G. Patterson, & L. Snyder (Eds.), *Antisocial behavior in children and adolescents: A developmental analysis and model for intervention* (pp. 101–122). Washington, DC: American Psychological Association.

Walker, H., Ramsey, E., & Gresham, F. (Winter 2003–2004). Heading off disruptive behavior. *The American Educator.*

C H A P T E R

4

Differentiating Instruction to Meet the Needs of Diverse Learners (Learning Styles, Learning Rate and Cultural Differences): With Strategies for Closing the Achievement Gap

Objectives for the Chapter

After reading the chapter, the reader will be able to

a. define differentiated instruction to a colleague
b. plan lessons that flexibly provide reteaching, practice and extension as needed
c. manage differentiated activities in a single lesson
d. use graphic organizers and other strategies that attend to various learning styles
e. use a variety of instructional strategies to differentiate instruction

What Is Differentiated Instruction?

The aim is clear. Each child—each of the young—should be able to advance to full capacity in accordance with general and special ability and aptitude.

Paul Brandwein, *Memorandum: On Renewing Schooling and Education*

Differentiating instruction is adapting curriculum (what is taught or *content*), instruction (how it is taught or *process*) and assessment (how it is assessed or *product*), based on the different levels of readiness, learning styles and interests of the students (Tomlinson, 1995a). Today's classrooms are very different than those of the past. Teachers today must contend with learners possessing a wide range of abilities and talents. The standards to which both teachers and students are held have become more rigorous and comprehensive as students must be prepared to face and succeed in an ever-changing, technologically advanced world. It is highly unlikely that a teacher will be able to achieve all students' mastering of the required standards as well as maximize the learning potential of each student unless differentiated instruction is provided. Fortunately, we understand much more about the teaching and learning dyad than we did even a decade ago.

It is highly unlikely that a teacher will be able to achieve all students' mastering of the required standards as well as maximize the learning potential of each student unless differentiated instruction is provided.

Table 4-1

Differentiated Instruction is...	Differentiated Instruction is not...
Multiple approaches to content, process and product	Individualized instruction
Student-centered	Teacher-centered
Variety of groupings that are in a constant state of change or **flexible grouping**	Homogeneous, static groupings
Organized	Chaotic
Concept-focused	Focused on memorization of discrete facts or skills
On-going assessment to inform instruction to better meet the needs of each student	Only summative assessments given at the end of the lesson or unit
Proactively planning instruction to meet the needs of your group	Assignments are the same for all the students
Expectations are the same for all students	Grading some students harder than others
Providing new and different challenges	Asking students to do more of what they already know

Differentiated instruction is good instruction for many reasons. Recent research suggests that classrooms that cultivate individuality are most effective. The following three research findings about students as learners support the importance of differentiating instruction in the classroom.

1. Students' *intelligences*[1] at the start of a task are variable.
2. The brain hungers for meaning.
3. Humans learn best when they are appropriately challenged.

Intelligence is Variable

Intelligence is multifaceted. Howard Gardner (1991, 1993, 1997) describes eight intelligences that humans possess in varying degrees. These eight intelligences are as follows: *verbal–linguistic, logical–mathematical, visual–spatial, bodily–kinesthetic, musical–rhythmic, interpersonal, intrapersonal* and *naturalistic.* As a result, students arrive at each task with a different intelligence level related to that task. Teachers must seek to understand how each student learns and thinks. We may then use teaching processes and require student products that maximize the likelihood that each student will learn the information and skills being taught. In Chapter 7, we look at ways teachers may use the knowledge about human intelligence to increase the level of student success. It is critical that teachers provide students with a variety of learning experiences in order to help all students achieve their learning potential.

The Brain Learns Best When It Connects to Something That Already Has Meaning

First, as we discussed in Chapter 2, the brain seeks meaningful patterns and connections. It is important for learners to be able to connect new information to their existing schemas. Second, the brain learns best when it is able to make sense out of information rather than having information imposed on it. For example, if you are teaching students how to find equivalent fractions, you tell students they need to multiply both the denominator and numerator by the same number. Most students will be able to easily follow these steps, however, this process holds little or no meaning for students as it is simply a set of memorized steps. A more effective way in which to teach children about equivalent fractions is to use a concrete manipulative such as fraction bars. By working with manipulatives, students are able to arrive at their own understanding of equivalent fractions. Using manipulatives to teach abstract mathematical concepts allows children to make sense out of how equivalent fractions work. Finally, a third way in which the brain learns best is when information is deemed relevant and meaningful to one's own life.

An effective curriculum must be meaningful and relevant to all students. Teachers must create learning experiences for students in such a way that they are able to connect new information and understandings to the old and existing knowledge, that is, their schemas.

Chapter 2 describes the ways in which teachers make learning connected, meaningful and relevant to students. Chapter 8 describes the way in which teachers best use their knowledge of the brain to facilitate the highest levels of student learning.

Learning Is Maximized With Appropriate Challenge

Through research, we now know that humans learn best when they are presented with a moderate challenge. If a task is too difficult, learners will experience frustration, and, if a task is too easy, learners will become bored. In both situations, learners lose their motivation and desire for learning.

It is important for educators to understand this principle as they plan lessons for their students. What may be challenging for one student may be too simplistic for another. For

---

[1] Chapter 7 explains the authors' belief that intelligence is learnable rather than a fixed entity. It also contains information about the multiple intelligences mentioned in the following paragraph.

this reason as well as many others, it is important for teachers to provide differentiated learning experiences for their students. In this way, all students will be able to achieve their learning potential. As you read this chapter, you will learn how to manage providing differentiated experiences in classrooms in which there are many students and only one of you!

Role of Teacher

Knowing one's students is paramount to effectively differentiating instruction for students.

Knowing one's students is paramount to effectively differentiating instruction for students. Fortunately, educators have a wide variety of tools to use in gathering information about their students. The following list provides some ways in which teachers learn about their students.

- preassessments
- interest inventories
- informal conversations
- questions (recall, comprehension, higher order thinking)
- observations
- tests, quizzes
- performance assessments
- self-assessments
- student portfolios
- academic histories
- parent questionnaires
- student questionnaires
- K-W-L charts

In a classroom in which differentiated instruction is being utilized, the primary role of the teacher is that of a facilitator. It is the responsibility of the teacher to provide a variety of different learning opportunities for students. The teacher will choose some of the activities for students to complete, while at other times, the students will choose what activities they will do.

The teacher must also appropriately organize students for learning. Will the students work individually, in pairs, in flexible groups or as a whole class? In addition, the teacher must decide if students will be differentiated based upon readiness, interest or learning profile.

Teachers using differentiated instruction must be flexible in terms of how they use their time. Students who need more explanation, review or practice, must be provided with such opportunities. Students who have already mastered skills and concepts being taught must be given opportunities to expand their thinking (Heacox, 2002).

Differentiating instruction in the classroom requires much time and effort, particularly when first getting started. For this reason, it is important to work collaboratively with colleagues. The following are ideas for working with others.

- Work with teachers at your grade level or in your department. Divide up the task of creating remediation and extension activities for each of the concepts in the curriculum. Sharing the resources and work with colleagues decreases the burden on any one teacher.
- Designate blocks of professional development time for differentiating curriculum. Activities such as lesson study may be extremely valuable in modifying lessons to meet the differentiated needs of students. Chapters 10 and 11 describe ways in which teachers may conduct this type of professional development.

- Work with the media or technology specialist in your school. They can help with finding web sites and other valuable sources of information that students may readily access independently or with minimal teacher prompting.
- Work with other specialists, such as the reading or math specialists (in elementary and middle schools), special educators, English as a second language teachers, etc. These teachers have much experience and a substantial knowledge base related to working with students who may need more reteaching than the majority of the students and/or extensions for students who master concepts more quickly than the majority of the students.

Tomlinson (2001) outlines several general guidelines that teachers should attend to in order to make differentiating instruction possible.

- **The key concepts and generalizations that give meaning to the topic of study should be clear.** Focusing on key concepts within a unit helps all learners gain a better understanding that will serve as a building block for future learning. When planning a unit of study, we start with determining the most important information and skills we would like our students to have mastered at the end of the unit. Chapter 1 describes this process in more depth.
- **Assessment should serve as a guide to our thinking and planning.** We should use assessments as a way in which to learn about our students. Observing students, homework, collaborative work, projects, tests, quizzes and oral presentations are just some of many ways to assess or better understand where our students are in terms of their learning and understanding. Chapter 6 explains the ways in which teachers may use assessments of student learning to inform instruction.
- **All lessons for students should encourage higher order thinking skills.** All students, regardless of their abilities, should be required to engage in tasks that require students to think at higher levels. While some students may need more support and scaffolding with this process, others may benefit from being challenged with more advanced materials and/or activities. Chapter 6 describes ways in which questioning practices promote higher order thinking skills. Later in this chapter, we will look at graphic organizers as another means of developing higher order thinking skills.
- **All lessons for students should be engaging.** Although all students may need to engage in drill and practice to master required skills, it is important that *all* students are provided with opportunities to use this information in more meaningful ways. Although some students will need more time to grasp basic skills, these students need opportunities to apply the concepts and/or skills in more complex ways that are meaningful to their own lives.
- **A balance of student-selected and teacher-assigned tasks should exist in a differentiated classroom.** This balance will vary from student to student based upon his or her needs, however, it is critical that all students have choices as well as curricula that are appropriate to their levels of readiness, interests and learning profiles. Although the choices the teacher presents to students will vary from student to student based upon specific needs, it is important that all students have choices in some part of their curricula. In this way, students feel as though they have more ownership over their learning.
- **Fairness is redefined.** In a differentiated classroom, fairness means every student gets what he or she needs in order to maximize his or her learning. This means that students will be working on different tasks at times. It may be helpful to have a discussion on fairness with students so that they understand what fairness looks like in a classroom. Students need to understand that fairness means all students get what they need in order to maximize their learning. This means that there will be times

when different students will be working on different tasks and different supports will be provided for students.

Differentiating by Readiness

As teachers, it is our responsibility to provide struggling students with more basic, foundation-building instruction while providing advanced learners with more complex, challenging tasks. Vygotsky, a developmental theorist and researcher of the 1920s and 1930s, felt that children's learning is maximized when instruction is appropriate to each child's cognitive development. To ask students to complete a complex task in which a more capable "other" is needed to guide them through unfamiliar territory without providing the necessary support will create frustration in children and inhibit student learning and growth. At the same time, asking students to complete tasks that are too simplistic will create boredom, and students may become less motivated to learn. It is imperative that educators provide students with appropriate assistance as well as develop instruction geared to a child's "zone of proximal development" which is defined by Vygotsky as

As teachers, it is our responsibility to provide struggling students with more basic, foundation-building instruction while providing advanced learners with more complex, challenging tasks.

> [the] distance between the child's actual development as determined by independent problem solving and the level of potential development as determined through problem solving under adult guidance or in collaboration with more capable peers (Vygotsky, 1978, p. 88).

In other words, the **zone of proximal development** is the distance between what a student knows and what he or she may learn without being over-challenged (or frustrated) or under-challenged (or bored).

Teachers who use students' readiness levels to differentiate content, process or product, design tasks that will push students beyond their current levels of understanding. A task that is designed to meet a student at his or her appropriate level of learning will extend that student's level of understanding and knowledge to a level beyond his or her independent level. It is important to remember that readiness is always changing, and students should move in and out of groups as they meet the stated learning goals. Later in this chapter, we will discuss the importance of flexible grouping as well as how to manage such groups.

Teachers may create "readiness-based adjustments" by offering students a range of learning tasks developed along one or more of the following continua (Tomlinson, 1995a, 2001):

1. concrete to abstract
2. simple to complex
3. fewer steps to multi-steps
4. smaller leaps to greater leaps
5. more structured to more open
6. less independence to greater independence
7. quicker to slower

As you read on, you will see that differentiating instruction in these ways is not as daunting as it may initially appear when looking at this list. A single teaching activity often incorporates several of the items on this list, as noted in the sample lesson later in this chapter. Differentiating instruction in several of these areas may be as simple as asking a well worded higher order thinking skills question and asking the students to address the question using the group questions strategy.

After you read a brief explanation and example of each of the above ways in which to differentiate instruction, you will find a differentiating lesson plan exemplar for an elementary mathematics class which uses *Investigations* as its math program. As you read through it, you will find that the activities move from a more concrete level in which manipulatives are used (i.e., pennies in this case) to a more abstract level. The problems that students are asked to complete at the beginning of the lesson are simple and become more complex as students become more proficient. In addition, as students become more competent, they will be asked to solve problems in which more steps are required and less structure is provided. Finally, when students are at the application mastery level, they are asked to solve a problem of the day in which they must carefully read the problem, determine the important and relevant information, choose an appropriate strategy, carry out their plan, find a correct solution and write about the steps they took to solve this problem. This problem is more abstract and open in nature and requires more complex thinking. In addition, this multi-step problem requires students to take greater leaps in transferring their knowledge of multiplication. Finally, you will notice this lesson allows all students to move at a pace which is appropriate for them.

Concrete to abstract. Information, ideas and concepts are **concrete** if they can be physically manipulated and/or if they are specific events. They are **abstract** if they focus more on meanings, implications or principles. When students are first introduced to a concept or skill, they often need to become familiar with the new information in a more basic, hands-on manner. Once this new information has become part of their schemas, students will benefit from tasks that involve more abstract materials, representations, ideas or applications than peers who are less advanced in their mastery. For example, students may need to work with concrete arrays when first introduced to multiplication. Once a basic understanding of multiplication has been mastered, students may be able to move on to applying multiplication in a problem-solving activity. The pace in which students move from concrete to abstract will vary from student to student.

Simple to complex. Information is in **simple** form if problems or concepts are presented in such a way that only a single meaning or a few meanings may be derived from a chunk of content. Events are also presented in simple form when the student is given the general overview at the outset. If many meanings may be ascertained or multiple events are presented in a more detailed manner, the material is considered **complex.** Students need to see the *big picture* of a topic when it is first introduced, however, once the big picture is understood, learners will benefit from and be better able to complete classroom activities that

- require more complex resources
- have more complex research requirements
- contain more complex issues
- address more complex problems
- require more complex skills
- contain more complex goals

For example, a teacher introducing a unit of study on simple machines first presents students with the general concept that simple machines help people to do work more easily. Once this general concept is understood by students, it is appropriate for the teacher to begin describing the complexities of how each of the six simple machines helps people to do work more easily. After the whole class introduction, the rate at which students will move from simple to more complex resources, research, issues, problems, skills and goals will vary from student to student.

Fewer steps to multi-steps.[2] Some projects, problems and activities require students to take fewer steps, while others involve more steps and applications. Some students may need to work on projects, activities or problems in which only a few steps are involved. Learners who are more advanced in a subject gain from tasks that have more complex directions or more connections within or across subjects or from tasks that require more complex planning and execution. The following two problems represent how to differentiate a mathematical problem-solving situation to better meet the needs of different learners. In the first problem, students need only work through a few steps in order to find the correct solution; they need to find the percent of each number. However, in the second example students are asked to think in more complex ways, and they will need to go through several steps to effectively solve the problem.

Problem 1: You are the owner of a running store who sold 400 pairs of running shoes in the previous quarter. Fifty percent of those pairs of shoes were Nike, fifteen percent were Reebok, fifteen percent were New Balance and twenty percent were Adidas. How many pairs of each brand of shoe did you sell?

Problem 2: You are the owner of a running store. The following table shows data about your sneaker sales in a recent week.

Type of Sneaker	Number Sold
Adidas	124
Nike	64
Reebok	49
New Balance	42
Asics	21

Next week you plan to order 36 dozen sneakers. Explain how you would use the data to decide how many dozen of each type to order, and state how many dozen of each you plan to order.

Smaller leaps to greater leaps. When students apply ideas in ways that are familiar to them or make connections to familiar ideas, they are considered to be making **smaller leaps** of transferring information. If students are asked to use ideas in new and unfamiliar ways or to make connections between previously unrelated ideas, they will need to make **greater leaps** of transferring information. All learners must make leaps in their learning for it to be meaningful. Learning in which memorization of facts is the goal is of little long-term benefit until the memorized information is used to make leaps to higher order thinking. For example, for students learning about perimeter, some may be able to determine how much fencing would be needed to enclose a 36-foot square pen for their dog. Other students may be able to find the solution in which the least amount of fencing is needed and approximate the cost. In addition, these students might be asked to find the additional costs if the pen is enlarged by varying amounts, and then provide a written rationale and recommendation of a size for the pen. Learners advanced in a subject often benefit from tasks that require greater mental leaps in insight, application or transfer than less advanced peers.

More structured to more open. Some students need to complete tasks that are direct and in which they are required to follow a specific format with clear directions. As stu-

[2] Fewer steps to multi-steps and smaller leaps to greater leaps are two differentiating instruction structures that special education teachers say are particularly important for special needs students.

dents become more proficient in a particular area of study, however, they will benefit from tasks that are more open with regards to solutions, decisions and approaches. For example, some students may need more structure in the area of problem-solving. For these students it might be necessary to help them set up an organized table (assuming that this is the appropriate strategy to use with this specific mathematics problem) before they solve the problem independently. More advanced learners would be expected to choose an appropriate strategy and implement this strategy on their own. They may even be asked to solve the problem using two or more different strategies.

The Lemonade Stand

The following problem illustrates how one teacher provided more support for those students who needed it with regards to solving a mathematical problem. In this instance, the additional support some of the students were given was a table constructed by the teacher.

Jack and Susan found they were collecting more and more money from their lemonade stand each day. On the first day, they collected $5.35, then, on the second day, they collected $6.45. On the third day, they collected $8.70, $9.80 on the fourth day and $12.05 on the fifth day. On what day did they collect $22.10?

Day	Money Collected
Day 1	$5.35
Day 2	$6.45
Day 3	
Day 4	
Day 5	
Day 6	
Day 7	
Day 8	
Day 9	
Day 10	
Day 11	
Day 12	

Providing a table for students at lower levels of mastery enabled them to organize the information so that they were able to solve the problem successfully. By providing students with the support they need, these students will develop the ability to solve similar problems with less scaffolding over time.

For more capable students, the teacher gave them the same problem without the table. These students were expected to organize the information and select a strategy that made most sense for them.

Answer to the Lemonade Stand Problem

Day	Money Collected
Day 1	$5.35
Day 2	$6.45
Day 3	*$8.70*
Day 4	*$9.80*
Day 5	*$12.05*
Day 6	*$13.15*
Day 7	*$15.40*
Day 8	*$16.50*
Day 9	*$18.75*
Day 10	*$19.85*
Day 11	*$22.10*
Day 12	

Less independence (more teacher-guided) to greater independence (less teacher-guided). Less independent tasks are those which are primarily designed and modeled by the teacher. As students become **more independent,** they become more responsible for the planning, designing and execution of the particular task at hand. A goal for *all* students is to become independent learners, however, learners reach varying levels of independence at different rates. More advanced learners in a subject will be able to be more independent in terms of planning, designing and self-monitoring than less advanced peers. For example, when first introducing literature circles to students, it is important to model the process for them as well as provide them with a structured format. Each student is assigned a specific role and given directions with regard to fulfilling the role. As the teacher scaffolds the students' learning, students become more competent, responsibility is gradually released to the students and they may modify the structure presented to them to better fit their group. Some groups may even create new roles. It is important to note that each group will reach varying levels of independence at different rates.

A goal for all students is to become independent learners, however, learners reach varying levels of independence at different rates.

Slower to quicker. In Chapter 1, we looked at the various levels of mastery that students progress through when learning new information and skills. Students require differing amounts of time to reach each of the mastery levels when they are taught information and skills. Some students will grasp the new information and skills immediately, while other learners will require more modeling and practice before moving to the next level of mastering the same information and skills. Sometimes learners advanced in their grasp of the information or skill will benefit from moving quickly through prescribed materials and tasks. At other times, they may need a greater amount of time with a particular area of study than less advanced peers in order to explore the topic in greater depth and/or breadth. By differentiating the pace for learners, the more advanced students are able to move forward and the struggling learners are provided the time and reteaching they need.

Students require differing amounts of time to reach each of the mastery levels when they are taught information and skills.

Below is an example of a differentiated instruction mathematics lesson. We have inserted the words "author's notes" in places where we point out to the reader the type of differentiation demonstrated by that part of the lesson.

Differentiating Instruction Exemplar: Elementary Mathematics

1. **What do I want the students to know and be able to do by the end of the lesson (my mastery objectives)?**
   By the end of the lesson, students will be able to correctly complete a two-digit by two-digit multiplication problem using cluster problems up to 49 * 49.
2. **How will I formatively and summatively assess the students' level of mastery?**
   a. **How will I pre-assess the students' level of knowledge? (*If you are not planning to do a mini-lesson, go directly to differentiating, which is question 3b after this pre-assessment*).**
      I will put the example 12 * 12 on the white board. All students will be asked to complete the problem by using smaller cluster problems on their white board. Those students who do not know how to complete the problem using this strategy will write the problem on their white boards and stop when they are stuck. I will then put up the example 24 * 25 and have the students follow the same procedure on their white boards.
   b. **How will I formatively assess after the mini-lesson to determine each student's level of mastery?**
      - The colored cups will enable me to constantly dipstick.
      - I will have some idea of the rate at which students are moving to mastery based on their white board work.
      - During the independent work, I will circulate around the room with the class list on a clipboard and observe the students working. I will record an i (introductory), g (guided practice), im (immediate mastery) or iam (immediate application mastery) for each student.
3. **Describe the sequence of events.**
   a. **What information and skills will I teach during the whole class mini-lesson?**
      - I will explain to students that cluster problems are smaller multiplication problems that you solve in your head (without paper and pencil) and may be combined to solve more complicated multiplication problems.

This allows the teacher to monitor the level of each student's success and provide higher levels of independence (or teacher direction) based on the needs of individual students.

The students' pace will be determined by their level of mastery as demonstrated by the process each student followed in solving the problem and each student's answer. Students who demonstrate mastery will be able to move more quickly to more complex tasks.

This gives the teacher a summative record of each student's level of mastery for use in flexibly grouping the students. It may be determined that some students are capable of greater leaps and, therefore, would be better challenged by skipping altogether some of the activities noted below. Other students may need to be given smaller leaps by using activities with a smaller gradation than those noted below.

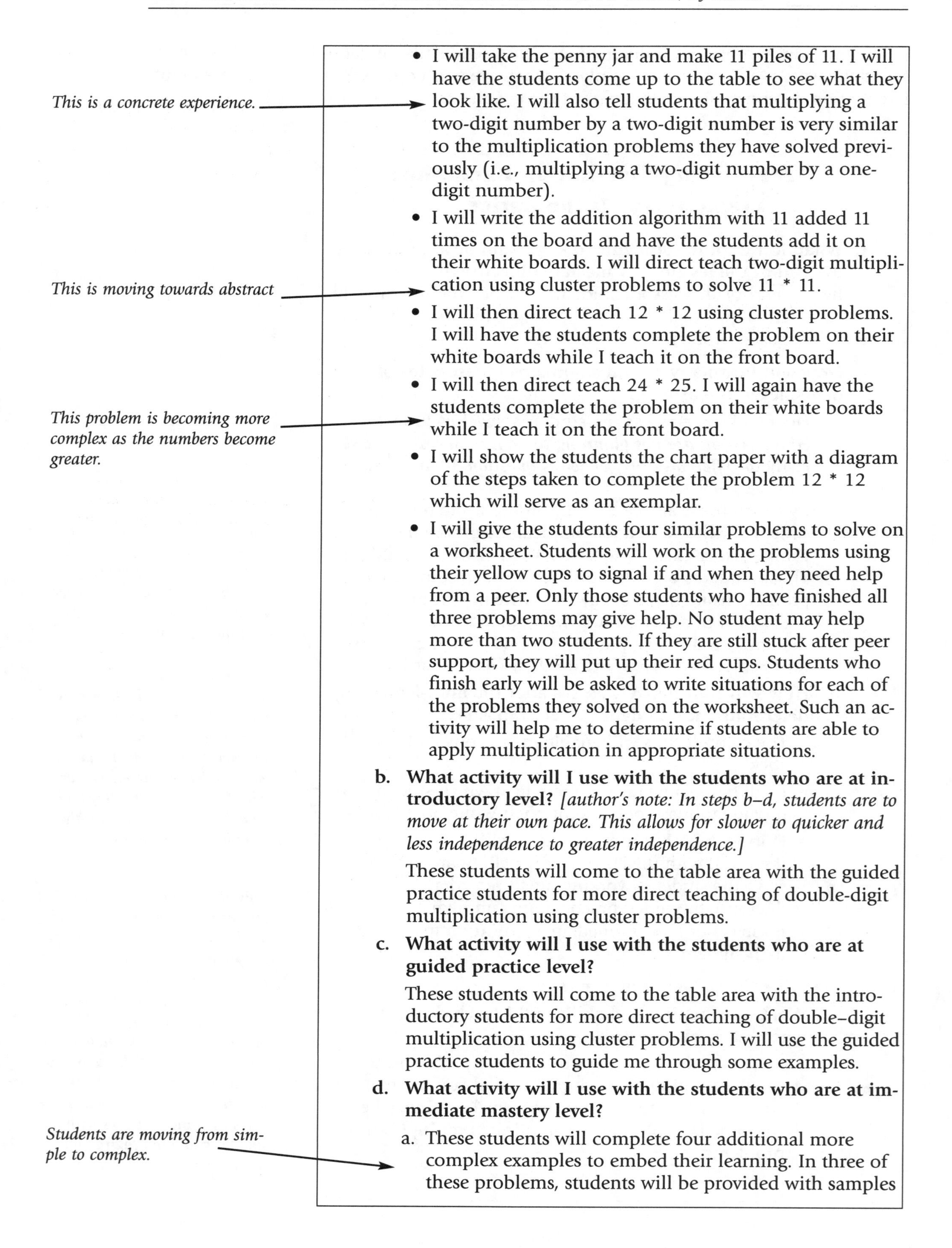

- I will take the penny jar and make 11 piles of 11. I will have the students come up to the table to see what they look like. I will also tell students that multiplying a two-digit number by a two-digit number is very similar to the multiplication problems they have solved previously (i.e., multiplying a two-digit number by a one-digit number).

This is a concrete experience.

- I will write the addition algorithm with 11 added 11 times on the board and have the students add it on their white boards. I will direct teach two-digit multiplication using cluster problems to solve 11 * 11.

This is moving towards abstract

- I will then direct teach 12 * 12 using cluster problems. I will have the students complete the problem on their white boards while I teach it on the front board.
- I will then direct teach 24 * 25. I will again have the students complete the problem on their white boards while I teach it on the front board.

This problem is becoming more complex as the numbers become greater.

- I will show the students the chart paper with a diagram of the steps taken to complete the problem 12 * 12 which will serve as an exemplar.
- I will give the students four similar problems to solve on a worksheet. Students will work on the problems using their yellow cups to signal if and when they need help from a peer. Only those students who have finished all three problems may give help. No student may help more than two students. If they are still stuck after peer support, they will put up their red cups. Students who finish early will be asked to write situations for each of the problems they solved on the worksheet. Such an activity will help me to determine if students are able to apply multiplication in appropriate situations.

b. **What activity will I use with the students who are at introductory level?** *[author's note: In steps b–d, students are to move at their own pace. This allows for slower to quicker and less independence to greater independence.]*

   These students will come to the table area with the guided practice students for more direct teaching of double-digit multiplication using cluster problems.

c. **What activity will I use with the students who are at guided practice level?**

   These students will come to the table area with the introductory students for more direct teaching of double–digit multiplication using cluster problems. I will use the guided practice students to guide me through some examples.

d. **What activity will I use with the students who are at immediate mastery level?**

   a. These students will complete four additional more complex examples to embed their learning. In three of these problems, students will be provided with samples

Students are moving from simple to complex.

of cluster problems to use. In the last problem, students will be asked to create their own clusters to solve each of the original problems. In addition, students will also be asked to choose one of the problems and show how it may be solved in two different ways. They will then check their work with another student in this level. If they have different answers, they will do the problem together to determine the error(s) and find a solution(s) to which they both agree. If both have the same answers and agree, they will move on to the problem of the day.

Students are moving from structured to more open and the problems are requiring a greater number of steps.

b. The problem of the day will be completed individually, using the problem-solving format sheet which may be found in Chapter 7. When a student finishes, he or she will check the work with another student who has completed the problem of the day. If they have different answers, they will do the problem together to determine where they differ and find a solution(s) to which they both agree. When both agree on a solution(s), they will move on to the web site, **http://www.coolmath4kids.com.**

This allows for a high level of independence (non-teacher directed) where appropriate.

e. **What activity will I use with the students who are at the immediate application mastery level?** These students will move on to the problem of the day. The problem of the day will be completed individually using the problem-solving format sheet. When a student finishes the problem, he or she will check the work with another student in this level. If they have different answers, they will do the problem together to determine where they differ and find a solution(s) to which they both agree. When both agree on a solution(s), they will work with their partners on one of the problems found on **http://www.coolmath4kids.com.** The problem(s) they complete will be printed out and placed in their math problem-solving folder.

4. **What other person can assist me with planning this lesson?** I will ask the other fourth-grade teacher to make and copy one of the worksheets and I will make and copy the other.

5. **What materials do I need?** I need dipsticking cups, two worksheets, class list and clipboard, white boards and dry erase markers, problem of the day chart-size sheets and problem-solving format sheets.

Differentiated Instruction Planning Template

1. **What do I want the students to know and be able to do by the end of the lesson (my mastery objectives)?**
2. **How will I formatively and summatively assess the students' level of mastery?**
   a. **How will I pre-assess the students' level of knowledge? *(If you are not planning to do a mini-lesson, go directly to differentiating, which is question 3b after this pre-assessment).***
   b. **How will I formatively assess after the mini-lesson to determine each student's level of mastery?**
3. **Describe the sequence of events**
   a. **What information and skills will I teach during the whole class mini-lesson?**
   b. **What activity will I use with the students who are at introductory level?**
   c. **What activity will I use with the students who are at guided practice level?**
   d. **What activity will I use with the students who are at immediate mastery level?**
   e. **What activity will I use with the students who are at the immediate application mastery level?**
4. **What other person can assist me with planning this lesson?**
5. **What materials do I need?**

The next three pages are the chart-sized sheets noted in the materials section above. Some teachers make these charts on easel papers. Others make the charts on the computer on standard-size paper. The charts are then printed out, taken to a copy center and enlarged to four foot by three foot charts. After they are used, the charts may be folded up and stored in a file cabinet until the next time the concept is taught (during review or in a subsequent year). As noted earlier, planning a differentiated instruction lesson is time-consuming during the initial planning, however, if we save the lesson and charts, the planning time is significantly reduced during the subsequent teaching of the lessons.

Using Cluster Problems to Solve 12 × 12

12 × 12=

Step 1

$12 \times 10 = 120$

Step 2

$12 \times 10 = 120$

$12 \times 2 = 24$

Step 3

$$\begin{array}{rr} 12 \times 10 = & 120 \\ 12 \times 2 = & +\ 24 \\ \hline & 144 \end{array}$$

Using Cluster Problems to Solve 24 × 25

$$24 \times 25 =$$

Step 1

$$25 \times 20 = 500$$

Step 2

$$25 \times 20 = 500$$
$$25 \times 4 = 100$$

Step 3

$$25 \times 20 = 500$$
$$25 \times 4 = +\ 100$$
$$600$$

Problem of the day: Two-digit multiplication

Each soccer team puts eleven players on the field at one time. Ninety-seven teams will enter this year's soccer tournament. Each team has enough players on its roster to make three eleven-man teams. Each team has three coaches and three water carriers who are not players. What is the total number of players who will come to the tournament?

Bonus: 48 teams will be eliminated in the first round. How many players will play in the second round?

Answer: 3201
Answer for bonus: 1617

Worksheet for Students

1. Solve the cluster problems below.

25 × 45 =

25 × 10
25 × 40

25 × 5
25 × 50

15 × 15 =

15 × 1
15 × 10
15 × 5

15 × 2
15 × 20

75 × 25 =

25 × 7
25 × 70
25 × 5

25 × 8
25 × 80

85 × 40 =

2. Choose one of the problems above and solve it using a different set of clusters.

3. When you have finished steps 1 and 2, check your work with another student who has also finished steps 1 and 2, and compare your answers. If you have different answers on a problem, do the problem together to determine the error(s) and find a solution(s) until you both agree. Once you both have the same answers and agree, move on to the problem of the day.

Differentiating Instruction for Varied Learning Style, Culture and Gender

In Chapter 7, we will take a comprehensive look at intelligence and how this impacts instruction. In Chapter 8, we look in depth at the brain and its impact on differentiating our instruction. In the next section, we will focus on four student characteristics that generate a need for varying instruction to meet their learning needs. These four characteristics are learning style, cultural influences, gender and the needs of second language learners.

Learning Style Differences

Environmental Preferences

Learning style has to do with one's environment and personal likes and dislikes. Some students prefer working in a quiet environment, while others prefer to have noise or music in the background. Some students prefer a bright, colorful room, while others prefer a darker, more subdued room. Some students learn better through oral presentation, and some students are visual learners. Some students need to move around and touch things. Although it is impossible for a teacher to present all of these elements at the same time, it is important to use a variety of teaching methods when presenting a new skill, concept or strategy in order to maximize learning for all students. A teacher might also set up the classroom such that some of these different learning preferences might be addressed at the same time.

One teacher found some of her students who preferred working in a quiet environment had a very difficult time with collaborative activities as the noise level was always higher. To accommodate this aspect of their learning style, she had these students work with their group in the hallway at a table when possible.

In another case, a teacher had students who preferred working alone rather than in a group. Because it is critical that students develop the skills needed to work collaboratively, these students were still required to participate in group work. At times, however, these students were permitted to work independently on their tasks. Their independent work would later become part of the group project or activity. As tasks were divided among the group members, this would be the student assigned to do the library research or go on the computer and search the Web for new resources.

Oral Learners and Visual Learners

Some students are oral rather than visual learners. They need to talk through their ideas orally before they begin writing. In these situations, students may dictate their ideas into a tape recorder as the first step in the writing process. These students are able to then listen to their ideas through earphones before making a decision about which idea to use in their writing piece.

Students who are visual learners particularly benefit from using *graphic organizers*. Graphic organizers are especially helpful in writing activities in which students need to organize their ideas and thoughts. In addition, graphic organizers are effective for outlining the structure of a story as these tools help children develop a deeper understanding.

Another way in which to utilize graphic organizers is when introducing major concepts. For example, one teacher presents the concept of the water cycle using a cyclical graphic organizer. It is interesting to note that when students were asked to explain the water cycle in their own words, the visual learners represented this information in a graphic organizer, while many of the other learners wrote out the steps and/or drew pictures. You will read more about graphic organizers later in this chapter.

Figure 4-1

Water comes to earth as rain or snow.

Water collects in clouds as rain or snow.

Water collects in oceans and lakes.

Water evaporates back up into the atmosphere.

Concrete Experiences

Although most students benefit from having concrete experiences with mathematical concepts before moving to a more abstract understanding, some students prefer to work with *manipulatives* even after they have developed a deeper understanding of the concept. For example, many teachers use fraction bars to introduce adding fractions with unlike denominators to students. Through manipulation of these bars, students are able to see and understand how to add such fractions. Some students, as a result of their particular learning styles, rely on these fraction bars even after they develop an understanding of how and why fractions need to have a common denominator in order to add them. For those students who need this concrete support to work independently, teachers may want to keep several bins of fraction bars easily accessible to students so that they may bring them to their desks during group and individual work.

Cultural Influences on Learning (a.k.a. The Achievement Gap)

The following example illustrates the importance of understanding different cultural values in relation to how children learn. The information on Latino students noted in this section comes primarily from a long-term project that studied the learning styles of Latino/Hispanic students in the Los Angeles, CA, public schools. They found that because Latino/Hispanic children are often raised in families which emphasize collectivism, it is important that educators understand how such values will impact learning in the classroom. "**Collectivism** is a cluster of interrelated values that emphasize the interdependence of family members. Within this value system, children are taught to be helpful to others and to contribute to the success of any group they belong to—beginning with the family" (Rothstein-Fisch, Greenfield, & Trumbell, 1999, p64).

Further, collectivism emphasizes scientific information as being part of social experiences. In contrast, individualism focuses on scientific information as being separate from social contexts (Rothstein-Fisch, Greenfield, & Trumbell, 1999). In order to most effectively teach Latino students about scientific concepts, it is important that teachers understand that these students need to first explore scientific concepts in the context of shared family experiences. One teacher who was teaching her students about birds first asked students to share their family stories about birds. This teacher wrote the highlights of the story on one side of the chalkboard and the corresponding scientific aspects of these experiences on the other side. By doing so, the teacher demonstrated that both the children's stories and the scientific information were equally valued in the classroom (Rothstein-Fisch, Greenfield, & Trumbell, 1999).

Culture also influences how students learn. Geneva Gay (2000), a professor of education at the University of Washington-Seattle, suggests that children begin school with a learning style that has been internalized through the experiences that are part of one's culture. The following cultural differences may impact learning and should be considered when planning learning experiences for children.

- reserved or outspoken
- whole to part or part to whole
- contextual, personal material versus discrete, impersonal material
- group or individual orientation
- creativity or conformity

Unlike the more homogeneous societies found in countries like Japan, schools in the United States, Canada and many European countries often have students from a wide variety of cultures with varying learning styles. In recent years, we have become very aware of the achievement gap that exists between the achievement of Asian-American, white, African-American and Latino/Hispanic students. This gap is due in part to differing learning styles based on culture and also to the lack of training that teachers have received to better enable them to meet these varied styles.

There is a significant, well documented gap between the achievement of Asian and white students as compared to that of the African-American and Latino/Hispanic students. The research (Ferguson, 2002) indicates that part of that achievement gap may be explained by the parents' education levels and the families' socio-economic levels. However, the gap lessens, but continues to exist even when the students from the same parent education and socio-economic levels are compared.

However, the gap lessens, but continues to exist even when the students from the same parent education and socio-economic levels are compared.

Below is a table which compares fourth-grade and eighth-grade achievement for each group from a select group of states. The data from the scale scores are from the National Assessment of Educational Progress (NAEP)[3]. The NAEP is the test data reporting required by the federal law No Child Left Behind (NCLB). The data for Asian and Native American students was not available at the time this book went to press.

Table 4-2

Fourth Grade Reading 2003

State	*African–American*	*Latino/Hispanic*	*White*
California	193	191	224
Connecticut	201	206	238
Florida	198	211	229
Maryland	200	209	231
Massachusetts	207	202	234
Michigan	189		228
New York	203	208	235
Texas	202	205	227
Virginia	206		231

Table 4-3

Fourth Grade Math 2003

State	*African–American*	*Latino/Hispanic*	*White*
California	213	216	243
Connecticut	217	223	250
Florida	215	232	243
Maryland	216	227	244
Massachusetts	222	222	247
Michigan	209	223	244
New York	219	221	246
Texas	226	230	248
Virginia	223	230	246

[3] Scale scores are used when comparing results from different tests that report results in unlike forms. Since the scores from unlike tests are not readily comparable, the scores are converted to scale scores that are based on a numeric scale with intervals of equal size. This allows the varying measures to be joined together for an accurate comparison. The raw scores from the various state tests were converted to scale scores to aid in interpretation by providing a quantitative measure of each student's performance relative to a comparison group across the states. A scale has been applied to these state tests so that direct comparisons among students, between individual scores and groups or among the scores within a specific subject area across grades can be made in a way that is statistically valid. This comparison cannot be done with the percentile or grade equivalent scores that these tests typically produce.

Table 4-4

Eighth Grade Math 2003

State	*African–American*	*Latino/Hispanic*	*White*
California	246	250	283
Connecticut	255	259	293
Florida	249	264	286
Maryland	256	262	289
Massachusetts			
Michigan	245	267	286
New York	255	262	293
Texas	260	267	290
Virginia	262	268	290

Education Watch Achievement Gap Summary Tables, 2004

Some of the recommendations for closing this gap are out of the control of a classroom teacher. For example, the class size is determined by the school district. It is more difficult for teachers to adequately meet the needs of all learners with a greater number of students. The socioeconomic status of students as well as the amount of support received at home and learning resources in the home are, for the most part,[4] also out of the control of the teacher. There are, however, a number of things we as teachers may do to improve the achievement of African–American and Latino/Hispanic students. For example:

- African–American and Latino/Hispanic students report less understanding of teacher lessons related to the material they read for school. Teachers may address this issue by employing more responsive instructional strategies to meet these students' learning needs. These students may also need to be retaught certain skills and concepts. In addition, teachers should require *all* students to read and write in complete sentences on a daily basis in order to improve writing skills (Bell, 2003).
- Higher order thinking skills should be taught to all students as all children need to possess such skills to succeed in today's world. Many Latino/Hispanic students have not yet fully mastered English. As a result, they master curriculum more slowly because of the need to translate concepts from English to Spanish and vice versa. This need to translate may cause these students to be placed in groups in which concepts are taught at a slower pace. Many of these groups don't receive the same level of thinking-skills training as the other groups. The result is that these students fall farther and farther behind the others in their ability to successfully complete higher order thinking tasks. This gap in their knowledge is then reflected in state (or province) and national test scores. It is important that we remember that such gaps are due to the students' experiences and not to their innate intelligence.
- Teacher encouragement has been found to be particularly important for nonwhite students as a source of achievement motivation. It is important for teachers to establish a trusting, caring relationship with all students at the beginning of the year. However, research indicates that doing so will have a greater impact on both African–American and Latino/Hispanic students (Ferguson, 2002) than on whites or

[4] Chapter 9 gives descriptions of ways in which districts and individual teachers have successfully worked with parents to improve their abilities to support their children's learning at home.

Asian–Americans. Ferguson's research indicates that the explicit and implicit messages teachers send these students about their ability to achieve at high levels has a greater influence on African–American and Latino/Hispanic students' perception of their ability than it does on white and Asian–American students.

Ferguson (2002) lists several implications for schools and communities based upon his research of the achievement gap. These recommendations are as follows:

1. **Assume no motivational differences.** Teachers should assume no differences in effort or motivation to succeed based upon a particular race, although observable differences in behavior and academic performance may be seen.
2. **Address specific skill deficits.** Schools need to identify and address any gaps in knowledge and/or skills that certain groups of students may have that result from influences such as fewer experiences at home that develop academic skills (e.g., more TV and less reading), second language issues or previous school experiences. These students will typically need an infusion of skills teaching to catch up to the others.
3. **Supply ample encouragement routinely.** Teachers need to provide effective encouragement for students routinely. African–American and Latino/Hispanic students respond particularly well to such encouragement. Chapter 5 and Chapter 7 both contain a description of the types of praise that have the greatest impact on furthering student achievement.
4. **Provide access to resources and learning experiences.** Due to the differences in learning resources in the home, schools should provide more books, computers and extracurricular activities to those families that are in need of such supports.

Ferguson (2002) has also developed a project, coined the *Tripod Project,* which is based upon his research with regards to the achievement gap. Content, pedagogy and relationships are the three legs of what he calls the **"instructional tripod."** Professional development opportunities should equip teachers to attend to all three of these legs.

Ferguson (2002) outlines five tasks that are part of the Tripod Project. He indicates that students will be more likely to succeed if the following conditions are met:

1. "Students begin the semester feeling trustful of the teacher and interested, instead of feeling mistrustful and uninterested.
2. Students experience a good balance between teacher control and student autonomy, instead of too little or too much of either.
3. Students are goal-oriented in their learning, rather than feeling ambivalent.
4. Students work industriously in pursuing their goals for learning, instead of becoming discouraged in the face of difficulty or disengaged due to boredom.
5. Teachers help students consolidate their new knowledge and, thus equipped, students are well prepared for future classes and life experiences."

Chapter 7 explains in depth how a teacher may help students with the previous items 1, 3 and 4. We strongly recommend that establishing a project in your school, such as the one described below, include professional development on the concepts explained in Chapter 7.

The Tripod Project is centered on five school–wide faculty workshops. At each meeting, one of the five stages listed above is explored, and teachers work in small groups, sharing their ideas with regard to each task and stage. As teachers share their best practices with others, they will find themselves strengthening each leg of the tripod within their own classrooms.

Teachers should be encouraged to test the strategies described by their colleagues in their own classrooms. After teachers try these strategies, it is important that teachers have opportunities to come together with their colleagues to discuss the following:

1. what worked and why it worked
2. what did not work, why it did not work and how they might try it again differently

Chapters 10 and 11 describe structures that enable teachers to examine their own practice independently and/or with their colleagues.

Although generalizations may be made for particular cultures, students will vary in their preferences, and it is important that a teacher discovers the ways in which individual students are able to work most productively.

Although generalizations may be made for particular cultures, students will vary in their preferences, and it is important that a teacher discovers the ways in which individual students are able to work most productively.

Second Language Learners

Unfortunately, many schools find it difficult to provide adequate instruction and resources for second language learners. This is due in part to a lack of available funding, however, it is also due in part to misconceptions about how these students learn. According to the research, reading, speaking, listening and writing are highly interdependent and interrelated processes that both first and second language learners should be engaged (Gebhard, 2002–2003). Given this understanding, it is important that educators provide second language learners with opportunities in which they use these processes simultaneously, rather than presenting these learners with a step-by-step curriculum in which students practice these as discrete entities.

Previewing reading materials and concepts—One teacher helped a second language learner acquire reading skills by providing extra support for this student prior to the literature circles. The student listened to an audiotape of the story at home the night before his literature circle met to discuss the book. In another instance, a teacher had the good fortune of having a teaching assistant. Prior to the student's listening to the story at home, the teaching assistant read the assigned chapter with this student and helped clarify any misunderstandings. In addition, when necessary, the assistant reviewed what the student had prepared and had him practice how he was going to present his work in the literature circle. In some schools, parent and senior citizen volunteers (or even reading partners from higher grades) perform the teaching assistant role with these students.

Small group guided instruction—Another way to help second language learners acquire important reading skills is through guided instruction. It is often easier for students to participate, ask questions and offer opinions in smaller groups. In addition, a teacher may more effectively target specific weak areas with smaller groups.

Previewing math concepts—A strategy for helping second language students acquire mathematical skills is to have a teacher, a teaching assistant (or volunteer) or some other adult preview math concepts before they are introduced to the class. Students should also be familiarized with important vocabulary words. Students, with the help of a teaching assistant (or volunteer), may construct flash cards with the word, a definition, an example and a visual illustrating the word. In addition, in order to help these students develop a conceptual understanding, they should work with manipulatives whenever possible. The manipulatives serve two purposes for second language learners. They both assist with conceptual understanding *and* serve as a visual that does not require an oral explanation that they need to translate before understanding.

Group projects with a bilingual student who helps the second language learner—In schools with a high percentage of second language learners, there are usually some students in the class who are fluent in both English and their primary languages. Teachers with such classes may want to have students work in collaborative groups on longer term projects.

Certain groups should have both a second language learner and a bilingual student. In this way, second language learners have opportunities when necessary to practice articulating their thinking as well as receive support from peers who are fluent in both languages.

Visuals—Above we spoke about the positive impact of mathematical manipulative materials because they serve as visual representations of the concepts. Another visual teachers may use with these learners is a graphic organizer so that the most important points are highlighted in an organized manner. The graphic organizers also glean out the key terms from the text, enabling the students to focus on these terms without translating all of the text. Whenever unfamiliar vocabulary is going to be used in a lesson, second language learners should be provided with a visual representation of the word, and, when possible, a preview of all important words. Pictures are also important visuals to use when teaching a class with second language learners. Foreign language teachers have long been aware of the importance of using pictures to reinforce instruction in the target language. Pictures that represent the information being provided in English are of tremendous value to students who do not yet have a strong grasp of the English language.

Working in pairs—As noted above, classrooms with high percentages of second language learners often have students who are fluent in both English and the primary language. It may be helpful to pair second language learners with bilingual students, particularly when students will be required to take notes.

Gender Differences

Gender also plays a role in how we learn. Michael Gurian's (2001) brain research on boys concluded that boys tend to master reading more slowly than girls. They also show early mathematical ability and reasoning with three-dimensional objects. Further, in one study, boys were more likely to name a boy as the best student in mathematics, while girls named boys and girls nearly equally as best in math (Matthews, Binkley, Crisp, & Gregg, 1997–1998).

The classroom teachers we work with often report that male students ask for math challenges more frequently than female students, whereas the girls in many of these classrooms gravitate more often to writing activities when given a choice.

Karen Roger's (1990) educational research on girls suggests that girls learn best when tasks have many possible solutions and there are opportunities for discussion and questions. It is important, however for teachers to call on both sexes equally. In one study, students suggested that "when you're calling on people, call on a girl, then a boy, then a girl, then a boy next." Or, "Call on everybody, even the ones not raising their hand" (Matthews, Binkley, Crisp, & Gregg, 1997–1998). In this way, students will perceive the teacher as being fair rather than favoring one sex over the other. Chapter 5 discusses strategies for improving our patterns for calling on students.

General patterns, such as the patterns of males tending to favor competitive learning more than females and females tending to prefer collaborative learning more than males may also be prevalent. Although, girls may tend to prefer group work more than boys do, boys often tend to dominate collaborative activities. For example, in one study, fifth-grade students were asked to work in groups and then to share their findings. Of the six groups, five boys and only one girl gave reports (Matthews, Binkley, Crisp, & Gregg, 1997–1998). Teachers we work with also report findings that are fairly consistent with this research. Girls often reported boys dominating the conversation and/or activity as a major problem within the group. Although the girls recognized this problem and were even able to articulate it, they often had difficulty mitigating it, and, at times, the classroom teacher had to become involved in the resolution.

It is important to note that the generalizations discussed above are not always the case, however, being aware of the possibility of these gender differences helps educators address these issues and create more equitable classrooms.

First Steps to Differentiating Your Instruction Based on Learning Profile

Tomlinson (2001) offers the following guidelines for implementing learning-profile-based differentiated instruction.

1. Keep in mind that not all students share your learning preferences.
2. Help students recognize their learning preferences.
3. Start small as you begin. Select only one or two learning profiles to differentiate instruction.

Step 1: Keep in mind that not all students share your learning preferences. It is important to remember that you are teaching to diverse learners and that a variety of learning preferences should be addressed. If you are an auditory learner and teacher, you may be more inclined to present your lessons auditorily. However, it is important to use a variety of teaching methods in order to reach all of your students.

It is important to remember that you are teaching to diverse learners and that a variety of learning preferences should be addressed.

Step 2: Help students recognize their learning preferences. It is important to help students understand how they learn best. In addition, let students know what type of learning they will be doing in a particular activity. For example, if you are presenting a lesson in which students will participate in visual, oral and kinesthetic activities, let the students know what type of activity they are doing as they are doing it. After, ask students which mode of learning was most effective for them and which was most difficult.

The following form is one which students complete at the beginning of the year to help both students and the classroom teacher better understand each student's learning profile with regard to learning mathematics.

Figure 4-2
Personal Mathematics Learning Profile

Please check the learning preferences that apply to you.

In math, I generally

_____ demand attention
_____ want to please
_____ am slow to get started
_____ ask questions
_____ am unhappy
_____ am well organized
_____ keep working on a task until I finish
_____ like teacher encouragement
_____ like to work alone
_____ am comfortable/happy

I am most successful in math when I

_____ get enough practice on the skills/concepts we are working on
_____ am not absent or I make up my work (with teacher help if needed) when I am absent
_____ put forth extra effort to really pay attention in class
_____ do all of my homework
_____ get extra help outside of class
_____ ask questions in class

I am least successful in math when

_____ students around me are distracting
_____ the teacher goes too quickly and I do not ask him or her to slow down
_____ I let other things on my mind interfere with my listening in class
_____ I do not complete my homework
_____ I am absent a lot
_____ I do not ask for extra help when I need it

My teacher helps me achieve success in math class when he or she

_____ provides lots of practice before a test
_____ works with me one-on-one
_____ allows me to correct the wrong answers on a test
_____ keeps the class quiet so I may concentrate
_____ makes sure I am not sitting next to someone who may distract me
_____ provides lots of concrete examples of what we are learning
_____ uses manipulatives when we are learning new concepts
_____ makes it clear exactly what we are supposed to do
_____ has us work alone
_____ has us work in pairs
_____ has us work in groups
_____ enforces the classroom rules

I prefer to be assessed by

_____ teacher observation
_____ paper and pencil tests/quizzes
_____ performance assessments (project-based assessments)
_____ take-home/open-book tests
_____ writing a report
_____ oral presentations

My biggest success in math last year was ______________________________.

In math class, it is difficult for me to ______________________________.

These are my recommendations to my teacher this year to help me be a successful learner:

____
____
____
____

Step 3: Start small as you begin. Select only one or two learning differences to address by differentiating your instruction. Differentiating lessons based on learning profiles may be a daunting task, as there are so many different ways to look at learning differences in students. Once you feel confident in using one or two strategies for differentiating instruction, branch out and try new ones. For example, you may want to begin by differentiating instruction according to intelligence style preference. You might present a lesson in which students are expected to learn the same content, but are able to choose to complete verbal, visual or kinesthetic activities to demonstrate their understanding.

The following example illustrates how one of our colleagues differentiated instruction according to learning styles for a fifth-grade unit of study in science. The class was studying endangered animals, specifically, the causes of endangerment of specific animals and what may be done to preserve the particular species being studied. In order to help students decide how to present their findings, the teacher brainstormed with the class about different ways to complete this project. The list included ideas such as creating a PowerPoint® presentation, making a poster, writing a report, making up a song, constructing a diorama, role playing, etc.

The visual learners drew pictures illustrating the required information. The auditory learners prepared an oral presentation based on the information they found. The kinesthetic learners role-played the causes of endangerment as well as what may be done to help these animals. The following figure outlines this particular project.

Figure 4-3
Endangered Animal Project

You are about to embark upon an exciting journey into the wild world of endangered animals. You will have the opportunity to choose an endangered animal and will be responsible for representing your findings to the class. There are several components that must be included in your representation. These components are as follows:

1. description of your animal (including a picture)
2. description of animal's habitat (including a map showing where the animal lives)
3. explanation of why this animal is endangered
4. explanation of things people may do to help save this animal
5. at least three resources must be used
6. bibliography must be included

The following steps should be followed to help you organize your time:

1. Choose an endangered animal
   Due Date: ______________________
2. Collect at least three resources
   Due Date: ______________________
3. Read and take notes using note-taking organizer
   Due Date: ______________________
4. Decide how information will be represented
   Due Date: ______________________
5. Draft of project
   Due Date: ______________________
6. Final project
   Due Date: ______________________

In this example, the content learned was the same for all students, however, the manner in which the students processed the information as well as how students represented their findings varied according to their learning styles.

Differentiating by Interest Through Project-Based Work

Teachers may also use students' interests as a way in which to differentiate information and skills, process and product. Students are more inclined to be motivated when they are pursuing an interest and have a choice in their learning.

Tomlinson (2001) offers the following guidelines to follow when implementing interest-based differentiation.

1. Link interest-based exploration with key areas of the curriculum.
2. Provide students with structures to help them succeed.
3. Create efficient ways for students to share their work.
4. Encourage students to discover new ways of learning.
5. Combine interest-based differentiation with other forms of differentiation.

Interest-based exploration should be linked with key areas of the curriculum. It is important for teachers to connect students' interests with information and/or skills that are integral to the curriculum. In this way, both the goals of the student and curriculum may be met at the same time. For example, if part of the reading curriculum specifies that students should develop strategies for reading nonfiction, a student who is passionate about frogs might develop these reading strategies by reading nonfiction articles or books about frogs.

Provide students with structures to help them succeed. When students are working on interest-based projects, there will be an element of independence as students will be working on different things. Some students are capable of greater independence, while others need more scaffolding in order to succeed. The teacher will need to provide the appropriate level of scaffolding to ensure success for each student. One technique that benefits all students is clearly outlining for students the criteria they are expected to meet to be successful.[5] Students perform at high levels when they know ahead of time how they are going to be assessed. For example, if a rubric or criteria sheet is going to be used to assess student success, the teacher should share it with the students before they begin working on their tasks. The following list provides more ideas for helping students in this process.

One technique that benefits all students is clearly outlining for students the criteria they are expected to meet to be successful.

- checklists
- timelines
- check-ins with the teacher
- rubrics
- criteria sheets
- exemplars
- step-by-step directions
- mini-lessons related to skills and/or strategies needed to complete the task

[5] See Chapter 1 for an explanation of how to create mastery objectives that clearly describe for students what they will know and be able to do at the end of the learning time. Chapter 6 contains examples of rubrics and criteria sheets that also may be used to clearly outline for students the criteria for success.

Create efficient ways for students to share their work about their areas of interest. It is a time-consuming process to have twenty-five students present their work to the class. Instead, you may want to ask students to share their work in small groups or pairs. Or, you may have students share one aspect of their projects with the class. It is important that students are taught both how to appropriately share their work as well as how to be a good listener while others are presenting. As a class, you may want to create and post a list of what a good listener looks like. Student responses may include things such as maintaining eye contact, not doodling or playing with objects, asking appropriate and related questions and giving specific feedback to the presenter. These behaviors should be modeled for students. It may also be beneficial to have students role-play being both a good listener and a poor listener. Finally, teachers may want to ask students to reflect upon themselves as listeners after role-playing and after students present their work.

Encourage students to discover new ways of learning. Invite students to propose new ideas for tasks and projects, and let them know you will help them in their endeavors. Doing so instills a greater sense of shared ownership in learners and ignites creativity and greater enthusiasm for learning.

The following teaching experience took place in one teacher's fifth-grade classroom.

This particular teacher had divided her class into four different groups for an author study of Avi. Each group read a different book written by Avi according to its instructional reading level. At one point, one of the groups approached the teacher and asked if each group could present a Reader's Theater to the class, based on its particular book. In this way, the students would have an opportunity to compare and contrast some of the different books written by Avi. After giving it some thought, the teacher agreed to this idea. As a class, they established guidelines: students needed to present a summary of their stories, including a clear problem and solution, as well as the overriding theme. Students were quite enthusiastic and worked diligently to put together a well organized Reader's Theater.

Each group presented its book in a competent and innovative way. In addition, all groups incorporated all of the required components. After the groups made their presentations, the class had a rich discussion on the differences and similarities found among these books. The students uncovered a very surprising element that appeared to be present in these particular books written by Avi. Contrary to the previous reading experiences of most of the students, these books did not end in a completely happy, fairy tale manner. Instead, the endings of each of these books had an element of disappointment and surprise as part of the resolution. They talked about how this made Avi's stories more realistic as well as unpredictable. It was interesting to listen to students' comments with regard to this new revelation. Some students preferred knowing a story was going to end happily, while others preferred the element of surprise which was sometimes accompanied by disappointment.

Although this project did take a good amount of time to complete, according to the teacher, it was an invaluable learning process as students developed a new and more sophisticated understanding of story structure.

Interest-based differentiation may be combined with other forms of differentiation. It is possible to design a task which is differentiated by readiness, interest and learning profile. In the inventor example presented below, the project was differentiated by readiness in that students were provided with research materials appropriate to their reading levels and understanding. The task was differentiated by interest in that students were given the opportunity to choose the inventor they wished to further explore. This project was also differentiated according to learning profile as students were able to create a final product that most closely matched their learning style.

Part of the science curriculum that fifth-grade teachers were expected to teach each year involved learning about different inventors and how their work impacted society. In order to generate greater enthusiasm for this unit of study, the fifth-grade teachers differentiated the information and skills by having students select inventors who were of interest to them. The process was also differentiated as the teachers helped guide the students in selecting appropriate research materials. Some students were capable of using multiple sources that were more complex in nature, while others needed to read more basic sources (e.g., lower reading levels, fewer primary source materials) in order to understand the information. Further, some students needed a more structured format to follow, while other students were able to conduct their research using their own ideas for organizing information. The final product was also differentiated in that students had a wide range of choices available to them among ways to present their information. These choices were generated from the students as they brainstormed different ways of representing the information they had acquired. Some students created a PowerPoint® presentation, while others created a visual poster and oral report. Some students created a game show and others wrote a standard research report. This project was one of the students' favorite projects of the year, as they were able to pursue their genuine interests as well as choose how to present their work. The actual project is provided in the following boxes.

Figure 4-4
Welcome to the World of Inventors and Inventions

Why do people invent? People invent for a variety of reasons. They are curious about that which is new, untried and unknown. They are stimulated by a natural desire to learn. Because of past inventions, they have a certain amount of leisure time in which to dream and experiment with new ideas. They want to solve a problem, improve a product, achieve fame or help humanity.

Now, with this activity, you will take an exciting journey into the mind of a famous inventor. You will need to follow several guidelines, however, you will have an opportunity to make several decisions along the way.

Guidelines

1. Choose an inventor about whom you would like to learn more. If you need help with selecting an inventor, see the attached list for some ideas.
2. Fill out the planning sheet I have provided for you. You will need to decide
   - how you would like to represent the knowledge you gain from your research
   - which materials you will need
   - if you would like to work alone or with another person.
3. Turn in your planning sheet for my approval.
4. Gather information about your inventor and his or her invention. You need to use at least three resources. You will be given time at the library and the computer lab to look for your resources. I also have several books on inventors in the classroom.
5. Take notes using the note-taking sheet I have provided for you.
6. Execute the plan you chose on your planning sheet.

Note: You will have class time to work on this project. However, you may need to work on parts of this project at home in order to meet the agreed-upon deadline.

Figure 4-5
My Planning Sheet for Inventors and Inventions

Name(s): ______________________________ Date: ____________

I am going to research ________________ who invented ________________

I plan to work (check one): _____ alone _____ with ____________________

I need to demonstrate my knowledge about my chosen inventor in the following areas:

1. a description of the inventor, including how he or she came up with his or her ideas
2. a description of the invention created by the inventor
3. how the invention changed the lives of people at the time that it was invented
4. why this invention is important to us today

I/we plan to demonstrate our knowledge by

____

Materials I/we will need to complete this project are

____

____

Resources (at least 3) I/we will use are

____

____

____

Deadline: ________________ Teacher Approval: ________________

Figure 4-6
Note-Taking Sheet

Inventor: ____________________

Invention: ____________________

Description of inventor: ____________________

____

____

Description of invention: ____________________

____

____

How this invention changed the lives of people at the time the invention was created:

____

____

____

Why this invention is important to us today: ____________________

____

____

Resources used:

1. ____________________
2. ____________________
3. ____________________

Figure 4-7
Inventor Project Timeline

1. Select inventor to research
   Due Date: ____________________
2. Planning sheet completed
   Due Date: ____________________
3. Gather resources (at least 3)
   Due Date: ____________________
4. Notes completed
   Due Date: ____________________
5. Draft of project
   Due Date: ____________________
6. Project completed
   Due Date: ____________________
7. Project presentation
   Due Date: ____________________

Differentiating Content (Information and Skills), Process and Product

This section discusses differentiating instruction by content (information and skills), process and product as separate components. It is important to note, however, that these elements are interrelated and often the lines are blurred between how and what is being differentiated. These elements will be discussed separately for purposes of more clearly defining how to differentiate instruction in each of these ways.

Differentiating Content

Content refers to information and skills being taught and is often mandated by the state or district. In other words, the prescribed content is often found in state curriculum standards. Content may be differentiated by emphasizing the highest priority information and skills or by making the learning more complex. Some students may need more practice and direct instruction in order to master information or a skill, while other students are able to quickly master the same content and need a greater challenge (Heacox, 2002).

Content may be differentiated by emphasizing the highest priority information and skills or by making the learning more complex.

Content may be differentiated in a variety of ways according to readiness, interests or learning profile. Tomlinson (2001) outlines the following strategies that may be used to differentiate content.

- **Curriculum Compacting**—More information about using this strategy may be found later in this chapter.
- **Using Varied Text and Resource Materials**
- **Learning Contracts**—More information about using this strategy may be found later in this chapter.

- **Mini-lessons**—Mini-lessons are brief lessons which a teacher may use to reteach a lesson, present a lesson in a different manner or extend a lesson. These lessons may be used with a whole class or with smaller groups of students.
- **Varied Support Systems**
  - Audio–Video recorders
  - Note-taking organizers
  - Highlighted print materials
  - Digests of key ideas—A **digest of key ideas** is a 1–2 page graphic organizer, list or summary of key ideas within a unit of study. It may also include important vocabulary words as well as essential questions.
  - Peer and adult mentors

The following example illustrates how one colleague of ours differentiated content for a weather disaster reading unit. Students were required to read one of several books based on a weather disaster. The selection of books reflected a variety of reading levels, and students were matched to books that were appropriate to their instructional reading levels. All students were asked to describe both the causes and effects of the weather disaster. As a culminating activity, the class as a whole created a chart of causes and effects of the different weather disasters studied. In addition, those students who needed more challenging work or had a strong interest in weather events were encouraged to conduct further research using more technical and more sophisticated materials.

In this example, although students read different texts of varying difficulty, they were all required to master the skill of cause and effect and were able to do so using text that was at a reading level appropriate to their levels of understanding. Further, those students who were ready to explore more sophisticated information were provided the opportunity. These students were then able to share their findings in science class.

Early in this chapter, we talked about the importance of sharing the work of differentiating by planning with other teachers. Both of the previous two projects would be much more *doable* if the work were divided among several teachers teaching the same curriculum. For example, for the inventor project, assuming there were four fifth-grade teachers in the school, the teachers might divide the list of inventors and each locate resources for their assigned inventors. The building literacy teacher might give the teachers advice on the reading level of each resource so they might be assigned to students with appropriate reading levels. The teachers might even divide the students based on the inventors they chose, so that each teacher is responsible for being knowledgeable about only one-fourth of the inventors.

Differentiating Process

Instruction may be differentiated by varying the process or the means by which the content is being taught. Your teaching, when feasible, should reflect the styles and preferences of your learners. You may differentiate the process in three ways:

1. increasing the complexity of a task
2. providing tasks that require greater creativity and critical thinking
3. requiring the students to learn in a variety of ways (Heacox, 2002)

The following strategies may be used to differentiate process.

- journals
- graphic organizers
- literature circles
- interactive journals
- creative problem-solving

- think-pair-share
- mind-mapping

Students may be provided the opportunity to learn the information and skills using the strategy that is best matched to their learning styles. For example, some students working on the previous weather disaster unit may be given the opportunity to describe the disaster and note the cause and effect by writing a journal about the events from the point of view of a meteorologist reporting on the event. Other students may choose to describe the same information by creating both a sequence of events and a cause and effect graphic organizer. A group of students reading the same book may choose to conduct a literature circle (with or without the teacher) in a small circle, while the remainder of the class sits around them in a larger circle, listening to the discussion.

In addition to offering a variety of strategies, each of the strategies in this example may be structured to vary the level of complexity and/or to require differing levels of creativity and critical thinking.

The previous item 3 talks about requiring students to learn in a variety of ways. It is important to remember that there are times when we want to require students to use processes that are not in their greatest areas of strength. Processes such as those listed in the bullets above are important for all students to learn. If they never choose some of the options, then it is important that from time to time we assign them to use learning processes that they need work in developing.

It is important to remember that there are times when we want to require students to use processes that are not in their greatest areas of strength.

Differentiating Product

The manner in which students are assessed may also be varied as a means of differentiating instruction. His or her product demonstrates a student's understanding at the end of a unit of study. Many of the items listed as processes in the previous bulleted list may also result in differentiated products. Products may be differentiated by providing students with choices of the way in which they demonstrate their mastery of the information and skills and/or by providing greater levels of challenge. Units of study in which learning may be represented in a multitude of ways are examples of lessons planned to allow for differentiating products (Heacox, 2002).

The following strategies may be utilized for differentiating products.

- build assignments around a theme, concept or issue that is central to the topic being studied
- use variations on a theme to address individual interests and readiness
- design assignments to help children connect key ideas to their own world
- support students' use of varied modes of expression and materials
- give clear criteria for success—more information about creating and using rubrics may be found in chapter 6.

The following example represents a way in which one of our colleagues differentiated the product at the culmination of a mathematics unit on decimals, fractions and percents. The *concept* students were required to demonstrate was the relationship among decimals, fractions and percents. All students were required to demonstrate that decimals, fractions and percents are different ways to express numbers that are less than one whole. To demonstrate knowledge or *variations of the theme* and *connect to their own world,* students were required to describe the importance of having different ways of expressing the same number. (For example, when dealing with money, we use a decimal and when we talk about the chance of rain, we use a percentage, etc.) Students were asked to provide an example showing when each mode of expression would be most appropriately used. Students were also asked to choose a fraction and express it as both a decimal and percent.

The description of the activity piqued students' *interests* and they were given *the option to use varied modes of expression and materials*. Some students wrote a song to demonstrate the connection among the three concepts. Some students created a game in which players had to use their knowledge of the relationship among these three concepts to play. Other students created a poster that visually showed the relationships, and others wrote a picture book both explaining and illustrating how decimals, fractions and percents are connected. Each option was accompanied by a rubric that *clearly stated the criteria* for successfully completing the assessment.[6]

Using Instructional Strategies to Differentiate Instruction

A multitude of instructional strategies may be used to differentiate instruction by content, process and product according to learners' readiness, interests and learning styles. Often, you will use a variety of instructional strategies to differentiate instruction in more than one way simultaneously. This section highlights instructional strategies that teachers have found to be particularly effective for differentiating instruction.

Flexible Grouping

Flexible grouping is a central practice of differentiated instruction, and it is accomplished by assigning students to a variety of instructional groups based on levels of readiness, learning styles and interests. The composition of the groups varies. Sometimes these groups are homogeneous, sometimes heterogeneous, sometimes random, and sometimes composed of the whole class, depending on learning goals and students' needs and interests.

One of our colleagues used flexible grouping in her reading program in the following manner. When doing an author study with students, the teacher selected a variety of books of varying levels and themes but written by the same author, Avi. Although students needed to choose a book that was at their instructional reading levels, they did have some choice in determining which book they would read, as there were a few books at each reading level. By using different books by the same author, the teacher was able to capitalize on students' interests, while, at the same time, grouping students according to their levels of readiness. Moreover, throughout this unit, the teacher often met at the same time with students reading different books when they needed more direct teaching and/or practice with one of the comprehension strategies they were learning.

Heacox (2002) offers the following tips when implementing flexible grouping.

1. When using flexible grouping, try to keep the groups small, around four to five students. Smaller groups are more manageable and students will have greater opportunities for participation.
2. Do not feel as though you need to spend equal amounts of time with each group. Some groups will need more support and structure than others.
3. If you recognize in advance that you will need to spend a large amount of time with a particular group, plan activities for other groups in which minimal direction is needed.
4. Construct tasks so that students will be able to complete them independently after you explain the directions. Provide students with step-by-step directions and clear criteria for assessment, such as rubrics or criteria sheets. If possible, share exemplars of student work that successfully meets the criteria.

---

[6] More information about assessing student learning may be found in Chapter 5.

5. Set clear expectations with regards to behavior. It may be helpful to post a list of rules that clearly outlines your expectations.

Set clear expectations with regards to behavior. It may be helpful to post a list of rules that clearly outlines your expectations.

6. Establish a system of how students may get assistance from you when needed. Some teachers use a designated spot on the board in which students write their names when they need help. When the teacher is available, they know the teacher will either call them to his or her desk or will come to visit with them. They also understand that they are to continue working (on an alternative activity if necessary) until the teacher is able to meet with them. Another strategy is to give the students three colored plastic twelve-ounce cups (preferably red, green and yellow). The students begin the independent work time with the cups stacked on the corner of their desks, so only the green one is showing. The green signals to the teacher that the student is working well and does not need any help. When the student needs the teacher but has an alternative activity on which to work, the student puts the yellow cup on top. When the student is completely stuck and has no alternative work, the red cup is placed on top of the stack. The teacher attends to the red cups showing before going to the students with the yellow cups on top. Some teachers use a variation of this activity. When the yellow cup is on top, a student with a green cup may go and assist the student. A red cup on top indicates that the student has already received peer help but still needs the teacher's assistance.
7. Create a system in which students are held accountable for the progress made during each class period. Some teachers have students place their work in a *work-in-progress folder* which the teacher may view at any time. At other times, students turn in the work they completed during the class period so the teacher is able to make comments and return their work the following day.
8. Establish procedures for what students should do when they have completed the assigned task. Should they turn in their finished work? If so, where? What should they do when they are done?
9. In order to bring the whole class together, make time either at the beginning or end of the class session for students to share their work. Doing so sends the message to students that everyone's work is valuable.

Anchor Activities

Anchor activities are familiar activities that are engaging and self-sustaining. They are assigned to students so that the teacher may work with individuals or small groups of students on more differentiated tasks. Some teachers present students with a list of activities they may do when they have completed assigned work. These activities must be appropriate to the needs of the students and relevant to the curriculum, and students should be able to access the activities and complete them on their own.

The following examples illustrate how one of our colleagues uses anchor activities in her classroom.

Reading When students finish their assigned reading work for the day, they know they need to read their independent reading books. In order to establish more accountability for students, the teacher provides students with focus questions which they are to answer after reading an assigned number of pages in their independent reading books. These questions usually relate to the particular skill or strategy the class is focusing on at the time. For example, when students are working on making connections to the texts they are reading, their anchor activity is to explain three different connections (e.g., text-to-text, text-to-self and text-to-world) they make while reading from their independent reading books.

The teacher collects journals weekly to read student responses. Often, she responds in writing, however, at times, she only reads over student work to check for understanding and completion. Then, she asks for student volunteers to share their responses in class or in small groups. It is important for students to listen to how other students respond in their reading journals, and the teacher has found that it gives other students different ideas about responding to texts.

Mathematics An example of using anchor activities in mathematics is setting up a problem-solving station at which students select different problems to solve. If the current unit of study were fractions, the problem-solving center might include different activities of varying complexity for which students need to use their knowledge of fractions or related concepts. In addition, students would be required to follow a particular format when they solve these problems. They would also be asked to turn in their work (finished or unfinished) at the end of each class period, so the classroom teacher may check it, make comments and clarify any misunderstandings. Because students would be able to choose which activities to complete, they would enjoy working on these activities and would not view them as "extra work."

A variation of this strategy that is often used in upper elementary, middle school and high school is featuring a problem of the day or of the week. The teacher posts a mathematics problem on a bulletin board or writes it on a white board. Students who complete the assigned task before the others work on the problem. Typically, a multi-step problem is used. The problems that teachers find work best are those that interest students. For example, a class with a high number of students interested in sports may have problems that use the batting averages of the local major league baseball team.

One teacher uses this technique in a very time-efficient manner. She downloads problems from mathematics web sites and collects them from other teachers. She has the problems enlarged to three-foot by four-foot charts. Her collection of problems is kept folded up in a drawer. She need only take out the problem that best matches the group, topic being taught and/or time of year and thumbtack it to a bulletin board. In doing this, she has successfully differentiated her lesson for the day or week in less than three minutes!

Co-Teaching

Having more than one adult in the classroom enables a teacher to provide more individualized support to students, while, simultaneously, students may learn from one another through collaborative work. This is an invaluable process. An elementary teacher describes one of her most valuable experiences as a teacher as one in which the literacy specialist and she worked closely together and co-taught two reading lessons weekly in the classroom. They chose to co-teach rather than have the reading specialist work with students outside of the class. By doing so, the teacher found that they were able to more effectively support those students who needed it as well as provide more challenging activities for those students who were ready to move forward. When teaching students the comprehension strategy of summarizing, the teachers found that some students quickly grasped the concepts and were able to identify key points in a chapter and succinctly explain these ideas in a well-written and organized summary. At the same time, many students were unable to identify the main points, and, consequently, retold the entire chapter, including all minor points in addition to the major points. These students needed more direct instruction and practice to master summarizing, while other students were ready to apply the strategy on their own. Because there were two teachers in the classroom, they were able to meet students at their current levels of understanding.

Many special education teachers identify co-teaching as an effective means for meeting the needs of special education students for the following reasons:

1. The classroom teacher and the special education teacher may alternate between teaching the students who master concepts quickly and teaching those who need additional guided practice. Special education teachers report that this alternating decreases some of the stigma students with special needs may feel when they are removed from class.
2. The special education teacher is always fully aware of what is being taught in the classroom, enabling him or her to ensure classroom success for the special needs students.
3. The special education teacher gets firsthand information about the ways in which the special needs students interact with the teacher and the other students in the regular classroom.

At Least

At Least is a very simple strategy that provides some differentiation with relatively little effort on the part of teachers. When asking students independently, or with a partner or group, to make a list of items, we insert the words *at least* into the explanation. For example,

With your partner, name four presidents who served during a time of war.
becomes
With your partner, name *at least* four presidents who served during a time of war.

In your group, list three causes for the Civil War.
becomes
In your group, list *at least* three causes for the Civil War.

By inserting the words *at least,* we require those students who think of the four causes of the Civil War quickly to push their thinking to include other causes. It also generates a discussion using higher order thinking skills as the students look at the more subtle and more complex causes. For example, some students may expand their discussion to talk about the impact that England had in encouraging secession because of its trade with the southern cotton industry.

Tiered Assignment

A **tiered assignment** is one in which a teacher provides a series of related tasks at levels of varying complexity. These assignments are usually presented at three levels. Some teachers use a pre-assessment to determine which tasks are most appropriate for which students. Students complete tasks most suitable to their academic readiness. All activities should focus on the key concepts that students are expected to master.

Heacox (2001) suggests four different ways to structure tiered assignments: by challenge, resources, outcome and process. The following section will identify and briefly describe each of these approaches.

1. **Tier by challenge level**—Bloom's Taxonomy, found in Table 4-7 in this chapter, is helpful in creating tiered activities ranging from basic to more challenging. This method of tiered assignments works well when some students are at introductory (or exposure) levels of learning, while others are at more advanced levels. This type of tiered activity is also effective when some students need more time to work on skills, strategies or content, while others are ready to work with more advanced skills, strategies or content. The activities listed in Table 4-7, Bloom's Taxonomy, provide an example of how to tier assignments by challenge level.

2. **Tier by resources**—Tiering activities by resources takes into account the differences in students' reading abilities as well as their knowledge about the topic. When you tier by resources, you choose reading materials of varying degrees of difficulty with regard to content. This type of tiered task works well when varied levels of resources may be used to match students' levels of readiness with appropriate materials. For example, you would like all students to learn about endangered species and write a research report based on their findings. To best meet the needs of all learners, you provide varied reading materials and match students with the resources most suitable for them.
3. **Tier by outcome**—At times, you will want all students to have experiences with the same content and material. However, some students may be more ready than others to work on more advanced applications of their learning. Differentiating in this way requires you to possess a deep understanding of each of your students' readiness levels. This type of tiered task works well when students may use the same materials to work on both basic and more advanced outcomes. The example in Figure 4-3 in which students were required to demonstrate their understanding of endangered species represents a project tiered by outcome. Students had experiences with the same content, however, some students were able to express their knowledge in more sophisticated and complex ways than others.
4. **Tier by process**—Sometimes you will want students to have the same outcomes, but different students may need to get there through different means, that is, by using a different process. For example, a class has just finished a unit of study based on weather disasters. A question for this unit might be, "What are the effects of two different weather disasters we have studied?" The following two assignments which are tiered by process address this question.

    Basic level—Choose two different weather disasters we have studied. Using the resources we have used throughout this unit of study, compare and contrast the effects of these two disasters.

    Advanced level—Choose two different weather disasters we have studied. Interview at least two survivors for each disaster. Using the information received from these persons, compare and contrast the effects of these two disasters.

Curriculum Compacting

To **compact the curriculum,** a teacher assesses students' information and skills at the beginning of a unit of study and moves students who demonstrate they have mastered the information and skills to alternative activities. Compacting works well in classrooms in which there are both high-achieving and gifted and talented students whose content knowledge and skills are far more advanced than their peers. The regular classwork is replaced with an advanced, interest-based project that these students may work on during class time. For example, in a math class, a teacher may pre-assess students for mastery on coordinate graphing. After determining the high-achieving[7] students who already understand this concept, the teacher might have these students create pictures for other students to solve by listing the ordered pairs to be connected to complete the drawing.

If you decide to use compacting, be careful that more advanced learners do not feel as though they are being given *more* work. This strategy may work well for short periods of time when students are given specific choices of additional activities. Many teachers who use this pedagogy send letters home to parents, explaining the rationale and expectations of using such a strategy (Benjamin, 2003).

[7] We make a distinction between high-achieving students and gifted students. We consider as gifted students only those who are achieving in the top 1% of all students in their age group.

Learning Centers

Learning centers are small group and individual projects which offer students opportunities to review, practice or extend classroom lessons through a variety of activities and allow a teacher to better meet the students' varying needs. These tasks should be designed to meet students' levels of readiness, interests and/or learning profiles.

One teacher used learning centers in her classroom when she wanted students to have different experiences during a science unit on simple machines. She set up ten stations in the classroom, and students rotated around the room. The stations were based on the different simple machines, that is, wheel and axles, screws, pulleys, levers, inclined planes and wedges. Some of the stations required students to build, some to manipulate objects, and others to draw, conduct an experiment or identify the particular simple machine. Students were encouraged to visit particular stations based upon readiness, interests and learning styles. All students were expected to have at least one experience with each of the six simple machines in order to develop a basic understanding of how each machine works and how to apply its use in everyday life.

Learning Contracts

A **learning contract** is an agreement between the teacher and student in which students work independently to complete tasks that are designed to match skills and/or content to their readiness, interests and/or learning profiles. The contract should state the particular task the student is expected to complete as well as establish a deadline. Such contracts help students set daily or weekly work goals and manage their time.

The following table illustrates an example of a learning contract that was used throughout a unit of study on poetry. Students chose three of the nine activities to complete, and were given class time each week to work on these activities. As students finished an activity, they placed their completed work in a spot designated by the teacher.

Table 4-5
Poetry Contract

Create a Rhyming Wheel Use your spelling lists as a way to get started.	**Use Your Rhyming Wheel** Write a poem that sounds like Shel Silverstein might have written it.	**Write an Acrostic Poem** Be sure it includes alliteration.
Write Write a cinquain. (Check with another cinquain writer to make sure you got the pattern right.)	**Computer Art** Use clip art to illustrate a simile, metaphor or analogy on our class list or ones you create.	**Write About You** Use good descriptive words in a poem that helps us know and understand something important about you.
Interpret "How to Eat a Poem"	**Research a Famous Person** Take notes. Write a clerihew that uses what you learned.	**Illustrate a Poem** Find a poem we've read that you like or find one on your own. Illustrate it. Write about why you illustrated it as you did.
Student Choice #1	**Student Choice #2**	**Student Choice #3**

From Tomlinson, 1999

Adjusting Questions

In whole class discussions, tests, quizzes and homework, a teacher may adjust questions to better meet the needs of students based on their readiness, interests and learning profiles. However, all students should be expected to answer important questions which require them to think. Some teachers keep a list of Bloom's verbs (see the column labeled "Activities" in the Bloom's Taxonomy Table, 4-7) readily accessible to assist them in differentiating questions. More information about questioning techniques may be found in Chapter 5.

However, all students should be expected to answer important questions which require them to think.

Independent Study

An independent study is a research project in which students develop skills for independent learning through research. The student and teacher identify problems or topics of interest to the student, decide how to investigate the problems or topic and determine the product the student will create to demonstrate his or her learning. This strategy works well with older, more independent students. Specialists in gifted and talented education highly recommend this technique, provided that students have adequate levels of teacher contact.

Reading Buddies

In using the **reading buddies** strategy, students are paired and gain additional reading practice away from the teacher. This strategy is most appropriate for elementary students. It is important that students read for a specific purpose set forth by the teacher and are given an opportunity to discuss what was read. For example, a teacher may want students to focus on making predictions. Before reading the assigned text, students would be asked to make predictions based on prior readings, the chapter title or book title. After reading the assigned text, they would be asked to confirm their predictions and reflect upon the accuracy of them. Finally, students may be asked to make new predictions using what they learned from their reading that day. Reading buddies may be reading at different or similar levels, however, the follow-up tasks and/or questions should be assigned based on readiness levels. Some teachers use this strategy across grade levels.

Graphic Organizers

A **graphic organizer** is any kind of diagram or outline which assists children in visually arranging information in such a way that the information is made more accessible. Graphic organizers have many names, including *visual maps, mind maps, visual organizers* and *concept maps* or *webs.* Graphic organizers may be created by teachers and/or students using either pencil and paper or technology tools. They may be used during all phases of learning, from brainstorming to presentation of findings. In addition, teachers may use these organizers with the whole class or with individual students.

Graphic organizers may be used to help students of all ages in

- clarifying concepts
- organizing and remembering information
- explaining complex relationships in a more simplistic manner
- speeding up communication of information
- focusing on essential information

There are many instructional uses for graphic organizers. They are as follows:

- teach students to think about information in new ways
- review and summarize concepts
- represent large chunks of information in a concise manner or in the big picture
- edit and revise easily

(The two lists above were adapted and reprinted with the permission of Jeanette Bastien, a middle school teacher in Westfield, MA.)

Graphic organizers are categorized as *hierarchical, sequential, conceptual* or *cyclical.* The following table highlights some of the uses of each of these organizers.

Table 4-6

Hierarchical	• main concept with ranks, levels or subconcepts • generalizations • classifications • main idea
Sequential	• chronological order • cause and effect • events in a story • explanation of a process • problem/solution
Conceptual	• central idea, category or class with supporting ideas • description • compare/contrast • charts, tables, matrixes
Cyclical	• series of events in a circular formation • continuous sequence of events having no beginning or end

Author unknown

Hierarchical

The most common type of hierarchical graphic organizer we see is the flowchart for the hierarchy of positions in an organization. The following graphic organizer tells us that the West coast director of marketing, the East coast director of marketing and the Midwest director of marketing all report to the vice president for marketing. All the vice presidents report to the company president.

Figure 4-8

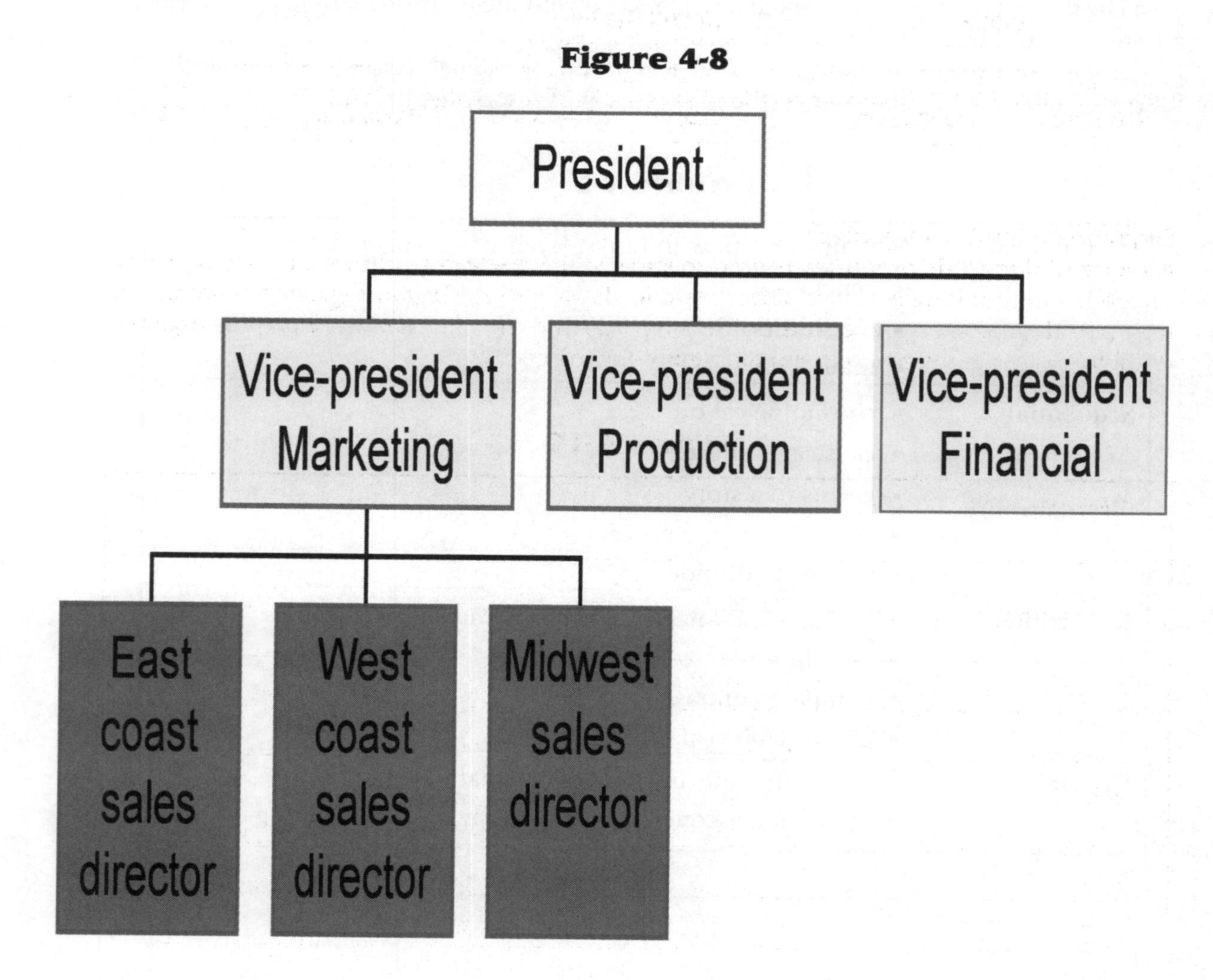

In an educational context, we might use a hierarchical graphic organizer to show the relationship between continents, countries and cities as in the one that follows.

Figure 4-9

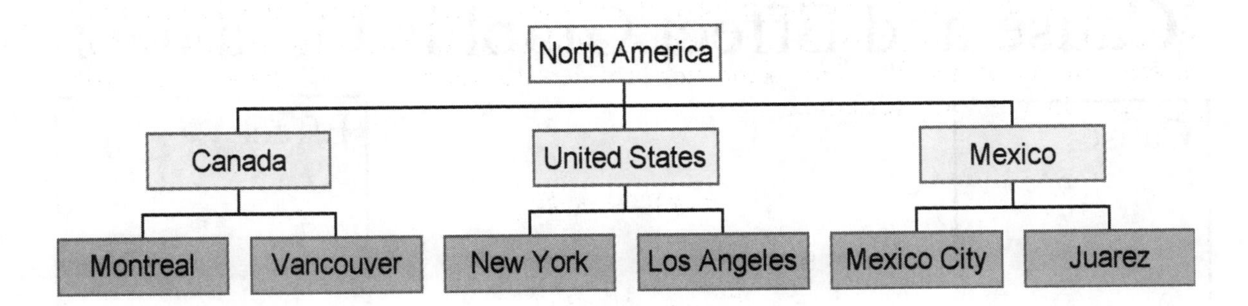

Sequential Graphic Organizer

A **sequential graphic organizer** is used to show when one thing follows another, however, the events do not have a cyclical nature that leads back to the beginning, such as we saw in the cyclical graphic organizer earlier. The *story map* and the *cause and effect* graphic organizers below are examples of sequential graphic organizers.

Figure 4-10

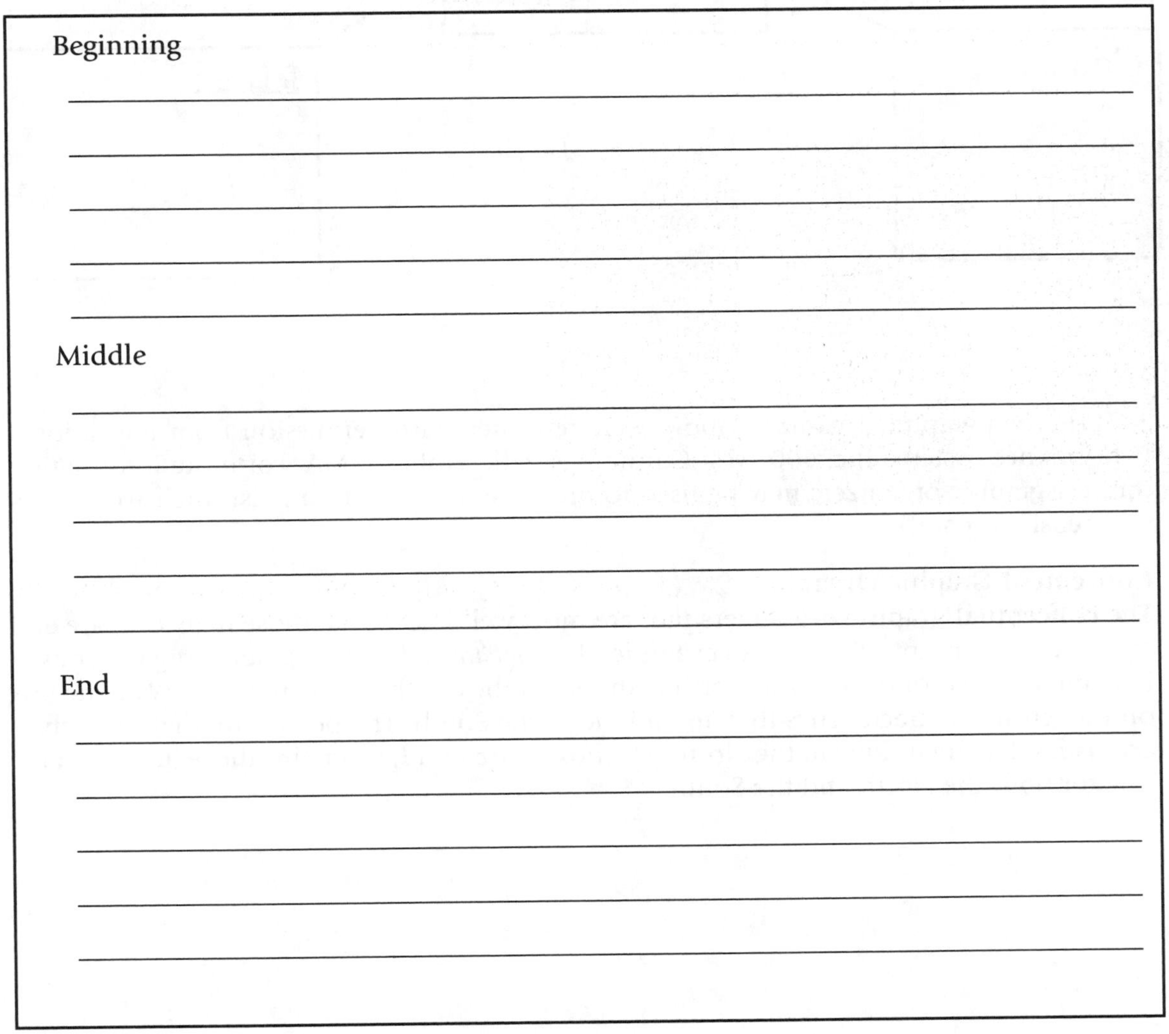

Beginning

Middle

End

Figure 4-11

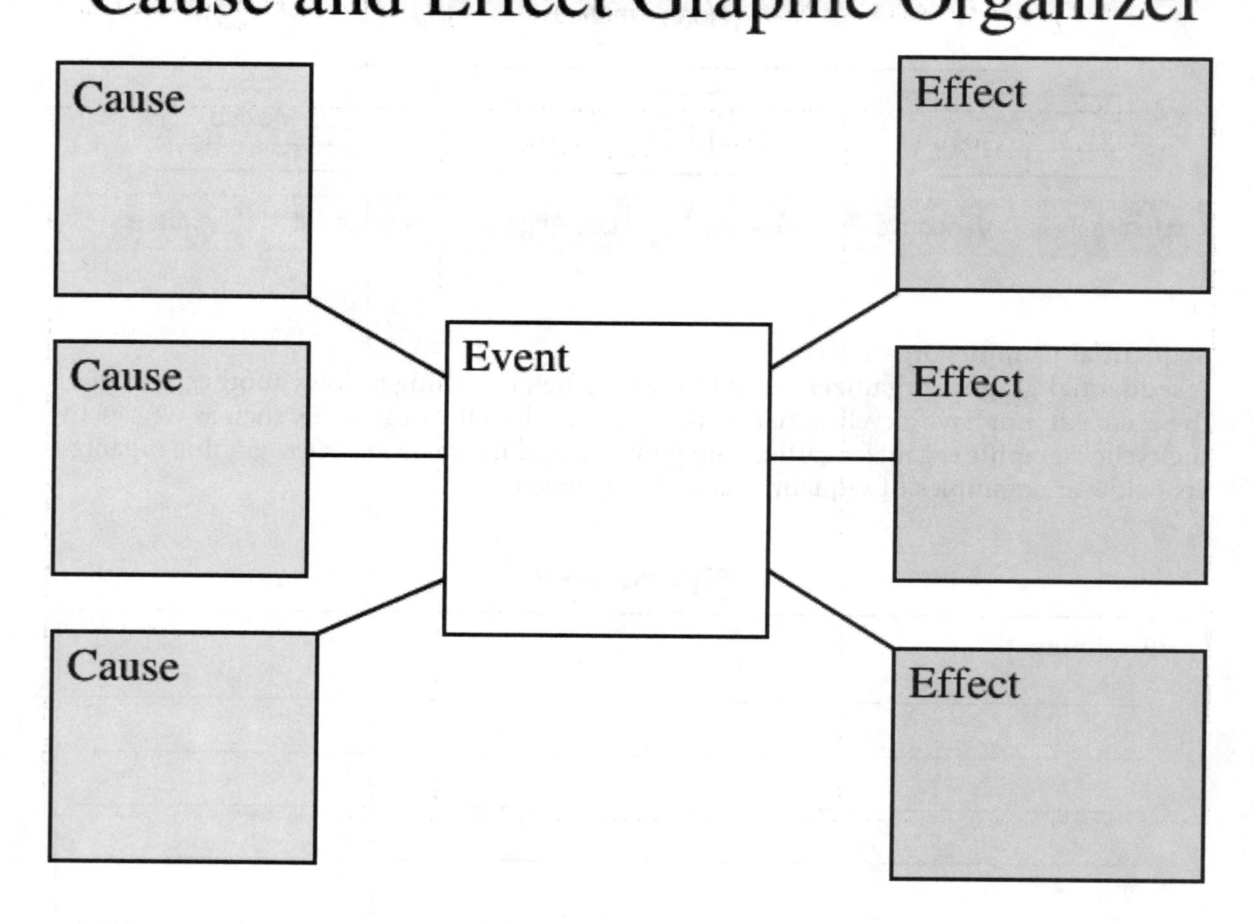

(The two graphic organizers above were reprinted with permission from Educational Performance Systems Inc. 600 West Cummings Park, Woburn, MA. For more information on how graphic organizers may be used to promote metacognition, visit their web site at www.epsi-usa.com.)

Conceptual Graphic Organizer

The **conceptual graphic organizers** that are most well known are those that compare and contrast two concepts. Below is an example of a *compare and contrast* graphic organizer used to compare the economy of the North with that of the South during the Civil War. The box on the left has characteristics that are unique to the South. The box on the right has characteristics that are unique to the North. The box in the middle contains those items that are true for both the North and the South.

Figure 4-12

Compare and Contrast Graphic Organizer

The South	Both Regions	The North

The above compare and contrast may also be done with the interlocking circles commonly referred to as a Venn Diagram.

The following web sites provide blank graphic organizers that you may print out to use with your students.

- www.teachervision.com
- www.graphic.org
- www.eduplace.com/kids
- www.sdcoe.k12.ca.us
- www.writedesignonline.com

www.teach-nology.com will allow you to customize a graphic organizer to meet the needs of your students.

Inspiration® (or Kidspiration® for younger students) is a software program made for creating graphic organizers. It allows students and/or teachers to create a variety of graphic organizers. We have found this program to be very kid-friendly and easy to navigate. Students with fine-motor issues have found this to be an invaluable program for helping them to organize their thoughts and ideas. Words, clipart and actual photographs may be used with this program. The Inspiration web site (www.inspiration.com) has many ideas for classroom applications and also allows you to download a free trial version.

Community Mentors

Gifted and very high-achieving students present unique challenges to classroom teachers. Sometimes their intellectual needs extend beyond available differentiated challenges and extensions within the classroom. These students who have extraordinary abilities and academic appetites in a particular area such as math or science may benefit tremendously from mentors. Possible mentors include an older student in the school with expertise in the area of strength as well as collaborative ability, an older student in another school, a parent volunteer, a college student or a community mentor, such as a retired physicist or mathematician. A mentor may teach the gifted student new and unfamiliar aspects of their favored subjects. The mentor–student relationship may provide a positive and powerful social experience as well. Lastly, a mentor may provide resources that meet the gifted student's needs within the school community.

Strategies Discussed in Other Chapters

Many of the strategies discussed in Chapters 2, 7 and 8 enable us to differentiate by learning style. For example, *giving the mastery objectives at the start of the lesson* particularly helps those students who learn from whole to part. *Posting and reviewing the agenda* helps those students who need to know at the outset what will happen at each stage of the lesson, before they are able to focus on the content. *Group activators* of the students' previous learning on the topic helps those students who were only at the introductory, guided practice or immediate mastery level the last time the topic was addressed. *Connecting to the students' own world* is important for students with particular learning styles to move the information and skills into their long-term memories. Summarizers are particularly important for students with learning styles that need the information pulled together at the end of the learning period before they move it into their long-term memory. *Learnable intelligence* strategies are particularly important for students who have low confidence as learners.

Bloom's Taxonomy

Another effective way in which to differentiate instruction is to use Bloom's taxonomy as a guide. Bloom's different levels of learning help you determine the level of complexity of a particular task. Keep in mind that all students need to use higher order thinking skills, and that the higher level of learning may be used to reteach and reinforce basic content (Heacox, 2001). The following table outlines Bloom's six varying levels of learning from most basic to most complex.

Keep in mind that all students need to use higher order thinking skills, and that the higher level of learning may be used to reteach and reinforce basic content (Heacox, 2001).

Table 4-7

Level	Definition	Action	Activities
Knowledge	Recall facts and information	Know it	Tell, list, define, label, recite, memorize, repeat, find, name, record, fill in, recall, relate
Comprehension	Show your understanding	Understand it	Locate, explain, summarize, identify, describe, report, discuss, locate, review, paraphrase, restate, retell, show, outline, rewrite
Application	Use what you have learned	Use it	Demonstrate, construct, record, use, diagram, revise, reformat, illustrate, interpret, dramatize, practice, organize, translate, manipulate, convert, adapt, research, calculate, operate, model, order, display, implement, sequence, integrate, incorporate
Analysis	Examine critically	Examine it	Compare, contrast, classify, critique, categorize, solve, deduce, examine, differentiate, appraise, distinguish, experiment, question, investigate, categorize, infer
Evaluation	Determine worth or value, based on criteria	Judge it	Judge, predict, verify, assess, justify, rate, prioritize, determine, select, decide, value, choose, forecast, estimate
Synthesis	Put together in a new or different way	Create it	Compose, hypothesize, design, formulate, create, invent, develop, refine, produce, transform

Based on *Taxonomy of Educational Objectives: Book 1 Cognitive Domain* by Benjamin S. Bloom, et al. (New York: Longman, 1984) in Heacox, 2001 (p. 69)

Some teachers may use these different levels of learning in planning a differentiated instruction lesson. You may use the verbs listed below to assign levels to the mastery objectives for the tasks.[8] The following activities are examples of different levels of objectives for students' learning in a unit on immigration. They are arranged so that 1 requires the lowest level of thinking and 6 requires the highest level of thinking.

[8] Chapter 1 explains the writing of mastery objectives for planning lessons and units. It includes a list of verbs teachers can use to develop mastery objectives that require higher order thinking skills.

By the end of the class you will be able to

(Level 1) *List* four different immigrant groups that came to America during the 1800's and *tell* why they wanted to come to America.

(Level 2) Pretend you are an immigrant in steerage class in the late 1800's and *describe* your life when coming to America on a ship.

(Level 3) *Research* the procedures that immigrants had to endure once they arrived at Ellis Island during the 1800s and demonstrate the knowledge acquired in your research by *dramatizing* an immigrant arriving at Ellis Island during this time.

(Level 4) *Compare and contrast* the reasons two different immigrant groups came to America.

(Level 5) *Predict* specific ways (e.g., food, language, holidays, economy, etc.) in which our country would be different today if immigration was outlawed during the 1800s.

(Level 6) It is 1850 and you are a quality control expert hired to improve the procedures for processing immigrants on Ellis Island. You are given three charges. First, you must increase the thoroughness with which immigrants are screened. Second, you must increase the speed with which immigrants are processed. Third, you must improve the conditions for the immigrants while they are on the island. Your report should describe the present procedures and your recommendation for improving those procedures.

Assessing and Improving Your Lessons by Increasing Differentiation

Effective differentiated instruction begins with lesson planning such as that described in Chapter 1. It is then followed by teaching the lesson and assessing its success. It is important when you first start differentiating your lessons that you don't try to plan the perfectly differentiated lesson the first time. This will only lead to frustration and disappointment. We recommend that you initially take a few manageable steps toward differentiating your lesson based on the concepts in this chapter. You should then assess the success of the lesson and make additional modifications. You will probably need to repeat this process several times before you feel as though the lesson has sufficient differentiation. The following template may be used to assess your lesson when you have determined that the current lesson is not differentiated sufficiently to meet the varied needs of students in your classroom.[9]

[9] The question—How can I differentiate this lesson to better meet the needs of all my students?—is an excellent research question for a lesson study project. In Chapter 11, we explain the process of professional development through lesson study.

Figure 4-13
Using Differentiated Instruction to Modify a Lesson that Is a Mismatch for Some Students

What are the mastery objectives for the lesson? Do they address higher order thinking skills? If not, what high level objectives do I want to add?

Which students do not receive sufficient challenge in the lesson as planned?

Which students are frustrated because activities do not provide sufficient scaffolding for them to master the concepts?

Are there other factors in the lesson that are not working?

How may I modify or change the lesson to better extend or scaffold the learning? Do I need to differentiate content, process or product?

Which differentiated instructional strategy would be most effective?

Are there other modifications that would make the lesson more successful?

What resources do I need to make these modifications?

What will the differentiated lesson look like? How will it be different than the lesson as presently planned?

Conclusion

Successful differentiation takes time to plan and prepare. The steps in this chapter are designed to give you a road map for increasing the level of differentiated instruction that you provide for students. Differentiated instruction becomes more manageable when we undertake it in doable steps and share the work with our colleagues.

The result of differentiating our teaching is higher student achievement, increased student interest and better student behavior.

Differentiated instruction becomes more manageable when we undertake it in doable steps and share the work with our colleagues.

References

Anonymous. Graphic organizers. Woburn, MA: Educational Performance Systems.

Bastien, Jeannette, (2003). Unpublished paper used with teachers and students in the Westfield, MA Public Schools.

Bell, L. (2003, December/January). Strategies that close the gap. *Educational Leadership*, 32–34.

Benjamin, A. (2003). *Differentiated instruction: A guide for elementary school teachers.* Larchmont, NY: Eye on Education.

Bloom, B. S. (1984). *Taxonomy of educational objectives. Book 1: Cognitive domain.* Reading, MA: Addison Wesley.

Ferguson, R. (2002, November) *What doesn't meet the eye: Understanding and addressing racial disparities in high-achieving suburban schools.* Naperville, IL: Learning Point Associates.

Gay, G. (2000). *Culturally responsive teaching: Theory, research, and practice.* New York: Teachers College Press.

Gebhard, M. (2002–2003, December/January). Getting past "see spot run." *Educational Leadership*, 35–39.

Gurian, M. (2001). *Boys and girls learn differently!* New York: John Wiley & Sons.

Heacox, D. (2002). *Differentiating instruction in the regular classroom: How to reach and teach all learners, grades 3–12.* Minneapolis, MN: Free Spirit Publishing, Inc.

Rogers, K. (1990). *Challenges of promise.* Edina, MN, Public Schools.

Rothstein-Fisch, C., Greenfield, P., & Trumbell, E. (1999, April). Bridging cultures with classroom strategies. *Educational Leadership*, 64–66.

Tomlinson, C. (1995a). *How to differentiate instruction in mixed-ability classrooms.* Alexandria, VA: Association for Supervision and Curriculum Development (ASCD).

Tomlinson, C. (1995b). Deciding to differentiate instruction in middle school: One school's journey. *Gifted Child Quarterly, 39*, 77–87.

Tomlinson, C. (1999). *The differentiated classroom: Responding to the needs of all learners.* Alexandria, VA: Association for Supervision and Curriculum Development (ASCD).

Tomlinson, C. (2001). *How to differentiate instruction in mixed-ability classrooms* (2nd ed.). Alexandria, VA: Association for Supervision and Curriculum Development (ASCD).

Tomlinson, C. (2003). *Fulfilling the promise of the differentiated classroom: Strategies and tools for responsive teaching.* Alexandria, VA: Association for Supervision and Curriculum Development (ASCD).

Vygotsky, L. S. (1978). *Mind in society*. Cambridge, MA: Harvard University Press.

C H A P T E R

5

Questioning Practices That Improve Student Performance and Promote Higher Order Thinking

Objectives for the Chapter

After reading the chapter, the reader will be able to

a. describe the different purposes for which teachers ask questions and the various types of questions used to achieve these purposes
b. increase the number of students who ask and answer questions in class
c. raise the thinking level of the answers from students
d. use questions and dipsticking to formatively assess student understanding
e. use questions and dipsticking to inform instruction
f. respond effectively to students' correct and incorrect responses

Introduction

Virtually all of us have at least one memory from our own student days of an episode involving one of our teachers and a particularly challenging question or string of questions. For some, that memory is of turning bright red as the other students in the class turned in our direction, waiting expectantly for our response. For others, that memory is of a particular question during which a "light bulb" clicked on and a whole new level of understanding emerged. Or perhaps your most vivid recollection of questioning hearkens back to the *one time* you came to class unprepared. You remember sitting at your desk as your teacher posed questions all around you, fervently hoping not to be called upon while simultaneously vowing never to put yourself in this position again. Whichever experience rings most true for you, there is no question that our own experiences as students affect our philosophies and practices as educators, perhaps particularly so in the case of questioning practices. Some teachers flatly refuse to "cold call" students, preferring, instead, to rely on volunteers. Other teachers utilize a Socratic pedagogy in which a student is called upon and then each of that student's responses generates an additional question. In this chapter, we will consider in detail the various purposes that questioning serves within a classroom as well as the different questioning practices that best achieve these purposes. We will also discuss strategies for increasing the number of students in your classroom who actively respond to questions as well as improving the depth of the responses these students provide.

In this chapter, we will consider in detail the various purposes that questioning serves within a classroom as well as the different questioning practices that best achieve these purposes.

Purposes of Questioning

There are several different reasons *why* teachers ask students questions: to assess student learning, to inform instruction, to activate previous learning, to deepen understanding, to promote higher order thinking and to keep students engaged. In this section, we will examine each of these motivations for asking students questions as well as the particular strategies and types of questions most effective for achieving the desired results. Figure 5-1 briefly summarizes the various purposes for questions.

Assessing Student Learning to Inform Instruction

In *Highly Effective Questioning*, Ivan Hannel (2003, p. 41) writes that a common and appropriate time for teachers to ask students questions is upon completing a "mini-lesson" of direct instruction. Such questioning "helps to indicate to the teacher whether or not a student has learned something that was assigned." Hannel (2003) also notes that an intense period of questioning following direct instruction enables the teacher to understand *how* the students understand the content to which they have been exposed. For example, upon completing a read-aloud of the final scene from *A Raisin in the Sun* in which different students have taken on the roles of various characters, we might follow this activity with several questions concerning the plot, themes and literary elements that emerge during the scene. Some typical questions that might be utilized for assessing student knowledge of this scene are the following:

An intense period of questioning following direct instruction enables the teacher to understand how the students understand the content to which they have been exposed.

1. What is the final object that "Mama" takes with her as she leaves the apartment?
2. Why was that old plant so important to her?
3. What kind of look do the stage directions describe as coming over Mama's face as she takes one final look around her apartment?
4. What kind of challenges might the Younger family face in their new neighborhood?
5. How would you describe this play's resolution?

Figure 5-1

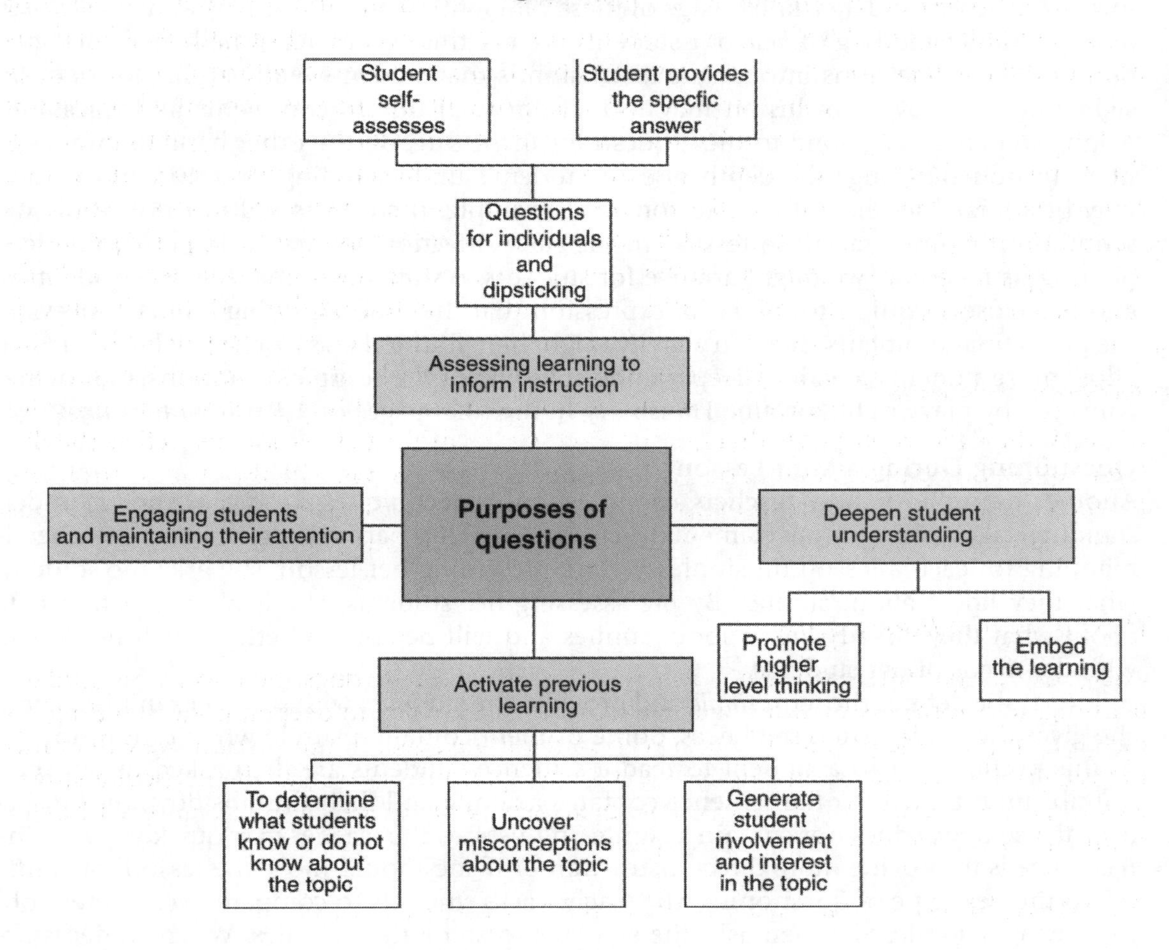

In different ways, each of these questions seeks to assess the degree to which students understand the play's conclusion. As you may be able to ascertain from these questions, or from having read the play yourself, the final scene in *A Raisin in the Sun* depends upon a few small symbols and gestures to make some powerful points. As teachers, we utilize these questions to determine whether students note the significance of events such as Mama personally carrying her withered old houseplant with her from the apartment. *The first two questions* are checking whether students remember that Mama had purchased this plant several decades previously when she and her husband first moved into the apartment and that, earlier in the play, Mama had spoken admiringly of the plant's ability to stay alive despite the scarcity of light the apartment receives. (A higher order thinking question, described in subsequent pages of this chapter, might ask students to note the ways in which the plant's life is symbolic of Mama's life.) *The third question*—concerning Mama's facial expression as described by the stage directions—seeks to determine whether students noted this subtle but important descriptor and, more importantly, whether they understand why Mama's face might betray a wide range of emotions as she leaves behind the apartment in which she has raised her family and experienced her husband's death.

Finally, *questions four and five* seek to ascertain whether students understand the complexity of the play's resolution— that the African-American Younger family is ready to leave behind their decrepit old apartment, but that uncertainty and danger may await them in their new, all-white neighborhood. Also, there is always something sad about leaving one's past behind, even when that past has been a challenging one. Asking these questions allows us to assess students' knowledge of these different aspects of the play and also to gain a deeper understanding of *how* our students are reacting to the play. The benefit of incorporating these questions into a class discussion is that students with varying levels of insight into the play's conclusion may learn from each other's comments and questions. Asking students to respond to these questions in writing, on the other hand, allows us to more thoroughly gauge the depth of each student's understanding, and this information may be utilized to shape future lessons. For example, if students did not notice the description of Mama's facial expression in the stage directions or are having difficulty deciphering its meaning, we might arrange for students to watch this final scene on videotape and pay close attention to the facial expression that the actress playing Mama conveys in the play's final moments. Such an activity might benefit the class's more visual learners and allow more students to gain a deeper understanding of the complex emotions and themes conveyed by playwright Lorraine Hansberry in the final pages of *A Raisin in the Sun*.

Questioning During a Mini-Lesson

Another example of how teachers use questioning techniques to assess student understanding takes place in an elementary classroom. This particular elementary teacher is planning to teach a lesson on similes. Before presenting her lesson, she asks the students what they know about similes. By pre-assessing her students, she is able to gather data about what they already know about similes and will be able to better match her lesson with the needs of her students.

Next, she defines the term *simile* and provides the students with several examples. Then, she gives the students ten sentences. Some of them contain a simile while others do not. At this point, she asks a student to read a sentence. Students are then asked to put their thumbs up if they think the sentence contains a simile and their thumbs down if they believe the sentence does not contain a simile. In this way, the teacher may quickly determine if she needs to provide more direct instruction or if she should move the lesson forward.

In the next type of questioning, the teacher asks students to compare two different objects using a simile. She then asks the students to share their similes. When students are able to successfully write similes, they are asked to begin incorporating them into their writing assignments.

Dipsticking to Decide Whether to Move On, ReTeach or Differentiate

It is also valuable for a teacher to ask students questions *as* he or she is providing direct instruction or directing another type of learning activity. This method is often referred to as "dipsticking," a term first coined by Madeline Hunter (1982). Just as one uses a dipstick to gauge a car's oil level, a teacher utilizes questions to gauge the level of understanding of his or her students. And just as the prudent car owner regularly checks his or her oil level in order to detect potential problems in their early stages, dipsticking makes a teacher much more likely to pick up on miscommunications and misunderstandings as they occur rather than after the fact. By dipsticking to gauge students' comprehension of a particular lesson, a teacher can make the decision to reteach a concept to the entire class, move on to the next activity if students demonstrate keen understanding of the lesson or differentiate instruction to allow some students who "get it" to move on while simultaneously reteaching to students still struggling for mastery of the particular skill or concept. More information on differentiating instruction may be found in Chapter 4.

> *Just as one uses a dipstick to gauge a car's oil level, a teacher utilizes questions to gauge the level of understanding of his or her students.*

While the term *dipsticking* may refer to teachers asking questions of individual students over the course of a lesson, it is more typically used to describe a system that allows a teacher to quickly "check in" with each student in the class simultaneously. For example, a middle school teacher we know purchased a large dry-erase board from a local hardware store and asked the hardware store to cut up the board into small one-foot by one-foot squares. At the beginning of this teacher's class, each student would pick up a mini dry-erase board and a dry-erase marker from the back of the classroom and keep it on their desks for the entire class. At various points in a given lesson, the teacher would pose a question to the entire class and then instruct students to inscribe their response on the dry-erase boards. After a minute or two had passed, the teacher would ask students to hold up their responses, and then one student would be called upon to explain his or her solution. In this way, the teacher could quickly and easily gauge his students' various depths of understanding of the particular skill or concept being taught.

Lest you fear that dipsticking requires large outlays of cash for supplies or an expertise with power machinery, here is another example of dipsticking from our own classrooms. In order to assess students' understanding of the parts of speech, we hand out to each student an envelope containing five slips of paper labeled *verb, noun, adjective, pronoun* and *adverb.* With the aid of an overhead projector, we flash a sentence in front of our class and then point out a particular word. Students are expected to hold up the slip of paper that describes the function of the word in that particular sentence. As in the last example, this system allows us to gauge quickly and easily our students' understanding of the different parts of speech. If this activity reveals that the majority of the class has a strong understanding of the parts of speech but that four or five students are struggling, we might make the decision to let the majority of the class get a jump on their homework for the last ten or fifteen minutes of class while working as a small group in the back of the classroom with those students who are struggling. In this way, students already "getting it" are not exposed to needless repetition, and students who do not yet firmly understand the parts of speech receive individualized instruction prior to embarking upon a homework assignment that, otherwise, might prove a frustrating exercise in futility.

The technique of dipsticking may be carried out with even less preparation than in the previous example. For dipsticking "on the fly," a math teacher might put a problem on the board for students to solve and also offer four possible solutions—#1, #2, #3 and #4—only one of which is correct. Students solve the problem at their seats and then at the given prompt hold up the number of fingers that corresponds to the solution they believe is correct. Alternatively, this math teacher might take his or her cue from a professional sports announcer exhorting fans to guess the day's attendance at a sporting event. The teacher asks students to raise their hands or cheer for the solution they believe to be correct and then, with great fanfare, reveals the answer—"If you guessed #2, you're... absolutely... right!" While such an activity represents a less pure form of dipsticking, in that students may be tempted to change their answer based on the responses of other students, such an activity may have the added benefit of more fully engaging students in the lesson, a purpose of questioning practices discussed in more detail in subsequent pages.

Dipsticking in Which Students Assess Their Own Learning

It should also be noted that the term *dipsticking* may be used to refer to a system through which individual students are responsible for assessing their own learning and then reporting back to the teacher. For example, in Chapter 4 we described the dipsticking method used by one of our elementary school colleagues during independent seatwork. Prior to beginning work on their assignments, each student is given three plastic cups: one red, one yellow and one green. As students work at their desks, they utilize these multi-colored cups to signal their progress to their teacher. Students who find themselves cruising through the assignment with a high degree of understanding place the green cup in view of the teacher on their desks. Students who are progressing through their assignment with reasonable success, but believe they occasionally might need to leave their seat and consult with a fellow student, place the yellow cup in view of the teacher. Finally, the students who are "stuck" and in need of assistance from their teacher place the red cup out on their desks. Here then, one sees a system in place that allows the teacher to focus her attention on those students most in need of help. Moreover, the system allows the teacher at any given time to take a quick gauge of the depth of understanding of each student in the class. If at any point, the teacher observes a high proportion of yellow or red cups, she may make the decision to interrupt the independent seatwork in order to re-teach the particular concept central to completing the assignment. By the same token, if the teacher observes there to be a preponderance of green cups, she might conclude that the vast majority of the class has this particular skill or concept firmly in hand and may make the decision to interrupt this independent work in order to move on to the next topic of study.

Activate Previous Learning

Marzano, Pickering and Pollock (2001, p. 111) note in *Classroom Instruction That Works* that "educational researchers have shown that the activation of prior knowledge is critical to learning of all types. Indeed, our background knowledge can even influence what we perceive." How does this work? Marzano et al. (2001, p. 114) explain that "teachers can use questions *before* a learning experience to establish a mental set with which students process the learning experience." There are several ways in which we utilize this strategy in our classroom.

Brainstorming

Prior to beginning the study of a new historical time period, we like to ask our students what they know about this time period already. One way in which such an activity may be organized is by first giving students the opportunity to brainstorm independently at their desks and then transcribing the results of their brainstorming on the blackboard. For example, imagine that we are beginning a unit on the Salem witch trials. We might hand out paper for our students to use in jotting down anything and everything they know about the Salem witch trials before calling on students to share their thoughts with the class. From the standpoint of questioning practices, one asset of allowing students the opportunity to brainstorm independently prior to noting ideas on that blackboard is that, having provided this opportunity for independent thought, every student may be expected to contribute to the master list being compiled on the blackboard. Rather than seeking volunteers—a practice that might only draw in the most engaged students—the teacher might simply go around the room, expecting each student to contribute an idea to the master list. A student who claims, "I don't know," may gently be asked simply to read an idea on the piece of paper in front of him or her. The teacher might even explain that it is fine for students to note that one of their ideas has already been placed on the blackboard, as long as they explain specifically which idea they had conceived of as well. Finally, a teacher utilizing such an activity to activate previous learning might consider sporadically collecting the papers on which students have done their independent brainstorming. While time-consuming, occasionally looking over these papers may be a valuable tool for assessing students' prior knowledge of an upcoming unit as well as the effort they are expending on this class activity. Moreover, the act of occasionally collecting and grading this classwork is likely to serve as a motivator for students to take this work seriously.

Making Predictions

Another related method of activating student learning involves asking students to make predictions about an upcoming unit of study, For example, prior to starting a new literary work, we might ask our students to predict what they think the work is going to be about based on the title, the front cover or even the blurb in the back. This strategy of asking students to make predictions may be continued throughout our study of this literary work. For example, upon assigning a new chapter of *To Kill a Mockingbird* to read for homework, we might ask students to make predictions about what events they believe will occur in the upcoming chapter. As explained by Marzano, Pickering and Pollock (2001), this strategy activates students' thinking. As they complete their reading assignment that evening at home, they will be actively comparing the events they are reading in *To Kill a Mockingbird* to those they predicted several hours earlier in class. Such a "mental comparison" makes students sharper readers, more likely to focus on what they are reading and to remember it the next day in class or later that semester. Moreover, such an activity provides a natural lead-in to a literary discussion the next day in class comparing what students expected to occur plot-wise in *To Kill a Mockingbird* with what actually happened. Of course, such a question ("How did the events in last night's chapter compare to what you expected?") may also serve as a means of assessing students' knowledge and understanding of the chapters they read for homework and provide an opportunity for the teacher to determine the degree to which these chapters should be focused on during the current class period. For example, students we have worked with tend to find the final chapter of *To Kill a Mockingbird* quite confusing at even the basic plot level. If our question about students' expectations for the novel's conclusion reveal this to be the case, we might choose to hold off on a more abstract discussion of symbolism and theme in favor of taking the class period to clarify what occurred in the final pages of the novel.

The strategy of making predictions also works well in an elementary mathematics classroom. Before beginning a unit on fractions, decimals and percents, we ask students to predict the relationships among fractions, decimals and percents. They are also asked to think about how these concepts are used in their everyday lives. Throughout the unit of study, we continually refer to the list of our students' ideas to determine the accuracy of their initial predictions. The value of such an activity is similar to that described above for ninth-grade students reading *To Kill a Mockingbird*. As our students increase their knowledge about fractions, decimals and percents, they actively compare the information and skills they are acquiring to their initial predictions. Such comparisons sharpen their ability to understand and remember the functions of these various mathematical representations.

The Do Now

A third way in which teachers activate students' previous learning is through an activity that Dr. Lorraine Monroe calls a "Do Now" (Checkley, 2004). The Do Now, described in more detail in Chapter 2, is an activity written on the chalkboard that students are expected to begin upon entering the classroom and taking their seats. Many teachers combine the practice of Do Now's with journals or reflection logs. For these teachers, the Do Now takes the form of a "reflection question" related to the day's lesson. Students begin the class by answering a question in their logs that will activate their thinking about the learning they will embark upon for the rest of the period. For example, a graphics arts teacher beginning a unit on "creating an effective ad campaign" might utilize a Do Now to activate students' thinking about advertisements they have recently seen in magazines and on billboards. In this case, the Do Now may serve as a means of helping students to start thinking about the different components of effective campaigns. Such an activity pushes students to connect the learning they are about to embark upon to their own previous experiences and, as Marzano, Pickering and Pollock (2001, p. 114) explain, "establish a mental set with which students process the learning experience."

Deepen Understanding

The **deepening of understanding** refers to two processes: embedding the learning and utilizing higher order thinking skills.

Embedding the Learning

When we ask a question to embed the learning, we cause students to reflect again upon the knowledge just taught so that it is better implanted in their memories. For example, upon teaching the parts of speech *noun, verb, adjective* and *adverb* we may choose a student to define the terms in his or her own words. We may then ask four other students to give an example of each word. By doing this, the students again hear the information that was just taught, creating deeper understanding and better retention.

When we ask a question to embed the learning, we cause students to reflect again upon the knowledge just taught so that it is better implanted in their memories.

Higher Order Thinking Skills

The second way we deepen understanding is through questions that push students to think at high levels. Marzano, Pickering and Pollock (2001) emphasize the importance of asking questions that push students to utilize the higher order thinking skills of *analysis, synthesis* and *evaluation*. An example of a teacher utilizing questioning practices to strengthen students' higher order thinking skills and deepen understanding may be seen in a lesson on metaphysical poet John Donne's "A Valediction Forbidding Mourning." One of the images in this poem describes the closeness of two people in love, comparing them to the legs of a compass (the type used to draw circles as opposed to that used to gauge direction). Donne writes the following lines:

Thy soul, the fix'd foot, makes no show
To move, but doth, if th' other do.
And though it in the centre sit,
Yet, when the other far doth roam,
It leans, and hearkens after it,
And grows erect, as that comes home.

(Rosengarten, H. & Goldrick-Jones, A, pp. 42-43)

A question that engages students' lower order thinking skills might be simply, "What is a compass?" However, asking students to interpret the meaning of Donne's extended metaphor comparing two people in love to the "legs" of a compass pushes students to analyze Donne's words and draw a comparison between a concrete object such as a compass and the more abstract love that exists between two people. For example, the astute student will be able to deconstruct Donne's extended metaphor above and note that, because the two legs of a compass are attached to each other, one cannot move without affecting the other. A student must utilize his or her higher order thinking skills, however, in order to understand that Donne makes this observation to suggest that, likewise, the actions or words of one person will affect or "move" that of the other person in the couple. Likewise, it requires higher order thinking on the part of a student to understand that when Donne describes the way in which the fixed (stationary) leg of the compass seems to "lean and hearken" in the direction of the compass's other leg, Donne is suggesting that people in love will also instinctively move (whether mentally or literally) in the direction of one another. Finally, when Donne describes the way in which the legs of a compass "grow erect" as they are pushed closer to each other, a student utilizing his or her higher order thinking skills might observe that, similar to the legs of this compass, two people in love returning to each other's company might "straighten up" or "bloom" in the sense that they feel more whole or complete in each other's presence.

In closing, Donne's poetry is unquestionably challenging, and utilizing the higher order thinking skills necessary to make sense of his metaphors requires hard work on the part of students (and teachers). Questions that push students in the right direction may greatly facilitate their ability to make sense of Donne's metaphors and abstractions. Examples of questions that a teacher might utilize in this example include the following:

1. How could Donne's lines about how the legs of a compass move relate to the actions of two people in love?
2. When you draw a circle with a compass, what does the "center leg" do? How could this be similar to a lonely lover?
3. How could the way in which the two legs of a compass straighten up when you push them towards each other be symbolic of the actions or emotions of two people in love who are brought together?

These questions offer some preliminary examples of the type of questions that promote higher order thinking on the part of students. Later in this chapter, we will look in more detail at the difference between questions intended to recall information and questions such as those given above that promote higher levels of understanding and thinking.

Using Processing Partners to Raise the Level of Student Answers in Response to Higher Order Thinking Questions

It is often helpful for students to discuss higher order questions with a partner. Doing so enables them to build upon one another's thinking, thereby producing high level answers. One strategy teachers use to get students to effectively process with a partner the information requested with a higher order thinking question is **processing partners**[1]. In this strategy, students quickly discuss a higher level (or any) question with a partner and then quickly return to their own seats, ready to listen to the teacher. Teachers create a partner sheet using terms they want the students to learn through repetition. The students then follow the questions below to get their partners.

The instructions given to the students are as follows (see Figure 5-2):

1. When the teacher gives the direction, find one class partner for each of the Generals noted below.
2. Be certain that for any space in which you have the name of a classmate, that your classmate has your name in the same space. For example, if you have John Doe's name in your Stonewall Jackson space, then John Doe should have your name in his Stonewall Jackson space.
3. You may not have any partners who sit at your table (or sit at a contiguous desk).
4. You many not have a partner more than once.
5. Fill as many slots as you can in the five minutes given. Don't worry if you don't fill them all. We will help you to do so after the five minutes are up

After the five minutes have passed, students are asked to return to their seats. At this time the teacher asks, "Who does not have a Robert E. Lee?" If an even number of students raise their hands, then the teacher has them take each other's names to fill that slot on their sheets. If some students still have blanks, it is fine to bend the rules at this point and let students partner with someone at their table or someone they already have had as a partner. If there is an odd number of students with a blank slot, the teacher pairs up as many as possible and assigns the one remaining student the name "wild card." The teacher completes this process for all the spaces on the sheet. When it comes time to share, the "wild card" student partners with someone whose partner is absent or is assigned as a third person joining a pair of partners.

[1] Processing partners is also an excellent strategy to use with recall and comprehension questions when teachers want to firmly embed a piece of information.

The teacher is now ready to ask a higher order thinking question, and he or she tells the students to find their partners for a particular category. For example, the teacher might say, "Pair up with your Stonewall Jackson partner." Once the students are sitting with their partners, the teacher then asks the higher order thinking question for the pairs to discuss. This higher order question is typically *not* about the term (Stonewall Jackson) that names the partner. The reason teachers use curriculum-related terms is only to keep the terms in front of the students for learning through repetition. *It is important the first time you use the partners list that you stress to students that they are not to talk about the term on the list. Repeat the higher order thinking question they will be discussing.* After the students finish discussing the higher order thinking question in pairs, they return to their original seats and either share their answers orally or write them in their response journals.[2]
Civil War General Processing Partners

Figure 5-2

Robert E. Lee ______________________

Ulysses S. Grant ______________________

Stonewall Jackson ______________________

George Meade ______________________

William T. Sherman ______________________

Joseph Johnston ______________________

Joseph Hooker ______________________

Pierre Beauregard ______________________

William Hayes ______________________

Alfred Sully ______________________

John Jones ______________________

James Longstreet ______________________

Using Teacher Think-Alouds to Model Answering Higher Order Thinking Questions

A strategy that teachers use to demonstrate the cognitive strategies students may employ to answer a higher order thinking question is that of modeling out loud the thinking necessary to answer such a question. To do this, the teacher answers a question or solves a problem in front of the class and verbalizes to the class each step of his or her thinking.

1. The teacher presents the class with a higher order thinking question.
2. The teacher works out the answer to the question, verbalizing all of his or her thinking.

[2] The following sample is for a high school history class. Teachers in other disciplines have used terms such as *the being verbs, poets of the 19th century, titles of Shakespeare plays, elements from the periodic table, the continents, words that are difficult to spell,* etc. A partner sheet can be made from any list of content-related terms a teacher wishes to have students frequently review.

3. The students listen to the teacher and note what the teacher did in the process of thinking through the answer. It is important to tell students that they may not offer answers or help the teacher in any way.
4. After the verbalization is completed, the class analyzes the teacher's thinking and identifies the strategies the teacher used to answer the question.

For example, when teaching students to solve the analogy *mason:stone,* the teacher might use the following script to model answering the following question:

A mason is to stone what a ________________ is to ________________.

A. soldier: weapon
B. lawyer: law
C. blacksmith: forge
D. teacher: pupil
E. carpenter: wood

"A mason is to stone what a soldier is to a weapon. That seems to work because a mason uses stone and a soldier uses a weapon. Let me try the next answer to see whether or not it is a better fit. A mason is to stone what a lawyer is to law. That seems to work also because a lawyer works with the law, however, stone is something the worker physically moves around while the law is something you work with more intellectually than physically. I think I still prefer A. Let me try the next one. A mason is to stone what a blacksmith is to a forge. That seems to fit the criteria I used for A. The blacksmith uses a forge, and he uses it with physical activity, however, stone is the actual substance from which the mason makes a product. The blacksmith uses the forge as tool rather than it being the actual substance used to make a product. Using that definition then, soldier and weapon doesn't appear to work any more. Certainly, the soldier physically uses the weapon, but he uses it as a tool. It is not a substance used to make a product. It appears A and C have some characteristics that match the mason:stone analogy, but they also have at least one part that does not seem to fit. Teacher and pupil work in that the pupil is the raw material the teacher develops into a final product, however, the teacher does not physically handle the pupil to make the product. Finally, let me try carpenter and wood. A carpenter uses the wood to make a product. The carpenter physically manipulates the wood to make the product. The carpenter uses tools on the wood to make the final product. I think carpenter:wood is the analogy that is most similar to mason:stone."

The students now analyze the strategies that the teacher used to solve the analogy. For example, the teacher took each option in sequential order. While working with each option, the teacher found those characteristics about the option that were the same as the original analogy. Even though an early option appeared to work, the teacher continued to assess the other options in order to find the option that worked best. As the teacher progressed through the options, he or she noted those options that had more similar characteristics than the others and began to eliminate some of the options.

Student-Generated Questions

While asking questions may push students to utilize higher order thinking skills, giving students the opportunity to develop their own questions may also result in higher order thinking. As Shira Lubliner (2001, p. 3) notes, "To form a question, the student must [first] make sense of the text." One activity that we have used to encourage students to develop meaningful questions takes place on the day prior to a test or quiz. We divide the students into groups and ask them to develop questions that they believe would be appropriate for the following day's exam. We give students specific instructions for the types of questions they should create (i.e., ten multiple choice, five short answer, two open response questions, etc.). At the end of the period, we collect the questions that students have produced and create a test or quiz using the best of the submitted questions.

Writing Their Own Test

Another teacher we know utilizes a similar activity. On the day before a test, she divides the class into groups, gives directions for the type of test she wants them to create and collects one test from each group at the end of the period. She then chooses the best of these tests to give to the entire class. The students in the group that created the test automatically receive A's and don't have to take the test at all (though they do have to write an answer sheet while the rest of the class is taking the test). The catch is that the winner of the test-writing contest isn't announced until the next day, when students come in to take the test, so all students must study for the test without knowing whether or not their test has been selected as the winner. The benefit to such an activity, of course, is that all students get off to a strong start in their studying through the process of devising the test questions that they believe should appear on the next day's exam. More than just serving as a means of reviewing content, however, asking students to devise the questions that they believe to be most relevant to the unit of study pushes them to choose the most important and fundamental concepts within the just-completed unit of study. Simultaneously, this activity pushes students to see their input as "real." Their teacher is not simply questioning them to determine what they do and do not know (as if in a game of "gotcha") but rather has suggested through her actions that their questions and insights are important enough to form the content of the test that will be used to assess the class's learning. Such an explicit vote of confidence in students' abilities conveys a powerful message about their learning and knowledge.

Engage Students and Maintain Their Attention

Questioning may also be utilized to keep students engaged in the class's work. As Hannel (2003, p. 1) writes, "Questioning reduces the stream of information coming at the student to bite-size pieces and better attends to active listening." In other words, a teacher who intersperses questions throughout direct instruction is more likely to keep a class focused and attentive and less likely to "leave anyone behind." For example, a science teacher explaining the seven or eight steps necessary to run an experiment would be well advised to intersperse several questions throughout his or her explanation in order to ensure that students remain focused and attentive throughout. Questions this teacher might ask include

A teacher who intersperses questions throughout direct instruction is more likely to keep a class focused and attentive and less likely to "leave anyone behind.

1. Who remembers the first step of every lab we do?
2. What did I say to do after putting on your safety goggles?
3. What should the other lab partner be doing while one of you is mixing the chemicals?

Even at the high school level, don't hesitate to ask a question that amounts to "What did I just say?" For an attentive student, such a question represents a chance to receive some "easy" validation, and such questions serve to remind less attentive students to refocus their attention on the teacher's words.

Calling on Students Who Have Not Volunteered

Many teachers feel understandably uneasy about "cold calling" students to answer questions, rather than asking for volunteers, but such a technique may be invaluable for keeping students engaged and "on their toes" as well as for re-engaging students who may have lost focus or are "spacing out." As is always the case, the point of questioning is not to "catch" students who have lost focus but to keep students engaged and attentive. Towards this end, questions should never be asked in an aggressive or irritated tone but, rather, in a pleasant or neutral tone. Our goal is very much to convey that we are interested to hear this particular student's contribution to the lesson. For those teachers still reluctant to call on students who have not volunteered, it seems important to note that there will be some segment of the student population that, out of shyness or other reasons, will literally *never* volunteer on its own to answer a question. Allowing these students not to participate in answering questions denies them important opportunities for learning. Moreover, it seems unlikely that future employers will be as accommodating to an employee either incapable or unwilling to contribute to meetings or planning sessions. While it is difficult for us as educators who care about children to pose a question to a child who we know would prefer to remain silent, we encourage you to take the long view in terms of what will ultimately be best for that child. In our classes, we make it clear on the first day of school that sometimes we will be soliciting volunteers to answer questions and at other times we will be calling on students to answer. Strategies for working with shy students will be offered later in this chapter.

> *We make it clear on the first day of school that sometimes we will be soliciting volunteers to answer questions and at other times we will be calling on students to answer.*

"I Don't Know"

In *Highly Effective Questioning*, Hannel (2003) suggests that teachers do not accept "I don't know" as an acceptable response to a query. If a student does respond with "I don't know," Hannel (2003, p. 82) advises teachers to either (1) change the phrasing of the original question or (2) narrow the scope of the question. In this way, students who answer with "I don't know" to avoid doing the thinking necessary to answer the question will quickly learn that a response of "I don't know" only leads to additional questioning.

The following two scenarios stand as an example of this questioning strategy in action.

Teacher: Bobby, what do you remember from our unit on civil rights?
Bobby: I don't know.
Teacher: (rephrasing) Bobby, tell me something that interested you from the unit we finished yesterday on civil rights.
Bobby: I thought the stuff about the Black Panther Party was interesting.
Teacher: What interested you about the Black Panthers?

Here, the teacher responds to Bobby's initial "I don't know" response by simply rephrasing his or her question. Then the teacher asks Bobby to expand upon his response that he had found their study of the Black Panther Party to be particularly engaging. By asking an additional two questions, rather than simply calling on the student beside Bobby who is frantically waving her hand, the teacher successfully encourages Bobby to make a genuine contribution to the class's review of the previous unit. The Black Panther Party may well have been an aspect of the unit upon which the teacher had placed little emphasis. This exchange could potentially lead to Bobby preparing a report or presentation on the Black Panthers for extra credit.

In the first scenario above, the teacher chose to simply rephrase the question for Bobby's benefit. Had the teacher believed Bobby to be genuinely stymied by the initial question, however, he or she might have chosen to narrow the question's scope, as in the example below.

> **Teacher:** Bobby, what do you remember from our unit on civil rights?
> **Bobby:** I don't know.
> **Teacher** (narrowing the question's scope): Bobby, name one person from our unit on civil rights that interested you.
> **Bobby:** John Lewis.
> **Teacher:** Really? Why, Congressman Lewis?

In this scenario as well, the teacher chose to stick with Bobby and narrow the scope of the question instead of moving on to another student. Here again, Bobby's response may well lead to an unanticipated but productive class discussion about civil rights activist and current Congressman John Lewis or perhaps to Bobby carrying out some additional research on his own. In short, then, while we respect the intentions of those teachers who feel uncomfortable pushing their shyer students to participate in class, we encourage educators to regard the ability to answer questions and contribute to class discussions as a skill as or more important for students to acquire than writing strong topic sentences or deriving the quadratic formula. As Hannel (2003, p. 54) reminds us, "This is not to say that every student must answer each question correctly or perfectly, but to say that students may not opt out of participating in the questioning process" (p. 54).

Asking Students Questions

Having discussed the different purposes for which teachers ask questions, we now turn to the different types of questions that teachers ask to achieve these purposes. The three types of questions that teachers ask are generally broken down into the following three categories: *recall questions, comprehension questions* and *higher order thinking questions.* It should be noted at the outset, however, that there is some overlap between these categories. A challenging recall question might legitimately be classified as a comprehension question; likewise, a more complex comprehension question could be regarded as a higher order thinking question. In describing the different types of questions then, our aim is less on erecting concrete boundaries between these three categories and more on the type of question or questions we may ask to successfully achieve our purposes. Rather than slotting different types of questions into distinct categories, we suggest that questions are better categorized along a continuum such as that shown in Figure 5-3.

Rather than slotting different types of questions into distinct categories, we suggest that questions are better categorized along a continuum.

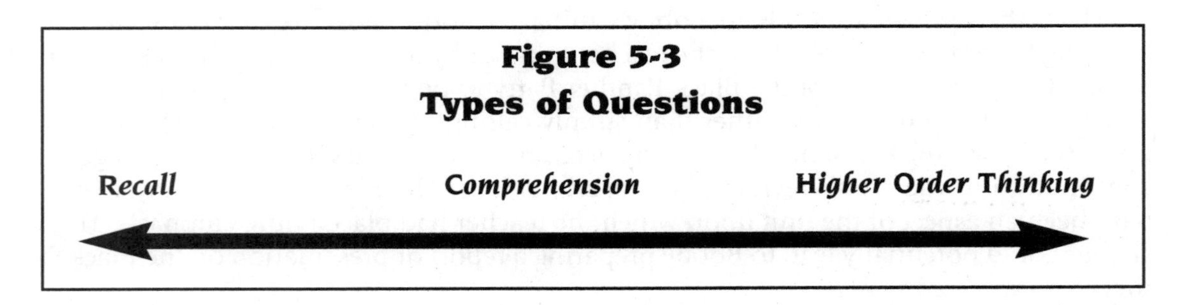

Moving from left to right, questions require more complex student thinking.

Recall Questions

- What is the name of the main character of the story?
- Who remembers the quadratic formula?
- In what year did the Civil War begin?

As may be seen in the three examples above, a **recall question** calls for a factual response which a student either knows or does not know; there is nothing to calculate or analyze. A teacher utilizes recall questions in order to activate students' previous learning and/or assess students' knowledge of a particular skill or concept.

Recall Questions to Activate Previous Learning

In a social studies class focusing on the Boston Tea Party, we might begin the class with a series of questions that push students to recall the previously studied actions and laws imposed by the British government that angered the Colonists. What was the Stamp Act? What law forced colonists to board British soldiers in their homes? The purpose of such questions is to activate students' prior learning so as to allow them to connect previously held knowledge to the day's lesson. In *Accessing the General Curriculum*, Nolet and McLaughlin (2000, p. 360) explain that when a student's brain takes in new information, "[This] information is held in working memory temporarily while it is compared with information already stored in long-term memory. If the new information is related to some prior knowledge, it is moved out of working memory and stored along with that related information in long-term memory." In other words, there is a physiological reason why students can remember information longer if this information is connected to their previous learning[3].

> *There is a physiological reason why students can remember information longer if this information is connected to their previous learning.*

Recall Questions to Assess New Learning

Another way in which we utilize recall questions is in the form of a one-question quiz at the start of class. When we assign students to read an article or book chapter for homework, we will often begin class the next day with a one-question quiz. The question is merely a recall question, which should result in an "easy A" for students who have completed their homework assignment. The purpose of such an assessment is to determine which students in the class have completed their homework assignment. For students who answer this recall question incorrectly, a private conversation after class may be appropriate in order to learn why the student has not completed his or her assigned reading and to devise a plan for getting that student back on track.

It is important for a teacher to bear in mind a caveat offered by Marzano, Pickering and Pollock (2001, p. 113) that recall questions "should focus on what is important as opposed to what is unusual." A question such as "What color was the protagonist's shirt?" could certainly be categorized as a recall question but not as one that represents a valuable use of instructional time. Instead, we focus our recall questions on what is important to the story, for example, "What did the protagonist find in the forest?"

Comprehension Questions

- Which of the words in this sentence is an adjective?
- If an object's mass is 8 kilograms and it is accelerating at 9.8 m/s/s, what is its force?
- What does "No taxation without representation" mean?

---

[3] Chapter 2 discusses in more detail the importance of connecting new information and skills to previous learning.

As may be seen in the three examples above, **comprehension questions** are those that assess whether or not students understand a particular concept, operation or idea. A comprehension question, then, is more complex than a recall question, because to answer a comprehension question correctly, a student must not only recall a previously learned piece of information but also apply this information to something new. For example, a recall question given in the previous section was, "Who remembers the quadratic formula?" Correctly answering this question merely requires a student to *recall* the particular formula. In contrast, a comprehension question might be, "What is x in the equation $5x^2 - x + 6$?" To answer this question correctly, students must not only *recall* the quadratic formula but *comprehend* how to utilize this formula to solve for x.

Use Comprehension Questions to Inform Instruction

Comprehension questions are the type of question that should be interspersed throughout a period of direct instruction in order to ensure that students are keeping pace with the teacher's lesson. For example, midway through a Spanish teacher's lesson on when to use the preterit tense versus the imperfect tense, the teacher might ask students to conjugate a verb in the preterit tense. If students falter in answering this question correctly, the teacher may need to reteach the conjugations of the two tenses. On the other hand, if the students easily conjugate the given verb in the preterit tense, the teacher may confidently move ahead to helping students understand *when* each of these verb tenses should be used in a sentence.

Higher Order Thinking Questions

- What might the colonists involved in the Boston Tea Party have been thinking as they threw the tea overboard?
- What information is conveyed in this advertisement? How is this information misleading?
- What evidence supports the claim that Romeo and Juliet were not truly in love?

The most difficult type of question for a teacher to form and for students to answer is a question that pushes students to utilize their higher order thinking skills. "Higher order thinking" was a term first popularized by educator Benjamin Bloom in 1956. He developed an instructional model that categorized thinking skills from the most concrete to the most abstract. In Bloom's model, a concrete form of thinking such as memorization is classified as an example of a "lower order thinking skill" whereas "higher order thinking skills" constitute more abstract forms of thinking such as *analysis*, *synthesis* and *evaluation*. More information on Bloom's taxonomy of thinking skills may be found in Chapter 4.

In *Classroom Instruction That Works*, Marzano, Pickering and Pollock (2001) describe four types of questioning that help students to hone their higher order thinking skills: questions that push students to make inferences, analyze an error, construct support and analyze perspectives. Each of these analytic skills and the questions that push students to use such skills will be examined here briefly.

Making Inferences

The Merriam-Webster Dictionary (1994, p. 598) defines **making an inference** as "the act of passing from one proposition, statement or judgment considered as true to another whose truth is believed to follow from that of the former." In other words, making an inference involves drawing upon something we already know to be true in order to make an educated guess about something we believe to be true. An example of a question that pushes students to make an inference might be the following: "What were the colonists who participated in the Boston Tea Party thinking as they threw the tea overboard?" Of course, students don't have a telepathic understanding of the thoughts that were running through these colonists' minds; however, their learning about the actions and laws imposed upon the colonists by the British in the months leading up to the Boston Tea Party should provide them with a factual base upon which to draw a reasonable inference about the colonists' mindset on that fateful evening.

Analyzing Errors

Teachers who have taken the GRE (Graduate Record Examination) or looked over recent versions of the S.A.T. (Scholastic Aptitude Test) will recall a number of questions that require the test-taker to read a short passage and then identify the error in the passage's line of reasoning. Such a question is assessing the test-taker's ability to analyze errors, a higher order thinking skill. Similarly, teachers may utilize questions to strengthen and assess their students' analytic skill in this regard. For example, a teacher might ask students to examine various magazine advertisements during a lesson on propaganda and to identify both the "message" the advertisement is attempting to convey to its audience about the benefits of using the given product as well as the error in reasoning that such an advertisement encourages its audience to make.

An elementary teacher shares with her students several double-digit addition problems in which errors exist. She asks her students to determine the nature of the error and then asks them to solve the problems correctly. For example, 25 + 39 = 54. In this case, the error is such that the ten that should have been carried over from 5 + 9 was never taken into account. The correct answer to this problem is 64.

Constructing Support

Perhaps the most important analytic skill for students to hone is the ability to construct support for a particular viewpoint. Virtually every academic discipline and profession requires its practitioners to effectively state ideas or plans of action and then construct support for why such a plan should be implemented. For example, lawyers are expected to provide evidence in the form of previous case law to support their clients' claims. Accountants responding to an auditors' queries must be able to reference specific tax codes that support the manner in which they have managed their clients' finances. Businesspeople proposing that their organizations develop new products will be expected to cite market research that demonstrates the wisdom of such a change. The examples go on and on.

> *Virtually every academic discipline and profession requires its practitioners to effectively state ideas or plans of action and then construct support for why such a plan should be implemented.*

In class, we might ask students to construct support for various statements such as the following two examples:

Do you believe Odysseus acted heroically? Why or why not?

To answer this question, students will need not only to state their opinions, but also to offer textual evidence to support them. For example, a student claiming that Odysseus did act heroically might note that he devised a brilliant plan to save himself and members of his crew from being eaten by the Cyclops. A student arguing that Odysseus did not act heroically, however, might counter that it was Odysseus's foolhardiness that led to his crew's imprisonment in the Cyclops' cave in the first place. Neither of these responses is necessarily more correct than the other. Rather, in allowing these two students to debate Odysseus's heroism, both students are strengthening their higher order thinking skills as long as their teacher continually pushes them to utilize textual evidence to support their respective views.

How can you prove to someone who doesn't know anything about math that 3/4 is greater than 2/3?

This question, a variation of which we once heard posed by Professor Eleanor Duckworth to a classroom of teachers, is more challenging than it initially appears. Were it not for the phrase, "to someone who doesn't know anything about math," this question might simply be a comprehension question assessing whether or not students understand the process of finding the least common denominator of two fractions or, alternatively, the process of cross-multiplying. Asking students to prove that 3/4 is greater than 2/3 without using mathematical terms in their explanation, however, requires students to come up with a different form of evidence. How can a student prove that one fraction is greater than the other? One student might transpose two circles on top of each other, one of which has 3/4 of its area shaded and the other 2/3 of its area. By transposing one on top of the other, the student could demonstrate that 3/4 of a circle covers more area than 2/3. Other students might come up with entirely different strategies. Again, the goal is to push students to find the evidence that will prove the statement, rather than simply relying on a memorized formula for comparing fractions.

Both of these questions push students to construct support in the form of textual or mathematical evidence, a skill that they will likely rely upon heavily throughout their academic and professional careers.

Analyzing Perspectives

Before beginning a unit on poetry, an English teacher we know likes to begin by asking his class two questions: (1) "What is the point of poetry?" and (2) "How is studying poetry going to improve your lives?"

Students offer various responses, many of which focus on the beauty of poetry and its ability to enrich one's life. The teacher acknowledges the value of each of these responses, but also makes sure to note that poetry is an excellent tool for improving one's ability to understand others' perspectives, or for putting oneself "in someone else's shoes." This English teacher then asks students to consider how an ability to understand others' perspectives might serve one well out in the "real world." In this way, the teacher managed to engage the future engineers, lawyers, accountants, etc. who might otherwise have been tempted to shrug off poetry as irrelevant to their future goals.

So how may teachers ask questions that push students to analyze other people's perspectives? To take poetry as an example, one poem that we enjoy teaching is "Traveling Through the Dark" by William Stafford, a poem that describes a motorist coming upon a dead deer on a deserted mountain road. The deer, though dead, is heavily pregnant, and the narrator can feel the unborn fawn still alive in its mother's belly. Should he take some action to rescue the unborn fawn? Should he load the deer into his car and seek help? After a moment's indecision, the narrator chooses to push the dead deer off the side of the mountain road to protect the safety of other drivers following this path. After reading this poem with our students, we discuss the action the narrator takes and ask our students to analyze the motivation that may have prompted such an action. We ask if they would have made a similar decision. In this way, we utilize questions to encourage our students to examine a situation through another's perspective.

Of course, such questioning is not limited to poetry. Going back to the unit on the Boston Tea Party, we might ask our students how they would expect English citizens reading about the Boston Tea Party in their weekly newspapers to react to the actions of the colonists. What might have been their thoughts and feelings? How might the King of England have reacted to this news? By pondering these questions, students strengthen their ability to examine a scenario or situation from multiple perspectives, an important higher order thinking skill.

For elementary school students, one way to help them understand others' perspectives during a unit on immigration might involve asking them construct a diary, written from the perspective of an immigrant child coming to America. In their journal entries, students are required to address their trip over to America, how they feel about being different and being in a strange land and about how others treat them. In addition, the teacher provides the students with several readings about immigration to help students write more realistic journals.

Asking Questions

How to Ask Questions

Having reflected upon the different purposes for which educators utilize questions and the different types of questions that suit these purposes, we now turn to the actual act itself of asking questions.

Avoiding Happy Talk

Perhaps the most important skill for a teacher to keep in mind in regards to questioning practices is clarity. In *Accessing the General Curriculum,* Nolet and McLaughlin (2000, p. 34) make the following observation:

> To allocate attention to something, a student must select it from among many sensory inputs that occur simultaneously. Teachers can assist students in this process by limiting the amount of information to which they ask students to attend at any one time. For example, teachers who use clear concise wording in their presentations often are better able to maintain and focus student attention than those who require their students to pick the most important information out of an endless stream of superfluous 'happy talk.'

In other words, the most effective questions are those that are expressed succinctly. Teachers who surround their questions with superfluous commentary only serve to confuse students. Note, for example, the difference between the following two examples:

> *Teachers who surround their questions with superfluous commentary only serve to confuse students.*

Teacher #1: Romeo and Juliet are probably the most famous couple in the history of literature. Their story is known all over the world. But were they really in love? When you think back over the course of the play, do their actions and thoughts, their innermost feelings, reveal them to be two people deeply, truly in love with each other, or is this just a case of childish flirtation or perhaps even adolescent lust?

Teacher #2: Do you think Romeo and Juliet were truly in love with each other? Why or why not?

Clearly, Teacher #2 expresses his or her question in a more succinct manner than Teacher #1. The students of Teacher #2 may immediately begin to consider the question at hand, whereas the students of Teacher #1 must first sift through all of the superfluous "happy talk" to determine precisely what they are being asked. On paper, the question asked by Teacher #1 may strike us as so exaggerated an example as to constitute caricature; however, when we consciously focus in and listen to our own questioning practices or those of our colleagues, we often find ourselves to be perilously close to the happy talk level achieved by Teacher #1. In Chapter 10, we talk about conducting classroom research in our own classroom. Audiotaping a lesson we are teaching and analyzing our questions to determine the extent to which they are succinct is an excellent way to self-assess and thereby improve our teaching.

Avoiding Multiple Questions in Quick Succession

Related to the concept of happy talk is the tendency on the part of many of us to pose several questions in a row before giving our students the opportunity to respond. Take, for example, the questioning pattern of Teacher #3.

Teacher #3: Should President Harry Truman have made the decision to drop the atomic bomb on Hiroshima and Nagasaki? Do you think racism against Asians played a role in this decision? Would Truman have been willing to drop an atomic bomb on Berlin or Rome? What decision would you have made?

All of these questions posed by Teacher #3 have the potential to form the basis of a powerful class discussion, however, firing all four questions at the class in quick succession only serves to confuse students. Some students will simply forget the first two or three questions posed and focus only on the final question they hear. Other students will be uncertain about which question they are expected to answer. Still other students will be reflecting upon the potential racism behind the decision to drop the atomic bomb on Hiroshima and Nagasaki while other students are volunteering their thoughts on what they would have done in Truman's place. As a result, Teacher #3 will have difficulty leading a coherent, focused discussion. He or she has simply floated out too many different ideas for students to consider at one time. Instead, Teacher #3 needs to focus on one of these questions and solicit student responses before moving on to the next question.

Why do we as educators sometimes fall into the trap of posing multiple questions in quick succession to our students? One reason seems to be that we have seen this technique utilized with great success in speeches by politicians and graduation speakers as well as TV lawyers making closing statements. We must remind ourselves, however, that an effective oratory technique in front of a passive audience does not meet with the same success in a student-centered classroom. Another reason is the discomfort some of us feel when silence ensues after we ask a question. Teachers unfamiliar with the use of wait time after asking a question often assume that students don't know the answer, rather than that they are thinking about the answer. In these instances, we often fill the silence with additional questions. The role of silence and wait time in classrooms will be examined in detail in the next section, but we wish to note here that students benefit deeply when we resist the urge to follow a question we have just posed with an additional question or comment. We must give students the opportunity to reflect and formulate a response to our first question before posing another.

Avoiding Overly Vague Questions

Also related to the issue of our clarity is avoiding overly vague questions. An example of an overly vague question might be the following:

Teacher #4: What do you think about World War I?

Such a question provides no clue to students about the type of response for which the teacher is looking. These questions typically occur when the teacher has not thoroughly considered the type of answers he or she wishes to get from the students. You'll recall that in our discussion earlier in this chapter of the types of questions that teachers pose to students—recall questions, comprehension questions, higher order thinking questions—there was no category of questions that involved students simply offering up guesses. Questions that lead to wild guessing are likely too vague and result in students feeling unclear about the purpose of such questions or the responses for which the teacher is searching.

> *Such a question provides no clue to students about the type of response for which the teacher is looking.*

The Importance of Strong Preparation

In our experience, the best defense against the pitfalls of happy talk, questions in a series and overly vague questions is strong preparation. As young educators and even now as experienced educators teaching a new unit or concept, we find it crucial to write into our lesson plans the specific questions that we intend to pose to our class. Having these questions written on paper to glance down at as we teach a particular lesson means that we aren't struggling in front of our students to find the right wording or phrasing for a particular query; that work has already been done.

A novice teacher with whom we recently worked initially resisted this idea of planning questions to pose to the class ahead of time. His contention was that he wanted to pose questions to his students that sprung naturally from the class's own comments and that he could think quickly enough "on the fly" to form these questions as the lesson occurred. While this young teacher was unquestionably a bright young man, his on-the-fly strategy led him to practice many bad habits such as happy talk described in this section. Additionally, we have found that, rather than negatively impacting the spontaneity of a classroom discussion, a teacher who spends time anticipating the direction that an upcoming classroom discussion might take and developing questions relevant to such a discussion is a more effective discussion leader, even when the discussion does not unfold precisely as anticipated. The time the educator has spent reflecting and planning for this lesson enables him or her to be *more*—not less—flexible if students raise unanticipated ideas or points.[4]

Diverse Questioning Practices

Finally, in *Accessing the General Curriculum*, Nolet and McLaughlin (2000, p. 35) suggest that teachers "ask a variety of related questions that require students to recall declarative information, make inferences, form opinions, and make evaluations." In other words, within the course of a particular lesson, students are more likely to remain engaged when teachers ask a range of recall, comprehension and higher order thinking questions, rather than exclusively favoring just one of these types of questions. For example, a teacher leading a review of the Cold War might ask the following questions over the course of the lesson:

1. In what year was the Berlin Wall erected?
   This is a recall question. Students simply do or do not remember the year the wall was erected.
2. How did the theory of Mutually Assured Destruction (MAD) affect America's nuclear arms policies during the Cold War?
   This is a comprehension question. Students must not only recall the definition of Mutually Assured Destruction but also understand how this theory played out in American nuclear policy during the Cold War.
3. What would you say represented the start of the Cold War, and what evidence can you give to support this view?
   This is a higher order thinking question. Students must develop their own opinions about the particular event that set off the Cold War and then construct support in the form of historical facts to support this viewpoint.

Asking different types of questions, such as those listed above, pushes students to engage in different kinds of thinking, encourages a variety of students to volunteer responses and keeps students more engaged in the lesson. While the suggestion to vary the types of questions we ask may seem like an obvious one, we have found that actually putting this

---

[4] In Chapter 1, we discussed mastery-based planning. Teachers who use that model find that their questions become more succinct and better enhance student learning.

Striving to pose a balanced mix of recall, comprehension and higher order thinking questions "on the fly" is a challenge we find nearly impossible to meet well.

concept into practice also requires the preparation described in the previous section. Preparation for the lesson, including diligent lesson planning and developing the questions we plan to pose, provides an opportunity to monitor the diversity of the questions that will be asked. In contrast, striving to pose a balanced mix of recall, comprehension and higher order thinking questions "on the fly" is a challenge we find nearly impossible to meet well.

Wait Time

Educator Mary Budd Rowe conducted the pioneering research on wait time in the late 1960s. In her article, "Wait Time: Slowing Down May Be a Way of Speeding Up!", Rowe (1987, p. 38) identifies two types of "wait time" that teachers may utilize to have a significant impact on students' learning. As she explains, "If teachers can increase the average length of the pauses at both points, namely, after a question and, even more important, after a student response there are pronounced changes in student use of language and logic as well as in student and teacher attitudes and expectations." In this section, we will examine the mechanics of both types of wait time in more detail.

Rowe (1987) describes **"Wait Time I"** as the length of time that passes between a teacher asking a question of his or her class and a student starting to respond. Rowe defines **"Wait Time II"** as the length of time that passes before a teacher responds to a student's comment or question. In a study of wait time in both elementary and high school classrooms, Rowe (1987) found that the average wait time for both situations is less than one second. Having made this observation, Rowe (1987) then embarked on a series of experiments that sought to observe the impact of increasing Wait Time I and Wait Time II from an average of less than one second to an average of three seconds. Her study uncovered results that follow.

Impact of Increased Wait Time on Student Learning

1) *When wait time is increased, the length of students' responses increase between 300% and 700%.* Students are less likely to answer in short phrases and more likely to give explanations of their responses. The reasoning for this increase is likely two-fold. First, increased wait time means that students who are slower, more methodical thinkers are less likely to have their thinking time cut off prematurely by the teacher or another student. Second, students reluctant to exert the mental energy necessary to provide a well reasoned, well constructed answer will learn that they cannot avoid the work of responding thoughtfully by simply delaying until their teacher supplies the answer for them or calls on someone else. Rather, their teacher will wait patiently until students attempt thoughtful responses.

2) *When wait time is increased, students are more likely to offer evidence to support their points.* Again, the reasoning behind this finding seems two-fold. Given more time to reflect upon questions, students are more likely to come up with evidence that supports their responses. Simultaneously, those students interested in providing their teacher with as hasty a response as possible will discover that their teacher is not going to "let them off the hook" by supplementing their hasty answer or calling upon another student in the class to do so. Rather, these students quickly learn that their teacher is willing to wait silently until both an answer and evidence supporting this answer are provided.

3) *When wait time is increased, students ask more questions of the teacher.* Slowing down the pace of the exchange between a teacher and his or her students allows students the opportunity to form questions and then to put those questions into words. In contrast, in a class in which a teacher responds instantly to students' responses, a student with a question for the teacher will often find that the topic under discussion has already moved on by the time the student has fully formulated the question in his or her mind.

4) *When wait time is increased, students are more likely to interact with each other, answering and responding to each other's questions.* This finding by Rowe suggests that increasing wait time not only benefits the specific student who has been called upon by the teacher, but that other students in the class also take advantage of this slower pace to form questions and thoughts as well. Given the time to formulate these thoughts and questions, students may then begin to speak and question each other, rather than interacting solely with the teacher. Experienced teachers will agree that encouraging students to speak to each other, rather than simply responding to the teacher, is one of the more challenging feats to accomplish. This finding by Rowe that increased wait time positively affects student-to-student interactions is an exciting one.

> *Experienced teachers will agree that encouraging students to speak to each other, rather than simply responding to the teacher, is one of the more challenging feats to accomplish.*

5) *When wait time is increased, students are less likely to answer with "I don't know."* Here again, it would seem that increasing wait time sends the dual message to students that, when called upon, they will be given an adequate amount of time to formulate an answer and, additionally, that they will not simply be "let off the hook" with a hasty or inadequate response. In a previous section of this chapter, we discussed the importance of rephrasing the question or narrowing the scope of the question when a student responds with "I don't know." Both of these strategies remain sound ones, but Rowe's research suggests that an effective initial strategy to this type of response is simply to increase wait time.

6) *When wait time is increased, disciplinary problems within the class decrease.* This finding by Rowe initially strikes teachers as counterintuitive. We assume that increasing the amount of time in which the class is sitting silently will lead to an increase in opportunities for mischief. It would seem that the reverse is true, however, most likely because increasing wait time provides students with more opportunities to think about the content they are learning, to ask questions and to express their own ideas about this content. As a result, students are less likely to become frustrated and confused during the course of a lesson, and these are the emotions that often lead students to act out.

7) *When wait time increases, a broader scope of students volunteers responses to questions.* It is unquestionably the case that different students process information at varying speeds. Thus, a teacher who fires questions at his or her class and then immediately calls upon the first student to volunteer is inadvertently favoring those students who can most quickly process the teacher's question. In contrast, a teacher who poses a question and then waits for several seconds before calling on a student to respond will provide those students who process information more slowly (but perhaps more deeply) with an opportunity to participate in the class's discussion.

Obstacles to Increasing Wait Time

In short, Rowe (1987) uncovered a number of dramatic improvements in student performance that come with increasing Wait Time I and Wait Time II from the typical one second to approximately three seconds. Unfortunately, learning to slow down and increase wait time between asking a question and eliciting a response (Wait Time I) and responding to a student's question or comment (Wait Time II) may be challenging for teachers. There seem to be several reasons for this finding. First, many teachers simply aren't familiar with the proven benefits of consciously increasing one's wait time. The topic may not have come up in the course of their teacher education programs or subsequent professional development, and it seems safe to speculate that, prior to beginning her research, even Rowe herself would not have guessed at the degree to which increased wait time impacts student achievement.

Second, Rowe (1987) has observed that increasing the length of Wait Time II may be particularly challenging for teachers as many of us have gotten into the habit of repeating our students' responses to a given question. Why do we do this? The answer seems to lie in a societal discomfort with silence. For example, imagine yourself at a cocktail party in which you are chatting with a group of four or five other people. If a break in the conversation occurs, we tend to find this silence uncomfortable, and our minds race for something to say to fill the silence. In short, we seem to live in a society that regards silence during verbal interactions to be a negative occurrence and something to be eliminated as quickly as possible. While the implications of this societal norm at cocktail parties don't seem overly troublesome, Rowe's work suggests that teachers' discomfort with silence does in fact have a negative impact on teaching and learning.

Third, teachers seemingly fail to increase their wait time out of a desire for validation that they have taught their content well. In other words, imagine completing a lesson on the scientific method and then asking the class a question about the final step of this process. If the question is met with total silence, we immediately conclude that we have not successfully taught this material to our students, and this is a frustrating discovery. Imagine now that we ask our question about the final step of the scientific method, and one student's hand shoots up in the air. We immediately call upon this student to answer, relieved by this validation that our students "get it." Of course, such validation is not necessarily warranted. What has really been proven is that one student—not the entire class—gets it., Too often, however, we accept this single response as representative of the entire class's level of comprehension and make the decision to move on to the next concept to be studied. A dipsticking technique (described earlier in this chapter) that assesses the entire class's understanding of the particular skill or concept up for discussion would be more effective.

Finally, a teacher's efforts to increase wait time may be derailed by students in the class who simply shout out answers without waiting to be called upon. Teachers consciously working to allow three full seconds to pass during Wait Time I and Wait Time II grow understandably frustrated if their efforts are thwarted by over-eager students. Waiting to be called upon without shouting out is an important skill for students—elementary through high school—to develop and practice. The most important defense against students' shouting out is defining clear expectations for class behavior during the first days of school. In our own classrooms, one of our primary expectations for students is that only one person in the classroom will speak at a time, and this policy requires students to wait to be called upon before volunteering an answer. If a student shouts out an answer, we gently remind that student to raise his or her hand and then call upon another student to provide the answer. (Immediately calling on that same student once he or she raises a hand unintentionally rewards the student for calling out the answer in the first place.) If the tendency to shout out answers persists, we may need to meet privately with such a student to devise a plan that will allow us to jointly monitor his or her responses. Such a plan might involve "good participation points" or perhaps even a small reward if the student can make it through an entire class period without shouting out an answer. Perhaps most powerfully, however, we try to positively reinforce this student's good behavior by immediately calling upon him or her to speak when he or she raises a hand to volunteer. In this way, we work to condition this student to raise his or her hand prior to making a contribution to the class's discussion.

> *Rowe (1987) and other researchers have found that the most effective technique for helping teachers to lengthen their wait times is for a teacher to tape-record a typical lesson and then listen to the recording with a stopwatch in hand in order to monitor his or her wait times.*

Techniques to Increase Wait Time

Rowe (1987) and other researchers have found that the most effective technique for helping teachers to lengthen their wait times is for a teacher to tape-record a typical lesson and then listen to the recording with a stopwatch in hand in order to monitor his or her wait times. This technique must be repeated regularly, however, in order to prevent a teacher from slipping back into his or her previous patterns. Another technique that may be effective is inviting a colleague to observe one's teaching and then offer feedback on the average length of wait times observed. Finally, some teachers have had success actually utilizing their own students to help them to monitor wait time. By explaining to students what they would like to accomplish in terms of increasing Wait Time I and Wait Time II, students may play a role in ensuring that both they and the teacher are leaving adequate pauses after both teacher and student responses. In Chapter 10, we discuss ways in which teachers may conduct their own classroom research. In Chapter 11, we discuss ways in which teachers may work as partners or in teams to analyze their own classroom practices.

Since Rowe's pioneering work on wait time, other researchers and educators have added to this area of research. In fact, other opportunities for wait time in a typical classroom have been identified, such as the amount of time a student pauses in the process of answering a teacher's question. Robert Stahl (1994) writes that a teacher typically cuts a student off if a pause extends beyond one-half second. Stahl also comments on the value of teachers creating wait time in the midst of their own presentations. He writes, "Within-teacher presentation pause-time occurs when teachers deliberately stop the flow of information and give students three or more seconds of uninterrupted silence to process the just-presented information. This period of silence provides students uninterrupted time to momentarily consider the information of the teacher's presentation in smaller, bite-sized chunks" (Stahl, 1994, p. 2). In short then, the work of various researchers suggests that students benefit when teachers deliberately create opportunities for pauses of approximately three seconds during periods of both direct instruction and rounds of questions and answers. We speak from experience that it can be incredibly challenging for a teacher to allow a student who is responding to a question a full three seconds of silence to collect his or her thoughts while the rest of the students in the class sit and wait. And yet the work of researchers such as Rowe and Stahl suggests that allowing these pauses to occur is ultimately quite beneficial to the entire class's learning.

Responding to Students' Correct Answers: Diversify the Praise to Match the Student or the Student's Response

On the surface, responding to students who have answered a question correctly seems significantly easier than responding to students who have answered incorrectly, however, this is not always the case. A college professor of ours had the habit of responding, "Well done!" in a bright, enthusiastic tone to virtually every comment a student made. Initially, students in the class beamed at this enthusiastic praise, but after a few weeks, it became apparent that virtually every correct response received a "Well done!" in that same enthusiastic tone. In short, the praise lost its luster through overuse.

There was much that this college professor was doing correctly when it came to responding to our correct answers. Perhaps most importantly, his tone conveyed warmth and enthusiasm. This educator's method also serves as a cautionary tale, however, in that he came to rely too heavily on one particular phrase. Whether we realize it or not, students are paying close attention to our every move, and that includes the ways in which we offer praise. Thus, we must consciously work to diversify the ways in which we praise student responses. Here are just a few examples:

"Thank you."
"That's exactly right."
"Great point."
"Interesting idea."
"That's a very astute answer."
"Great contribution to our discussion."
"I think you're right on target."

While each of these sentences or phrases represent examples of praise, each one would be more effective if coupled with the specific response that the student offered. Take the conversation that begins the following section as an example.

Be Specific About What is Praiseworthy

Teacher: What do you consider to be the start of the Cold War?

Student: I think the Cold War was getting started even before World War II ended. I think that President Truman began to see Russia as a future competitor, and some historians say that Truman dropped the atomic bomb on Hiroshima to intimidate Stalin.

Teacher: Your point about why Truman used the atomic bomb is a great contribution to our discussion.

As may be seen in this dialogue, the teacher's praise goes beyond simply, "That's a great contribution." Rather, the teacher explicitly notes the point the student made that contributed to the class's discussion. Such praise is more likely to strike the student as authentic than would a generic compliment such as, "Great point."

Tone

Of course, not even the most specific praise will validate a student's response unless the teacher's tone of voice and body language complement his or her words. In other words, telling a student, "Your point about Truman is very smart" is less likely to be regarded as authentic if you have already turned away from that student and are facing in the other direction.

Body Language

Likewise, responding to a student's contribution by muttering "Great point" as you scan your lesson plan for the night's homework is equally unlikely to appeal very much to that student. Instead, make sure that you are not only looking at the student but facing squarely in his or her direction when you are offering praise. Speak loudly and clearly. Only after you have finished expressing your praise should you turn to the next student interested in volunteering or back toward the blackboard to provide further instruction.

Direct Praise

Finally, some useful suggestions for responding to students may be found in Bob Kegan and Lisa Lahey's *How the Way We Talk Can Change the Way We Work*. Kegan and Lahey (2000) argue that praise is most powerful when it is direct and non-attributive. By direct, Kegan and Lahey suggest that praise should be directed *toward* the recipient of the praise rather than spoken *about* the recipient. For example, if Albert answered a question correctly, we would say "Albert, you did a great job." This is a more effective way of praising Albert than stating more generally to the entire class, "Albert is absolutely right."

Non-Attributive

Kegan and Lahey (2000) also suggest that praise is most effective when it is non-attributive. By non-attributive, they mean that in praising a student, we should try to avoid making a declaration about that student's intellect, personality or skill-set. Instead, we should describe the way in which we personally appreciate that aspect of the student's personality or skill-set. In other words, don't tell the person about themselves, tell them what effect his or her qualities had on you. For example, rather than saying, "Alex, you are an excellent writer," we might choose to say, "Alex, we enjoy reading your papers because we find the writing so clear." What is the difference between these two sentences? In the first example, Alex might think to himself or even say out-loud, "No, I'm not really a good writer." In the second example, however, we are describing the way in which we experience Alex's writing, a statement that Alex cannot internally or verbally refute.

In addition to communicating praise more effectively, remembering the suggestions offered in this section serves an additional benefit as well. If we are committed to offering praise that is direct, specific and non-attributive, we are unlikely to fall into the trap described in this section's opening paragraph of the teacher who uses the same clichéd phrase each time he expresses praise. Instead, our praise will be tailored to the specific student response that elicited the praise, causing the praise itself to resonate far more strongly with our students.

Summary of Characteristics of Effective Praise

_____ diverse phrases

_____ warm tone

_____ attentive body language

_____ specific praise

_____ direct praise

_____ non-attributive praise

Responding to Incorrect Answers or Partially Incorrect Answers

There is no single way to respond to a student's incorrect or partially incorrect answer. Different students have varying personalities and thus require responses tailored to their particular styles. For each of the examples below, we can think of students for whom each response would have been appropriate and other students for whom each response would have been inappropriate.

Different students have varying personalities and thus require responses tailored to their particular styles.

"That's a good try, Judy."
"You're close, Evan."
"Anne, you're a little off the mark."
"Can someone else add to Frank's answer?"
"You're right on track with the first part of what you said, Selma. Do you want to try again on the second part?"

The important principle to remember when responding to a student's incorrect answer is to respond in such a way that the student won't be put off from volunteering again later in the class period or in future class periods. Determining which responses will accomplish this goal for particular students requires us to know our students well and to utilize this knowledge in formulating a response. While responding to a student's incorrect answers is heavily dependent upon the personality of that student, there are some strategies to keep mind.

1. *Try to hear something in the student's response with which you can agree.* This strategy was utilized in the case of Selma in the examples above. Selma had given a response that

was partly right and partly wrong. In pointing out that the second part of her response was incorrect, the teacher made sure to observe that the first half of Selma's answer was correct. When possible, start with praise and move on to constructive criticism. By starting with praise, a teacher's ensuing constructive criticism is more likely to be heard and processed by the student. In contrast, if a teacher starts with criticism and then finishes with a word of praise, the student's defensive response to the initial criticism may prevent him or her from hearing the ensuing praise.

2. *Don't pretend an incorrect answer is correct.* While our goal is to respond to students' answers in a way that won't inhibit them from volunteering in the future, this goal does not mean that we should avoid telling a student he or she is incorrect. Such a move will only serve to confuse or provide inaccurate information to the entire class. Often, this aversion to telling a student that his or her response is incorrect results in the teacher speaking ambiguously. Take the following example:

> **Ellen:** I think the assassination of Ferdinand was an underlying cause of World War I.
>
> **Teacher:** That's an interesting point, Ellen. Does anyone else have an alternative theory?

While the assassination of Francis Ferdinand certainly played a role in the start of World War I, we would be hard pressed to find historians who consider it one of the *underlying* causes of the War. Unfortunately, in her response to Ellen, the teacher's desire to encourage Ellen's participation leads her to avoid explicitly stating that Ellen's response is incorrect. The danger is that Ellen and her classmates now likely regard Ellen's statement to be an accurate one. A more appropriate response to Ellen might have been the following:

> **Teacher:** Ellen, you're right that Ferdinand's assassination played a role in the start of World War II; however, the assassination of Ferdinand is not considered an *underlying cause* of the war. Do you remember how his assassination contributed to the start of the war?
>
> **Ellen:** His assassination set off a conflict between Austro-Hungary and Serbia that escalated into World War I.
>
> **Teacher:** If that's the specific event that started the fighting, can you name one of the forces that may have led that one assassination to turn into a worldwide war?

As you may see here, the teacher explicitly notes that Ellen's response is incorrect; however, the teacher also finds something to praise in Ellen's response and then follows up this praise with additional questions that will draw out Ellen's knowledge. In this way, the teacher allows Ellen to demonstrate that she knows quite a bit about the start of World War I. In contrast, a teacher who responded, "No, that's not right" and then asked another student to supply the correct answer might be hard pressed to convince Ellen to volunteer in the future.

3. *Question to make sure you understand the student's response.* There are two components of answering a teacher's question correctly. A student must possess the knowledge to supply the answer, but, additionally, the student must express that knowledge in an articulate way. Sometimes, the source of a student's incorrect response lies more with the second component, articulateness, than with the first, lack of knowledge. For this reason, a teacher is often well served to ask additional questions that might help a student reshape his or her knowledge into an answer that makes sense. Take the following conversation, for example.

Teacher: Allan, why did Mercutio say on his deathbed, "A curse on both your houses?"

Allan: I think he felt mad that he was dying alone.

Teacher: Why do you say that?

Allan: Because the reason Tybalt was looking to fight someone in the first place was because of the feud between the Montagues and the Capulets, and then Mercutio sort of got caught up in the middle of it.

Teacher: So why do you think he cursed both families?

Allan: I bet he wanted them to be cursed since he was dying because of their feud with each other.

In this scenario, the teacher easily could have declared Allan's initial response— that Mercutio was angry to be dying alone—incorrect and then moved on to another student. Instead, the teacher asked several probing questions to better understand Allan's thinking, and it turned out that Allan did understand the motivation behind Mercutio's final words; his initial response hadn't revealed all that he knew. Moreover, it is notable that the teacher's initial probing question to Allan was, "Why do you say that?" In this instance, the teacher's follow-up question unearthed a mother lode of additional information that the student possessed. The right answer was "in there" but the student needed help "digging it out."

Monitoring the Responses of Other Students to Incorrect Answers

A colleague of ours who worked as a supervisor in a homeless shelter prior to transitioning into a career in teaching used to say there were some surprising similarities between the two jobs. At the homeless shelter, his job was partly to ensure that all of the different men and women staying at the shelter felt safe, and while a teacher's classroom is typically a safer place than a homeless shelter, one of a teacher's primary responsibilities is to foster a culture in which students feel safe while answering questions and contributing to class discussion. Teachers may take several steps to ensure that the responses of students to the incorrect answers of their peers foster a safe environment.

Teachers may take several steps to ensure that the responses of students to the incorrect answers of their peers foster a safe environment.

Setting Explicit Expectations and Consequences

It is important that teachers explicitly set out expectations on the first day of class regarding appropriate student behavior. One urban high school expects all students, faculty and visitors to follow its "safety rule" of "No Shame, Blame or Attack." This safety rule is taught to all incoming ninth graders on the first day of school and is posted in literally every classroom and corridor. Moreover, in teaching this safety rule to their students, teachers emphasize the importance of responding respectfully to other students' ideas, comments, questions and opinions. Teachers also know they must act to "nip in the bud" any attempts by students to subvert these expectations. In other words, if one student jeers or teases another for an incorrect answer, the teacher must react. It may be appropriate to issue a stern warning for a first offense, but a student who repeatedly makes fun of other students' responses is not acting as a positive member of the classroom community and should not be allowed to remain in the classroom. (Chapter 3 gives an in-depth explanation of how to establish effective classroom routines.[5])

[5] More information can be found in Chapter 3 about an important classroom routine for how students respond to an incorrect answer given by another student

Perhaps the ideal reaction from a high school teacher is to ask an offending student to leave the classroom for the remainder of the period and to return at the end of the period or the end of the school day for a private conversation. It is important to note here that we don't necessarily need to send such a student to the assistant principal's office, but rather the student may go to the library, computer lab, cafeteria, etc. What is crucial is that the student who is making the classroom culture a less safe space for students to volunteer is removed immediately from that classroom. The teacher may meet later with this student privately and discuss the importance of maintaining a classroom culture in which everyone feels free to volunteer his or her thoughts. We emphasize here the importance of immediate action in the face of a student who is disrespectful to his or her peers because such a student may have a significant (and negative) effect upon a teacher's ability to increase the number of students who answer during a given lesson.

Increasing the Number of Students Who Answer During the Lesson

Different teachers utilize different techniques to encourage students to more readily volunteer to respond to questions. Many teachers utilize a class participation grade primarily gauged by students' willingness to participate in class.[6] During student presentations, one teacher that we know offers candy to any student willing to *ask* a question of that student presenter at the conclusion of his or her presentation. Such a bit of bribery may encourage both active listening to the presentation as well as eager questioners following the presentation.

The Ball of Knowledge

Other "gimmicks" may encourage increased volunteering as well. One teacher with a class of particularly chatty students brought a foam ball into class and made a rule that only the student holding the ball could speak. While the intended purpose of this strategy was to encourage only one student to speak at a time, this teacher discovered another unintended benefit: students were intrigued by the prospect of having the ball thrown to them and then getting to throw the ball back to the teacher following their comments. As a result, the number of student volunteers to respond to the teacher's questions increased dramatically. On a side note, this exercise with the ball had a second unintended benefit related to questioning as well. Such an activity created a concrete tool for the teacher to observe the number of times within a class period that students responded directly to each other, instead of communicating solely with the teacher. The teacher could count the number of times within the period that a student threw the ball to another student as opposed to throwing it straight back to the teacher.

Processing in Writing Prior to Answering

Another technique we use to increase the number of student participants in class discussion is posing a question to students but then asking them to write out an answer to the question prior to asking for volunteers. When the time comes to solicit responses, students who may have been hesitant to speak "off the cuff" will feel more confident speaking out with a written response in front of them. This is particularly helpful to those students who use writing as a form of processing. Many adults have learned that they can best think through a problem by writing about the problem. This is sometimes referred to as "writing to think." Many students also think best through writing.

[6] Chapter 3 includes an example of how one teacher incorporates participation into a student's grade.

Processing Partners

In a similar vein, we sometimes pose a question to students and ask them to discuss that question with a partner for two minutes. Using a stopwatch, we will ask one student to share his or her thoughts for sixty seconds, and then we will ask the other student to share his or her thoughts for sixty seconds. At the conclusion of this "pair-share" activity, we might ask for volunteers to explain their partners' perspectives. Some students who are hesitant to share their own opinions are less inhibited about sharing someone else's. Sharing the perspective of the other also helps students learn to be better listeners. Earlier in this chapter, we described a management technique known as *processing partners* for getting students quickly into and out of partner pairs.

Calling Sticks

For teachers reluctant to "cold call" students, one technique we have used that might be more agreeable is writing the name of each student in the class on a Popsicle stick and placing all of the Popsicle sticks in a hat. When the time comes for a student response, the teacher simply reaches into the bag and pulls out a Popsicle stick with a student's name on it. That student is then responsible for answering the question.[7] Students often respond better to this type of randomization then they do to the teacher's choosing a person who does not have his or her hand raised. Students tend to feel this is more fair. In some cases, the teacher will remove the stick once a student is called. This helps the teacher keep track of who has been called and who has not been called. When using this strategy, it is important to occasionally go back to the "already called pile" to ensure that students don't tune out once they have answered a question. Other teachers put the stick back into the container after a student answers, thereby giving that student an equal opportunity to be randomly chosen later in the class period.

Encouraging Shy and/or Reluctant Participants

Stratifying the Randomization of the Calling Sticks

One way to help shy or reluctant students when using the calling sticks is to only choose their sticks when asking a question the teacher is reasonably sure they can answer correctly. Although we don't usually recommend deception as a teaching strategy, this is one time when it may be beneficial to surreptitiously choose a specific student without the other students knowing that you have co-opted the random process.

Providing the Question to the Student Prior to the Class

Another strategy for working with shy students is to initiate a private discussion after class one day during which a deal is struck. At this meeting, we might first explain to this shy student that we recognize his or her reluctance to volunteer in class but that public speaking is an important skill to develop. Towards this end, we strike a deal with this student in which he or she agrees to volunteer a response once per class. If a student is particularly shy, we might even sit down together with the student to look over the next day's lesson plan and plan out ahead of time the question that we will ask and the student will answer. Actually giving the student a question ahead of time may go a long way toward calming his or her nerves. If necessary, we might meet with this student for the first several days after the deal has gone into effect, choosing the question ahead of time that the student will answer. We might even work out a secret signal to alert the student when we are on the verge of posing the previously determined question. For example, we might agree to casually approach the student's desk a moment or two before posing the question. Even after such planning

[7] Some teachers prefer to use index cards (referred to as *calling cards*).

is no longer necessary, we would keep this student's reluctance to volunteer in mind and immediately call upon this student to answer whenever he or she raises a hand. In this way, we try to positively reinforce the student's attempts to contribute to the class's discussion.

Alerting the Student That He or She Will Be Asked the Next Question and Providing the Question in Advance

Some students reluctant to answer questions in class feel this way not because they are shy but because they find it difficult to collect their thoughts quickly enough to offer a coherent answer. Increasing wait time is one response to this situation. Students who fit this description might also benefit from the teacher giving them a question ahead of time and telling them that they will soon be called upon to answer it. For example, imagine the following scenario.

> **Teacher:** In *Of Mice and Men*, was Lenny really a good friend to George?
>
> *Teacher allows a full three seconds of wait time.*
>
> **Teacher:** I'm going to call on Michelle to answer this question, but, Allison, would you think about specific examples of ways in which Lenny *was* a good friend to George and, Peter, would you think about specific examples of ways in which Lenny *was not* a good friend to George? I'm going to call on you both after we hear Michelle's answer.

In this way, the teacher has given both Allison and Peter a few moments to think about the question each will be asked and to formulate a response.

Group Questions

This technique creates a safe environment for students in which they may answer questions about something that has just been taught. The students are placed in small groups usually composed of three or four students. The group is presented with one or more comprehension questions related to the information or skills that were just taught. Students discuss the question together until they reach consensus on the correct answer. Any questions for which they cannot find consensus answers are listed by the group scribe. Also added to the list are any additional questions raised by members of the group that were not sufficiently answered. The questions on the list are then read to the class by the scribe without attributing them to any one member of the group. In this activity, reticent students are more willing to ask questions when it will not be known by the class that they orginated the questions.

Pygmalion Effect

We also believe that the way in which a teacher responds to students' comments or ideas has a dramatic impact upon the willingness of students within that class to become regular volunteers and contributors. In asking students questions and then responding to students' answers, teachers need to convey through their tone of voice, body language and responses that they deeply value their students' contributions to class discussion and instruction. Conveying these beliefs to students has a dramatic impact on their performance. In the classic 1968 work, *Pygmalion in the Classroom*, Rosenthal and Jacobson describe an experiment in which they measured the IQs of the elementary school students in a particular school, chose 20% of these students at random and informed these students' teachers that these particular students were extremely bright and could be expected to make great gains academically over the course of the year. At the end of the school year, Rosenthal and Jacobson measured the IQs of all of these elementary school students once again and discovered that the students they had chosen at random and described to the teachers as extremely bright had increased their IQ scores significantly more than had their peers. The implications of this experiment suggest that a teacher's expectations for his or her students and the way in which these expectations are conveyed through tone of voice, body language, etc. have a significant impact on these students' achievement. Suggestions for responding to students' correct and incorrect answers were offered in previous sections of this chapter.

Improving Patterns for Calling on Students

In recent years, much research has been done on the topic of teachers' patterns for calling on students. In racially diverse classrooms, are teachers more likely to call upon students of one race than another? Are teachers more likely to call on boys than girls? Are teachers more likely to call on regular education students than special education students or students who sit in the front of the classroom in comparison to students who sit in the back? Do right-handed teachers favor students seated on the right side of the room and vice versa for left-handed teachers? To some degree, despite our best intentions, it seems likely that virtually all of us end up favoring one group of students or another in our solicitation of student responses if only because the student sitting in the front row is more likely to catch our attention or the young man who waves his arms so frantically that he practically falls out of his seat distracts us from the young lady quietly raising her hand behind him. Determining our own selection patterns for calling on students, like anything else, requires some action research. Probably the easiest way to conduct this research is to ask a colleague or department head to observe your teaching and to keep track of the students whom you call upon to answer questions. Providing this observer with a seating chart will enable the two of you afterwards during your debriefing session to note whether students on one side of the room answered a disproportionately higher or lower number of questions than the rest of the class. You may also break your data down by race, gender, special education, etc. While we recognize that such a process may be time-consuming, there is unquestionable value in taking the time necessary to ensure that all students within your class are being provided with equitable learning opportunities. We would suggest, for veteran teachers in particular, asking your department head or administrator to focus on your questioning patterns during his or her annual observation. This focus is far more likely to be of benefit to you when added to the observation standards that these administrators are using to supervise younger, novice teachers. Moreover, if you wanted to take the issue of questioning and patterns one step further, you might ask a colleague to keep track of the number of times that students respond to each other rather than to you directly. As was mentioned in the section of this chapter discussing wait time, even the most skilled teachers are sometimes surprised by the rarity with which students in a given classroom are actually questioning and responding to each other. Yet, for many of us, our most exciting moments as teachers are those times when students become so engaged in a discussion or activity that we feel confident we could leave the room without the discussion faltering or perhaps even anyone noticing. For most of us, such an occurrence is not an everyday affair, and yet, paying attention to the volunteering patterns in our classrooms and enlisting the aid of colleagues or supervisors in this endeavor may lead to significant gains in both the quantity and quality of student responses to our questioning practices. More information about action research and peer observation may be found in Chapters 10 and 11.

Conclusion

In closing, it is tempting for us as educators to assume that asking students questions and responding to their answers are skills that we instinctively possess. In reality, asking and responding to questions are complex acts that require preparation, reflection and practice to perform effectively. We began this chapter by discussing the different purposes for which teachers utilize questions and then matched these purposes with the types of questions that can best achieve them. We then moved into the mechanics of asking questions, focusing on the importance of clarity, wait time and diversifying the types of questions asked within a lesson. Finally, we examined effective ways to respond to both correct and incorrect answers as well as strategies for encouraging wider student participation during question and answer sessions. Our goal has been to share the experience we have gained in our own classrooms along with the most current research on questioning practices in order to offer concrete techniques and strategies for using questions to enhance teaching and learning. Questions have the power to transform the act of teaching from a monologue into a dialogue. They pull students into the conversation, thereby encouraging them to play a role in their own learning. A classroom in which students are challenged by frequent and diverse questions and have the opportunity to pose questions themselves is a classroom in which deep learning is taking place.

References

Checkley, K. (2004, April). A is for audacity: Lessons in leadership from Lorraine Monroe. *Educational Leadership,* 70–72.

Donne, J. "A Valediction Forbidding Mourning." In H. Rosengarten & A. Goldnick-Jones (Eds.), *The Broadview anthology of poetry.* (pp. 42–43). Ontario: The Broadview Press.

Hannel, G. (2003). *Highly effective questioning: Developing the seven steps of critical thinking.* Phoenix, AZ: Hannel Publications.

Hannel, G. (2003, October). Highly effective questioning. *Texas Association for Bilingual Education Newsletter,* 1.

Hunter, M. (1982). *Mastery teaching.* El Segundo, California: TIP Publications.

Kegan, R., & Lahey, L. (2000). *How the way we talk can change the way we work: Seven languages for transformation.* San Francisco: Jossey-Bass.

Lubliner, S. (2001, November). Reciprocal teaching: An alternative to gatekeeping practices. *Classroom Leadership,* 1–5.

Marzano, R., Pickering, D., & Pollock, J. (2001). *Classroom instruction that works: Research-based strategies for increasing student achievement.* Alexandria, VA: Association for Supervision and Curriculum Development (ASCD).

Woolf, H (ed). (1994). *Merriam-Webster dictionary,* (10th ed.). Springfield, MA: Merriam-Webster.

Monroe, L. (2003). *The Monroe Doctrine.* New York: Public Affairs Inc.

Nolet, V., & McLaughlin, M. (2000). *Accessing the general curriculum: Including students with disabilities in standards-based reform.* Thousand Oaks, CA: Corwin Press Inc.

Rosenthal, R., & Jacobson, L. (1968). *Pygmalion in the classroom: Teacher expectations and pupils' intellectual ability.* New York: Holt, Rinehart & Winston Inc.

Rowe, M. (1987, Spring). Wait time: Slowing down may be a way of speeding up. *American Educator,* 38–43.

Stahl, R. (1994, May). Using think time and wait time skillfully in the classroom. *ERIC Clearinghouse for Social Studies/Social Science Education,* 1–4.

CHAPTER

6

Using Teacher-Made, Local and State Assessments to Inform Your Instruction

Objectives for the Chapter
After reading the chapter, the reader will be able to
a. describe the various purposes for assessment
b. define the similarities and differences between summative and formative assessments
c. define the similarities and differences between product and performance assessments
d. create teacher-made product and performance assessments that assess the level of student mastery on the stated objectives both formatively and summatively
e. write rubrics that assess student products and performances on those concepts that are difficult to quantify for assessment

Definition and Purpose of Assessment

What is it that we want to know about our students? What tools will help us best gather this information? What will we do with this information once we have interpreted and analyzed the results? Most importantly, how will this assessment further the learning and teaching process? These are all questions that we as teachers must ask ourselves as we plan and prepare our curriculum goals and assessments.

In order to truly understand assessment, one must think about how we view learning. What is learning? How do we measure it? Grant Wiggins (1993) differentiates between learning and measurement. His view is such that "understanding[1] is not cued knowledge; performance is never the sum of drills; problems are not exercises; mastery is not achieved by the unthinking of algorithms. In other words, we cannot be said to understand something unless we employ our knowledge wisely, fluently, and aptly in particular and diverse contexts" (p. 200). **Learning** should be viewed as the process of constructing meaning rather than accumulating a number of skills.

Today, **assessment** encompasses *observing, teaching, describing, collecting, recording, scoring* and *interpreting* information about a student's learning. Assessment is interwoven into the teaching and learning process and it occurs on a continual basis. It is a process that requires two-way communication between the teacher and the students to provide accurate and meaningful information that the teacher and the student may use for improving student learning, instructional practices and educational options in the classroom.

The three major purposes of assessment may be categorized as follows: to improve student learning and performance, to improve teaching and to improve schools (Stuart, 2003).

Improving student learning and performance is the primary reason to assess students, however, assessments must be aligned with the instructional practices of the teacher in order to be truly effective. It is important that the teacher communicates a student's progress relative to the stated learning goal to both the parents and the student. The assessment should provide evidence of what a student understands as well as how learning may be furthered in a particular area of study. "It is an ongoing process with a cycle of learning, teaching, assessing, providing feedback,[2] reflecting, more learning, and around again" (Stuart, 2003, p. 34).

Assessments also provide teachers with *tools to help improve instruction,* assuming they are aligned with instructional practices. As teachers document students' learning, they are better able to make appropriate adjustments to meet the needs of individual students. Such reflective teaching fosters improved teaching and learning. Figure 6-1 (author unknown) provides a form that a teacher may use, after an assessment is given, to help students improve their performance.

Figure 6-1
Using Results to Improve Performance

What have I determined that the student knows from this assessment?

What is the student ready to learn?

What does this student need to practice?

What does this student need to be retaught?

---

[1] In this book, we use the term *application mastery* for the level of learning that Wiggins calls *"understanding."*

[2] You will see the word *feedback* used frequently in this chapter. When it appears in quotes from other authors, we have left the term as it appears in those authors' works. In those instances when we use the term *feedback* we are referring to a very specific type of information that the teacher provides the student about his/or her performance. Feedback as we use it is neither praise, recommendations, nor criticism. It is specific information about the student's performance as it relates to the desired performance. It is only used when the student clearly knows the standard for success. An example of feedback given to a student who has been taught that a paragraph needs a topic sentence, at least three supporting sentences and a closing sentence would be as follows:

Your paragraph contains a topic sentence and three supporting sentences. It does not have a closing sentence.

Assessments may also be used to improve schools as their use connects all members of the school community in striving towards continuous improvement. A school-wide assessment system encourages the participation of the whole school community. "As community support for assessment expands through greater understanding of the school's goals and achievements, the ongoing school improvement needs are also recognized and addressed" (Stuart, 2003, p. 35).

Assessment for Learning

Assessment for learning may be described as the process of seeking and interpreting evidence to be used by teachers and students in determining where learners are in their learning, where they need to go and how best to get there. Such assessment is critical to maximizing learning for all students. However, assessment *for* learning is not to be confused with assessment *of* learning which is often intended to be used for grading and reporting purposes (ARG, 1999). Research has shown (Black and Wiliam, 1998) that one of the most powerful ways of improving learning and raising standards is through assessment for learning. Assessment for learning is in contrast to traditional modes of assessment in many ways. Figure 6-2 outlines the differences between the characteristics of assessment for learning and those of assessment of learning.

However, assessment *for* learning is not to be confused with assessment *of* learning which is often intended to be used for grading and reporting purposes (ARG, 1999).

Figure 6-2

Assessment for Learning	*Assessment of Learning*
Embedded in the teaching and learning process and is ongoing	Typically occurs at the end of a unit of study
Focuses on how and what students learn	Focuses solely on what students have learned
Teachers work in teams to construct assessments	Teachers use commercially produced tests
Focuses on constructive feedback	Focuses on grade or mark
At the outset of the learning, students understand the learning goals and criteria that will be used for assessment	Learning goals and criteria used to assess are unknown to students
Fosters motivation for learning	Fosters motivation for grades
Main goal is to improve understanding	High marks/grades are celebrated
Self-assessment is key ingredient	Self-assessment is not used
All educational achievement is recognized	

The following twelve characteristics of assessment for learning are based in part on the 10 research-based principles created by The Assessment Reform Group (2002).

Assessment for learning is part of effective planning of teaching and learning. A teacher's plans should include opportunities for both the students and the teacher to acquire and use information about the progress students have made towards the stated learning goal(s).

Learners need to understand the goals they are pursuing as well as the criteria that will be used to assess their work. In addition, a teacher needs to clearly state how the students will receive feedback, how students will participate in assessing their own learning and how they will be helped to make further progress towards the stated goal(s). In Chapter 1, we discussed planning our teaching in ways that facilitate this type of assessment.

Assessment for learning should focus on how students learn. Both teachers and students should be concerned with the process of learning when the assessment is planned and carried out. It is essential that learners be as aware of *how* they learn as they are of *what* they learn in order to promote growth and understanding of the content. Students should be aware of how they are going to be assessed, that is, what tools or techniques will be used by the teacher. For example, if a rubric is going to be used, it should be shared with the students beforehand. Later in this chapter, we provide a comprehensive explanation of rubrics and their use.

For example, if a rubric is going to be used, it should be shared with the students beforehand.

Teachers need to inform students about why they are being assessed and how the results are going to be used. Too often, teachers neglect to tell students the purpose of a particular assessment. As students better understand the purposes of assessment, they will be able to more effectively use the results and feedback to improve their learning.

Assessment for learning is central to classroom practice. Much of what teachers and students do in the classroom may be described as assessment. Effective assessment practices will mirror instructional activities. The lines among instructional practices, lesson activities and assessment tasks should be blurred. The tasks and questions teachers ask of students encourage them to show their knowledge, understanding and skills. As a teacher observes and interprets what learners say and do, they are able to more effectively plan instruction so as to best meet the needs of all students. Such assessment processes are critical to maximizing learning, and they include teachers and learners in reflection, dialogue and decision-making.

Assessment for learning is a key professional skill. Teachers must clearly understand how to plan assessments, observe learning, analyze and interpret evidence of learning, give feedback to students in a constructive manner and support students in self-assessment. Later in the chapter, we discuss in depth the developing of students' skills of self-assessment. Teachers must be given opportunities to develop and maintain these critical skills through initial and on-going professional development. Chapters 10 and 11 describe examples of high quality professional development that helps teachers to develop these skills.

Assessment for learning is sensitive and constructive. Teachers' comments and grades may greatly impact a learner's confidence and motivation. As such, comments should be as constructive as possible. Teacher comments should focus on the quality of the work, rather than on the student. When teacher comments are properly focused, student performance improves.

Assessment for learning fosters motivation. In order to encourage students' learning and motivation, progress and achievement should be emphasized, rather than failure. Comparison to other students should be avoided as it has a negative impact on the learning environment. Assessments should

- protect the student's autonomy by comparing their work to the standard, rather than to that of other students
- provide students some choice as to the method by which they demonstrate the concept

- offer constructive comments
- create opportunities for self-direction

Assessment for learning promotes understanding of goals and criteria. Learners need to both understand their learning goals and desire to achieve them in order for effective learning to occur. When students participate in the decision-making process—for example, by deciding the criteria for assessing their progress and using the information from the assessment to set their individual learning goals—they will better understand what is expected of them and consequently be more committed to the learning process. Teachers should discuss assessment criteria with their students in terms they understand and provide specific examples of how students may meet the established criteria. Students and parents[3] need to understand the process of how the students will be assessed. They must be informed about what students need to know and how they are expected to illustrate their knowledge. Learners should also be engaged in both peer- and self-assessment.

When students participate in the decision-making process—for example, by deciding the criteria for assessing their progress and using the information from the assessment to set their individual learning goals—they will better understand what is expected of them and consequently be more committed to the learning process.

Assessment for learning helps learners know how to improve. Teachers are responsible for guiding students in their learning. Teachers should highlight the student's strengths and offer guidance for further developing them. Weaknesses should be clearly addressed in a manner that is constructive to the student so that the student understands how learning may be furthered. Finally, teachers must provide students with opportunities to improve their work and demonstrate any new understandings.

Assessment for learning develops capacity for self-assessment. Students need to learn how to gain new skills, knowledge and understanding. It is essential that they are able to self-reflect and identify the next steps to further their learning. Teachers may help students acquire these lifelong skills by helping them understand how to self-assess or reflect on what they are learning and how well they are doing. Later in this chapter, we take an in-depth look at student self-assessment.

Assessment for learning recognizes all educational achievement. Assessment for learning should be utilized to help all learners achieve their maximum potential in all areas of the curriculum.

Assessment for learning minimizes the following factors which have been found to be inhibitors of assessment for learning (Assessment Reform Group, 2002).

- a tendency for teachers to assess quantity of work and quality of presentation, rather than the quality of learning
- greater attention is given to grading, tending to lower the self-esteem of the pupils, rather than providing suggestions for improvement
- strong emphasis is placed on comparing students which demoralizes the lower achieving students
- teachers' feedback to students often provides a social and managerial purpose, rather than helping the students to learn more effectively
- teachers not clearly understanding the needs of the learners

[3] Chapter 9 takes an in-depth look at techniques for effectively communicating with parents.

Formative and Summative Assessments

Teachers assess students for a myriad of reasons. Both teachers and students need to clearly understand the specific purpose of an assessment, and a particular assessment should be used for only one purpose at a time. Mixed purpose assessments do not work well. Inevitably, they shortchange one of the purposes because different design demands exist for different types of assessments (Bloom et al. 1981 in Saphier & Gower, 1997). For example, an assessment designed to provide feedback to students about their strengths and weaknesses would look very different from an assessment developed to make summative statements about how well students have done overall in meeting unit objectives. It is critical that teachers are clear about the purpose of a planned assessment because of the design requirements of various types.

Summative assessments may be described as ongoing assessments that are separated from teaching and provide a mark in the form of a grade, score on a criteria reference test or a local or national norm score for the student. Such assessments are often used by teachers at the culmination of a unit to sum up the learning that has occurred in a particular area of study. The purpose for which a teacher is assessing in large part determines which type of assessment will be given to students.

> *The purpose for which a teacher is assessing in large part determines which type of assessment will be given to students.*

The following are some of the purposes for summative assessment.

1. States use summative assessment data from competency tests to certify that the student acquired the requisite skills and knowledge for a particular grade.
2. States use summative assessment data from competency tests to determine the level of success or failure of a particular district.
3. In support of the No Child Left Behind Act, the federal government uses summative assessment data from competency tests to determine "adequate yearly progress."
4. Districts use summative assessment data to evaluate whether or not the curriculum is teaching the desired skills and knowledge in a particular subject area and/or at a particular grade level.
5. Districts use summative assessment data to sort students for participation in certain courses and to determine which level (e.g., standard, honors, advanced placement) of a specific course the student should be enrolled.
6. Schools use summative assessment data to rank or compare students for honors and awards or for admission into programs with limited enrollment.
7. Summative assessment data is used to norm students or groups of students in comparing their achievement relative to national groups or other populations. (Later in this chapter, we discuss standardized testing and district, state and national assessments.)
8. The Scholastic Aptitude Test (SAT) uses summative assessment data to predict students' potential for success in their first year of college.
9. Employers and the military use summative assessment data to predict their staff's potential for success in certain jobs.
10. For the purpose of giving a grade, teachers use quizzes at the end of unit sections to assess each student's and the class' levels of mastery on the information and skills taught in each section of the unit.
11. For the purpose of giving a grade, teachers use tests at the end of units to check each student's and the class' levels of mastery on the information and skills taught in each unit.
12. Teachers use activators to assess students' present knowledge at the outset of teaching a new unit.

Formative assessments may be described as assessments that are that are embedded in the teaching. They provide the teacher and students with information about the students' levels of mastery during instruction. The teacher uses this information to modify the teaching to better meet the needs of the students. The students use the information to determine what they know and do not know, so they may ask questions or seek information in other ways to fill in the gaps in their learning. The following are some examples of formative assessment.

1. The teacher asks a recall question about some specific information that has been presented thus far during the lesson.[4]
2. The teacher asks a comprehension question that requires students to apply the information that has been presented thus far in the lesson.
3. The teacher displays on the overhead a math problem that reflects the concept that has been taught thus far in the lesson. Students solve the problem on their individual white boards. The students all hold their boards up together, so the teacher may scan the room and see who has solved the problem correctly, who has not and where students have difficulty in solving it.[5]
4. Students self-assess their progress against a criteria sheet, rubric and/or an exemplar.
5. Students peer-assess each other's work based on a criteria sheet, rubric and/or an exemplar.
6. The teacher observes students working independently or in groups and takes anecdotal notes.
7. For the purpose of deciding whether to move the class on to new concepts or reteach, remediate and/or extend the previously taught concepts, teachers use quizzes at the end of unit sections to assess each student's and the class' levels of mastery on the information and skills taught in each section .
8. For the purpose of deciding whether to move the class on to a new unit or reteach, remediate and/or extend the previously taught concepts, teachers use tests at the end of units to check each student's and the class' levels of mastery on the information and skills taught in each unit.
9. Teachers use in-class assignments to check students' ability to apply the learning independently. The teacher checks these assignments and uses the information gathered to plan instruction for the next day of class.
10. Teachers use homework assignments to check the students' ability to apply the learning independently at home.

Types of Assessment

Wiggins and McTighe (1998) have identified and classified three different categories of assessments. These categories are *quiz and test items, academic prompts* and *performance tasks and projects.* Wiggins and McTighe (1998) describe **quiz and test items** as including simplistic, content-focused items and questions. They

- assess for factual information, concepts and/or discrete skills
- use selected-response or short answer formats

[4] More information on questioning techniques that check student understanding can be found in Chapter 5.

[5] Strategies for checking the understanding of all the students at one time are known by a term coined by Madeline Hunter, *dipsticking.* More information on dipsticking can be found in Chapter 5.

- are convergent and usually have one best answer
- may be easily corrected with an answer key
- are typically unknown to the students in advance

Wiggins and McTighe (1998) describe **academic prompts** as "open-ended questions or problems in which the student must think critically and apply acquired knowledge to prepare a response, product, or performance." More information on questions that promote higher order thinking can be found in Chapter 5.

Wiggins and McTighe (1998) describe **performance tasks and projects** "as complex challenges that are realistic and authentic. They may range in length from short-term to long-term, and require a final product or performance. They are in contrast to academic prompts in that they

- feature a setting that is real and authentic, one students and/or adults may encounter in their everyday life.
- usually require a student to address a particular audience.
- are based on a specific purpose related to the audience.
- allow the student greater opportunity to personalize the task.
- are known in advance. The task, criteria, and standards help guide the student throughout the process."

An example of a performance assessment developed for use with the book *Night of the Twisters* by Ivy Ruckman may be found later in this chapter.

As educators understand how assessment may be used in more productive ways, more students will be successful learners in the classroom environment. Assessment should be a means of promoting success, not simply measuring it. According to Black and Wiliam (1998), students achieved unprecedented score gains on standardized tests when the principles of assessment for learning were applied by teachers. Teachers may improve their daily assessments, make their comments to students more constructive and more actively involve students in the assessment process with appropriate training and understanding of the process. "In this way, classroom assessment for learning becomes a school improvement tool that helps create responsible, engaged, and self-directed learners" (Chappuis & Stiggins, 2002, p. 43).

Assessment should be a means of promoting success, not simply measuring it.

Performance Assessment and Product Assessment

Performance assessment may be defined as any assessment in which students demonstrate the knowledge they have acquired in a meaningful context. Performance assessments should also be authentic in that they provide students with tasks that are realistic and measure skills and outcomes that students need to use in their daily lives. **Product assessments** are the results of a performance assessment being completed, and they are what the teacher examines to determine what students have learned. Performance and product assessments may take on a variety of forms. Performance assessments may appear on standardized tests as well as in the classroom, however, these assessments must be designed in such a way that students are afforded the opportunity to connect, explain and demonstrate their knowledge in a broader context that makes it their own.

Performance Assessments: Guidelines for Success

Performance tasks contribute to the authenticity and richness of a curriculum. Students are required to use multiple skills as well as apply knowledge they have gained in a meaningful way. It is important, however, that both teachers and students carefully plan the task. In addition, teachers must provide students with consistent and constructive feedback throughout the process. Figure 6-3 highlights the guidelines that teachers should follow in order to ensure a successful experience for their students.

Figure 6-3
Creating an Effective Performance Assessment

1. Performance tasks must take into account both process and product. At every stage of the process, feedback should be provided.
2. Performance tasks should be manageable for both students and teachers.
3. Performance tasks should be purposeful and should include clearly defined criteria and standards. Well-defined steps should help guide the students through this process.
4. Performance tasks should be developmentally appropriate. Teachers must scaffold and differentiate tasks in order for all students to achieve success. Students should be encouraged to take risks. Teachers need to provide encouragement and direction.
5. Performance tasks are more successful when developed by a team of teachers as they are complex and take time to construct.
6. Performance assessment tasks may require an authentic performance that uses ideas and skills that are part of our everyday lives. These tasks may also require the use of discrete skills.
7. Performance tasks should encourage students to think in new ways, develop a deeper understanding and demonstrate greater complexity in their thinking.

Adapted from Stuart (2003)

Figure 6-4 illustrates a performance assessment task that was given to fifth-grade students after completing a literature unit based on the book *Night of the Twisters* by Ivy Ruckman. This book was used to teach students a variety of comprehension strategies as well as the elements of a story. In addition to demonstrating their understanding of this particular story, students were also asked to show their knowledge of the comprehension strategies and elements of a story on this assessment. Students were given a week to work on this task in class. The teacher observed students as they worked and offered both written and oral constructive feedback regarding their progress. In some cases, students needed suggestions as to how to include all of the expected elements to meet the criteria. Other students needed redirection to correctly sequence the events of the story. In some cases, students needed assistance in getting started, that is, coming up with a workable plan. The rubric used to assess their work was shared and discussed with the students before they began working.

Figure 6-4
Night of the Twisters Assessment

You will have the opportunity to choose one of the following projects to complete as your assessment for this literature unit of study. Although every project will be different, all students must include the following components.

1. *Comprehension Strategies*
   Show your understanding of the text through one or more of the following strategies:
   - *visualizing/sensory images*
   - *making connections (self–text, text–text, text–world)*
   - *summarizing*
   - *understanding difficult vocabulary words*
2. *Elements of a Story*
   Be sure to include these story elements.
   - *character*
   - *setting*
   - *main events in chronological order*
3. *Mechanics*
   Please be sure you have proofread for the following:
   - *correct paragraphing*
   - *correct punctuation*
   - *correct capitalization*
   - *correct spelling*

Projects

1. ***In paragraph form, retell*** *the story of how the* Night of the Twisters *traveled through* Grand Island, Nebraska, *and how it changed the lives of the characters. Organize your story in sequential order. Use the story map graphic organizer to help you organize your thoughts and ideas.*
2. ***Create a picture book.*** *List and describe all important events and characters in the story. Draw pictures illustrating each event and character from your list. Arrange the events and corresponding pictures in the order that reflects the sequence of the story.*
3. ***Create a cause and effect flowchart.*** *Use the cause–effect graphic organizer to help you organize your work. On the left-hand side, write the different causes of a tornado. On the right-hand side, write the effects of a tornado hitting a town. Pay attention to the sequence of events as you prepare your chart. Use the text as well as other resources (books, internet, etc.) to gather your information.*
4. ***Compose a message.*** *Recall information from the book about tornadoes. Tell how you think the characters felt during this weather disaster and tell about a similar experience (or connection) that you have had. Create a message, poem, song or some other token that expresses feelings of sympathy for the tornado victims and how the tornado changed their lives.*
5. **TV Weather Forecaster.** *Using vocabulary words from* Night of the Twisters, *write a weather forecast including the events before, during and after the tornadoes swept through* Grand Island, Nebraska, *on June 4, 1980.*
6. ***Create a PowerPoint® presentation.*** *Imagine that you are making a documentary video about the Nebraska tornadoes. Plan how you would present the story of the tornadoes in a documentary and make a list of the important scenes and characters you would cover. Based on your plan, create a PowerPoint® presentation for the documentary. Include as many vocabulary words as you can. (Refer to your reading journal for ideas.)*

Night of the Twisters Assessment Rubric

4	3	2	1	*Student Score and Comments*	*Teacher Score and Comments*
One or more comprehension strategies reflected in detail	*One or more comprehension strategies reflected*	*One or more comprehension strategies not accurately reflected*	*One or more comprehension strategies not reflected*		
All elements of a story accurately incorporated	*Most elements of a story accurately incorporated*	*Some elements of a story incorporated*	*Elements of a story not incorporated*		
Your paragraphing, punctuation, spelling, and capitalization reflect your wonderful abilities.	*Your paragraphing, punctuation, spelling, and capitalization need some editing.*	*Your paragraphing, punctuation, spelling, and capitalization need some editing.*	*Your paragraphing, punctuation, spelling, and capitalization need much editing.*		

Characteristics of Good Assessment Tasks

A **good assessment task** is one that is meaningful, purposeful and connected to everyday life. Figure 6-5 highlights the essential criteria for assessment tasks that foster higher level learning.

Figure 6-5

Authenticity	• Does the task reflect real-life situations? • Does it require multiple levels of understanding?
Credibility	• Is the task purposeful in that it helps students achieve the learning goals established for the unit? • Is the task aligned with other standards set at the district, state and/or national level? • Is the task connected to an overarching question?
Validity	• Does the task assess what it claims to assess? • Does the task provide sufficient evidence of learning? • Does the task require multiple forms of written and oral evidence of learning? • Does the evidence allow us to make accurate inferences about student understanding?
Reliability	• Does the evidence accurately reflect a student's abilities? • May the task be used over time to show a student's progress in a particular area?
Feasibility	• Can the task be completed in a timely manner? • Is the task feasible in terms of logistics and resources?
User-Friendliness	• Is the task appropriate, engaging and beneficial to the teacher and student? • Does the task challenge the students? • Does the task make sense to the students? • Are there clear instructions, guidelines and criteria for the task?
Fairness	• Is the assessment equitable for all students? • Are the standards and criteria clearly established?

Adapted from Stuart (2003), Wiggins and McTighe (1998), Herman, Aschbacher and Winters (1992), and Mitchell, Wills, and the Chicago Teachers Union Quest Center (1995)

Gathering Information

Teaching and learning are interconnected, occur simultaneously and, as such, must be interwoven to function effectively. Teachers must clearly understand their students' strengths and weaknesses in learning in order to adapt their teaching to best meet the needs of their learners. These needs are often unpredictable and vary from student to student, adding to the complexity of a teacher's work (Black & Wiliam, 1998).

Teaching and learning are interconnected, occur simultaneously and, as such, must be interwoven to function effectively.

Fortunately, teachers have a variety of tools and techniques they may use to gather information about their students, that is, to assess the progress of their students. General sources of assessment evidence that may be collected in the classroom may be categorized as follows: *observations* of learning, *products* students create and *conversations* discussing learning with students (Primary Program, 1990, 2000, in Davies, 2000). It is important for teachers to collect evidence from different sources over time in order to increase the reliability and validity of classroom evidence (Davies, 2000).

Observations of Learning

Observations are a powerful source of information. They include a teacher's observance of either anything a student is doing or the performance of a task he or she has asked a student to do. Observations are critical to ensuring the validity and reliability of classroom assessment as some learning may only be observed. Some students, particularly younger children, have difficulty writing about what they know and need opportunities to present their knowledge in action. Observation may also be effectively used with projects "under construction" as a teacher may observe and offer feedback to students as they are engaged in the learning process (Davies, 2000).

The purpose of the activity will determine the focus of your observations. The following questions may be useful when designing focused observations and will be helpful in designing subsequent learning activities (Davies, 2000).

- What is the purpose of the learning activity? What are students to learn?
- What particular focus will I choose for this observation?
- How will I record and organize my observations so they are useful?

Figure 6-6 outlines some possible activities that teachers might observe.

Figure 6-6
Observing Learning

Oral/Kinesthetic Presentations	***Labs/Project-Based Work***
• Formal and informal presentations • Drama presentations • Music-related activities • Reading aloud • Talking about one's work • Persuading • Giving opinions • Debating • Charades • Dances • Demonstrations • Giving instructions • Reader's Theater	• Scientific method being applied • Planning and designing a Web page • Planning and designing a PowerPoint® presentation • Measuring objects • Cartooning • Simulations
Written Reports • Persuading • Writing opinions • Writing instructions • Following instructions • Journal entries • Reflections	***Group Work*** • Group or partner activities • Listening to others • Debating • Communicating ideas to others • Conflict resolution • Discussions • Giving and receiving descriptive feedback

Tools and Techniques for Observing and Documenting Student Learning

Teachers may keep track of their observations in a variety of ways. It is essential that as teachers observe their students, they are recording information that is pertinent to the established learning goals. This section highlights methods that teachers have found particularly helpful when keeping track of students' learning.

- *Clipboard with class list, checklist or observation guide.* For example, if you are observing students engaged in literature circles, it is not enough to observe that a student has come prepared to the discussion. Rather, you might choose to observe that the summarizer has properly summarized the main points of the chapter or the vocabulary enricher has correctly defined identified terms as well as used these words appropriately in sentences. The teacher might then use information from these observations to address the group's problem areas when teaching a mini-lesson, determining how to group students or providing students with additional practice activities. These observations will also provide evidence of progress for students.
- *Spiral notebook with tabs for each student to be used in recording observations.* This tool may be helpful for looking at student growth over time, and the information gathered may be particularly useful during parent–teacher conferences and when writing progress reports.
- *White board to record comments and observations.*
- *Classroom computer for students or teachers to use in making conference notes.*
- *Tape recorder to record group presentations, literature circles, collaborative mathematical activities, writing conferences, etc.* (You will learn more about how to do this in Chapters 3 and 10.)
- *Video recorder to film group presentations, literature circles, collaborative math activities, writing conferences, etc.*
- *Journals or notebooks to use in documenting student work.* Interactive observational assessment is a technique in which students write in journals about their thinking and/or the processes they use to complete a task and the teacher responds in writing by asking questions or making comments to promote further thinking. Such interaction helps the student to move to deeper levels of understanding of the content. This strategy can be used as an on-going assessment piece, serving as a record that can be revisited in the future (Albert, Mayotte, & Sohn, 2002).

Although using the strategy of interactive observation may seem unwieldy, it may be a manageable and effective strategy if used in situations that are conducive to circulating around the classroom to interact with individual students in which specific comments may be necessary to further students' thinking. In addition, it may be helpful to tentatively determine ahead of time when you are going to interact with each of your students. It is not feasible to write in more than 5–8 journals during one class period.

One teacher who uses the interactive observational strategy in her mathematics class finds it works well with activities that involve algorithms and open-ended problems with which students work independently. As students work on problem-solving activities, they are asked to record step-by-step in their math journals the processes they use to solve each particular problem. As the students record their thinking, the teacher circulates around the classroom and reads their developing thoughts. She responds to the students' thoughts in their notebooks by posing a question or commenting in a way that promotes further thinking. See Figure 6-7 for an excerpt from a journal during an interactive session. "Writing descriptions of mathematical reasoning allows students to reflect on their own work, explain their thoughts, and gain insight into their own thinking" (Albert, 2000).

Figure 6-7
Paragraph on Probability

Student Response: I think that the coin lands on heads 50% of the time because there are 2 sides of the coin. If there were 6 sides of a die, you would have a 1/6 chance of it landing on your number.

Teacher Response: If you rolled again...(a six sided die) would it still be a 1/6 of a chance that you would get a particular number?

Student Response: Yes, it would because there are 6 sides and the chances of it landing on that particular number will still be the same. (Some people would say that it would be less of a chance, but I think that is a superstition.)

Teacher Response: Good logic...We'll learn about six-sided die rolling a little later. I think you will be surprised at the results.

From Sheila Cutler Sohn's Classroom (2002)

This particular teacher uses this strategy one to two times per week and occasionally collects her students' journals to allow for additional time to assess student work. For students who have difficulty with writing or are not native speakers of English, special arrangements should be made with the special educator or an assistant when this form of assessment is being implemented. Students with fine motor difficulties may need to type their work on a computer (Albert, Mayotte, & Sohn, 2002).

Figure 6-8 offers suggestions for teachers implementing an interactive observational assessment during mathematics instruction.

Figure 6-8

- *Maximize classroom space for easy movement.* Seating students in groups allows a teacher to access students more easily. In addition, you may decide to target a cluster of students seated together to write in their journals. In this way, it may be easier to keep track of students with whom you have interacted.
- *Use a variety of problem-solving and critical thinking activities.* A variety of written questions and comments helps teachers better assess students' mathematical thinking and, consequently, scaffold their learning. Comments should be as specific as possible.
- *Write in every student's notebook.* Interacting with all students over the course of several sessions is important. In order for students to value this process, they need to know that the teacher might write in their journals during any of the interactive sessions. A special educator or assistant might also write in the journals if assisting in the classroom at the time.
- *Revisit students a second or even third time to write in their journals.* Teachers should let students know that they may revisit their work more than once during an interactive session to encourage new and deeper ways of thinking. Revisiting journals sends the message to students that they are accountable for responding to your comments.
- *Write brief, clear and direct questions and comments.* Write something to which the student may respond immediately. Keeping questions brief will help students to write more precisely with regards to their mathematical reasoning.
- *Use this strategy with other assessment techniques.* After using this strategy, the teacher should follow up with whole class discussions as both oral and written communication are important in mathematics.

Adapted from Albert, Mayotte, & Sohn, 2002

Collecting Products

Teachers collect a variety of evidence to show what knowledge students possess. Such evidence includes projects, assignments, notebooks, journals, quizzes and tests. As Gardner's theories of multiple intelligences are becoming more widespread and better understood, teachers are providing students with expanded opportunities to express their knowledge in a manner that is appropriate to their particular learning styles (Gardner 1984; Sternberg, 1996 in Davies, 2000). More teachers are providing students with choice with regard to the form their final product will take. Some teachers and students generate a list of ideas of how they may represent their work. Figure 6-9 highlights possible products students might create.

Figure 6-9
Ideas for Student Products

Oral/Written Reports	***Technology Projects***	***Creative Projects***
• Write a story. • Make an oral presentation. • Write a poem. • Write a report. • Write a song/rap. • Write a play. • Write a journal entry.	• Design a Web page. • Create a PowerPoint® presentation. • Make a video. • Make an audiotape.	• Draw a diagram. • Make a timeline. • Make a poster. • Build a model. • Create a puzzle. • Design a t-shirt. • Create a collage. • Build a diorama/model.

Adapted from Davies (2000)

Providing learners with guidance and support in the form of constructive comments along the way is necessary to ensure that optimal learning occurs.

It is important to clearly outline the criteria and expectations for students for any given product. Later in this chapter, creating and using rubrics with students will be discussed. Providing learners with guidance and support in the form of constructive comments along the way is necessary to ensure that optimal learning occurs.

Conversations Centered Around Learning

Conversations about learning allow teachers to acquire information about a students' thoughts, understandings and feelings about their learning in a given subject area. Such conversations may occur in writing or in person and may take place during class meetings or during individual or group conferences as well as when students' self-assessments are read.

We encourage students to think about their learning when we engage in conversations with students in these ways. We gather evidence about students' knowledge and understanding as we listen to them think and explain. Through such dialogue, it becomes apparent what was difficult or easy for students, what risks they took and what they might do differently next time (Davies, 2000). With this knowledge, teachers are better able to support students in the most effective manner. When teachers take the time to engage students in self-assessment, learning is maximized (Black & Wiliam, 1998; Young, 2000).

Teachers may use the following questions to obtain information about their students. These questions may be used either in an oral conversation or through a written activity. It is important to prepare a list of questions ahead of time, however, student responses may necessitate asking different questions from those originally planned.

When students solve open-ended mathematical problems, they often misinterpret what the question is asking them to do. The following questions may be used to determine whether or not the student is properly interpreting a problem-solving activity (Stenmark, 1991).

- What is the task about?
- How would you interpret that?
- What can you tell me about it?
- Would you explain that in your own words?
- Can any information be eliminated or is there any missing information?

In addition, it is important to help students formulate a plan. Students need an organized approach to the task. The following questions may be used to assess whether or not students have chosen an appropriate plan and strategy (Stenmark, 1991).

- Where might you find the needed information?
- What have you tried? What steps did you take?
- How did you organize the information? Do you have a system or strategy to solve this problem?
- Can you explain your strategy or plan to me?

The following example illustrates how this questioning technique was used during a problem-solving task.

Problem: Derrick is planning his tenth birthday party. He invited ten classmates and plans to order 3 eight-slice pizzas. If Derrick and his friends (who happen to really love pizza!) eat 3 pieces each, will he run out of food at this birthday pizza party? Explain and show how you determined your answer.

Teacher: In your own words, tell me what this problem is asking you to do.

Student: I need to find out if Derrick will have enough pizza for his friends at his birthday party.

Teacher: How many people will be eating pizza?

Student: Ten.

Teacher: Let's go back to the problem and carefully reread the highlighted information. (Teacher gives the student time to reread the problem.)

Student: Oh, we need to include Derrick in our count for pizza, too. So there will be eleven people eating pizza.

Teacher: What other information will you use to help you figure out this problem?

Student: We need to know how many pizzas they are ordering, and in the problem it says 3 eight-slice pizzas.

Teacher: What strategy or strategies will you use?

Student: I might draw a visual.

Student: Making an equation.

Student: Guess, check and revise.

Teacher: Can you explain how you would use that strategy?

In this example, the conversation that occurred between the teacher and student allowed the teacher to understand where the student was experiencing confusion. It became clear to the teacher that the student was not correctly identifying what the problem was asking him to do, and he was not using all the important information that was given in the problem. Fortunately, by prompting the student with guiding questions, the teacher was able to help the student clearly understand the problem. In this case, the student was able to find an accurate solution to the problem.

The following resource may be used for more information on this topic:

Stenmark, J. K. (1991). *Modern assessment: Myths, models, good questions, and practical suggestions*. Reston, VA: National Council of Teachers of Mathematics.

Student Self-Assessment: A Key Ingredient in the Assessment Process

Involving learners in the process of assessment, that is, providing them with opportunities to assess their own work, helps students deepen their understanding of the learning process. Students are able to learn more effectively when they are provided with opportunities to play an active role. Some of the strategies we use to promote self-assessment include

1. sharing the learning objectives to facilitate self-assessment as students better understand the learning goals for which they are striving
2. providing students with recommendations, commendations and feedback that helps students determine what steps they need to take next to further their learning
3. creating an environment that promotes risk-taking since students must feel supported and confident in their environment in order to take risks
4. using rubrics, criteria sheets, exemplars, anchor papers and other items that enable students to assess their performance against clearly evident standards
5. planning student self-assessment time into the lesson

Students must feel supported and confident in their environment in order to take risks.

Benefits of Self-Assessment for the Teacher and Student

Self-assessment is an essential component in assessment for learning, and, as such, it must be embedded in the learning and teaching that occurs in the classroom. Students take responsibility for their learning and become active in this process when they self-assess (Gator, Jones, et al., 2000). Figure 6-10 illustrates the benefits for both students and teachers when self-assessment is implemented.

Figure 6-10
Benefits of Self-Assessment

Students...	***Teachers...***
• become more responsible for own learning • are able to recognize next steps in learning • feel secure about not always being right • raise self-esteem • are actively involved in the learning process • become more independent and motivated	• shift more responsibility to students • are able to plan smoother, more efficient, challenging lessons as students are independent and motivated • benefit from feedback as it helps them identify students' progress • are better able to identify next steps for a group and/or individual • are able to identify thinking process as students explain their strategies

Adapted from Gator, C. et al. (2000, April 15)

Teachers should encourage students to think about the following questions in order to help facilitate self-reflection.

- Am I learning in the best way for me?
- What strategies help me learn best?
- What can I remember and understand?
- What questions do I still have?
- Where do I have to focus my revision?
- What are my learning goals?
- What are my strengths and weaknesses?
- How am I doing?
- What is really making me think?
- How will I know if my work is good?
- What do I need to do in order to improve?
- How am I going to make this improvement?

The ability to self-assess is within the realm of possibility for all students. When students consistently self-assess, they take more responsibility for their learning (Shephard, 2001, in Chappuis and Stiggins, 2002). It provides students with a means of monitoring and communicating to others the progress they have made in their learning.

Self-Assessment Forms

To help children reflect upon their own work, it is important for teachers to provide them with tools to help guide their thinking. This section provides a variety of self-assessment forms that are appropriate for different situations. Figure 6-11 is a general assessment form that may be used at the beginning, middle and end of year to help children think about where they are and where they are going in terms of their learning. It also encourages them to think about how they learn. It asks them to write about both their strengths and weaknesses as well as set goals for the remainder of the year. In addition, the teacher should follow up with the student either in writing or by conferencing with him or her.

Figure 6-11

All About My Learning

On a scale of 1–10 (1 being never, 10 being always), how well do I

- *Follow directions?* ___________
- *Manage my time?* ___________
- *Cooperate with others?* ___________
- *Participate in class discussions?* ___________
- *Work independently?* ___________
- *Work in groups?* ___________
- *Complete my work?* ___________
- *Bring in my homework?* ___________

1. *These are some things that are easy for me in class and why.*

2. *These are some things that are difficult for me in class and why.*

3. *These are some things I like in class and why.*

4. *This is something on which I should be working harder and an explanation of my choice.*

5. *This is the person with whom I work best and an explanation of why.*

6. *Reflections about subject areas:*

   a. Math

   b. Reading

   c. Writing

   d. Spelling

   e. Science

   f. Social Studies

7. *Two goals I have for the rest of the year are...*

8. *My plan for achieving each of these goals is...*

Adapted with permission from Joyce Silberman, fifth-grade teacher, Newman Elementary School, Needham, MA

The next student self-assessment form may be used in most subject areas. The first section is an activator that should be completed at the beginning of a lesson. The teacher might use this information as a pre-assessment to assess prior knowledge of a particular concept. The second section might be used at the midpoint of a lesson to gather information about a student's progress toward a specific learning goal. The third section is a summarizer that should be used at the end of a lesson to help both the student and teacher clarify what was learned, to ascertain whether a learning goal has been achieved and to adjust instruction so that any points of confusion are clarified. Lessons may range in length from one class period to many class sessions.

Figure 6-12
Student Self-Assessment

Section 1:

1. *What do I know about this topic?*
2. *What would I like to know about this topic?*
3. *How might I learn more about this topic?*

Section 2:

1. *What do I know now about this topic?*
2. *What questions do I still have?*
3. *Why am I learning about this topic?*
4. *How does this new information help me?*

Section 3:

1. *What have I learned about this topic?*
2. *What were the main points of this topic of study?*
3. *What confusions/questions do I still have?*

The next self-assessment form is specific to reading. This form may be adapted to be used at the beginning, middle or end of the year. The questions help children to think about themselves as readers as well as better understand their strengths and weaknesses in this area. The teacher is provided with information that may be used to inform instruction so that individual needs are more appropriately addressed. Again, a teacher should either comment in writing or orally after this form is completed by the students.

Figure 6-13
Self-Assessment: Reading

1. *How many books did you read this year?*

2. *What are the different kinds of books you read?* (*Genres: realistic fiction, fantasy, biography and autobiography, historical fiction, informational books, articles*)

3. *What are your favorite genres to read? Why?*

4. *Which were the best books you read this year? What made these books so good?*

5. *What are two of your favorite authors and why do you like them?*

6. *What is your favorite poem? Why do you like it?*

7. *What do you know how to do well as a reader?*

8. *What did you learn this year as a reader that you are proud of?*

9. *What did you learn about reading fiction this year?*

10. *What did you learn about reading nonfiction this year?*

11. *What is one skill you would like to improve in your reading? What is your plan for improving?*

Teacher Comments:

The following form might be used after a student has completed a problem-solving activity and the student work has been evaluated by the teacher. Providing students with such a form encourages them to use teacher feedback to improve their performance. Too many times, students are more concerned with their scores and do not take the necessary time to read and think about the comments and questions the teacher has posed.

Figure 6-14

Evaluating My Problem-Solving Skills

Carefully look over your corrected work and answer the following questions below.

1. *I used a strategy that made sense.*	Yes	No
2. *I found a correct solution.*	Yes	No
3. *I explained my strategy clearly and step-by-step.*	Yes	No

4. *My score was____________.*
5. *Explain what you feel you did well on this task.*
6. *Explain how you will improve your work in the future.*

These questions might be used in most content areas to help children think more deeply about how they are learning as well as how they are making progress toward a specific learning goal. The teacher is provided information about how students view themselves as learners.

Figure 6-15

Reflection Questions

1. *List three strategies (and provide possible examples) you used in...that helped you.*
2. *List three important things your teacher did to help you better understand...*
3. *Compare your________work now to the work you were doing at the beginning of the year. Compare the amount of effort you are putting forth now to the amount you were giving at the beginning of the year.*
4. *Describe the quality of your work.*
5. *Describe your focus during class.*
6. *Write a letter to yourself. Be sure to congratulate yourself on specific successes. Encourage yourself to improve those skills, strategies, ideas and understandings that you need to continue working on during the next few weeks. Include specifics that explain what works best for you.*
7. *I am confused about...*
8. *Now I understand...*

9. *The most important thing I learned today is...*
10. *I can use what I learned today when I...*
11. *When I don't know what to do, I...*
12. *When I work with a partner, I feel...*
13. *When I work with a group, I feel...*
14. *I need help on...*
15. *I get frustrated when...*
16. *If I could hear one lesson over again, it would be...*

The next assessment form might be used when students are engaged in discussion groups. It is important to share this form with students before they begin group work so that they are aware of group behaviors for which they should be striving. This form assists students in helping them to think about group dynamics, what actions benefit the group, what behaviors are detrimental to the learning process and how they might improve their performance next time they meet.

Figure 6-16
Assessment Form for Discussion Groups

Names:

Date:

Group's Discussion Topic:

Circle the appropriate responses. Provide evidence where possible.

1. *Everyone participated and shared in the discussion process.*
   Yes No Sometimes
   Evidence:

2. *The group is supportive of its individual members.*
   Yes No Sometimes
   Evidence:

3. *Group members often ask questions for clarification and elaboration.*
   Yes No Sometimes
   Evidence:

4. *The group discussion stays on topic.*
   Yes No Sometimes
   Evidence:

5. *The group is energetic and enthusiastic.*
   Yes No Sometimes
   Evidence:
6. *What was the best thing about the way this group worked together?*
7. *What was one problem this group had?*
8. *How did you solve it?*
9. *What else might you have done?*
10. *What specific plans do have for improving your group's performance the next time you meet?*

Adapted from Saskatchewan Education, 1996

The next self-assessment form should be completed by individual students after engaging in group work to help them reflect on their own interactions. Again, this form should be shared and discussed with students before they begin their collaborative work so as to help them better understand appropriate behaviors during group work.

Figure 6-17
My Contribution to Group Work

My group was discussing/solving...

Rate each entry as:
1-Needs Improving 2-Satisfactory 3-Excellent

Please also provide an example for each of the following questions.

1. *I shared my ideas and offered suggestions.* 1 2 3
   Example:
2. *I spoke clearly and slowly enough.* 1 2 3
   Example:
3. *I answered others' questions.* 1 2 3
   Example:
4. *I remained on topic and helped the group stay focused.* 1 2 3
   Example:
5. *I encouraged others to participate.* 1 2 3
   Example:
6. *I disagreed without hurting others' feelings.* 1 2 3
   Example:
7. *I summarized or repeated my ideas when necessary.* 1 2 3
   Example:

	1	2	3
8. *I gave reasons for my opinions.* *Example:*	1	2	3
9. *I listened courteously and effectively.* *Example:*	1	2	3
10. *I tried to understand and extend the suggestions of others.* *Example:*	1	2	3
11. *My most important contribution to the discussion was*			
12. *I would like to improve______________________the next time we meet.*			
13. *My plan for improvement is*			

Adapted from Saskatchewan Education, 1996

The next form is specific to students working on solving mathematical problems in collaborative groups. This form asks students to think about both the process used to complete the task and group interactions. This form should be completed by the group as a whole and should be shared and discussed before beginning the task. Again, sharing the form beforehand helps the students to focus on important parts of the problem-solving process and the behaviors that support a collaborative activity.

Figure 6-18
Assessment Form for Problem-Solving Groups

Names:

Title of Problem:

Circle the appropriate response. Provide evidence where possible.

1. *The group understood what the problem was asking.*
   Yes No Sometimes
   Evidence:

2. *The group formulated a plan and selected appropriate strategies.*
   Yes No Sometimes
   Evidence:

3. *The group solved the problem, labeled work and used visuals.*
   Yes No Sometimes
   Evidence:

4. *The group clearly explained how the problem was solved step by step.*
   Yes No Sometimes
   Evidence:

5. *Everyone participated in the problem-solving process.*
   Yes No Sometimes
   Evidence:

6. *The group was supportive of its members.*
   Yes No Sometimes
   Evidence:

7. *Group members asked questions for clarification.*
   Yes No Sometimes
   Evidence:

8. *The group discussion stayed on topic.*
   Yes No Sometimes
   Evidence:

9. *The group was enthusiastic.*
   Yes No Sometimes
   Evidence:

One problem we had was...

We will improve our work next time by....

Checklists are another tool that students may use to help them assess their own work. Such lists should highlight what students must do in order to successfully complete a task. Providing children with such lists gives them a means to monitor their progress toward a particular task. Checklists also encourage students to review and revise their work before turning it in to be assessed by their teacher. The following two checklists are specific to solving open-response mathematical problems and writing activities, respectively.

Figure 6-19
Assessing Open-Response Questions

Are all parts of the question answered?	*Yes*	*No*
Are all directions followed?	*Yes*	*No*
Are all parts and answers labeled?	*Yes*	*No*
Is the explanation clear for the reader?	*Yes*	*No*
Does the explanation include a combination of pictures, numbers or words?	*Yes*	*No*
Is appropriate math vocabulary and symbols included in the response?	*Yes*	*No*
Is the work neat, organized and spelled correctly?	*Yes*	*No*

Figure 6-20
Editing Checklist

Topic/Organization/Language

__ *My first paragraph begins with a topic sentence that restates the question.*
__ *Every paragraph begins with a topic sentence.*
__ *The sentences in each paragraph relate to the topic sentence.*
__ *I have introductory, supporting and concluding paragraphs.*
__ *My sentences begin in many different ways.*
__ *I remembered to indent each new paragraph.*
__ *I made an effort to use interesting vocabulary words by consulting a thesaurus.*

Mechanics

__ *I capitalized the first word in each sentence and all proper nouns.*
__ *I punctuated the end of each sentence.*
__ *I used commas and apostrophes appropriately.*
__ *My handwriting is legible.*

Spelling

Dictionary:

The following is a list of some words I corrected.

Thesaurus:

The following is a list of some words I looked up in the thesaurus to expand my written vocabulary. (Include the word you looked up and the word you found.)

Student Portfolios as a Means of Student Self-Assessment

What is the purpose of a portfolio? How should it be used? Who should select what goes in it? What types of pieces should go in it? Should it be evaluated and, if so, how? What should the process of implementing portfolios look like in a classroom? These are all questions teachers grapple with as they attempt to create a portfolio system which holds meaning for both students and teachers.

Purposes of Portfolio Assessment

A portfolio serves many purposes. It shows and documents students' actual work and progress over time. Teachers use portfolios to determine students' strengths and weaknesses, and, in this way, portfolios may inform instruction as teachers become more aware of students' needs. Portfolios also help students determine their own strengths and weaknesses. Once students clearly understand the areas they need to improve, they may set realistic and effective goals for themselves. In this way, a portfolio is a tool that may be used to help children self-reflect in a holistic way as the portfolio captures students' growth in all areas of the curriculum.

In this way, a portfolio is a tool that may be used to help children self-reflect in a holistic way as the portfolio captures students' growth in all areas of the curriculum.

Sharing a student's portfolio with parents during conferences is an effective way to show parents the progress their child has made over time. Parents may celebrate their child's successes and growth. As parents look at their child's work and are able to more clearly understand areas of weakness, they will better be able to support their child's learning at home.

Implementing Portfolios in the Elementary Classroom

The way in which one teacher implemented a classroom portfolio system in her elementary classroom evolved over the years. Although she felt her first few attempts were not very successful, she learned from these experiences and, consequently, was able to eventually construct the following system which works well for both her students and herself.

First, she begins by asking students what they know about portfolios. If necessary, she prompts them with questions such as, *What do they look like? What are they used for?* and *What goes in them?* After brainstorming as a class, they define *portfolio* in their own words.

Next, they discuss what types of things go into a portfolio and why. The teacher explains that work from all academic disciplines, such as math, reading, writing, science and social studies, should be included and will have a special section. There will also be a section for students to place work that may not fall under one of the specified categories. Most of the pieces will be selected by the students, however, the teacher explains to the class that she will, at times, ask them to include particular pieces.

Students typically think that only exemplary pieces should be placed in a portfolio. Therefore, it is important to help students understand why it is important to include work that they are not so proud of or that in which they did not perform well. The teacher talks about how *poor* work may be used to help set goals and determine areas in which they need more support. She also emphasizes that it takes time, practice and effort to become proficient in many things in school and that it is a rewarding experience to see firsthand how much progress they have made over time as they look through their portfolios. An example of items to include in a portfolio is as follows:

- tests and quizzes
- journal entries
- self-reflections
- homework
- group work assessment forms from literature circles or problem-solving groups
- problem of the week
- pictures taken of oral presentations or projects
- reports
- technology projects
- science lab reports
- art work
- work the student did really well on
- work the student didn't do very well on

Next, the teacher gives each student a white binder that has been divided into six sections with tabs. The sections are labeled as follows: *math, reading, writing, social studies, science, miscellaneous.*

After students understand the various pieces that are appropriate for a portfolio, the teacher explains the process they will use to place such items in the portfolio. For the pieces included, students are to use index cards to record the following:

- date and subject
- what they learned
- why they included these pieces

Once they have finished writing the required information on the index cards, they are to staple them to the pieces of work and place them in the appropriate sections in their portfolio binders. The teacher also explains to the students that it is not necessary to fill out index cards for the few pieces that she asks them to place in their portfolios. During the first year she implemented portfolios, she selected most pieces for students to place in their binders, however, she made the mistake of asking students to fill out index cards, including an explanation of why they included these pieces. She found many students wrote that they "included the piece because my teacher made me," a comment that was not very effective in terms of self-reflection. Figure 6-21 provides actual pieces that students in this teacher's fifth-grade class chose to include in their portfolios. The first is from science and second is from mathematics.

Figure 6-21

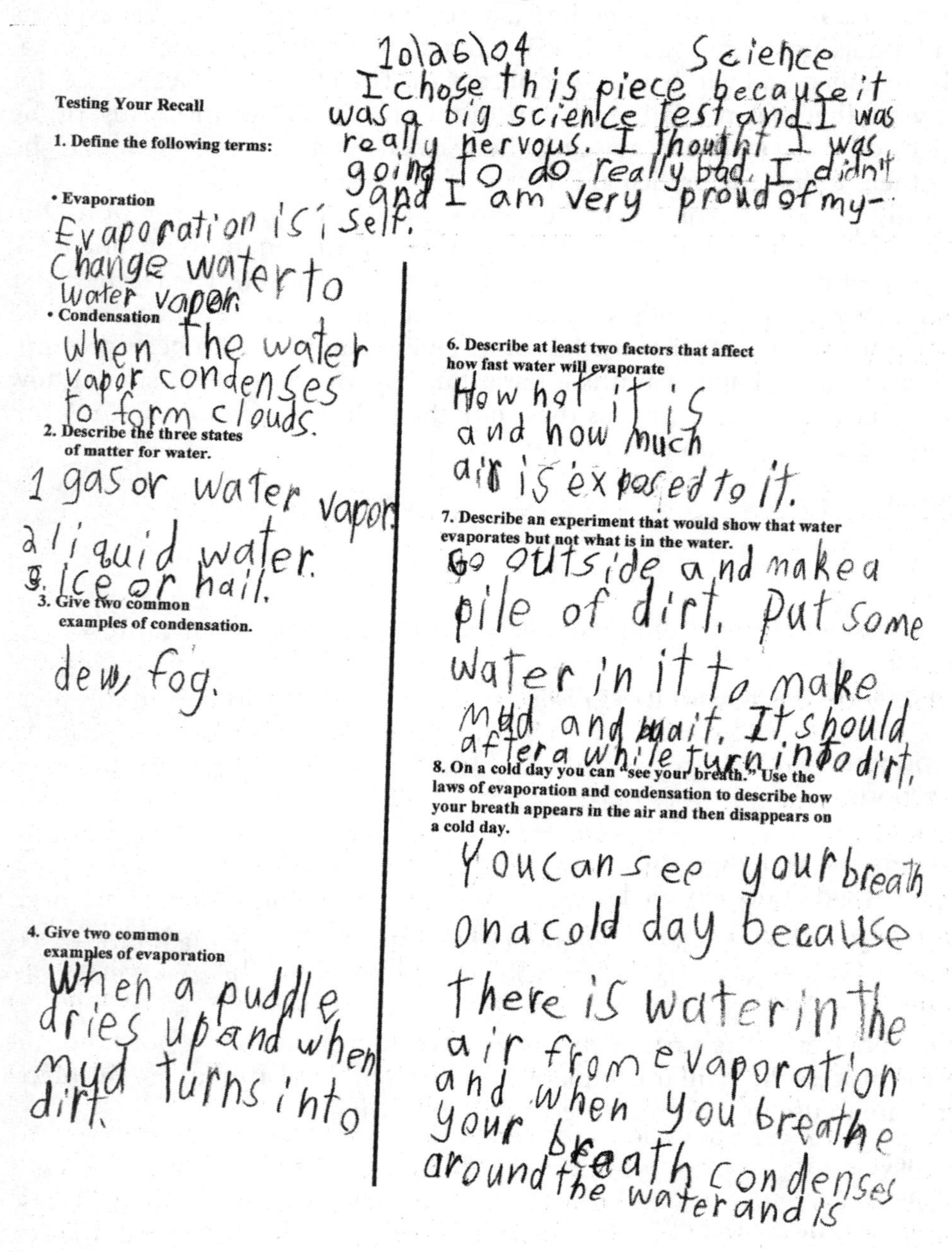

10\26\04 Science
I chose this piece because it was a big science test and I was really nervous. I thought I was going to do really bad. I didn't and I am very proud of my-self.

Testing Your Recall

1. Define the following terms:

• Evaporation

Evaporation is; change water to water vapor.

• Condensation

When the water vapor condenses to form clouds.

2. Describe the three states of matter for water.

1 gas or water vapor
2 liquid water.
3. Ice or hail.

3. Give two common examples of condensation.

dew, fog.

4. Give two common examples of evaporation

When a puddle dries up and when mud turns into dirt.

6. Describe at least two factors that affect how fast water will evaporate

How hot it is and how much air is exposed to it.

7. Describe an experiment that would show that water evaporates but not what is in the water.

Go outside and make a pile of dirt. Put some water in it to make mud and wait. It should after a while turn into dirt.

8. On a cold day you can "see your breath." Use the laws of evaporation and condensation to describe how your breath appears in the air and then disappears on a cold day.

You can see your breath on a cold day because there is water in the air from evaporation and when you breathe your breath condenses around the water and is

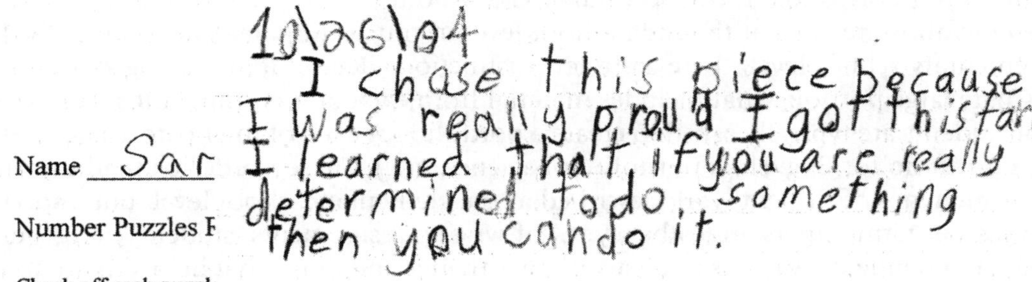
10\26\04
I chase this piece because
I was really proud I got this far.
I learned that if you are really
determined to do something
then you can do it.

Name Sar

Number Puzzles F

Check off each puzzl

Investigation 1 Number Puzzles

	Puzzle	Answer
✓	1	16
✓	2	24
✓	3	20, 40
✓	4	1, 3
✓	5	150
✓	6	120, 240
✓	7	30
✓	8	1, 7, 2

	Puzzle	Answer
	9*	
✓	10*	6, 14
✓	11*	trick question
✓	12*	350
	13*	
	14*	

Save this recording sheet for use in Investigations 4.

Investigation 4 Number Puzzles

	Puzzle	Answer
	15	
	16	
	17	
	18	
	19	
	20	
	21	
✓	22	750

	Puzzle	Answer
	23*	
	24*	
	25*	
✓	26*	900
✓	27*	16
✓	28*	impossible

Next, the teacher explains that students' work will be kept in file folders until Friday morning. Before school, she will pass out all student work from the week. She often asks for student volunteers to come in early to help save time by passing out papers, however, she makes sure she passes out any tests, quizzes or other items students may not want others to see. When students come into school on Friday, their morning work is to choose at least three items to place in their portfolios. They need to create index cards for each of these items and then place them in the portfolios. It is important to remind students they need to take home all other work and share it with their parents. It may also be helpful to explain this system to parents at Back to School Night and tell them that they are welcome to browse through their children's portfolios at any time (in addition to conference time) to better understand what their children are learning at school.

The students seem to take great pride in their portfolios and enjoy sharing them with their parents. This teacher also has students look through their work periodically to come up with particular goals for each academic area which they would like to achieve over the next couple of weeks or even months. It is important to have students determine successes and ask them to show evidence of their growth. Such concrete evidence really helps students understand their learning in terms of both areas of strengths and areas of weaknesses.

Implementing Portfolios in the Secondary Classroom

While portfolios are used at the high school level in much the same way as described for the elementary school level, there are a few distinctions. Rather than having students create a single large portfolio that includes material from each of their different subjects, high school students are typically asked to create a portfolio for each of their core academic subjects (a portfolio for English, a portfolio for science, etc.). These portfolios tend to consist of the same types of student work described at the elementary school level, but, especially in the case of term papers and other types of writing assignments, students are generally expected to include the various brainstorming activities and drafts that helped them to ultimately put together a final product. The last item that high school students typically place into their portfolios is a piece of reflective writing about the various pieces of work that they have included in their portfolios. Generally, such a reflection activity asks students to page through their own portfolios, looking for areas in which they see their own progress as learners as well as areas for which they recognize a need for continued improvement. Though this assignment is generally the last piece of student work added to the portfolio, it is placed at the very front of the portfolio in order to provide the portfolio's reader with an overview of the work contained therein.

Rubrics

What Is a Rubric?

Rubrics are used to assess students' learning of multifaceted concepts. **Rubrics** are essentially scoring guides in which specific criteria are used to discern among different levels of student proficiency. The critical elements of the task, process and/or product are specified. Often, rubrics are accompanied by examples of student work to illustrate the various scores. We talk more about anchor papers, projects and exemplars as examples of student work later in this chapter. A rubric may be used in conjunction with a variety of assessments and may help improve learning and instruction. An effective rubric will encompass the quality of the performance and will clearly delineate the levels of performance.

An effective rubric will encompass the quality of the performance and will clearly delineate the levels of performance.

Holistic and Analytical Rubrics

A rubric may be used either holistically or analytically in assessing student work. After the criteria for the task have been established, the teacher may look at the criteria as a whole and give one score for the task, which would be considered a **holistic assessment.** A teacher might also use an **analytical rubric** in which a product or performance is divided into essential dimensions so that they are judged separately. A separate score is assigned to each of the defined criteria. Figures 6-22 and 6-23 illustrate examples of a holistic rubric and analytical rubric, respectively.

Figure 6-22
Holistic Problem-Solving Rubric

1

* *didn't think through the problem*
* *didn't come up with an appropriate strategy and plan to solve the problem*
* *didn't answer all parts of the problem*
* *made basic mistakes in methods and calculations*
* *didn't explain the work in an organized, step-by-step manner*
* *didn't label the work and visuals*

2

* *gave some thought to the problem*
* *used a good strategy and plan to solve the problem*
* *answered most parts of the problem*
* *made some calculation errors*
* *explained the work in a semi-organized manner*
* *labeled some of the work and visuals*

3

* *thought carefully about the problem*
* *used an excellent strategy and plan to solve the problem*
* *answered all parts of the problem*
* *made only a few calculation errors*
* *explained the work in an organized, step-by-step manner*
* *labeled all work and visuals clearly*

4

* *thought carefully about the problem*
* *used an excellent strategy and plan to solve the problem*
* *answered all parts of the problem*
* *made no calculation errors*
* *explained the work in an organized, step-by-step manner*
* *labeled all work and visuals clearly*
* *used mathematical thinking to do something extra— for example, solved the problem in more than one way*

Figure 6-23
Oral Presentation Rubric

Criteria	Excellent 4	Proficient 3	Competent 2	Limited 1	Score
Content	Student shows a full understanding of the topic.	Student shows a good understanding of the topic.	Student shows a good understanding of parts of the topic.	Student does not seem to understand the topic very well.	
Organization	Presentation includes a strong introduction that gains audience attention, followed by organized progression of ideas.	Presentation includes a good introduction, followed by an organized progression of ideas.	Presentation includes an introduction followed by a relatively organized progression of ideas.	Presentation has a weak introduction and ideas are difficult to follow.	
Posture and Eye Contact	Student stands up straight and looks relaxed and confident. Student establishes eye contact with everyone in the room during the presentation.	Student stands up straight and establishes eye contact with everyone in the room during the presentation.	Student sometimes stands up straight and establishes eye contact.	Student slouches and/or does not establish eye contact during the presentation.	
Speaks Clearly	Student speaks clearly and distinctly all the time and mispronounces no words.	Student speaks clearly and distinctly all the time but mispronounces one word.	Student speaks clearly and distinctly most of the time and mispronounces no more than two words.	Student often mumbles and cannot be understood or mispronounces more than two words.	
Enthusiasm	Facial expressions and body language generate a strong interest and enthusiasm about the topic in others.	Facial expressions and body language sometimes generate a strong interest and enthusiasm about the topic in others.	Facial expressions and body language are used to try to generate enthusiasm but seem somewhat faked.	Facial expressions and body language are used very little and did not generate much interest in topic being presented.	
Comprehension	Student is able to answer accurately almost all questions posed by classmates about the topic.	Student is able to answer accurately most questions posed by classmates about the topic.	Student is able to answer accurately a few questions posed by classmates about the topic.	Student is unable to answer accurately any questions posed by classmates about the topic.	

Deciding which type of rubric to use, holistic or analytical, is dependent on a variety of factors. Each type of rubric has its advantages and disadvantages. Arter and McTighe (2001) recommend using an analytical rubric for daily classroom use in which on-going assessment is embedded in instruction and specific feedback is necessary for improving teaching and learning. For example, teachers may use the writing rubric (see Figure 6-24) on a regular basis during writing workshop sessions to help focus the students on the areas that they feel are important. Teachers may use it as both a self-assessment tool as well as an instrument with which they score their students' work. This rubric allows teachers to provide specific comments in an efficient manner and, consequently, provides students with an opportunity to improve their work in the weaker areas.

Holistic scoring is more appropriate for a summative assessment for which an overall score is needed, rather than detailed feedback. It is important to note, however, that if teachers decide to use a holistic rubric, they may still provide students with constructive feedback by posing questions and/or offering comments. In this way, a holistic rubric functions more like an analytical rubric in that it provides students with more detailed feedback, helps them to understand what a quality performance looks like and illustrates their strengths and weaknesses.

Developing Rubrics

Although commercially produced rubrics may be used, research shows that the most effective rubrics are those that have been created by the teacher and/or students for a particular task or tasks (Strickland & Strickland, 2000). One time-saving technique to find or quickly write your own comprehensive rubrics is the Internet site www.4teachers.org. This site contains a link to the *RubiStar* site. RubiStar (in www.4teachers.org) is a public domain site funded by the United States Department of Education so teachers may use it without cost to the teacher or the district. RubiStar allows teachers to

1. choose for their own use from hundreds of rubrics developed by other teachers
2. develop their own rubrics using the easy-to-use pull-down menus
3. write their own rubrics by modifying or rewriting the criteria contained in the pull-down menus

Rubrics, such as the ones seen earlier in this chapter, can be made in a matter of minutes using RubiStar. This excellent resource allows teachers to quickly create rubrics suitable and appropriate to the task at hand, and this site is appropriate for teachers of all grade levels and subject areas.

Goodrich (1996-1997) and Strickland & Strickland (2000) have developed several suggestions that are useful in writing rubrics. These recommendations are listed and explained in the following section.

List criteria. Start by listing the specific criteria. Generally speaking, four to six criteria define a task for most elementary situations. What components should the final product include? What elements will be considered when assessing the final product? For example, if creating a rubric for problem-solving activities, possible criteria may include mathematical strategies, mathematical reasoning, explanation and computational work.

Articulate gradations of quality. Typically, three to six gradations seem to be most appropriate at the elementary level. For many middle and high school tasks also, three to six is sufficient, however, some secondary tasks may require more that six gradations. There is an ongoing debate with regard to using either an odd or even number of gradations. Some feel that when an odd number of gradations is used, students tend to choose a middle score, while others believe this is not an issue. As a teacher, you will have to decide what works best for you and your students. Begin with the highest and lowest level of quality and then fill in the middle. If words such as *excellent, satisfactory* and *poor* are used, they need to be defined by providing examples of such quality of work. What makes a piece of persuasive writing excellent? Use models and discuss what makes a product excellent.

Avoid ABC conversions. Develop a rubric to assess what you want to assess, not to match an ABC grading system. Focus on articulating the quality of the work. The gradations should appropriately match the purposes of using a rubric. If you are required to grade, as most teachers in upper elementary and secondary schools are, you may convert the information from the rubric into grades at a later point.

Allow class time for the development and use of assessment tools such as rubrics. Creating a rubric is a time-consuming process. Assessment is part of the learning process, and it is a valuable process for both the students and the teacher. Keep in mind that it usually takes several revisions before you are able to design the "perfect" rubric. In the beginning, it is important to get your ideas on paper and come up with a framework for your rubric that you are able to live with. When teachers develop rubrics in committees, the charge they should be given is to come up with a rubric they can live with, not one that they all like. Asking a committee to come up with a rubric that everyone likes might lead to a very long and frustrating process that often does not yield results.

In the beginning, it is important to get your ideas on paper and come up with a framework for your rubric that you are able to live with.

Have trial runs with the rubric. After you get your ideas down on paper, use the rubric with your students. Make adjustments based on student work. Both teachers and students may practice using the rubric with student samples to better understand what is clear and what needs to be refined.

Be willing to revise the rubric. The rubric should be designed to help students revise their work, however, the rubric will also need to be revised as part of the rubric development process. As revisions are made to the rubric, it is important that students understand the changes that were made and why they were made.

Use the rubric for self- and peer-assessment. The rubric should be used as often as possible for both self- and peer-assessment which will further students' understanding of how to improve their performance. For example, we use a problem-solving rubric (see Figure 6-22) with students for the evaluation of their work, self-assessment and even peer-assessment. After students complete a problem-solving task, they are asked to assess their work and determine a score for it. They must provide a rationale for the particular score they give themselves. Doing this encourages students to review and reflect upon their work and make any changes or additions that are necessary. After the students turn in their work, we use the same rubric to evaluate it ourselves. In addition, from time to time, we give students samples of students' work (from previous years) and ask students to use the rubric to score the student work. Requiring students to assess other students' work provides them with an opportunity to look at student work from a different perspective.

Below is an example of a rubric used district-wide that went through the development steps noted above.

Figure 6-24
Needham Elementary School: Writing Rubric for Grade Five

(Levels three and four are acceptable ranges of grade five performance, mid-year; level 4 is the standard expectation for grade five students by the end of the year.)

5	4	3	2	1
The writer creatively approaches the topic with a strong voice and clear sense of audience and purpose. Organization and development are thorough and enhanced by effective elaboration of details and connections, as well as richness of language. Transitions are accomplished with ease. Very few, if any, mechanical or grammatical errors. **Topic** • *Clearly demonstrates awareness of audience, purpose, and task* • *Creative, unique approach* • *Multiple use of well-developed, clearly focused paragraphs* • *Topic and sub-topics supported with many elaborate details* **Organization** • *Compelling presentation; flows smoothly* • *Good organization and sequencing of ideas* • *Maintains clarity of expression and word choice throughout* • *Each paragraph is developed with topic and conclusion sentences* • *Transition words/phrases connect ideas and paragraphs* **Language** • *Creative, unique, original approach* • *Precise/powerful use of vocabulary; imagery relevant, vivid details enrich central theme* • *Rich variety and complexity of sentence structure* • *Transition words/phrases connect ideas and paragraphs* **Voice** • *Distinctive voice throughout* **Mechanics/Usage/Grammar** • *Few mechanical errors, if any, relative to length and complexity* • *Consistent use of correct, internal punctuation* • *Proper indentation* • *Conventional spelling* • *Correct grammar and usage for the most part*	The writer is able to develop and maintain focus throughout multiple paragraphs. Organization of paragraphs and sequence of ideas follow logical patterns. Theme is supported by relevant details with several elaborations of details. Sentence structure shows developing variety and complexity. Transitions and connecting paragraphs are usually evident. There are only minor errors in mechanics, usage, and grammar. **Topic** • Establishes and maintains clear purpose • Demonstrates awareness of audience and task • Strong introduction and conclusion paragraphs • Topic and sub-topics supported with relevant details and elaboration **Organization** • Sequencing of ideas moves reader smoothly along • Logical organization of paragraphs • Multiple paragraphs within body where appropriate • Topic sentences focus paragraphs • Transition words/phrases connect ideas and/or paragraphs **Language** • Most ideas expressed with deliberate, appropriate word choice • Expanded vocabulary and imagery • Sentence beginnings show further development (i.e., prepositional/adverbial phrases, etc.) • Variety of sentence types • Use of transition words and phrases to connect paragraphs **Voice** • Personal voice heard **Mechanics/Usage/Grammar** • Capitals and end punctuation used correctly • Internal punctuation correct with some minor errors • Indents used properly • Pronoun/subject/verb tense agreement • Accurate spelling appropriate to grade level	The writer is able to maintain the topic through several paragraphs. Ideas are supported with details. Some elaboration of details is evident. Organization utilizes the basic three-phase paragraph structure. There is evidence of varied sentence structure. Generally correct basic punctuation. Use of internal punctuation is emerging. Few agreement (pronoun/subject/verb tense) errors. Conventional spelling is generally accurate. **Topic** • Establishes and maintains clear purpose • Demonstrates awareness of audience and task • Three-phase paragraph structure used where appropriate • Introductory sentence/paragraph focuses reader • Conclusion sentence/paragraph pulls ideas together • Some body paragraphs are well-developed and expanded, but others are brief with one or two details **Organization** • Most ideas/paragraphs are organized • Most details are grouped and sequenced • Some topic sentences guide paragraphs • Emerging use of transition words and phrases **Language** • Deliberate word choice enhances meaning • Some variation in sentence structure and beginnings • May have occasional sentence run-ons/ fragments in more complex structure **Voice** • Personal voice is emerging **Mechanics/Usage/Grammar** • Capitals and punctuation used correctly • May have some errors in punctuation in complex sentence structure • Emerging use of correct internal punctuation • Indents for new paragraphs • Spelling demonstrates knowledge of spelling conventions and high frequency words • Pronoun/subject/verb tense agreement	The writer is able to focus the topic through two or three loosely connected paragraphs. Details usually support the theme, but with few if any elaborations. Introduction and conclusion are brief and simply stated. Minimal sentence variety and limited word choice as well as occasional lapses in clarity of expression are present. Mechanical errors may interfere with meaning. Difficulty is noted with punctuation of complex sentence structures and some spelling conventions. Word agreement (pronoun/ subject/verb tense) errors may occur frequently. **Topic** • Attempts to establish and maintain purpose • Demonstrates some awareness of audience and task • Topic focus maintained but may be simplistically stated • Topic supported with many details • Few details are elaborated **Organization** • Some inconsistent sequencing • May be some lapses in clarity of ideas • Evidence of paragraphing • Body paragraphs are short and not fully developed around sub-topic • Occasional loose connection of details • Weak or absent transitions **Language** • Common vocabulary • Little variety of sentence beginnings • Standard and predictable sentence structure for the most part • Run-on and sentence fragments in more complex sentences **Voice** • Personal voice may be emerging **Mechanics/Usage/Grammar** • Accurate punctuation for simple sentences • May be little understanding of correct punctuation when more complex sentence structure is used • Lack of understanding of internal punctuation • Conventional spelling of high frequency and phonetic words • Minor lapses in syntax	The writer is able to convey the basic theme using a few details. Organization is random, but shows beginning understanding of paragraphing. Many ideas are repeated. Mechanical errors may interfere significantly with meaning. Writer demonstrates an inconsistent use of punctuation. There may be some sentence fragments and run-on sentences. Common high frequency words may be misspelled. Word agreement errors may appear. **Topic** • Purpose may not be clear • Minimal awareness of audience and task • Basic topic may be conveyed or recognizable • Details support topic but with little or no elaboration **Organization** • Minimal sequencing • One-, two- or three-sentence paragraphs • May attempt to use three-phase paragraph structure, but little evidence of understanding of paragraph development • May lack clarity and cohesiveness • Some random and/or repeated ideas **Language** • Basic vocabulary • Some variety in sentence types **Voice** • Personal voice may be emerging **Mechanics/Usage/Grammar** • May be end-punctuation errors • Some sentence fragments and run-ons • Message confused because of spelling and/or punctuation errors • Pronoun/subject/verb tense disagreements • Errors in spelling of some common sight words

NS= nonscorable—illegible, incoherent, or blank paper OP= off prompt—does not answer prompt

Anchor Papers

Rubrics are beneficial to teachers in that they serve as guides in assessing student work, however, since rubrics are a collection of individual criteria, students are often in need of holistic examples of the finished product to fully understand the expectations. Holistic models, such as anchor papers, help us consistently assess the students' final products and increase students' understanding of how the criteria in the rubric are integrated into the final product.

Anchor papers are samples of actual student work that correspond to the different levels of proficiency within the rubric. The examples of anchor papers (and accompanying rubric and writing task) provided in Figure 6-25 are taken from a ninth-grade English classroom. The teacher began by presenting a writing task on *Romeo and Juliet* and sharing with students the rubric that would be used to assess this task. The teacher then distributed four anchor papers from the previous year (with the names concealed). Students read through each of these four anchor papers and utilized the assignment's rubric to assess each one. A discussion followed on the strengths and weaknesses of each of the four anchor papers, and, through this discussion, students were able to come to a deeper understanding of the teacher's expectations for the present writing assignment.

Figure 6-25

English 9 — Seider

Romeo and Juliet Writing Assignment, Act V, Scene i

In Act V, Scene i, of *Romeo and Juliet*, Romeo buys poison from an apothecary in order to kill himself because he believes that Juliet is dead. The apothecary is initially reluctant to sell Romeo the poison but ultimately agrees to do so explaining, "My poverty but not my will consents"(V,i). Was the apothecary wrong to sell Romeo the poison? Is he partly to blame for Romeo and Juliet's deaths?

As a means of exploring these questions, imagine that you have recently graduated from college with a degree in accounting. A prominent cigarette manufacturer offers you a six-figure salary to work as the company's accountant. Would you take the job? Why or why not?

English 9 Seider
Romeo and Juliet Writing Assignment, Act V, Scene i
Rubric for Writing Assignment

Mechanics

Criteria	0 points	1 point	2 points	3 points
Topic Sentence Provides	no topic sentence	topic sentence exists but does not describe content of paragraph	topic sentence conveys somewhat the content of the paragraph	topic sentence successfully conveys content of paragraph
Evidence	no evidence provided	evidence provided but does not support claim	evidence somewhat supports claim	evidence strongly supports claim
Concluding Sentence	no concluding sentence	concluding sentence exists but does not wrap up content of paragraph	concluding sentence successfully wraps up content of paragraph	concluding sentence successfully wraps up *and extends* content of paragraph
Grammar and Usage	many grammar and usage errors	several grammar or usage errors	1–2 grammar or usage errors	no grammar or usage errors

Content

Criteria	0 points	3 points	6 points	9 points
Claim	no claim stated in topic sentence	claim in topic sentence unrelated to assignment	claim stated with some ambiguity in topic sentence	claim clearly stated in topic sentence
Quality of Evidence Provided	no evidence to support claim made in topic sentence	evidence presented to support claim is confusing and unclear	evidence presented to support claim is clear	several clear, compelling pieces of evidence to support claim made in topic sentence

TOTAL POINTS: ____________/ 30

Student 1: 22/30

I would take the job if I could. People know exactly what they are doing when they start smoking. Everyone knows they're addictive and that you can die from smoking. I would feel kind of guilty going to work everyday, but people are responsible for themselves, not me for them. People make the decision to smoke on their own, no one forces them. People also don't buy cigarettes because their trying to kill themselves, they buy them for the enjoyment of smoking. In the book *Romeo and Juliet,* I don't think the apothecary should have sold Romeo the poison because the apothecary knows Romeo is going to kill himself immediately, that's why he wanted the poison. People aren't looking to kill themselves when they buy a pack of cigarettes but it is 100% their own decision to smoke, they know what they are getting into before they start. In conclusion, I would definitely take the job because I wouldn't be the one actually making or selling them, I would just be figuring out the company's taxes.

Student 2: 26/30

If given a fancy job at a tobacco company, I would absolutely turn it down. There are several reasons behind my decision. First, I don't want to do work that is selling a harmful substance. Cigarettes are harmful in many ways. They poison our air, they cause cancer in the people that smoke them, and their second hand smoke can cause cancer in millions of other innocent bystanders. It is amazing to think about how much damage cigarettes cause. Second, cigarettes bring no positive effects to the world, the only point of cigarette companies is to earn money. Cigarette companies value money over human beings. Working as an accountant for one of these companies would make me part of their business and as guilty as anyone else working there. Finally, I wouldn't work as an accountant for a cigarette company because cigarettes are so addictive. Cigarette companies make money off people's addictions. Smokers have no choice but to keep buying more cigarettes. Making money off people's addiction is practically evil. It is bad enough that cigarettes cause so much misery, but the fact that smokers can know what they're doing to their bodies and want to save themselves but can't, that is even worse. An addiction is like a disease. The tobacco companies take advantage of smoker's disease. If you saw a sick man lying in a hospital bed, would you run up and steal his wallet? Cigarette companies do this everyday, but it is even worse because it is not only a man's money they are taking, it is a man's life. I could not look at myself in the mirror if I helped do the accounting for companies that sell cigarettes. I would be as guilty as a CEO. I just couldn't do it.

Student 3: 28/30

If I were offered a high-paying job as an accountant for a cigarette company, I would definitely accept the position. My decision to accept the position is not because I believe that marketing and selling of cigarettes is okay, but because I believe that people make their own choices in life. Each person is capable of making his or her own decision about whether or not to smoke. With all of the anti-smoking advertisements today, it is hard to believe adults and even children do not know the risks they are taking when they start smoking. As long as cigarette companies do not lie to their customers about the risks and health hazards associated with smoking, these companies are doing nothing wrong. Rather, these companies are simply providing an option for people to take or not as they wish. Are automobile companies responsible for the people who die in automobile accidents? Of course not. People who purchase cars know that there are some risks associated with driving, and they make the decision to take their chances. The same is true with cigarette companies and these companies' clients. The men and women who purchase cigarettes do so knowing full well that there are risks associated with this habit. As a result of this belief— that men and women who purchase cigarettes understand the pro's and con's of smoking cigarettes— I feel certain that I *would* accept a position as an accountant for a cigarette company. In fact, the job sounds like a great opportunity. In exchange for doing the company's finances, I would receive a good paycheck and a nice home. And should the company ever go out of business or I need to move to another part of the country, I would have excellent accounting experience on my resume to help me find a new job. In closing, I don't see why anyone would hesitate to take this position, and I know that my belief that people are free to make their own decisions would lead me to accept the job if it were offered to me.

Criteria Sheets

Like a rubric, a **criteria sheet** specifically explains the criteria the students and the teacher will use to assess an assignment. A criteria sheet is used in place of a rubric when there are multiple parts to the assignment that are not easily categorized into a rubric. For example, in the following criteria for a high school lab report, the teacher chose to use a criteria sheet rather than a rubric because the various components of a lab report have different point values. An analytic rubric might have been used to describe each of the components, however, applying different point values to each area was deemed by the teacher as too unwieldy and confusing for the students to use effectively in self-assessment. A different holistic rubric might have been used for each component of the lab report, but the teacher again decided that multiple rubrics would prove unwieldy for the students and the teacher.

Honors Chemistry

Laboratory Report Format

Laboratory reports are written to communicate the work that you have done to others. When preparing your report, you should always write with the idea that the reader will be using your report and no other instructions to repeat the experiment. Therefore, you should be complete in all of your descriptions and calculations. The format given below is a typical format for a published research paper. Unless you are told otherwise, all of the laboratory reports that are turned in this year should follow this format.

Regarding the style of your report, don't use the active voice. Only use the passive voice. You should refrain from using pronouns such as *I, me, you* or *we*. For example, instead of writing, "I added 30.0 ml of water to the reaction flask," you should write, "30.0 ml of water were added to the reaction flask."

Standard Report Format

I. **Title** (5 pts.)—A report of any kind should have a title that gives the reader an idea of what was accomplished by the investigation. The title should be brief.

II. **Objective** (5 pts.)—This section should give a clear description of the problem being investigated and what you were attempting to accomplish in the investigation.

III. **Background** (15 pts.)—The background section should summarize all of the relevant information that the reader would need to carry out the experiment. This includes the definitions of the quantities being investigated and equations that are needed to calculate the quantities. The equations should be correctly written and clearly presented. Remember that your laboratory report should be written so that any reasonably knowledgeable reader should be able to use your report and no other directions to repeat the experiment.

IV. **Materials** (10 pts.)—Include any materials that were used to carry out the experiment that you are reporting. This includes the type of glassware used, whether you used a Bunsen burner, the types of substances, etc.

V. **Safety Issues** (5 pts.)—Include any areas in the investigation where safety is a concern. In most cases, the use of the proper eyewear is a minimum safety requirement, but there will be others, depending on the activity.

VI. **Procedure** (25 pts.)—This section will include the step-by-step procedure required to correctly carry out the experiment. It should include diagrams of the experimental setup. If a procedure that you use has been published in a textbook or other readily available source, you may reference the source with a complete MLA bibliographic reference in a reference section at the end of the report. Otherwise, you must write the complete procedure.

VII. **Results** (25 pts.)—Include all of the data (numerical and otherwise) collected in the experiment as well as all tables, graphs and calculations. All numbers should be justified, meaning, you should indicate where you obtained all of the numbers that are used in your calculations. The source of any known values that are used should be referenced in a reference section at the end of the report.

VIII. **Conclusion** (10 pts.)—Summarize the investigation and what you accomplished. You should also discuss any possible sources of error in your experiment that may have affected the accuracy and precision of your results and ways that these errors might be avoided in the future.

References (If this section is needed, points for it will be included in the point values for sections VI and VII).

District, State and National Assessments

Today, educators often feel pulled in different directions and believe they are asked to attain conflicting goals. Teachers are asked to teach for application mastery and higher order thinking, while at the same time ensuring that their students perform well on tests mandated by both the district and state. As the quality of these tests improve, they more accurately assess students' application mastery and higher order thinking skills.

Some teachers, however, find themselves in districts where the curriculum is not aligned to the state curriculum, and there is a mismatch between the content that students are taught in the classroom and the content on a standardized test. When this occurs, students are unable to demonstrate the extent of their knowledge and do not perform as well as expected. Even in circumstances when there is a mismatch between the test and the curriculum, teachers must continue to hold high expectations for their students and strive to meet curriculum goals set forth by the district and state. By doing so, performance on tests should naturally improve.

Standardized Testing

Standardized testing was developed about 100 years ago to address concerns of unfairness and bias in grading procedures. Despite the implementation of standardized testing, however, such unfairness and bias still exists today, as nothing we do may be said to be purely objective.

Standardized tests provide educators, administrators and policy makers with a snapshot of what students know in relation to what they are being tested on and how other groups of students perform on the test. These test results yield comparisons across years, grade levels and student populations both locally and nationally, and they may be used as one piece of data. "A data review of the test performance of a class, grade, or school can point out content that might not have been taught, aspects of test taking that are difficult for individual students or groups, and students' ability to read and follow directions" (Stuart, 2003, p. 217).

State Testing

The educational reform movement in the 1970s and 1980s brought about accountability changes such as graduation requirements, curriculum testing and minimum competency tests. Recently, however, standards-based education has become more prevalent, and many states have developed criterion-referenced assessments that are aligned with their state curriculum frameworks. In contrast to norm-referenced testing, these tests are intended to measure whether or not students have met the state curriculum standards. "Accountability in these states focuses on output evidence: How well do students perform on the state test?" (Stuart, 2003, p. 218).

Such high-stakes testing systems have a major impact on students, educators and schools. Since 2000, many states have implemented (or are planning to implement) a state testing graduation requirement. For example, in one state, students have up to five opportunities over the course of two years, beginning in tenth grade, to pass the English Language Arts and Mathematics portions of the test. Students who fail to pass these exams are denied a high school diploma. Many states now have similar requirements.

District-Based Assessments

District-based assessments provide school systems with measures of how the students are doing in particular content areas. Using this information, districts determine the students' overall strengths and weaknesses and make decisions about how to improve instruction in the weaker areas. Teachers and administrators use this information as a guide for where to add more supports, professional development, etc.

The following strategies have been used effectively by one school system to assess student learning.

- District-wide mathematical assessments developed by the district are administered at selected grade levels.
- A classroom-based, district-wide writing assessment is scored using a district-developed rubric by classroom teachers and placed in students' permanent portfolios to document growth over time.
- Permanent portfolios are maintained by teachers in which they are required to place certain items that demonstrate students' mastery on specifically designated performance competencies.
- Classroom-based portfolios (more student-centered than the permanent portfolios) demonstrate students' progress toward meeting the grade level competencies over the course of the school year.

Using the above district-wide classroom-based strategies may benefit practice at the classroom, school and district levels in many ways. For example, in one school system, in the first year a mathematics end-of-the-year assessment was administered, it was recognized that students with special needs did particularly poorly. When the test was given, it was not clear to the teachers what types of modifications were acceptable. As a result, classroom teachers made few necessary modifications for these students. In the following year, suggested modifications were made for the final assessment as well as for daily classroom use.

In another example in which a district-wide mathematics end-of-year assessment was beneficial, the results of the assessment were analyzed, and it was determined that, across-the-board, students did poorly in the area of measurement. After examining the reasons for the lack of success in this particular area, it was discovered that the program teachers were using did not adequately provide materials, activities, lessons and information on this topic. In addition, many teachers ran out of time before teaching this unit of study. Consequently, recommendations were made for prioritizing mathematical content to be taught throughout the year, that is, curriculum mapping, so that all mathematical strands were addressed in some capacity. Supplementary materials were also developed and given to teachers to support their instruction in this area.

Analyzing Test Results

Data plays a crucial role in assessment and accountability. It is important to understand what the results tell us and how they may be used to make improvements in the education system. Both district and state assessments should be used in conjunction with other sources of information documenting student progress to make effective decisions that support student learning.

How One School System Used District-Wide Assessments

In one particular school system, a district-wide mathematics assessment was administered to all elementary grades, kindergarten through fifth, at the end of each year. The construction of these assessments was based on the district's Mathematics Scope and Sequence, which encompasses both state and national standards. The results of this comprehensive mathematics assessment were entered into a spreadsheet and were analyzed in a variety of ways. Individual student's results were entered into the program, and data was collected for each test item number. A composite score was used to summarize each student's test results according to each of the five mathematical strands, *number and operations, algebra, geometry, measurement* and *data, statistics and probability.* The data was organized by school, grade and teacher, thus providing each teacher with a mean class percentage score for every item number and mathematical strand.

The test questions were then analyzed to document general strengths and weaknesses in specific schools. The strengths for both individual schools and the district were recognized by noting those strands in which average student performance exceeded 75%. Scores between 65% and 75% were considered average performance. The weaknesses were determined by examining each item and noting those questions for which the class average was below 65%. District weaknesses were determined by recording item numbers for which more than two schools averaged below 65%. These items in which students had more difficulty were categorized by mathematical strand. Each problematic question was studied to determine possible reasons for error. The possibilities included students' inability to follow directions, minimal exposure to a particular concept and poor test design.

Data was also organized by school and grade to determine the number of students who scored in each of the following intervals for each mathematical strand.

90–100% Advanced
80–89% Proficient
70–79% Proficient
60–69% Needs Improvement
50–59% Needs Improvement

Tables and bar graphs for each grade level were constructed to clearly show these results. See Figure 6-26 for an example of grade 4.

Figure 6-26
Grade 4—334 Students

	Number and Operations	***Algebra***	***Geometry***	***Measure-ment***	***Data***
90–100%	23%	36%	24%	14%	55%
80–89%	19%	35%	22%	17%	21%
70–79%	18%	0%	22%	10%	12%
60–69%	16%	18%	13%	18%	7%
0–59%	25%	11%	20%	40%	6%

Grade 4—Percentage of Student Scores in Each Interval

Points per Strand

Strand	**Points**
Number and Operations	12
Algebra	5
Geometry	4
Measurement	4
Data	5
Total	30 points

In addition, findings were summarized, trends noted and recommendations made for each grade level after the analysis was completed. The following paragraph was part of the final report, and it highlights the findings and recommendations at the fourth-grade level.

> The data indicates that measurement is a weakness in fourth grade. It has been recognized that the grade 4 mathematics program does not provide adequate experiences for conceptual understanding in measurement. Therefore, supplementary materials have been prepared to provide both students and teachers with the necessary experiences to meet the requirements of the Scope and Sequence for this strand. Similar to second and third graders, students in fourth grade also experienced difficulty completing in-out function machines and describing the rule. It is also evident students need consistent opportunities to answer open response questions. Teachers need to both model appropriate responses and clearly state expectations for adequate responses. It is recommended that teachers use word walls or vocabulary charts or journals that include a visual and explanation to reinforce mathematical language. Students at this grade level performed well on questions involving data analysis. Fourth graders were also able to successfully complete most algebra related questions (Levin & Deane, 2003).

Teachers at each grade level met as a group, and these results were shared and discussed. As a group, these teachers were able to strategize and plan how the noted weaknesses would be addressed in the classroom. Students who did particularly poorly were noted and their progress was documented by their teacher in the following year. Students and teachers who needed additional support were provided assistance by special educators, the mathematics instructional leader and the math coach. Supplementary materials were organized and given to classroom teachers for units of study in which resources were inadequate.

How a Secondary School Used Statewide Assessments

Secondary school teachers utilize standardized test data in much the same way as elementary school teachers. As you can see in the chart below, at one high school, the percentage of tenth-grade students who fell into each scoring category on the state math test was first compared to similar data from the previous two years.

Percentage of Glenbrook students scoring in each category

	2000–01	2001–02	2002–03
Advanced	3%	0%	4%
Proficient	21%	7%	26%
Needs Imp.	52%	60%	50%
Failing	24%	33%	20%

The information gleaned from this data was generally good news. More students moved out of the Failing and Needs Improvement categories and into the Proficient category.

Next, this data was broken down by the school's various demographics: race/ethnicity, gender, students eligible for free/reduced lunch, etc., and relevant observations were noted as follows:

87% of the students eligible for F/RP lunch passed the Math MCAS
74% of the students not eligible for F/RP lunch passed the Math MCAS

89% of Glenbrook's African–American students passed the Math MCAS
77% of Glenbrook's Mixed/Other students passed the Math MCAS
81% of Glenbrook's White students passed the Math MCAS

83% of Glenbrook's female students passed the Math MCAS
79% of Glenbrook's male students passed the Math MCAS

Next, the success of the tenth graders on the different types of questions that make up the math exam was examined in comparison to the results of their peers within the school district.

Average Percentage of Questions Answered Correctly by Category

	Number Sense	Patterns, Relations, Algebra	Geometry	Measurement	Statistics, Probability, Data Anal.
Glenbrook HS	42% correct	45% correct	31% correct	38% correct	47% correct
District HS's	45% correct	44% correct	40% correct	42% correct	51% correct

The data revealed that, in virtually all of the categories, a smaller percentage of Glenbrook's tenth graders correctly answered these questions than did the district's tenth graders as a whole. This data was a cause for concern. Why did the Glenbrook tenth graders score worse than those in the district as a whole? To answer this question, the administrators and teachers turned to an item analysis in which they examined each question on which the school's tenth graders fared worse than the district's tenth graders. They collected the following information.

#5 Square Root Question (Multiple Choice, Number Sense)

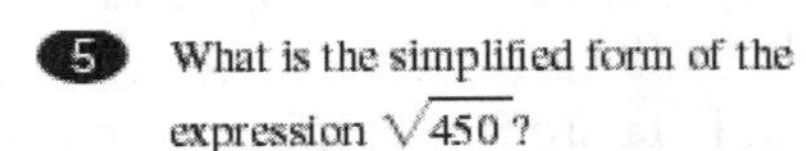

5 What is the simplified form of the expression $\sqrt{450}$?

A. $15\sqrt{2}$

B. $45\sqrt{2}$

C. $75\sqrt{2}$

D. $225\sqrt{2}$

17% of Glenbrook students answered correctly (A)
35% of District students answered correctly
63% of Glenbrook students answered "D"

It's interesting that so many students thought the answer was *D*.
Perhaps they saw the square root sign as indicating multiplication?

By noting not only how many of the students answered the question correctly but also whether there was another (incorrect) answer that students were drawn to, Glenbrook could start to understand how they should adjust their curriculum to meet the needs of their students. Upon completing an item analysis like this one for each question on the exam for which the students fared worse than the district as a whole, Glenbrook could then lay out recommendations for the math department to consider in adjusting its curriculum to support student success.

Conclusion

In conclusion, effective assessment and learning are interwoven and are ongoing. Today, assessment is far more global in that it encompasses observing, teaching, describing, collecting, recording, scoring and interpreting information about a student's learning. It is critical that teachers use these different means of gathering information about a student's learning. Both the teacher and the student must play an active role in the assessment process and must be able to communicate openly. The information derived from the assessment process is an invaluable source as it may be used to improve student learning, instructional practices and educational options in the classroom. As educators, it is our responsibility to use a variety of assessments in order to maximize success for each and every one of our students.

References

Albert, L. R. (2000). Outside in, inside out: Seventh grade students' mathematical thought processes. *Educational Studies in Mathematics, 41,* 109–42.

Albert, L., Mayotte, G., & Sohn, S. (2002). Making observations interactive. *Mathematics Teaching in the Middle School, 7*(7), 396–401.

Arter, J. A., & Busick, K. U. (2001). *Practice with student involved classroom assessment.* Portland, OR: Assessment Training Institute.

Arter, J., & McTighe, J. (2001). *Scoring rubrics in the classroom: Using performance criteria for assessing and improving student performance.* Thousand Oaks, CA: Corwin Press, Inc.

Assessment Reform Group. (2002). Assessment for learning: 10 principles. (a leaflet/poster available to download as a PDF file or HTML version at http://www.assessment-reform-group.org.uk/publications.html or available by mail from Ann Doyle, School of Curriculum, Pedagogy and Assessment, Institute of Education, 20 Bedford Way, London WC1H 0AL (minimum orders of 20 copies, £10 including postage).

Atkin, J. M., Black, P., & Coffey, J. (2001). *Classroom assessment and the national science education standards.* Washington, DC: National Academy Press.

Black, P., & Wiliam, D. (1998). Assessment and classroom learning. *Assessment in Education, 5*(1), 7–75.

Black, P., & Wiliam, D. (1998, October). Inside the black box: Raising standards through classroom assessment. *Phi Delta Kappan,* 139–148.

Bloom, B. S., Madaus, G. F., & Hastings, T. J. (1981). *Evaluation to improve learning.* New York: McGraw-Hill.

Chappuis, S., & Stiggens, R. J. (2002). Classroom assessment for learning. *Educational Leadership, 60,* 40–43.

Clarke, S. (2001). *Unlocking formative assessment.* London: Hodder and Stoughton.

Davies, A. (2000). *Making classroom assessment work.* British Columbia, Canada: Classroom Connections International, Inc.

Gardner, H. (1984). *Frames of mind: The theory of multiple intelligences.* New York: Basic Books.

Gator, C., Jones, J., O'Brien, A., Patterson, S., Rooney, R., Good, E. et al. *Pupil Self Assessment.* Retrieved April 15, 2004, from http://www.aaia.org.uk/pdf/aaiaformat4.pdf

Goodrich, H. (1996/1997). Understanding rubrics. *Educational Leadership, 54*(4), 14–17.

Herman, J., Aschbacher, P., & Winters, L. (1992). *A Practical Guide to Alternative Assessment.* Alexandria, VA: ASCD.

Levin, L., & Deane, J. (2003, October). Report to the School Committee of the Needham, MA, Public Schools.

Lincoln, Y., & Guba, E. (1984). *Naturalistic inquiry.* Beverly Hills, CA: Sage Publications.

Mitchell, R., Willis, M., & Chicago Teachers Union Quest Center. (1995). *Learning in overdrive: Designing curriculum, instruction, and assessment from standards.* Golden, CO: North American Press.

Rickards, D., & Cheek, E. (1999). *Designing rubrics for K–6 classroom assessment.* Norwood, MA: Christopher-Gordon Publishers, Inc.

Rutherford, P. (2002). *Instruction for all students*. Alexandria, VA: Just ASK Publications.

Sadler, R. (1989). Formative assessment and the design of instructional systems. *Instructional Science, 18,* 119–144.

Saphier, J., & Gower, R. (1997). *The skillful teacher.* Carlisle, MA: Research for Better Teaching.

Saskatchewan Education (1996).

Shepard, L. A. (2001, July). *Using assessment to help students think about learning.* Keynote address at the Assessment Training Institute Summer Conference, Portland, OR.

Stenmark, J. K. (1991). *Modern assessment: Myths, models, good questions, and practical suggestions.* Reston, VA: National Council of Teachers of Mathematics.

Sternberg, R. (1996). *Successful intelligence: How practical and creative intelligence determines success in life.* New York: Simon and Schuster.

Strickland, K., & Strickland, J. (2000). *Making assessment elementary.* Portsmouth, NH: Heinemann.

Stuart, L. F. (2003). *Assessment in practice: Creating a school culture of learning and assessment.* Newton Lower Falls, MA: Teachers 21.

Westley, J. (1994). *Puddle questions: Assessing mathematical thinking: grade 5.* Mountain View, CA: Creative Publications.

Wiggins, G. (1993). *Assessing student performance: Exploring the purpose and limits of testing.* San Francisco: Jossey-Bass Publishers.

Wiggins, G. (1998). *Educative Assessment: Designing assessments to inform and improve student performance.* San Francisco: Jossey-Bass.

Wiggins, G., & McTighe, J. (1998). *Understanding by design.* Alexandria, VA: Association for Supervision and Curriculum Development (ASCD).

Young, E. (2000). *Enhancing student writing by teaching self-assessment strategies that incorporate the criteria of good writers.* Unpublished doctoral dissertation, Department of Educational Psychology, State University of New Jersey, Graduate School of Education, Rutgers.

CHAPTER 7

Raising Students' Intelligence and Motivation by Teaching "Effective Effort" Strategies

Objectives for the Chapter

After reading the chapter, the reader will be able to

a. explain the key aspects of the following theories of intelligence
   - innate, single entity intelligence
   - learnable intelligence
   - multiple intelligences
   - attribution of intelligence

b. implement classroom strategies that move students toward the belief that success is due more to effort and acquired strategies than to innate ability and luck

c. increase students' motivation by helping them equate success with effort and the acquisition of effective strategies

d. provide students with strategies that make them "smarter"

Bob and Joe were brothers that were separated in age by four years. They lived in a housing project with their parents during the 1960s and early 1970s. Their mother supported the family with her job as a waitress in a diner. Their father was a drinking alcoholic who had no employment. Their father would eventually die of cirrhosis of the liver when the boys were approximately fifteen and eleven years of age.

Bob was the brother who appeared to have more potential for success (or more intelligence, as some would say). He attended the local public high from which the majority of the graduates went on to four-year colleges. He played on the basketball team and was in college track courses.

Joe was a likable young man who went to the regional vocational high school, rather than the high school attended by his brother. At that time in public education, the move to high school was a filtering process. Those who were smart enough for college went on to the local public high school. Those who were not went to the technical high school to acquire a trade.

Joe enjoyed his time at the technical high school and became a draftsman. He went to work for a local company. His boss noticed right away that Joe was a hard worker and had the potential to advance in the company. He encouraged Joe to go to college. Joe thought about this idea for a long time because he was unsure if he was "college material." After all, didn't his elementary and middle school teachers indicate he was not college material by recommending vocational high school rather than the local college preparatory high school? Joe finally decided he would give college a try. Since he was now married and needed the income from his job, he decided he would start going to college at night. Joe eventually received a bachelor's degree in business administration. His degree and hard work earned him a promotion in the company. His confidence in his ability to succeed in the professional and academic worlds rose significantly. Joe enrolled in an MBA program at night while he continued at his job. He completed the MBA and achieved further success in the company. During his MBA work, he developed a particular interest in business law since this area of study was most relevant to his present employment. He decided to enroll in a part-time law school program. He completed law school and passed the bar exam. Joe went on to become a successful attorney practicing business law.

What about Bob? During high school Bob worked as a cook in the diner where his mother waited tables. After high school, he continued in that position. During and after high school, Bob also began drinking alcohol to excess. Bob continued to work as a cook in the diner until his untimely death at the age of forty-seven due to alcohol-related physical problems.

The previous story is a true story. We provide it as context for the following discussion about the nature of intelligence.

For more than 125 years educators, social scientists and psychologists have debated the question of whether intelligence is innate or acquired. It is part of the age-old nature vs. nurture argument that continues to this day. In this chapter, we will look at the two perspectives on the nature of intelligence. The first is the idea that all or most of our *intelligence is genetic and a single entity.* Theorists in this school of thought say that there is relatively little that schools may do to impact the intelligence of a student. The second idea is that *intelligence is learnable and multifaceted.* This school of thought's proponents believe that most of a person's school and career success (up to 75%, according to some theorists) is the result of environment (school, home and others), effort and strategies for thinking and learning.

For more than 125 years educators, social scientists and psychologists have debated the question of whether intelligence is innate or acquired.

Intelligence as a Single Entity and Primarily Due to Heredity

As early as 1869, British scientist Francis Galton wrote the book *Hereditary Genius: Its Laws and Consequences.* In it he spoke about genetics as the primary determinant of intelligence. American psychologists extrapolated from this the concept of **Intelligence Quotient (IQ).** This was a measurable intelligence that was native and stayed constant throughout a person's life (Devlin, Fienberg, Resnick, & Roeder, 1997, p. 2).

In their book *Intelligence, Genes, and Success* (Devlin, Fienberg, Resnick, & Roeder, 1997, p. 5), the authors describe Galton's work as follows:

> Galton was a central figure in the founding of the eugenics (a term he coined in 1883) movement and the study of the relationship of heredity to race and talent. From his analysis of biographical dictionaries and encyclopedias, he became convinced that talent in science, the professions, and the arts ran in families so that it would be "quite practicable to produce a highly gifted race of men by judicious marriages during several consecutive generations (Kelves, 1985).

Interesting to note is that Galton was a cousin to Charles Darwin and was influenced by his cousin's work as it appeared in Darwin's famous book, *On the Origin of Species by Means of Natural Selection.*

Karl Pearsons, one of the founders of modern statistical methods, devised statistical methods for establishing the correlation between hereditary intelligence and success in society. Pearsons would later join the University of London and become the Galton Eugenics Professor. He went on to publish some 300 works dealing with the relationships between population traits and social behaviors, occupations and diseases. In describing intelligence, he was quoted as stating, "No training or education can create (it). You must breed it" (Kelves, 1985).

The person best known for developing a measurement for intelligence was Alfred Binet. Binet was a psychologist at the Sorbonne in France between 1894 and 1911. The first intelligence test described by Binet and a colleague in 1896 involved counting objects in pictures, noting similarities in familiar objects, filling in missing words in sentences and describing how terms had different meanings (Devlin, Fienberg, Resnick, & Roeder, 1997, p. 9). In 1904, Binet was asked to develop a way to determine which French schoolchildren needed extra help. He introduced his method for measuring a child's performance against the trends of other children in 1908. His system measured a child's mental age in relation to the child's physical age. This was the first step in developing the concept of *intelligence quotient* or *IQ* (Perkins, 1995, pp. 23–26).

Binet, however, was not a proponent of the idea that intelligence was a fixed, single entity that was established at birth. Perkins (1995) describes Binet's reticence to reach this conclusion as follows:

> *Binet, however, was not a proponent of the idea that intelligence was a fixed, single entity that was established at birth.*

> He (Binet) did not jump from the fact that some people behave more intelligently than others to the presumption that there was one essence, a single mental resource, that some people had more of and some less... He feared it would offer educators the excuse to ignore the plight of poorly performing students on the grounds that they lacked the intelligence to do better. It also might give educators grounds for dismissing under motivation and behavior problems as symptoms of low intelligence (p. 29).

Henry Goddard authored the first American version of this test in 1908 and administered it to 2000 school children in Vineland, New Jersey. It was the Americans, between 1908 and 1925, who took Binet's individually administered intelligence tests and turned them into paper and pencil, group-administered tests. To do this, they created a single entity IQ score to replace the mental age and chronological age scores developed by Binet that were difficult to interpret. Stanford psychologist Lewis Terman imported Binet's test to the U. S. and developed the Stanford–Binet IQ test (Gould, 1995, in Fraser, 1995, p. 11). Terman recognized that as long as IQ tests had to be administered one-on-one by a trained psychologist they would be too expensive to use widely. He and graduate student William Otis developed the first Army Alpha test that was administered to 1.7 million army recruits between 1917 and 1919. That test would eventually be renamed the Armed Services Vocational Battery and was used during World War II. It continues to be used today by all branches of the military service (Devlin, Fienberg, Resnick, & Roeder, 1997, pp. 9–10). Terman's belief that intelligence is hereditary is documented in his 1922 article "Were We Born That Way?" that appeared in the journal *World's Work*. In that article he states:

> The common opinion that the child from a cultured home does better in tests by reason of his superior home advantages is an entirely gratuitous assumption... The children of successful parents test higher than children from wretched and ignorant homes for the simple reason that their heredity is better.

The data derived from the Alpha tests began to drive the belief in American society that certain cultures were genetically more intelligent than others. Princeton psychology professor Carl C. Brigham wrote the book *A Study of American Intelligence* which is based on the findings from the Alpha tests. Brigham (1923) concluded that the immigration of southern and eastern Europeans to the United States would lower native American intelligence. One year later, Congress passed the Immigration Restriction Act of 1924 that enabled a disproportionate level of immigration by northern and western Europeans who were thought to be more intelligent. In the United States Supreme Court case Buck vs. Bell, 1927, the court supported sterilization laws passed in sixteen states between 1907 and 1917. In that opinion, noted justice Oliver Wendell Holmes wrote "Three generations of imbeciles are enough" (Hernstein & Murray, 1994, p. 5).

In 1912, German psychologist W. Stern improved on Binet's format for determing IQ. Stern (Perkins, 1995, pp. 26–28) developed a system in which a person's mental age was divided by his/her actual age. This number was then multiplied by 100. For example, a 10-year-old who had a mental age of 10 would have an IQ of 100. 10 divided by 10 equals 1. 1 multiplied by 100 equals 100. A ten-year-old with a mental age of eleven would have an IQ of 110. 11 divided by 10 equals 1.1 and 1.1 multiplied by 100 equals 110. A ten-year-old with a mental age of nine would have an IQ of 90. This gave rise to the bell curve with which we are all so familiar. (See Figure 7-1).

Stern's method worked well for children but became a problem when applied to adults. The mental versus chronological age comparison no longer worked when you applied it to forty- and fifty-year-olds. Another method was needed that might be applied to adults and children. Today, psychologists still use a bell-shaped curve such as the one in Figure 7-1. In today's model, IQ is no longer determined by dividing mental age by actual age. Instead, it is normed against the results of a large number of people who are tested to determine average scores and the various standard deviations from the average. The number 100 continued to be used for the average score solely to be consistent with Stern's model. The standard deviation of 15 was also used so as to continue with the familiar numbers from Stern's work. Stern found a standard deviation of approximately 15 or 16.

In today's model, IQ is no longer determined by dividing mental age by actual age. Instead, it is normed against the results of a large number of people who are tested to determine average scores and the various standard deviations from the average.

In the general population, more than 68.2% of the people have IQs between 85 and 115. 13.6% of the population has an IQ between 115 and 130. 2.1% of the population has an IQ between 130 and 145. Only .2% of the population has an IQ above 145. The same is true for the left side of the distribution, with 13.6% of the population having an IQ between 85 and 70, 2.1% with an IQ between 70 and 55 and only .2% with an IQ lower than 55.

Figure 7-1

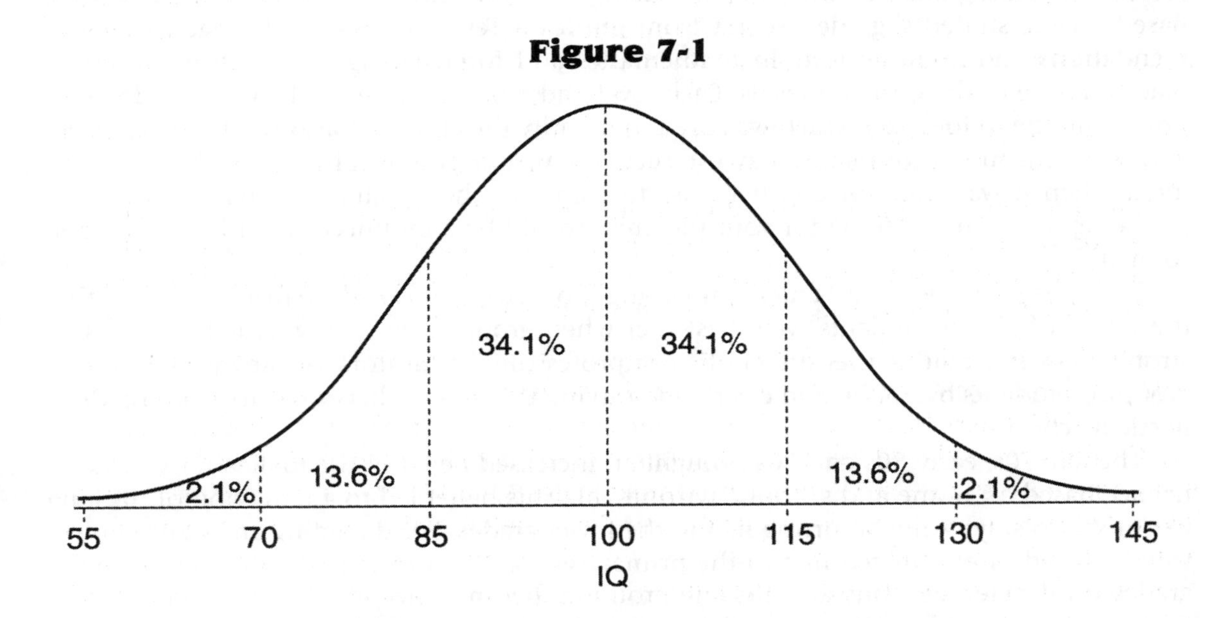

In the 1930s and 1940s, the United States' public was well on its way to believing that intelligence could be defined by a single score, was genetically inherited and varied by race. Everyone in education has at some time come across the Wechsler Intelligence Scale for Children commonly known as the WISC. Psychologist David Wechsler developed his first version of the test in the 1930s. This test, in its revised form, is still used in schools to determine student IQ.

In 1957, psychologist Ann Anastasi noted at meetings of the American Psychological Association that the nature vs. nurture debate about intelligence had subsided because geneticists, psychologists and social scientists had become convinced that nature and nurture were interactive and interrelated as they pertained to intelligence. In 1958, she indicated in an article in *Psychological Review* that the focus on the study of intelligence must be on the interaction of the both nature and nuture (Anastasi as cited in Devlin et al., 1994).

As the 1960s approached, most educators believed that some part of intelligence (or lack thereof) was developmental and not hereditary. Lyndon Johnson's Great Society program brought Head Start to schools in an effort to reverse the negative impact of the home environment in socioeconomically deprived homes. The belief was that early intervention would enable students to "catch-up" intellectually with their peers from socioeconomically advantaged homes.

> *Millions of baby boom children were placed in fixed-ability reading and math groups as early as first grade.*

Nevertheless, educators were not ready to let go of the concept that intelligence was fixed at some point early in a child's life. Educators determined that tracking by ability in schools was required to ensure that the less intelligent were not frustrated and overwhelmed and the more intelligent were not held back by the slow pace of the others. Millions of baby boom children were placed in fixed-ability reading and math groups as early as first grade. Junior high and high schools were tracked by ability. Junior high students such as Bob and Joe were even funneled to either academic college preparatory high schools or vocational high schools depending on whether or not they were intelligent enough to go to college.

One school district in southern Connecticut during the late sixties and early seventies went so far as to place eighth-graders into fourteen separate "divisions" based on ability. The elementary schools in the city were neighborhood schools from kindergarten to grade seven. All eighth grade students attended a single school before moving on to high school. Based on the students' grades, scores from the Iowa Tests of Basic Skills, teacher recommendations and aptitude tests in mathematics and foreign language, each student was placed in one of the fourteen levels. Each level had a distinct and public number designation from one to fourteen which was used to identify the class for various school activities. For example, on school picture day the secretary would periodically make an announcement when it was time for another class to come for their pictures. "Division fourteen, please report to the cafeteria for your pictures" would be announced in all fourteen classrooms!

These educators were not cruel or uncaring. Contemporary wisdom firmly believed that the needs of all the students were best met when grouped by ability. This belief was so strong in society that neither the public nor professional educators saw any problem with grouping students by ability and clearly identifying them as in this example from the Connecticut school.

The late 70s, early 80s and 90s brought an increased belief in the malleability of intelligence based on home and school environment. This belief led to a reduction of tracking in our schools, typically occurring first in the lower grades. Fixed reading and math groups were reduced or eliminated first in the primary grades. This change slowly moved up the grades until heterogeneous and flexible grouping became the primary structure in most schools through fifth grade. Many districts changed to the middle school concept (with sixth, seventh and eighth grades grouped together) and reduced the degree of tracking.

Even with these changes occurring in schools, proponents of the concept of intelligence as a single, fixed entity and primarily determined by heredity continued to promote these concepts. In 1994, the book *The Bell Curve* reestablished the concept of inherited, fixed, single entity intelligence as a viable theory of intelligence. The authors, Richard Hernstein and Charles Murray, used a comprehensive review of the research on intelligence over the previous 125 years to conclude that intelligence was primarily hereditary and that it varied by race and culture. The book reignited a fiery ideological debate in academia and among the general public between those who adhere to this theory and those who believe that intelligence has multiple components and may be enhanced by home and school environments.

Intelligence as Having Multiple Components That May Be Enhanced by Home and School Factors

The genesis of the idea that intelligence is actually a composite of multiple components was first suggested by Alfred Binet. David Perkins (1995, p. 25) credits Binet with presenting us with the first suggestion that there may be multiple intelligences. Perkins writes:

> Binet looked at a great variety of kinds of human behavior to gauge intelligence… He tested children every which way, and the more ways the better. So long as the task did not depend much on unusual rote knowledge or reading and writing it was fine with Binet… He took this approach because he believed that intelligence, far from being one thing, was a potpourri, a mix of this ability and that ability all jumbled together.

For the next fifty years, Binet's thoughts about intelligence containing multiple components were largely ignored as psychologists, educators and social scientists strove to find ways to establish a person's innate intelligence as a way of socially engineering aspects of society such as the military, education and the work force. As stated earlier, the largest body of work in this area at the turn of the twentieth century was for the purpose of efficiently determining job classifications for the military. Schools used the results to determine effective means of tracking students for efficient instruction. Bob was sent from junior high school to a high school to prepare him for college. Joe went off to a vocational school to prepare him to enter the work force with a trade upon high school graduation.

For the next fifty years, Binet's thoughts about intelligence containing multiple components were largely ignored as psychologists, educators and social scientists strove to find ways to establish a person's innate intelligence as a way of socially engineering aspects of society such as the military, education and the work force.

In the 1970s, University of Pennsylvania psychologist Jonathan Baron examined the relationship between strategies and intelligence. Baron's studies looked at the memories of mildly retarded and normal children. In his 1978 article *Intelligence and General Strategies,* Baron showed that the significant gap in the achievement on memory tasks that existed between normal children and mildly retarded children might be closed by teaching the mildly retarded children strategies that enhanced their memory.

Lloyd Humphreys (Perkins, 1995, pp. 77–79), a psychologist at the University of Illinois in Urbana, looked at the changes in the IQ test scores between soldiers tested in 1917 and those tested in 1942. Humphreys found a fifteen-point increase (one standard deviation) in the scores of those tested in 1942. Humphrey credits that increase to the expansion of public education during those years.

In the 1980s, University of Virginia psychologist Sandra Scarr examined the relationship between genetics and environment in a series of studies using identical twins. Identical twins were chosen because of their identical genetic makeup. Scarr identified groups of twins who were separated at birth and raised in different homes. Scarr's work combined with that of others established that IQ was 50% to 60% attributable to heredity and 40% to 50% attributable to genetics.

The research on the variability of IQ continues to uncover new evidence of the importance school and home environment play on increasing (or decreasing) IQ. Eric Turkeheimer, a psychologist at the University of Virginia in Charlottesville (Jacobson, 2003) found the correlation between IQ and heredity is even lower for children from homes with a low socioeconomic status than it is for children in socio-economically advantaged homes. Turkeheimer's research, based on twin studies, indicates that the correlation for children from homes with a low socioeconomic status is 0.1 on a scale with a maximum level of 1.0.[1] This would indicate that the environment, of which schools are an important part, is a significant component of the factors that shape the IQ of children from disadvantaged environments.

Perkins (1995, p. 61) explains to us that a person's IQ is only 50% due to genetics. He further explains that the correlation between IQ and a person's success in school and in the work force is approximately .5. That means that a person's genetic intelligence accounts for only 25% of his or her success in school and work. The remainder of a person's success is attributable to learned knowledge, strategies and effort. This means that 75% of

This means that 75% of a person's school and work success may be shaped by parents, teachers and other nurturing influences.

[1]Correlations between two factors range on a scale of –1.0 to 1.0. A 1.0 correlation between two factors means there is a perfect match. A –1.0 correlation indicates that each factor has an opposite correlation. For example, the correlation between a person's height and his shoe size is a positive correlation. On the other hand the correlation between days when the temperature is zero in a given region and the number of flowers that bloom on those days in that region is probably about –1.0.

a person's school and work success may be shaped by parents, teachers and other nurturing influences.

To better understand this idea, let's look again at our brothers, Bob and Joe. Let's assume that the decision for Bob to attend the college preparatory high school was based on his having an estimated IQ of 110 based on school grades, Iowa tests and teacher observations. Let's further assume that Joe's estimated IQ was 90 and that this score prompted the recommendation that he not attend the college preparatory high school. This would indicate a difference of more than one standard deviation between the brothers. If Perkins and others are correct, then 75% of what determined Bob's and Joe's ultimate academic and career achievements (or lack thereof) is attributable to family, school and other nurturing factors (such as the encouragement of his boss for Joe to attend college). To take this a step further, we may eliminate home as a factor in this example because both boys grew up in the same home with the same parents. One might then conclude that Bob's and Joe's career achievements are due to nurturing factors outside of the home.

During the twenty-five year span between Joe's entering ninth grade and his becoming a successful attorney practicing business law, Joe acquired on his own, or with the guidance of others, the mental capacity to achieve at a high level. He acquired the following:

1. confidence in his ability to succeed at academic tasks
2. the study, writing, verbal and problem-solving strategies needed to succeed in undergraduate, graduate and law school;
3. the work ethic to maintain a full-time job and part-time college study for a span of more than ten years
4. confidence in his ability to work successfully in a professional environment
5. the verbal, writing and problem-solving strategies needed to succeed in both the business and the legal professions
6. the work ethic to succeed in the competitive environment of business law

Learnable Intelligence

David Perkins' **theory of learnable intelligence** looks at intelligence as comprising three components. The first is **neural intelligence.** This is the part of our intelligence that is primarily determined by heredity and only changes as a result of the physical maturation of the brain, the *nature* portion of our intelligence. In his book *Outsmarting IQ* (1995, p. 102), Perkins defines neural intelligence as follows:

> The contribution of the efficiency and precision of the neurological system to intelligent behavior. This contribution may involve a single unified factor or some mix of several factors. In any case, it is influenced strongly by genetics and physical maturation.

The second component of intelligence described by Perkins is **experiential intelligence.** He supports this component of the theory by citing the work of Dutch psychologist A. D. de Groot (Perkins, 1995, pp. 80–81) and others. De Groot studied the similarities and differences between the cognitive abilities of amateur chess players and those of professional chess masters. He found that amateurs and professionals explored future moves with the same level of depth, however, the professionals easily beat the amateurs. To understand the reason for this, De Groot showed players a chessboard with a typical game situation and quickly removed the board from their sight and study. The amateurs could only remember the exact location of a fraction of the total number of the pieces on the chess board. The professionals, on the other hand, could remember *all the locations of all the chess pieces.* When he repeated the experiment with a random placement of the pieces that would not occur in a game situation, however, the amateurs and professionals had the same level of success in remembering the positions of the pieces. De Groot concluded that the professionals, who played much more frequently than the amateurs, had a much more highly developed memory based on the experience of studying chess pieces during game situations. It was their increased level of experience with the various configurations of pieces as they appeared in games that resulted in a greater ability to remember the location of the pieces during the experiment.

It was their increased level of experience with the various configurations of pieces as they appeared in games that resulted in a greater ability to remember the location of the pieces during the experiment.

Perkins describes experiential intelligence as follows:

> The contribution of context-specific knowledge to intelligent behavior. This contribution is learned, the result of extensive experience thinking and acting in particular situations over long periods of time. While there may be an initial ability to learn efficiently in a domain (for example musical giftedness), the accumulated knowledge and know-how of thinking in that domain constitutes experiential intelligence.

The third component of intelligence is **reflective intelligence.** Perkins (pp. 102–103) describes this as follows:

> The contribution to intelligent behavior of strategies for various intellectually challenging tasks, attitudes conducive to persistence, systematicity, and imagination in the use of one's mind, habits of self-monitoring and management. Reflective intelligence is in effect a control system for the resources afforded by neurological and experiential intelligence, bent on deploying them wisely.

In this model of intelligence, teachers, parents and the individual have little or no control over neural intelligence, however, teachers, parents and individuals have a great deal of control over the development of the experiential and reflective intelligences. Later in this chapter, we will look more at the role of teachers and parents in developing the motivation in students to maximize the growth of their experiential and reflective intelligences. (See the following section on Carol Dweck's work on self theory).

Let's place the three intelligences in the real life context of Bob and Joe. Bob and Joe came from the same parents, so in all likelihood they had similar neural intelligence. One might even argue that, based on Bob's early school success, his neural intelligence may have even been higher than Joe's. At some point in time, during their adolescence and into adulthood, Bob and Joe took very different paths related to their experiential and reflective intelligences. If we track Bob's life after high school, one might argue that Bob experienced no increase in experiential or reflective intelligence.

Joe, on the other hand, acquired increased experiential intelligence as academic and career building blocks. Joe's acquired knowledge at work and in high school led to a sufficient knowledge base to attend college and succeed in college. Joe's acquired learning in college and in his career lead to his ability to succeed when attending graduate school. His knowledge acquired in the MBA program and at work lead to his success when attending and successfully completing law school. The building blocks constructed to this point in academia and in his job ultimately lead to a successful career as an attorney.

Reflective intelligence also plays an important role in this story. Joe's decision to attend college at night while working requires a high level of self sacrifice, determination and the delay of the gratification of free time activities until some future time in his life. It is a decision almost anyone from any background might make, however, it is one that many people choose not to make. In this example, Joe increased his experiential intelligence and his reflective intelligence.

People who hear the story about Bob and Joe are often left asking themselves why Joe worked to increase his experiential intelligence while Bob chose to take no action in that direction. Columbia University social psychologist Carol Dweck offers interesting reasons for Joe's and Bob's behavior. Dweck, in her book *Self Theories* (2000, p. 3–5), indicates that some students respond to challenges with an "entity" belief in their intelligence. This is a belief that intelligence is a fixed entity and, therefore, if a task is difficult for me to do, it must be because I am not smart enough to do it. Other students, those who believe that intelligence is what Dweck calls **"incremental" intelligence,** or intelligence that may be increased with effort and new strategies, see challenges as interesting problems to be tackled step-by-step. Mistakes are seen as learning opportunities rather than failures. In her research, Dweck found, contrary to popular belief, that some students with low confidence in their intelligence still threw themselves wholeheartedly into difficult tasks and stick with them to fruition. These students had an incremental belief about intelligence. Other students, with high confidence, did not want their intelligence tested, and their high confidence was quickly shaken when confronted with a difficult task. These students had an entity belief in intelligence.

In another surprising finding, Dweck (2000, p. 53) found that students who had high achievement during their elementary and middle school years were most, rather than least, vulnerable to entity thinking when faced with a difficult task.

In another surprising finding, Dweck (2000, p. 53) found that students who had high achievement during their elementary and middle school years were most, rather than least, vulnerable to entity thinking when faced with a difficult task. They worried about failure, questioned their ability and were likely to wilt when they hit obstacles. The other students, those with a history of lower achievement, had developed the capacity to stay with a task even when their initial attempts lead to failure.

Making Kids Smarter in Schools

David Perkins tells us that our intelligence is 40% to 50% learned and our success in school and life is at least 75% due to the strategies we learn, the effort we exert and the people who guide the development of these two factors. Clinical psychologist Dr. Daniel Goldman (Goldman, 1999), the author of numerous books and articles on *emotional intelligence,* estimates that IQ only accounts for between 10% and 20% of a person's success in school and career. That means 80% to 90% of success in life is in the control of the individual and the people who impact their lives, such as teachers and parents. Social psychologist Carol Dweck has shown us that how we interact with children has a significant impact on how they react when confronting unfamiliar and challenging situations. What an exciting prospect for those of us who work in the education profession, which is primarily charged with preparing students for successful lives!

The next part of this chapter shares ideas that classroom teachers have used to help students get smarter. By that we mean developing students who

a. willingly exert more effort
b. use strategies to more efficiently learn new content and skills
c. use strategies to solve problems
d. stick with problems until they are solved
e. believe in their abilities to succeed in school and life by applying effort and strategies

Carol Dweck offers some techniques (2000, pp. 53–63) for assessing whether individual students have an entity or incremental approach to their intelligence. The following activity sheet may be used to assess students' beliefs about the nature of intelligence. This activity sheet is designed for use in upper elementary, middle or high school, however, it may be simplified or given orally to younger students.

Name: ____

Teacher's Name: ______________________________________

Date: ____________________

Please answer the following questions. It is important that you answer then as honestly as you can and are not influenced by what you think others will answer. **There are no right or wrong answers.**

1. Write a definition for intelligence.

2. Think of a person whom you consider intelligent. It might be someone you know personally or know of from the news or another source. Describe what this person does that causes you to think of him or her as intelligent.

3. Are there times when you feel intelligent? If so, when?

4. Is there a time or are there times when you have felt dumb (unintelligent)? If so, when?

5. Fill in the equation below so the total equals 100%:

Intelligence = ________% effort + _________% ability

In her research with fifth graders, Carol Dweck (2000, pp. 61–62) found that students with an entity mindset defined intelligence as

"What your IQ is or how smart you are."
"Intelligence is how smart you are."
"Very smart, brilliant, or bright."

But the incremental students defined intelligence as

"I think it is what you know."
"How much you look at a problem and check it over to find stuff wrong."
"I think it is to try your best."
"Studying hard."
"Intelligence is how hard you work to do something."

Entity theorists tended to answer question 5 with a higher percentage indicating ability. Incremental theorists assigned a higher percentage to effort.

Dweck speaks about the need to do "attribution retraining" (2000, p. 56) with all students and particularly with those who respond to challenges with the entity reaction of feeling dumb and giving up. By retraining students to think of intelligence as something we acquire with hard work and strategies, we develop the desire to work on challenging school assignments to completion. We motivate students not to give up when something is difficult, but to learn from their mistakes and try again.

By retraining students to think of intelligence as something we acquire with hard work and strategies, we develop the desire to work on challenging school assignments to completion.

The following are some strategies that teachers use to develop the belief that intelligence is incrementally achieved through effort and learning new strategies.

Strategies for Motivating Students by Developing an Incremental Belief About Intelligence

Incremental Messages Posted on Classroom Walls

Many teachers from elementary school through college have begun to post quotes that promote the belief that success and intelligence are due to acquiring new knowledge by using strategies and hard work. Some that we have seen include the following:

"Ballplayers are not born great. They're not born great hitters or pitchers or managers, and luck isn't a big factor. No one has come up with a substitute for hard work. I've never met a ballplayer who didn't have to work harder at learning to play ball than anything else he ever did." —*Ted Williams*

"I'm a great believer in luck and I find the harder I work, the more I have of it." —*Thomas Jefferson*

"The dictionary is the only place that success comes before work. Hard work is the price we must pay for success. I think you can accomplish anything if you're willing to pay the price." —*Vince Lombardi*

"Continuous effort—not strength or intelligence—is the key to unlocking our potential." —*Black Elk (1863–1950), —Native American*

"Genius is 1% inspiration and 99% perspiration."—*Thomas Edison*

"Measure a person not by the heights they achieve but from the depths from which they've come." —*Frederick Douglas*

"The journey of 1000 miles begins with the first step." —*Chinese proverb*

"All mankind is divided into three classes: those that are immovable, those that are movable, and those that move." —*Benjamin Franklin*

"The three great essentials to achieve anything worthwhile are, first, hard work; second, stick-to-itiveness; third, common sense." —*Thomas Edison*

"Smart is not something you are. It is something you become." —*unknown*

Incremental Stories About Celebrities Familiar to Students

This strategy becomes more effective as students leave the primary grades and enter a point in their lives when they become aware of the achievements of people in the news. Once students can identify famous people and the attention those people receive, they are ready for stories of incremental success. For example, many high school students have come to know Colin Powell because his picture appears frequently on the front of newspapers, his name is mentioned on the radio and he appears on television, however, students only see Colin Powell as the "finished product." They don't know the Colin Powell who started his military training in New York City in both a high school and a public college ROTC program. They don't know about Colin Powell's years as an officer taking troops on training missions that required a succession of sleepless nights. They don't know that Colin Powell volunteered for the rigors of airborne training at a time in his career when he was well established as an officer and a decade or more older than the majority of people who were in his airborne training class. They don't realize the obstacles he overcame to become chairman of the Joint Chiefs of Staff in a military hierarchy dominated by graduates of the military academies. As with Colin Powell, children often see famous people only as the finished product. They don't know the story of hard work, perseverance and incremental success that preceded their present levels of success. Many teachers are helping students to see that the finished products they admire and aspire to emulate are the result of significant effort, incremental growth and achievement.

Keep in the classroom the biographies of people who have achieved as a result of hard work and perseverance. In the past twenty years, there has been a proliferation of literature, including biographies, that has been written at age-appropriate reading levels for most students. Biographies of this type are an excellent source of information about the incremental growth to success of the famous people that students typically only know as finished products.

Biographies for Secondary School Students

Jacqueline Harris, *The Tuskegee Airmen: Heroes of World War II*

Elie Wiesel, *Night*

Jack Canfield and Mark Victor Hansen, *Chicken Soup for the Teenage Soul: 101 Stories of Life, Love, and Learning*

Viktor Frankl, *Man's Search for Meaning*

Maya Angelou, *I Know Why the Caged Bird Sings*

Arthur Ashe, *Days of Grace: A Memoir*

Cary Lorene, *Black Ice*

Richard P. Feynman, *Surely You're Joking, Mr. Feynman: Adventures of a Curious Character*

Jeanne Wakatsuki, *Farewell to Manzanar*

Ji-Li Jiang, *Red Scarf Girl: A Memoir of the Cultural Revolution*

Chris Mead, *Champion—Joe Louis, Black Hero in White America*

James McBride, *The Color of Water: A Black Man's Tribute to his White Mother*
Frank McCourt, *Angela's Ashes: A memoir*
Malcolm X, *The Autobiography of Malcolm X*
Libby Riddles, *Race Across Alaska: First Woman to Win the Iditarod Tells Her Story*
Tobias Wolff, *This Boy's Life: A Memoir*
Richard Wright, *Black Boy, A Record of Childhood and Youth*

Biographies for Elementary Students

Anne Frank, *The Diary of a Young Girl*
Russell Freedman, *Photobiography of Abraham Lincoln*
Rosa Parks, *I Am Rosa Parks*
Zlata Filipovik, *Zlata's Diary*
J. L. Wilkerson, *A Doctor to Her People: Dr. Susan LaFlesche Picotte*—first Native American Woman doctor

Incremental Stories About Ordinary People's Lives

Not all incremental success stories are about celebrities. Almost every adult has his or her own incremental story or stories. Tell students about times when you (their teacher) were faced with a difficult task and solved it through perseverance and by developing new strategies. As in the case of the celebrities discussed previously, students see you as a finished product also. They think you always read as well as you do now. They think you always solved math problems and spoke in front of the class as well. Bring in parent and community speakers to tell their incremental success stories.

Praise Student Effort

We often praise student achievement. It is a natural tendency to see success and praise the accomplishment. We need to make praising *effort* a frequent phenomenon in our classroom as well. We should praise effort and the use of effective strategies, and we should encourage students to praise one another when they witness effort and/or the use of effective strategies by their peers.

Help Students to Examine and Understand Strategies Used to Succeed

Students typically need help in examining and understanding the strategies they used to complete tasks. They will only be able to replicate a strategy if they know what strategy they used and how they used it. In Chapter 5, we look at questioning techniques that help students to understand the thinking processes they use when solving a problem.

Respond to Students' Successes with Praises of Their Efforts and the Strategies They Used

Carol Dweck found in her research (2000, p. 112–113) that students who were praised upon completing a task with statements that were what she calls **Person-oriented statements**

> "You're a good boy."
> "I'm proud of you."
> "You're smart."
> "You're very good at this."

made <u>no</u> movement away from entity thinking and toward incremental thinking.

Students who were praised with statements that she termed outcome-oriented made some movement away from entity thinking and toward incremental thinking. **Outcome-oriented statements** include the following examples:

"That's the right way to do it."
"You did an excellent job."

The students who made the greatest growth toward incremental thinking were those who were praised for their effort or strategies with statements or questions such as the following.

The students who made the greatest growth toward incremental thinking were those who were praised for their effort or strategies with statements or questions such as the following:

"You really tried hard."
"You found a way to do it."
"You found more than one way to do it."
"You kept trying even when you didn't get it right the first time."
"You've tried it that way and it didn't work. What is another way you might try to solve this problem?"
"You really put the time in to make this work pay off."
"All of these drafts really made this an excellent piece of work."
"You were determined to turn this into a really excellent piece of work."
"I'm impressed by your dedication to this assignment."

Teach Your Students About the Difference Between Entity Thinking and Incremental Thinking

In middle school, students are at the beginning stages of understanding the difference between attributing success to effort and strategies and attributing it to innate ability. It is particularly powerful to explain these theories in relation to the areas they find difficult. High school students respond very well to the direct teaching of the two theories. We may teach students that learning new strategies, trying new approaches after an initial failure and persevering will lead to more success. We may also teach them that getting down on themselves and giving up leads only to failure. A simple but effective method for doing this is to teach students to attribute success to effort and strategies using what has come to be known as "attribution theory" (Hunter, 1987).

Attribution Theory tells us that there are four forces that come into play when we confront a new task. These forces are effort, our ability in the area of the task (see the discussion later in this chapter about multiple intelligences), the difficulty of the task and luck or opportunity. When we first confront a task, the one area we have control over is our effort. Our ability is initially set at a certain level, however, we can increase our ability with preparation. The task difficulty is fixed. Running a mile or solving a two-digit multiplication problem or a quadratic equation is the same task no matter when we do it. Opportunity or luck[2] is fixed at the time we begin the task. Take, for example, a high school athlete who must run a mile in seven minutes to be eligible to play on the basketball team. Expending greater effort is going to lead to a better time than expending less effort would, however, different athletes come with different abilities at the outset.[3] A student who has run the mile

[2] Hunter (1987) talks about luck or opportunity as circumstances completely out of the control of the student. Others see an ability to maximize a lucky event or opportunity with preparation. There is an old saying that refers to a person's "ship coming in" as a time when they get the opportunity to succeed. We would argue that people's ships come in quite frequently during life. The difference between getting on it and sailing away to success and getting on the ship and ramming it into a reef is the level to which the person is prepared for the opportunity.

[3] In her article, Hunter (1987) talks about ability as being innate and completely out of a student's control. Others see ability as a combination of innate ability and ability that is changeable with practice and the development of strategies.

as an event in the fall track season will report for basketball season better able to run the mile than most of the other athletes. The task is the same for all. Everyone has to run a mile. No one gets to run a half-mile and no one has to run two miles. Luck or opportunity is variable by person and out of his or her control. The athlete who breaks an ankle will not be able to run the mile no matter how hard he or she tries.

In this example, the effort and ability are in the control of the athlete. As mentioned previously, trying harder will lead to a better running time. The athlete can increase his or her ability with practice and the development of strategies. Setting up a training schedule during the weeks prior to the first basketball practice will result in higher ability at the first basketball practice. Learning to run with a steady gait, longer strides and effective breathing are strategies that will also increase the athlete's ability. One might even argue that an athlete may impact the area of opportunity or luck. A well-established preparation program prior to the season will limit the possibility of injury. Running on an even surface such as a track or a road will decrease the likelihood of twisting and injuring an ankle prior to the first day of practice. Luck is an interesting concept. Teaching students that luck is an interaction between preparation and opportunity rather than a totally random and uncontrollable factor is empowering and motivating.

We are reminded of an interview with a professional golfer. The interviewer asked the golfer what part luck played in winning golf tournaments. The golfer replied, "Winning in golf is all luck. And, I find the more I practice the luckier I get."

Factor	Participant's Control Over the Factor	Consistency or Variability From Participant to Participant
Effort	Completely within the participant's control	Variable from person to person, based on levels of interest and perseverance
Task Difficulty	Completely out of the participant's control	Remains constant for all participants
Ability	Partially innate and out of the participant's control and partially determined by prior strategy development	Innate ability varies among participants; however, strategy acquisition varies among individuals.
Luck or Opportunity	Partially determined by circumstances out of the participant's control and partially determined by preparation	Some of the circumstances (such as how the person is feeling that day) are variable. Others (such as the weather on the day of the game) are constant for all participants.

Help Students Understand That Intelligences Are Multiple

When students are frustrated by a task, remind them of the fact that everyone has strengths in different intelligences. Success on tasks in those intelligences that come less easy to the student will require greater effort and the development of more strategies. Success on tasks in those intelligences in which the student has a more developed or innate ability at the outset of the task will require less effort to achieve the same level of success.

Howard Gardner's (1985) **theory of multiple intelligences** tells us that different people have different levels of innate ability in eight specific areas. He supports this theory with brain research that ties different tasks and their related intelligences to different parts of the brain. (See Chapter 8 for more information on how the brain functions). In his book, *Mul-*

tiple Intelligences in the Classroom (1994), Thomas Armstrong describes the eight intelligences as follows:

> **Linguistic Intelligence:** The capacity to use words effectively, whether orally or in writing. This intelligence includes the ability to manipulate the syntax or structure of language, phonology, or sounds of language, the semantics or meanings of language, and the pragmatic dimensions for practical uses of language.
>
> **Logical Mathematics Intelligence:** The capacity to use numbers effectively and reason well. This intelligence includes sensitivity to logical patterns and relationships, statements and propositions, functions, and other related abstractions.
>
> **Spatial Intelligence:** The ability to perceive the visual–spatial world accurately and to perform transformations upon those perceptions. This intelligence involves sensitivity to color, line shape, form, space, and the relationships that exist between these elements.
>
> **Bodily–Kinesthetic Intelligence:** Expertise in using one's whole body to express ideas and feelings and facility in using one's hands to produce or transform things. This intelligence includes specific physical skills such as coordination, balance, dexterity, strength, flexibility, and speed.
>
> **Musical Intelligence:** The capacity to perceive, transform, and express musical forms. This intelligence includes sensitivity to rhythm, pitch or melody, and timber or tone color of a musical piece.
>
> **Interpersonal Intelligence:** The ability to perceive and make distinctions in the mood, intentions, motivations, and feelings of other people. This may include sensitivity to facial expressions, voice, and gestures.
>
> **Intrapersonal Intelligence:** Self-knowledge and the ability to act adaptively on the basis of that knowledge. This intelligence includes having an accurate picture of oneself.
>
> **Naturalistic Intelligence** (Armstrong, 2003, p. 14): The capacity to recognize and classify numerous species of flora and fauna in one's environment (as well as natural phenomena such as mountains and clouds).

Sample Activities That Require Each of the Intelligences

Students who have low ability in an area need to expend more effort than those who have high ability in the same area, but they can eventually have a similar result. Let's look for a minute at the example of learning to ride a two-wheeled bike. A child with high bodily–kinesthetic intelligence may learn to ride in a couple of hours with the assistance of an adult. Another child may need several practice sessions with that adult over the course of several days. Ultimately almost every child, regardless of their bodily–kinesthetic intelligence, learns to ride a bike.

> *Students who have low ability in an area need to expend more effort than those who have high ability in the same area, but they might eventually have a similar result.*

Linguistic Intelligence

- writing an essay
- writing a short story
- writing from the perspective of an historical figure
- reciting a poem

- making an oral presentation
- explaining the solution of a math problem to the class
- writing a lab report

Logical Mathematics Intelligence

- solving a word problem
- solving a geometry proof
- deriving an equation

Spatial Intelligence

- interpreting a map
- interpreting various types of graphs
- drawing, painting or working on other types of art projects
- interpreting a painting

Bodily–Kinesthetic Intelligence

- performing an interpretive dance
- presenting a tableau
- acting out a scene
- miming
- taking part in an athletic event

Musical Intelligence

- singing
- playing an instrument
- interpreting a song
- writing music
- composing a song

Interpersonal Intelligence

- interpreting the mood, feelings and attitude of a literary character
- taking part in all types of group work
- role-playing
- taking part in simulations

Intrapersonal Intelligence

- reflecting activities
- working in groups
- taking part in simulations

Naturalistic Intelligence

- recognizing flora and fauna
- studying natural phenomena such as mountains and clouds

Figure 7-2 shows the different level of effort we need to assert depending on the level of intelligence, similar previous experience and personal interest we bring to the task. The greater our level of each of these three factors at the start of the task, the less effort we need to exert in order to succeed. Conversely, those tasks for which we have low intelligence, no similar previous experience and low interest require a great deal of effort to succeed. Thus it took much more effort for Joe to become a successful business attorney than it would take for a person who came from a family with a high parental education level, a high appreciation for education and a high socioeconomic level, and who also attended high-performing schools in grades K–12 and beyond.

Figure 7-2

When Confronted With New Information and/or Skill

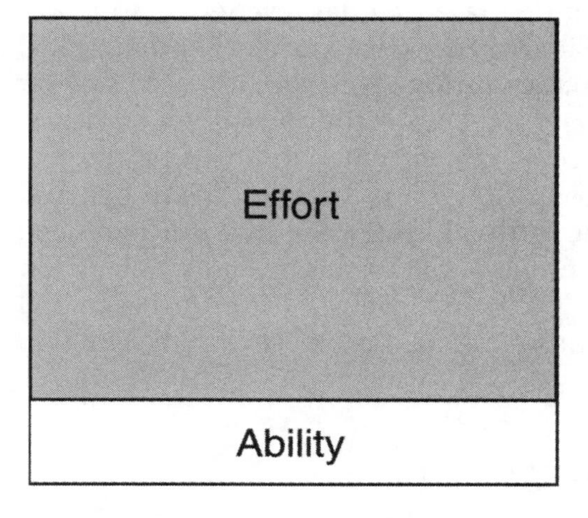

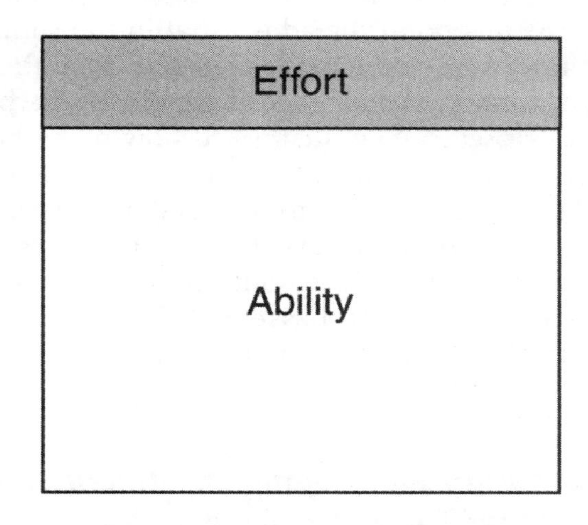

- Little or no previous experience with similar tasks and/or
- Area of lower aptitude (an area of weaker intelligence as defined by Gardner) and/or
- Area of low interest

- Many previous experiences with similar tasks and/or
- Area of high aptitude (a stronger intelligence as defined by Gardner) and/or
- Area of high interest

Remind Students About Previous Tasks That They Eventually Mastered

School days should be and are filled with situations in which students are confronting new learning. There is ample opportunity to become frustrated or feel dumb when a task is difficult. Reminding students of their previous successes and of how far they have come helps encourage and motivate their efforts. Take for example a high school student who starts out in calculus becomes discouraged and wants to drop the class when it becomes difficult. The student might be reminded that he or she felt the same way when first starting geometry and that he or she went on to eventually learn geometry and pass the class. An elementary student who is having difficulty with two-digit multiplication might be reminded of when he or she was first learning to add or first learning single-digit multiplication. Pausing to see how far he or she has come with these skills is a powerful motivator for tackling problems in the future.

One of our colleagues had the following experience with one of his high school students:

"I can remember working with a high school student who was frustrated by the challenge of understanding Shakespeare's *Romeo and Juliet.* I reminded him that, at the beginning of the year, he had believed that Homer's *Odyssey* was equally impossible, and yet we had actually managed to get him through and completely understand that work. So there was no doubt in my mind that he was going to succeed with *Romeo and Juliet* as well.

Have Students Analyze How They Got Good at Things That They Do Well

We have seen this technique used effectively with athletes who struggle in school. In one circumstance, a high school basketball player was very frustrated with mathematics. He felt and verbalized that he was dumb in math. The teacher asked him how he got to be so good in basketball. His initial response was that he "just was." The teacher went on to ask him how many hours in a typical week he plays basketball. He responded that it was about fifteen. She then said, "That means you play about sixty hours a month and 780 hours a year." At this point, he added that in the summer he played all day, every day, so it was probably more hours in the year than what the teacher had stated. The teacher then asked him how many hours a week he spent on mathematics during the school year. The answer was six or seven. She then asked how many hours a week he spent on mathematics during vacation. The student laughed and made the zero sign with his thumb and index finger. The teacher then summarized that he spent over 1000 hours a year on basketball and only about 220 hours a year on mathematics. She further pointed out that this had been something that had been going on in his life for ten years. That means he had spent almost 8,000 more hours on basketball than on math. "Of course you are better in basketball than math! Now, if you start to put more time into math, just as in basketball, you will get better and better."

Examples of Developing in Students Strategies That Will Make Them Smarter

Reading for Understanding: Helping Students Become Strategic Readers

Teachers may help their students become more active readers by teaching them a multitude of comprehension strategies. The following strategies are those that good readers use all the time as they read.

- visualizing
- predicting and confirming
- making connections
  - text-to-self
  - text-to-text
  - text-to-world
- analyzing vocabulary
- questioning what they have read and posing discussion questions
- summarizing
- highlighting important information
- noting questions

The following section illustrates how teachers might teach elementary and middle school students how to use visualization to help them better comprehend what they are reading.

Teaching the Comprehension Strategy of Visualizing

This particular comprehension strategy may be used with students as young as first grade and as old as fifth grade. Teachers should begin the lesson by modeling this strategy, that is, by thinking aloud about their own process of visualizing or evoking images while reading. Modeling should occur frequently, using short selections appropriate for the particular grade level. In addition, it is important that teachers use a variety of genres when modeling. Although modeling occurs primarily when this strategy is introduced, teachers should periodically model this strategy from time to time. Teachers should concentrate on visual images and on those that emanate from the other senses and should also focus on how they created those images. It is important for teachers to think aloud about how concentrating on visual images enhances comprehension. Gradually, teachers should ask the students to share their own images inspired by a variety of texts.

An example of how an elementary teacher might introduce this strategy by modeling visualization is as follows:

> Teacher reads the following passages from *Through Grandpa's Eyes* by Patricia MacLachlan.
>
> "In the morning, the sun pushes through the curtains into my eyes. I burrow down into the covers to get away, but the light follows. I give up, throw back the covers, and run into Grandpa's room."
>
> As I read this passage, I immediately think of myself waking up on a bright summer morning. In my mind, I can see the yellowish-orange-like sun filtering through blue and white curtains, while John tries to escape the light by trying to hide underneath his covers. I imagine him struggling to find darkness so that he can sleep a bit longer. Having no luck, I picture him quickly jumping out of bed. I hear the floorboards creaking as he runs with a grin from ear to ear to see Grandpa.

As students become more familiar with visualizing, teachers of both lower and upper elementary students might ask students to draw what they visualized as they read a short passage. Older students might meet in small groups or pairs to compare images and to discuss the components of the text that inspired those images. All children should be encouraged to discuss the ways in which their comprehension is enhanced by mental images.

During literature circles or book clubs, students might be asked to focus on this particular strategy in their conversations. In reading conferences with students, conversations might focus on the children's images and the parts of the text that evoked these images. Small flexible groups might be created for those students who need more modeling and explicit instruction. The teacher might focus sharing time on images that individual children discovered in their independent reading for the day, how those images were evoked and how thinking about important images enhanced their comprehension. As students read independently, they might use sticky notes to mark places in the text in which images were particularly vivid.

The following form may be used by students to encourage them to visualize as they read. Although this form is most appropriate for grades three through five, it may be adapted for younger grades.

Visualization

Good readers create pictures in their minds as they read. This strategy is known as visualization. Readers find their comprehension improves as these mental pictures help make the text more meaningful. Good readers practice this skill often as they read.

Directions:

As you read the assigned pages, practice the skill of visualization. Place sticky notes over parts of the text where you find yourself "painting pictures in your mind." After reading the entire selection, go back and select one of your favorite and/or most meaningful visualizations. Recreate this scene in color, copy the section of the text underneath and record the page number.

The following forms might also be used to help children read more actively by helping them focus on a particular strategy. Keep it in mind that these forms should only be used after a strategy has been introduced, modeled and practiced by the students. Again, these forms are most appropriate for students in grades three through five, but might certainly be adapted for younger children.

Predicting and Confirming

Good readers naturally make ***predictions*** *as they read, and like to think back as to how close their predictions were to the actual story events.*

Directions:

Make a ***minimum of two predictions*** *before you read the assigned chapter/pages. When you finish reading, make another prediction about what you think will happen in the next chapter.*

Record your predictions in the "Prediction" column, what actually happened in the "Confirmation" column, and document from the text the supporting evidence in the "Evidence" column. The supporting evidence should be a direct quote, so remember to use quotation marks and include the page number. Copy the following chart into your reading journal.

Prediction	Confirmation	Evidence

Making Connections

Good readers think about their own experiences as they read. They relate new text to their prior world knowledge, personal experiences and/or other books they have read. These connections take three different forms:

- *text-to-self connections*
- *text-to-text connections*
- *text-to-world connections*

Text-to-self connections

When the pictures or the story remind you of your own life, you are making a text-to-self connection.

Text-to-text connections

Readers who relate parts of the text or pictures to another book they have read are making text-to-text connections.

Text-to-world connections

When your world knowledge contributes to the understanding of a book you are reading, you are making a text-to-world connection.

Directions:

Keep track of the connections you make as you read in your reading journal. Be sure to mention the specific part of the text your connection relates to, note the page numbers and specify the type of connection you made.

Analyzing Vocabulary

Directions:

As you read, record two vocabulary words that you found interesting, difficult, unusual and/or relevant to the story. Complete the following tasks required for each new vocabulary word. This form will help guide you as you record this information in your reading journal.

Vocabulary Word: ______________________________

Definition: ______________________________

Source Used (dictionary, text) ______________________________

Use a thesaurus to find three synonyms for the word. __________

____

Part of Speech: ______________________________

Page Number: ______________________________

Original Sentence: ______________________________

Discussion Questions

Reading for meaning is a collaborative process. As we discuss it with others, we deepen our own understanding of a story. Your assignment is to create a minimum of three open-ended questions to present to your group as discussion prompts based on the assigned readings. The following are good examples of open-ended questions you are encouraged to include.

- *What might happen if...?*
- *How is ...like...?*
- *What do you think will happen after...?*
- *Do you agree with...and why?*
- *What feelings did you have when...?*
- *What was your first reaction to...?*
- *What did you consider to be the most important word or phrase within this assigned group of readings? Support with details from the text.*
- *Would you be friends with...? Why or why not? Be very specific. Support your opinion with details from the text.*
- *I like the way...said...or did.... How do you feel?*
- *How do you think...felt when...?*
- *What would you do if you were in the same situation as...on page...?*

The following question examples ARE NOT *good discussion starters. Do you know* WHY?

- *Who was the main character?*
- *Where does this story take place?*
- *What is the name of ...?*
- *Do you like...?*

Summarizing

When good readers read large chunks of a story or challenging text, they usually summarize what they have read.

Directions:

In your reading journal, write a brief summary of the text you have just read. Think about the main events and characters that are most important in the story. You may want to use the summarizing graphic organizer to help you organize the main events.

Secondary Reading Strategies

As students move to upper elementary and middle school, they are assigned content reading for classwork or homework with increasing frequency. One dilemma in assigning independent content reading is that the students often read the words as instructed; however, they are unable to extract the information they need from the reading. Successful content reading requires that we teach students specific strategies that allow them to extract important learning from the text. A second dilemma is when we assign content reading for homework. It is often difficult for teachers to determine which students have and have not completed (and comprehended) the assignment without administering quizzes and/or long sessions of recall question-and-answer periods that use up a great deal of class time. The following strategies are used by middle and high school teachers to increase students' comprehension of content area reading. Several of these are also good techniques for monitoring students' completion of the content reading when it is assigned for homework.

Graphic Organizers

During units on short stories or other such fictional reading, we assign our students to read a short story for homework and also to fill out the blank plot curve as they read. As you may see on the following example, the blank plot curve leaves room for students to fill in information about the plot's rising action, climax, falling action, resolution, conflict and main characters. We collect the plot curves at the beginning of class on which the assigned reading is due, not only as a means of ensuring that our students are doing their homework but also to better determine which students understood the story and which struggled with comprehension. These plot curves may also serve as useful study aides for an end-of-unit test or to help in locating particular quotes from the text for an essay assignment. The following is a sample of a plot curve graphic organizer.

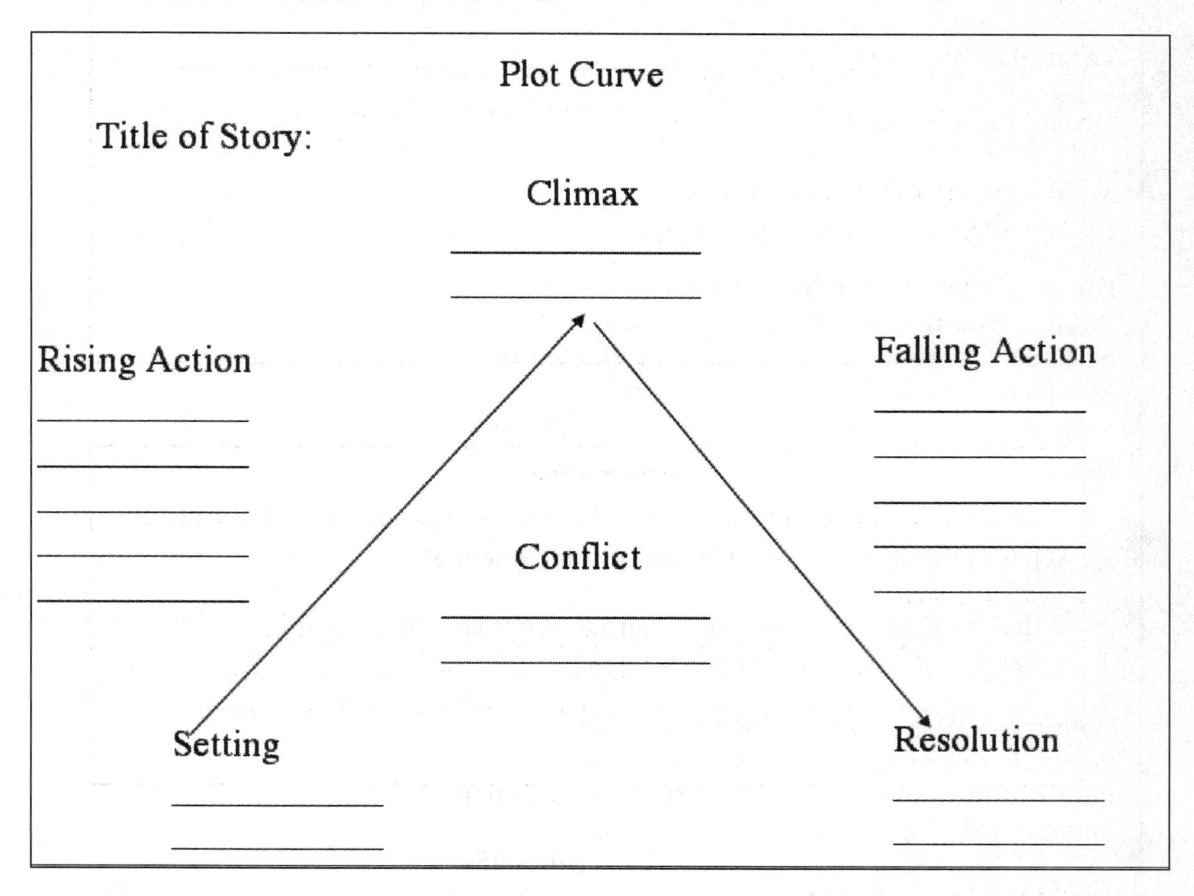

Guiding Questions

For a harder work such as Shakespeare's *Romeo and Juliet*, we give our student a sheet with six or seven plot-based questions to answer as they complete a night's reading. As with the graphic organizers, our goals were threefold: 1) to hold our students accountable for their assigned reading, 2) to give us a means of seeing which students were struggling with comprehension and 3) to provide checkpoints for keeping our students on track as they read. Chapter 5 gives a comprehensive explanation of questioning techniques. The following are questions related to a *Romeo and Juliet* reading assignment for Act II, scene iii.

Freedman *Literature Section*

Romeo and Juliet
Act II, scene iii

Summary:

____
____
____
____
____
____

Vocabulary Words: _______________, __________________, ______________

Discussion Questions:

1. What is the Friar collecting?

2a. What does the following mean?

For naught so vile that on earth doeth live,
But to the earth some special good doth give:
Nor aught so good but, strained from that fair use,
Revolts true birth, stumbling on abuse.
(lines18–21)

2b. What example does the Friar give of this principle?

2c. Where, besides in plants, does Friar Lawrence say this principle applies?

3. What does the Friar mean when he says,

Within the infant rind of this small flower
Poison hath residence, and medicine power.
For this, being smelt, with that part cheers each part
Being tasted, slays all sense with the heart.
(lines 25–28)

4. What does the Friar guess about Romeo?

5. Who does the Friar guess Romeo has been with?

6. How does Romeo respond to this guess?

7. What does Romeo want the Friar to do for him?

8. Why does the Friar criticize Romeo?

9. Why does the Friar agree to do what Romeo asks him to do?

10. What is the difference between Rosaline and Juliet?
    according to Romeo?

    according to Friar Lawrence?

11. What is the Friar's final piece of advice to Romeo? What does it mean?

Note-Taking

In college, students will be able to take notes in the margins of their assigned reading. In high school, however, we sometimes provide students with "sticky notes" (also called Post-it® notes) on which to take notes and then mark the pages in the night's reading from which the notes came. This method is particularly useful if students have been assigned to look for certain literary devices as they read. Students might jot down the term *foreshadowing* on the sticky note with an arrow directed at the paragraph in which they spotted the foreshadowing. The sticky notes technique may also be useful for students assigned essay or other writing assignments due upon completion of the book. As students read, they may mark scenes, quotations and incidents that they think might be useful as evidence for their papers. Toward this end, students might jot down 1–2 sentences noting why a page's text might be useful. Students might even draw an arrow directing their attention to the specific paragraph or sentence on the page that caught their attention. (See the following example.) It should be noted, however, that students with poor handwriting might find it frustrating to be asked to take notes on such a small surface area.

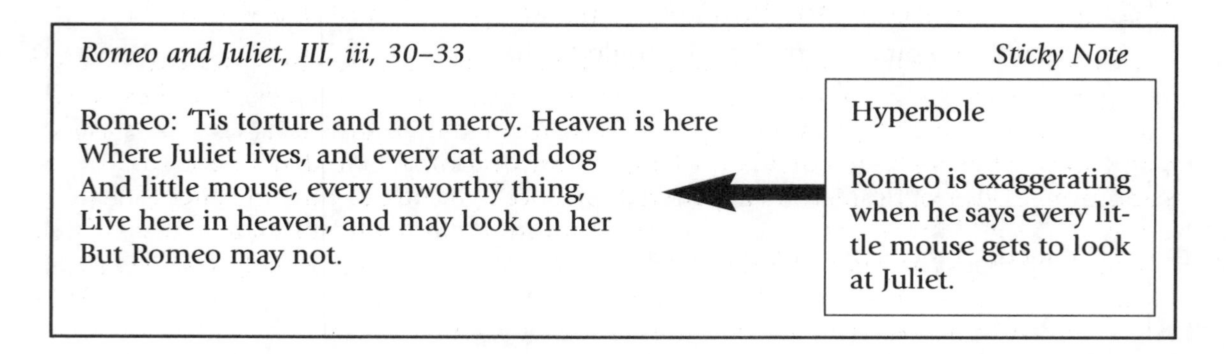

Romeo and Juliet, III, iii, 30–33
Sticky Note
Romeo: 'Tis torture and not mercy. Heaven is here
Where Juliet lives, and every cat and dog
And little mouse, every unworthy thing,
Live here in heaven, and may look on her
But Romeo may not.
Hyperbole
Romeo is exaggerating when he says every little mouse gets to look at Juliet.

Pre-Discussion

Before assigning students a short story or essay to read for homework, we often work with our students on some pre-reading brainstorming to activate their thinking about what they will read that night. For example, we might ask, "What did the title of the story make them think that this story might be about?" At the start of a new book, we might ask, "What does the cover of the book give away about the book's plot?" While students are working their way through a novel, we might ask, "What do you think is going to happen in the next chapter?" We then put our students' predictions on flipchart paper and begin class the next day by comparing their predictions to what actually occurred in the previous night's reading. By making predictions with our students, we are creating some "mental checkpoints" for them to consider as they read. Ideally, we want our students to be thinking as they read, "Oh, that's just like I predicted" or "Oh, that's not what I expected at all."

Differentiated Reading Assignments

To best support classes with heterogeneous reading levels, we often assign **semi-independent reading projects.** For these projects, we choose four different books from our school's multiple copy book collection and bring approximately ten copies of each book to class. We describe each of the four books to the students, giving a brief description of plot, page length and overall difficulty. Students are allowed to choose which of the four they want to read. Students write their choices on a slip of paper which they turn in to the teacher. On the next day, the teacher privately consults with students who he or she feels may have chosen a book that is either too challenging or not challenging enough. For the next few weeks, lessons are designed on literary elements, which students are then responsible for finding within the particular book that they have chosen to read. Concepts such as *foreshadowing, tone, foil, antagonist, falling action* and *internal conflict* are studied in class, and then students look for these elements in their respective books while reading for homework. The note-taking described previously is a good way for students to identify the elements in the book as they read, so they are prepared to talk about these elements the next day in class. For more information on differentiating instruction, see Chapter 4.

Choosing Good Material

Reading projects are unquestionably more successful when students are reading books and stories that genuinely interest them. A teacher of a twelfth-grade English class, for example, discovered that his students were absolutely fascinated by an autobiography written by a formerly homeless teenager who described living in New York's Grand Central Station (*Living at the Edge of the World* by Tina P.). His students loved reading a book written by a teenager and were fascinated by her tales from the tunnels of Grand Central Station. Students who claimed they'd never actually completed a book in high school reported they'd bought their own copies of the memoir so they could read it again.

Teaching the Strategies for Reading Content-Specific Material in All Classes

Math, science and social studies teachers sometimes believe that teaching students reading strategies should be left to the English and reading teachers, however, each of these disciplines requires its own type of reading. For mathematics, for example, standardized assessments in most states test students on lengthy word problems. Students need to practice reading these types of problems. They need to practice figuring out what the question is asking of them and how to draw out the relevant information. Different math teachers favor different strategies for guiding students in this type of reading. Some math teachers prefer for students to underline the relevant information provided in a word problem, while others encourage students to note this information in a table on a separate sheet of paper. Social Studies teachers who expect students to do Internet research for projects and papers need to work with students on how to read material they come across over the Internet. For example, they should teach their students to ask, "Who is the author of this source?" and "How credible is this source of information?" Finally, science teachers often assign reading in more traditional textbooks. For this type of assigned reading, students may be taught the **SQ3R method** (Robinson, 1970) of 1) examining the bold print section headings prior to reading a section, 2) mentally formulating a question that they believe this section of reading will attempt to answer and then 3) using this question as a mental checkpoint as they go on to read and consider the section's content. English and reading teachers may support their colleagues in improving their students' reading, but to some degree *all* teachers need to teach reading as it relates to their specific content areas.

Book Pals

A way in which one teacher managed to sneak in some extra reading practice for students was by creating a partnership with a third-grade class in a nearby school. Once a week, this teacher's students would travel to the third grade classroom and pair up with a "book pal," with whom they would read a story for approximately one-half hour. The high school students enjoyed working with their third-grade counterparts and, in the process of modeling good reading skills, unquestionably improved themselves.

Encourage Outside Reading

As people passionate about the subject matter we teach, the majority of us have shelves and shelves of books about or related to the courses we teach. If you feel comfortable doing so, bring in your books and fill up a bookshelf in the back of your classroom with a sign-out sheet for students or direct students to the relevant section of their school or public library. Offer students extra credit for reading one of these books on their own and then coming after school or during lunch to discuss the book with you. If your class load or teaching schedule precludes such an arrangement, consider asking students to tape-record themselves describing the book to a friend, sibling or parent and answering their questions about the book. Provide guidelines about the expected length of the conversation and questions that the friend, sibling or parent might be likely to ask. Perhaps you might start off each school week by profiling one of these books for the class, in a presentation similar to a coming attraction teaser for a recently released film.

Developing Proficient Mathematical Problem Solvers

Unfortunately, many students have the misconception that they are poor math students and will always be "bad" at math. As teachers, it is our job to instill confidence in children so they feel as though they are able to solve a variety of mathematical problems. In order to do so, we must equip students with tools to use, that is, strategies they may use to better understand and solve such problems.

To begin teaching students about problem solving, it is important to first understand what they believe problem solving is all about. As a class, create a problem-solving web, and elicit students' prior knowledge about this topic. If necessary, teachers may need to prompt students with questions such as,

"Is there one right way to solve mathematical problems? Explain."
"Is there always one right solution? Explain."

After brainstorming about problem solving, highlight the important points with regard to problem solving. The different problem solving strategies should be introduced and explained at this point. Each week, teachers may want to emphasize a different strategy until all strategies have been covered. Teachers will want to post a sign with the following strategies in the classroom.

- Look for a pattern.
- Write an equation.
- Draw a picture.
- Make a chart, table, graph or diagram.
- Make an organized list.
- Act it out.
- Use manipulatives.
- Guess, check and revise.
- Work backwards.
- Solve a simpler or similar problem.

The following format may be used to teach students how to systematically solve problems.

Problem-Solving Format

Please use this format as a guide when you solve the Problem of the Week. Remember to use your POW journal to record your work.

Title of Problem:

Thought: *Write a sentence that retells what the problem asks you to do.*

The problem is asking me...

Information: *Highlight the important information in the problem. Next, write a sentence that lists the important information in the problem.*

The information tells me...

Plan: *Choose a strategy that you plan to use. Remember, you may need to use several different strategies to help you solve the problem.*

I plan to solve the problem by...

Steps to Solution: *Show and label your work clearly and neatly. (Step 1...Step 2...Step 3...) Include visuals such as charts, graphs, pictures or tables. Clearly explain in order each step to the solution.*

Solution: *Label your answer. Be sure to ask yourself, "Does this answer make sense?" Check your work.*

My answer is...

Self-Assessment: *Read over your work. Are your steps clearly written? Did you proofread carefully and make appropriate changes? Does your solution make sense? Did you remember to include all of the above parts?*

I feel I deserve a ____________ because...

Created by Jenny Deane and Laurie Levin

Teachers should model the process of solving mathematical problems for students using the format described previously. Before solving a problem together as a class, share the rubric which will be used to evaluate their work. An example of a problem-solving rubric is outlined in Figure 6-22.

Begin by choosing a problem in which all students will be able to grasp the mathematical content fairly easily. Read the problem together and have students highlight or underline the important information, including what the problem is asking them to do.

Next, as a class, use the format to write a sentence that retells what the problem is asking students to do. Although this step seems straightforward, students often have difficulty determining what they are being asked to do, particularly with multi-step problems.

Then, as a class, write the important information in the problem. Be sure students are able to give reasons why the selected information is important. Students often tend to include irrelevant information, so it is important to discuss the difference between interesting information and information that is critical to solving the problem.

The next part of the process entails choosing a strategy and developing a plan to solve the problem. At this point, brainstorm a variety of strategies that might be used to solve the problem. Be sure to emphasize that a combination of strategies might be necessary and that sometimes the initial plan does not work. Students should also understand they should always use what they know to find out what they don't know.

After a plan is formulated, begin solving the problem as a class. As you solve the problem together, show and label all work. Keep track of the steps you take by recording each step in an organized manner. After the problem has been solved, check to make sure the solution makes sense. Reread your steps to solution, and add any necessary details.

At this point, share the following checklist with the students. They should use this form after completing a problem to ensure that they have completed all parts of the problem.

Assessing Open-Response Questions

Are all parts of the question answered?

Are all directions followed?

Are all parts and answers labeled?

Is the explanation clear for the reader?

Does the explanation include a combination of pictures, numbers or words?

Are appropriate math vocabulary and symbols included in the response?

Is the work organized, neat and spelled well enough to be understood by the reader?

Finally, students should assess their work and give specific reasons for giving themselves a particular score. Have them refer to the rubric when they assess their work. The rubric for this activity may be found in the chapter 6.

This problem-solving process should be modeled and practiced by students with guidance before they begin working independently. At times, you may wish to have students work in pairs or small groups. In this way, students may benefit from understanding others' perspectives and may experience firsthand how different strategies may be used to solve the same problem.

The problem-solving process may be used with both lower and upper elementary grade levels, however, the format that was outlined previously is most appropriate for grades three through five. Teachers of lower elementary grades may wish to modify and simplify this format for their students.

The following form is used by one high school teacher to aid students in solving mathematics problems in a similar way.

Problem #	Problem Illustration(s): Add explanation.	Equation: Show all your attempts.	Solution: Show the final equation and the answer.

Providing students with the necessary tools to use, that is, an organized process and an understanding of possible strategies, is imperative in order to help children develop the confidence and skills needed to solve higher order mathematical problems. All students have the ability to solve open-ended, complex mathematical problems. It is our responsibility as teachers to ensure that they are equipped to do so!

Conclusion

Bob and Joe were educated at a time when the concepts discussed in this chapter were not known to educators. Today, more and more educators are aware of the powerful impact that they may have on developing the intelligence of their students. Educators, with the right professional development and tools for instruction, may significantly increase the likelihood that all students will reach high levels of success in school and in life.

References

Armstrong, T. (1994). *Multiple intelligences in the classroom* (pp. 2–3). Alexandria, VA: The Association for Supervision and Curriculum Development (ASCD).

Armstrong, T. (2003). *The multiple intelligences of reading and writing* (p. 14). Alexandria, VA: The Association for Supervision and Curriculum Development (ASCD).

Barron, J. (1978). Intelligence and general strategies. In G. Underwood (Ed.), *Strategies in information processing* (pp. 403–450). London: Academic Press.

Brigham, C. (1923). Excerpts from *A study of American intelligence.* In D. J. Kelves, (1985). *In the name of eugenics: Genetics and the uses of human heredity.* New York: Alfred A. Knopf.

Devlin, B., Fienberg, S., Resnick, D., & Roeder, K. (1997). *Intelligence, genes, & success: Scientists respond to the bell curve.* New York: Springer-Verlag New York, Inc.

Devlin et al. (1994). Heredity, environment, and the question of "how?",

Psychological Review, 65, 197–208.

Dweck, C. (2000). *Essays in social psychology: Self theories.* Philadelphia, PA: Psychology Press of Taylor and Francis Group.

Fraser, S. (1995). *The bell curve wars: Race, intelligence, and the future of America.* New York: Perseus Books.

Gardner, H., & Walters, J. (1985). Excerpts from The development and education of intelligences. In *Essays on intellect* (pp. 1–13). Washington, DC: Association for Supervision and Curriculum Development (ASCD).

Goldman, D. (1999). *Emotional intelligence* [home video]. Washington, DC: Public Broadcasting Service.

Gould, S. (1994, November). Curve ball. *The New Yorker.*

Hernstein, R., & Murray, C. (1994) *The bell curve: Intelligence and class structure in American life.* New York: The Free Press.

Hunter, M. (1987, October). "If at first..": Attribution theory in the classroom. *Educational Leadership*, 50–53.

Jacobson, L. (2003, September). IQ study weighs genes and environment. *Education Week, XXIII*(2).

Kelves, D. J. (1985). *In the name of eugenics: Genetics and the uses of human heredity.* New York: Alfred A. Knopf.

Perkins, D. (1995). *Outsmarting IQ: The emerging science of learnable intelligence.* New York: The Free Press.

Robinson, F. (1970). *Effective study* (4th ed.). New York: Harper & Row.

Terman, L. (1922). Were we born that way? *World's Work*, *44*, 660.

CHAPTER

8

The Brain and Student Learning

Objectives for the Chapter

After reading the chapter, the reader will be able to

a. briefly explain to a colleague how the brain functions
b. explain to a colleague the basic physiological basis of left brain and right brain dominance and integration and multiple intelligences
c. explain to a colleague how the brain functions in relation to the teaching of mathematics
d. explain to a colleague how the brain functions in relation to the teaching of reading and writing
e. explain to a colleague how the brain functions in relation to remembering what is learned

Introduction

In books such as this one, there is often a temptation for us as educators to flip directly to the chapters on perennial challenges such as behavior management and lesson planning, while paying short shrift to the chapters covering more abstract topics such as this one: the brain and student learning. Yet, despite this understandable inclination, we have found through our own experiences as classroom teachers that gaining a deeper understanding of what *learning* actually means and what precisely is happening in our students' brains when we say that learning is taking place is crucial to fully utilizing and benefiting from the strategies laid out in this book's other chapters. Of course, we are

Gaining a deeper understanding of what learning actually means and what precisely is happening in our students' brains when we say that learning is taking place is crucial to fully utilizing and benefiting from the strategies laid out in this book's other chapters.

by no means the only educators who have come to realize the importance of utilizing psychologists, neuroscientists and medical doctors' most recent discoveries about the workings of the human brain to improve teaching and learning. Over the past ten years, literally dozens of books have been published specifically for educators detailing the importance of "brain-based education," "brain-compatible classrooms," "brain-compatible learning," etc. It seems accurate to say that there is something of a movement afoot to apply the latest advances in brain research to K-12 (and higher) education. In this chapter, then, we will seek to provide you with the content and concepts from this movement that are most directly relevant to our work as classroom teachers and which are most likely to impact the way in which teaching and learning occurs in our classrooms. We will begin with a brief overview of the different regions of our students' brains and the functions that each region serves. We will then utilize this nuts-and-bolts understanding of the brain to more deeply examine what is occurring in our students' brains when we ask them to *learn* and commit to *memory* a particular skill or piece of information. Finally, we will discuss the implications of our society's deeper understanding of the brain for teaching and learning, specifically, the strategies and activities we should incorporate into our classroom practices to take advantage of new discoveries about the brain and learning.

Nuts and Bolts of the Brain

The brain weighs approximately three pounds and is divided into two mirror-image hemispheres, the right and the left. The front of the brain is called the **anterior region,** and the back of the brain is called the **posterior region.** Each hemisphere is made up of four sections (also called *lobes*): *frontal, parietal, temporal* and *occipital.* Together, these four lobes make up what is referred to as the **cerebral cortex** or **neocortex.**

As you can see in Figure 8-1, the frontal lobe is in the anterior (front) section of the brain, the occipital lobe is in the posterior (back) and the parietal and temporal lobes lie between the two previously mentioned lobes. It is important to remember that, as the right and left hemispheres of the brain are mirror-images of each other, each hemisphere contains its own frontal, parietal, temporal and occipital lobe.

What role does each of these sections of the brain play in student learning? While the processes of learning and memory will be examined in more detail in the next section of this chapter, we can note here that the **frontal lobe** is utilized for higher order thinking and fine motor skills, the **occipital lobe** for processing visual information, the **temporal lobe** for processing auditory information and the **parietal lobe** for sensory information and spatial awareness.

The visual, auditory and sensory information processed by the various sections of the brain comes from the body's five senses and reaches the various lobes of the brain through the spinal cord and brain stem. (See Diagram 8-1.) In addition to serving as a conveyor of sensory information, the **brain stem** controls the body's heart rate, blood pressure and breathing. Behind the brain stem (and beneath the occipital lobe) is the **cerebellum,** which controls the body's motor coordination and motor learning.

Two other fundamental areas of the brain are **Broca's Area** and **Wernicke's Area.** Located in the frontal lobe and temporal lobes, respectively, (see Figure 8-1), these two areas of the brain are named for the doctors who discovered that these regions work together to produce and understand speech. People who experience brain damage in Broca's Area are able to understand the speech of others but cannot speak comprehensibly themselves. In contrast, people who experience brain damage in Wernicke's Area are able to speak (and, in fact, blather uncontrollably) but cannot understand the language of others.

Figure 8-1

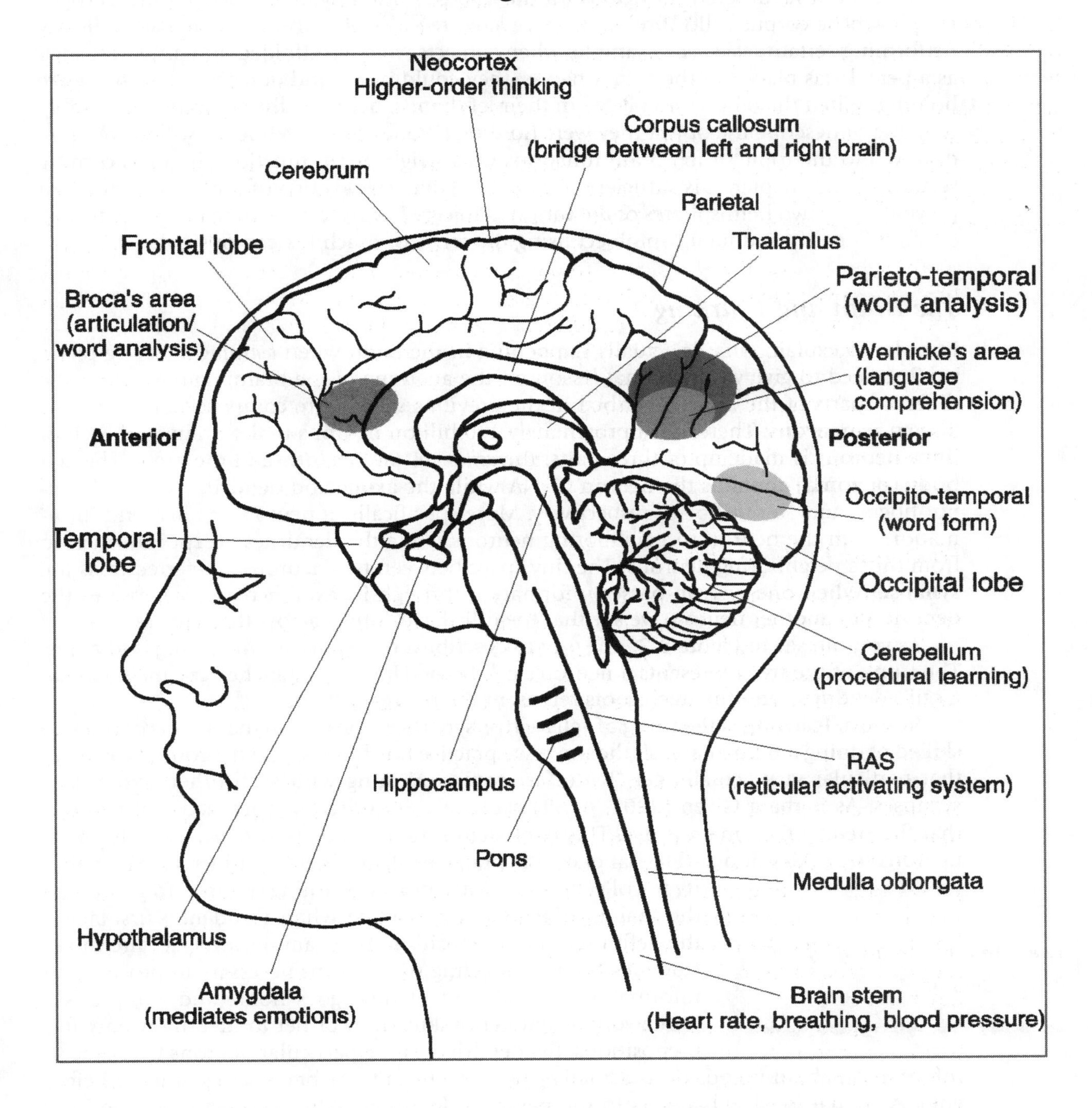

Located in the middle region of the brain (primarily in the temporal lobe) are the *hippocampus, thalamus, hypothalamus* and *amygdala*. (See Figure 8-1.) This area is sometimes referred to as the **limbic area** or the **limbic system,** and it controls body functions such as eating, drinking, sleeping and processing emotions.

Finally, the brain's right and left hemispheres are primarily connected by a bundle of nerve fibers called the **corpus callosum.** (See Figure 8-1.) Neuroscientists refer to the corpus callosum as the brain's "information superhighway" because it allows for communication between the two sides of the brain and for information collected in one hemisphere to be conveyed to the other. The corpus callosum is a key tool for allowing the brain to coordinate all of its different functions. In the 1960s, studies by Sperry, Bogen and Perry of people whose corpus callosum had been severed revealed that these people had difficulty performing certain tasks. For example, when subjects were blindfolded and an object such as a pencil was placed in their right hands, they could name and describe what they were holding. When the object was placed in their left hands, however, the subjects were unable to name or describe the object they were holding (Wolfe, 2001). While we will delve more deeply into the topic of left brain functions versus right brain functions in an upcoming section of this chapter, it is sufficient to note here that the severing of the corpus callosum prevented the two hemispheres of the various subjects' brains from working together to successfully identify and name an object using the sense of touch instead of sight.

The Brain and Learning

In order to explain what is actually happening in the brain when *learning* is taking place, we first need to give you one final lesson on the anatomy of the brain; namely, all of the different parts of the brain described in the previous section are composed of brain cells known as **neurons.** There are approximately 100 billion neurons in the brain, and each of these neurons is made up of three parts: the *cell body, the dendrites* and the *axons.* The **cell body** (or **soma**) contains the neuron's DNA while the **axons** and **dendrites** serve as "output fibers" and "input fibers" respectively. More specifically, a neuron's axons send information from the neuron to neighboring neurons while the dendrites accept information from those neighboring neurons. The tiny space between two neurons is referred to as the **synapse.** When one neuron passes information through its axon across a synapse to the dendrites of another neuron, we say that the cells have "fired" across the synapse.

As you can see in Figure 8-2, one way to describe a neuron is by comparing it to a tree. The trunk of the tree represents a neuron's cell body. The tree's branches are analogous to a cell's dendrites, and the tree's roots represent the neuron's axons.

In short, **learning** is the firing of cells across synapses. The reason that we become more skilled at doing a particular task the more we practice it is because the neurons involved in that particular task actually get "better" at communicating with each other across their synapses. As Barbara Given (2002, p. 69) explains, "Scientists have learned that neurons that fire frequently remain active. This consistent state is called *potentiation,* which causes neurons to . . . develop additional dendritic branches. Thus, [neurons] increase their ability to collect more information as learning occurs." To go back to the analogy of the neuron as a tree, when a student is first taught the definition of a preposition, for example, synapses fire in the student's brain connecting the neurons necessary to process that information. If that student then goes home and completes a homework assignment asking him or her to identify twenty-five prepositions, the dendrites of the particular neurons that process information about prepositions actually *grow.* Imagine a tree's branches expanding before your eyes; that is what happens to the neuron's dendrites. When the neurons' dendrites grow "bushier," information passes between them faster and more easily. Thus, the student becomes faster at identifying prepositions in a sentence. The neurons necessary for identifying prepositions are actually firing more efficiently than they were when this student first learned about prepositions in class earlier that same day. And the more he or she practices, the bushier the neuron's dendrites will get and the better those connections will be along that particular neural pathway. It is for this reason that Bransford, Brown and Cocking (1999, p. 15) write that, "the brain is a dynamic organ, shaped to a great extent by experience—by what a living body does and has done." The brain literally changes as learning occurs. Dendrites grow bushier, allowing synapses to fire more efficiently.

> ***Learning*** *is the firing of cells across synapses.*

Figure 8-2

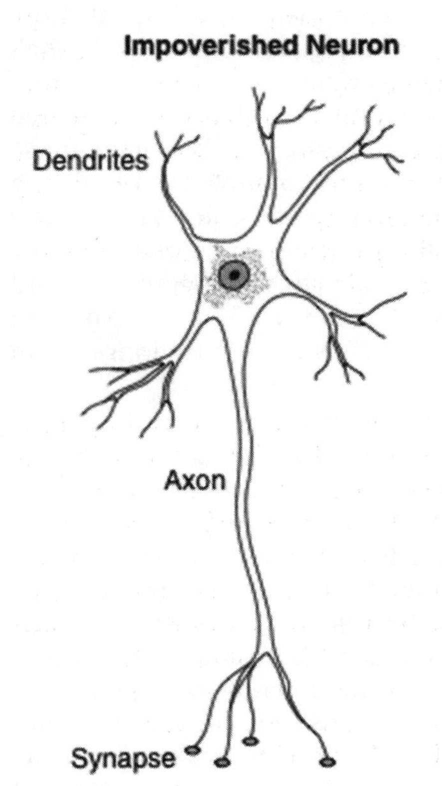

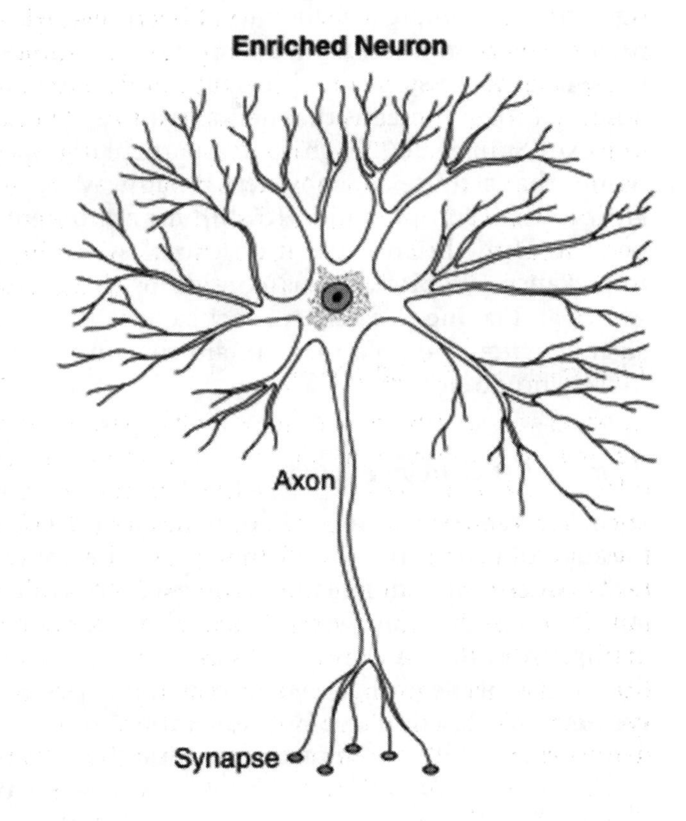

One way that neuroscientists sometimes describe this process of dendrites growing bushier is by comparing the dendrites' growth to that of an athlete's muscles growing stronger by lifting weights. Just as an athlete who regularly "activates" his or her muscles by following a consistent exercise regimen will increase the strength of these muscles, neurons along a particular neural pathway become better at communicating with each other the more that they are activated.

Just as an athlete who regularly "activates" his or her muscles by following a consistent exercise regimen will increase the strength of these muscles, neurons along a particular neural pathway become better at communicating with each other the more that they are activated.

A final point concerning the nuts and bolts of the brain relates to a fairly recent discovery about brain growth and adolescence. Prior to the late 1990s, the conventional wisdom concerning brain growth was that no *new* neurons developed in the brain after a child reached the age of eighteen months to two years. However, according to Dr. Jay Giedd, a scientist with the National Institute of Mental Health, recent studies have revealed that some parts of the brain continue growing long after early childhood. For example, the cerebellum continues growing into a person's twenties (Spinks, 2002). Moreover, the period of pre-adolescence directly before puberty represents a time of growth for the brain's frontal cortex. As was described in the previous section on the nuts and bolts of the brain, the frontal cortex is the area of the brain in which the mechanics of thinking and emotion occur. For this reason, it is particularly important that all children and particularly adolescents be exposed to a challenging school curriculum that pushes them to fully develop their cognitive skills. Remember that in the preceding paragraph we compared the constant activation of neural pathways to an athlete's increasing his or her muscle mass by lifting weights. Unfortunately, the reverse analogy is true as well. Just as the muscles of an athlete who stops exercising will gradually lose their strength and become weaker, a neural pathway that is not regularly activated through use will become slower and less efficient. As Dr. Jay Giedd explains, the brain's system of "use it or lose it" means that neural pathways not receiving sufficient use may be rendered inactive (Spinks, 2002). Thus, it is particularly important for children to participate in activities that activate as many neural pathways as possible in order to allow their brains to grow to their full potential. To shift for a moment to another demographic, it is precisely because of the brain's "use it or lose it" system that doctors have begun emphasizing the importance of senior citizens' continuing to "exercise" their brains by reading, playing card games and taking classes. Senior citizens who *use* their neural pathways by participating in such activities are able to maintain their intellectual capacities significantly longer than those who do not.

The Brain and Memory

It makes sense to follow up our discussion of learning with a discussion of memory because, of course, the two processes are interconnected. As teachers, we know that there is little value in our students learning a skill or concept if they are unable to remember that skill or concept a day, week or month later. Cognitively, learning and memory are interconnected as well. As Barbara Given (2002, p. 74) explains, "There is no single storage area for records of the past . . . Memory is not a 'thing' but a process of neuronal network activation." This description of what memory "looks like" in the brain should strike you as similar to our earlier description of what learning looks like in the brain. That is because the two processes are effectively the same. If *learning* a particular skill or concept results in the firing of neurons along a particular neural pathway, then *remembering* that skill or concept means that the neurons along that pathway communicate so effectively with each other that the brain can easily recall the particular skill or concept upon request.

> *If learning a particular skill or concept results in the firing of neurons along a particular neural pathway, then remembering that skill or concept means that the neurons along that pathway communicate so effectively with each other that the brain can easily recall the particular skill or concept upon request.*

Here is an example of this process playing out in the classroom. Imagine that a Spanish teacher is teaching her students how to conjugate a particular verb. Inside her students' brains, *learning* these six verb forms involves activating a particular neural pathway inside the temporal lobe on the left side of their brains. As students practice reciting the various forms of this verb, the dendrites of the neurons along this neural pathway grow bushier, allowing these neurons to communicate with each other more quickly. With enough practice, the communication of the neurons along this pathway becomes so efficient that the students can quickly *remember* the different conjugations of this particular verb. The teacher's goal, of course, is for her students to remember these verb forms well enough to instantly identify and utilize the correct form in conversation. Such automatic memory is achieved through practice.

While there is no single spot or system of neurons in the brain responsible for *all* memories, researchers have been able to determine the different locations in the brain in which various types of memories are stored. Eric Jensen (1998) explains that memories of sound are stored in the **auditory cortex.** The **hippocampus** stores memories related to speaking and reading and the **amygdala** stores negative emotional events such as an encounter with a bully. Memories of names, nouns and pronouns are stored in the **temporal lobe.** Information regarding vital life functions is stored in the **brain stem.** The **cerebellum** is responsible for recalling basic muscle movements such as pouring chemicals into a beaker.

Another expert in brain-based education, Marilee Sprenger (1999), breaks down the storing of memory in the brain in the following way.

Table 8-1

Type of Memory	***Definition***	***Section of the Brain in Which It Is Stored***
Semantic memory	Information learned from words such as a teacher's lecture or hand-out	Hippocampus (temporal lobe)
Episodic memory	Memory involving locations (such as the decorations on the walls of the classroom) in which learning occurs	Hippocampus (temporal lobe)
Procedural memory	Processes that the body does and remembers such as the various steps of a cheerleader's routine	Cerebellum
Automatic memory	The body's conditioned responses such as recalling the multiplication tables well enough to recite an answer instantly	Cerebellum
Emotional memory	Emotional information such as excitement over a fascinating lesson or anxiety for an impending exam	Amygdala

Specific strategies for utilizing each of these different aspects of our students' memories will be discussed later in this chapter.

There is one more aspect of memory that warrants discussion. In our discussion of various teaching strategies in both Chapters 2 and 5, we have noted that students are better able to remember information they are taught when that information is connected to knowledge already stored in their long-term memories. Here we would like to more fully explore the reasoning behind that strategy. In *Accessing the General Curriculum*, Victor Nolet and Margaret McLaughlin (2000, pp. 34–38) describe the process of committing something to memory in the following way:

> As a stimulus (or information) from the environment is detected through one of the senses, it is held briefly in *sensory memory* . . . Sensory memory has an extremely limited capacity. Visual information begins to fade after only one-half of a second and auditory stimuli are held for only about three seconds. Information that has been perceived and recognized is passed on to the *working memory* . . . Information is held in working memory temporarily while it is compared with information already stored in long-term memory. If the new information is related to some prior knowledge, it is moved out of working memory and stored along with that related information in long-term memory . . . If the new information cannot be connected to prior knowledge, it is less likely to be moved into long-term memory.

In this explanation, Nolet and McLaughlin describe how stimuli or information entering the brain is more likely to become part of the brain's long-term memory if that stimuli or information can be connected to knowledge already held in long-term memory. For example, a student in a geometry class who has already committed definitions of *triangles* and *quadrilaterals* to his long-term memory will find it much easier to learn and remember the definition of a *hexagon* as compared to a student who holds no prior knowledge of polygons. Why is this? Remember that, in cognitive terms, *learning* and *memory* both consist of laying down neural pathways by the firing of neurons across synapses. When a person is able to link new information to previously held knowledge, his or her brain is effectively linking that new information to neural pathways that have already been laid out. In contrast, brand new information unconnected to anything in a person's existing long-term memory necessitates the creation of a new neural pathway and the firing of synapses across neurons whose dendrites have not yet had the opportunity to become bushy, efficient communicators with each other. It is for this reason that in Chapters 1 and 2 we emphasize the importance of teachers planning with mastery objectives in mind and then giving students the mastery objectives at the outset of the learning. When we do this, we build a context for the upcoming learning in the long-term memory to which the new learning may connect.

The Brain and Reading

Despite the fact that reading instruction is perhaps the most researched area in the field of education, it is only in the last one to two years that brain imaging technology has become advanced enough to allow scientists to observe what is going on inside the brain when a student is reading. This technology has not only provided scientists with a deeper understanding of the cognitive processes that occur during reading but also of what is happening inside the brains of those students who have difficulty learning to read. One of the most important findings concerning reading and cognition is that that there are actually two different neural pathways for reading: "one is for beginning reading, for slowly sounding out words, and another that is a speedier pathway for skilled reading"(Shaywitz, 2003, p. 78). Both pathways involve multiple regions of the brain because reading involves both processing the visual information on the page as well as transforming this visual information into sounds and meaning (Shaywitz, 2003).

A child just learning to read utilizes the parietal and temporal lobes when reading. Called the **parieto–temporal system** and located in the middle of the brain, this system helps a child to recognize the different letters that make up a word and to then attach the appropriate sounds to these letters (Shaywitz, 2003). It is for this reason that a child learning to read may be heard very slowly sounding out each word on the page.

As a child becomes a more fluent reader, the area of the brain activated during reading shifts from the mid-brain to the lower brain, specifically, the **occipito–temporal area**. Why does this shift occur? Dr. Sally Shaywitz (2003, p. 79) explains that, after the child has read a particular word several times, he or she "forms an exact neural model of the specific word [in the lower brain] . . . reflecting the word's spelling, its pronunciation, and its meaning." As a result, the child can now automatically read the entire word upon seeing it in print in about a tenth of a second. In contrast, the child who is still relying upon the mid-brain for reading must mentally divide the word into separate letters, sound each letter out and then recombine the sounds into a single word. Later in this section, we will offer some strategies for supporting children in achieving reading fluency.

One reason why these new insights about reading and the brain are so important is that they provide us with a deeper understanding of what is occurring inside the brains of children who have difficulty becoming fluent readers. Shaywitz (2003) suggests that there are two major groups of poor readers: children who are dyslexic and children who are poor readers due to lack of experience. **Dyslexia** is a learning disability found in children of normal intelligence that impairs their ability to read fluently and accurately.

While approximately one in five children are estimated to be dyslexic, it is only in the last two years that researchers have come to understand the "glitch" in the brains of dyslexic children and adults. Specifically, children and adults with dyslexia have a glitch in the lower region of the brain that forces them to continue to rely on the mid-brain when reading, in contrast to other readers who transfer control of reading to the lower brain. Since we know that the mid-brain supports reading by breaking words into pieces, sounding them out and rejoining these sounds, while the lower-brain allows for nearly instantaneous sight-reading, Shaywitz (2003) suggests that children and adults with dyslexia are effectively forced to continue using a "manual" reading system when their non-dyslexic peers have shifted to "automatic." In other words, a child with dyslexia attempting to read a word such as *hamburger* will need to divide this word into syllables, sound out each syllable and then combine these sounds to form a single word. In contrast, a non-dyslexic child who has come across the word *hamburger* previously will automatically activate the neural pathway in his or her lower brain in which this word's meaning and pronunciation are stored, allowing the word to be read fluently. Dyslexia, then, is not something that a child grows out of as an adult; however, in Shaywitz's book *Overcoming Dyslexia*, she lays out many strategies that children and adults with dyslexia may utilize to strengthen their manual reading systems. For example, Shaywitz (2003, p. 269) explains that dyslexic children may benefit from **"fluency training"** which involves students reading and re-reading a particular passage until they can read this passage with a high degree of accuracy. Shaywitz compares this approach to athletic training in which one practices a particular dance move or jump shot until the movement is ingrained in one's neural pathways.

> *Children and adults with dyslexia are effectively forced to continue using a "manual" reading system when their non-dyslexic peers have shifted to "automatic."*

In contrast to dyslexics who literally have a glitch in their posterior brain system, the brains of children with poor reading skills have a working system in place that has not been activated appropriately. For these children, the often-heard quote of one of our old tennis coaches comes into play: "Learn the rules. Play the game. *Practice! Practice! Practice!"* As Shaywitz (2003, p. 188) explains, "New brain imaging technology shows the powerful positive effect of practice in creating neural circuits related to the development of what scientists call expertise or skill. Basically, the brain learns by practice." As is the case with other types of learning, children who practice reading strengthen the speed with which synapses fire along the neural pathways in their parieto–temporal and occipito–temporal regions. Achieving **reading fluency** means that the neural pathways have been exposed to a particular word enough times to process the word, decode it and attach it with meaning in less than a heartbeat. In *Overcoming Dyslexia,* Dr. Shaywitz (2003) describes a number of early intervention reading programs that have been effective at helping poor readers achieve this level of fluency. She notes that a common thread that runs through each of these reading programs is systematic and direct instruction in phonics, fluency training and enriched language experiences such as listening to and telling stories.

The Brain and Mathematics

The Third International Mathematics and Science Survey (TIMSS) reported that American schoolchildren studying mathematics are handicapped by curricula that emphasizes quantity over quality. As Bransford, Brown and Cocking (1999, chap. 3, p. 5) note in *How People Learn,* "Research on expertise suggests that superficial coverage of many topics in the domain may be a poor way to help students develop the competencies that will prepare them for future learning and work." They also express concern that too often students' knowledge of mathematics is conditional, meaning that they can solve a particular problem when it appears on a structured worksheet with similar problems but are unable to identify when and why to apply various problem-solving techniques when faced with randomly presented problems. For example, can an elementary school student who has learned the concept of perimeter and completed a worksheet with questions testing this concept then successfully find the perimeter of his or her classroom upon being handed a tape measure? In the introduction to this book, we refer to this process of applying problem-solving techniques in unfamiliar settings as application mastery.

In contrast to such students, Bransford, Brown and Cocking (1999, chap. 3, p. 3) report on research findings that "Mathematics experts are able to quickly recognize patterns of information such as particular problem types that involve specific classes of mathematical solutions." How can we as educators support students in their path towards attaining the skill level of such experts? Both researchers and educators suggest that mathematics curricula require an increased emphasis on application mastery, the application of learned skills to unfamiliar problems. Eric Jensen (1998, p. 35) writes in *Teaching with the Brain in Mind* that "the single best way to grow a better brain is through challenging problem solving. This creates new dendritic connections that allow us to make even more connections." An example of such a problem might be asking elementary school students who have recently learned how to add and subtract decimals to provide the appropriate change to a customer who has purchased a glass of lemonade that costs $0.60 with a $1 bill.

Interestingly, Jensen (1998) notes that, as far as a students' brain is concerned, it doesn't matter whether or not a particular problem is ultimately solved. Rather, the dendrites grow as a result of the process of solving the problem, not as a result of the solution. In other words, it is the process of reasoning and thinking about a problem that activates the neurons along a particular neural pathway, not the final step of achieving a solution. As long as the steps a student takes towards arriving at an answer are logical and reflective, the neuron activation inside that student's brain is the same whether the final answer is correct or not. For this reason, one might argue that there is a cognitive rationale for giving students partial credit when they complete several steps of a problem correctly but make a careless error that renders their final answer incorrect.

> *It is the process of reasoning and thinking about a problem that activates the neurons along a particular neural pathway, not the final step of achieving a solution.*

Finally, in *Brain Matters: Translating Research into Classroom Practice*, Patricia Wolfe (2001, p. 171) suggests that teachers consider helping students to develop their own word problems. As she explains, "The purpose of instruction in mathematics is to give students the skills they need to solve real-life problems involving numbers. Texts typically include word problems to provide practice in problem solving. Too often, however, these problems are abstract and meaningless. When students write their own word problems for others in the class to solve, the problems have more meaning and can be a lot of fun." For example, after students have been asked to determine the perimeter of their classroom, a teacher might assign as homework for students to choose a room in their house, measure its dimensions and then create a word problem with an accompanying diagram of the chosen room for other students in the class to solve. The next day in class, students will enjoy the opportunity to apply their problem-solving skills to the "real life" rooms in their classmates' homes. More information about the value of drawing problems from real life and other types of authentic assessments may be found in Chapter 2.

Later in her book, Wolfe (2001, p. 173) also suggests that teachers ask students to reflect in writing about the mathematical skills that they are acquiring. She asserts, "Writing about what they are learning in math helps students make sense of the information by putting the ideas and methods they are using into their own words." For example, the students in the earlier example, who applied their knowledge of decimals to solve a problem involving the purchase of lemonade, might be asked to write about the different situations in their current and future lives in which an understanding of how to add and subtract decimals might prove useful. In answering this question about when a learned skill might come in handy, students strengthen their procedural and conditional knowledge. **Procedural knowledge** is knowledge about *how* to do something, and **conditional knowledge** is knowledge about *when* to apply a particular skill or concept. Nolet and McLaughlin (2000) note that it is these types of knowledge—procedural and conditional—in which mathematics experts tend to far outstrip novices. Incorporating problem solving and reflective writing into a mathematics curriculum, then, may be important steps in guiding students toward mastery of the content and skills they will need to succeed in their future learning and chosen careers.

Left Brain vs Right Brain

One of the first things that most of us learned about the brain *as students* is that the left hemisphere of the brain controls the right side of the body and vice versa. This is generally true; however, virtually every book written about the brain in the past five years goes to great pains to note that many misconceptions exist about the activities controlled by the brain's right and left hemispheres. Eric Jensen (1998, p. 8) writes, "While each side of the brain processes things quite differently, some earlier assumptions about the left and right brain are outdated . . . The old biases about music and arts being 'right brained frills' are outdated." Marilee Sprenger (1999, p. 41) concurs, "Perhaps you have heard stories about 'right brained' people and 'left brained' people. These are simply that—stories. People are not 'right brained' or 'left brained' unless, of course, they have had a hemisphere removed." Thus, a passing fad in the education world in the late 1970s and early 1980s of teachers directing their instruction toward one hemisphere of the brain or the other has rightly faded off the radar screen.

> *Virtually every book written about the brain in the past five years goes to great pains to note that many misconceptions exist about the activities controlled by the brain's right and left hemispheres.*

All that said, the right and left hemispheres of the brain do not operate identically. For example, Given (2002, p. 25) reports that "the right side of the brain is associated with controlling negative emotions whereas the left hemisphere is associated with positive emotions." In school, a student's right hemisphere might be activated by the disappointment of receiving a low test grade while this same student's left hemisphere might register the pleasure activated by the teacher's offer of a retest. Moreover, the left hemisphere seems to play a primary role in producing and comprehending language, while the right hemisphere seems primarily responsible for processing visual, auditory and spatial information. This means that a French teacher who is holding up various objects for his students to describe in French is activating both sides of his students' brains. The right hemisphere controls the process of students' seeing and recognizing the objects, and the left hemisphere controls the process of students' orally naming the objects and describing their characteristics.

Marilee Sprenger (1999, p. 42) explains that "the left hemisphere is able to analyze; it deals with parts. The right hemisphere deals with wholes . . . .Analyzing music would occur in the left hemisphere and enjoying it in the right." In other words, a student in a music theory class might be asked to both identify the various types of chords and notes found in a particular piece and then to explain what emotions the piece instills in its audience. The student might utilize his or her left hemisphere to recognize the chords and notes of which the piece is composed but then utilize his or her right hemisphere to identify the different emotions that the song as a whole instills in its audience. This explanation differentiating between the right and left hemispheres helps to explain the research cited by Eric Jensen

(1998) that beginning chess players and mathematicians show intense left hemisphere activity during these activities while master chess players and mathematicians experience greater right hemisphere activation during these activities. The novice chess players and mathematicians are regarding their activities move-by-move or step-by-step, whereas the experts examine the chessboard or math problem more holistically. More information on novice and professional chess players may be found in Chapter 7. Readers may want to reread this section to get a better understanding of the reason for their different levels of performance.

In closing, there are some clear differences between the way in which the right and left hemispheres of the brain operate. Patricia Wolfe (2001, p. 47), however, seems to best express the point made by various researchers and brain-based educators that "although it now seems clear that our hemisphere each have their specialties . . . the responses of the two hemispheres are so closely connected that they produce a single view of the world, not two." To return to the example of the French teacher holding up objects for his students to identify and describe, both hemispheres of the brain are necessary to successfully carry out this activity. The right hemisphere allows students to process the visual information regarding these objects, and then the left hemisphere allows students to find the language to put this visual information into words.

Multiple Intelligence Theory

In 1983, Howard Gardner, a professor at the Harvard Graduate School of Education, published a work entitled *Frames of Mind: The Theory of Multiple Intelligences*. In this work, Gardner laid out his **theory of multiple intelligences**: namely, that society has defined intelligence too narrowly and, in fact, different people are intelligent in different ways. Gardner suggested that there were seven different types of basic "intelligences": *linguistic, logical–mathematical, spatial, bodily-kinesthetic, musical, interpersonal* and *intrapersonal.* In 1999, Gardner added an eighth intelligence—*naturalist intelligence.* Chapter 7 gives a brief description of each of these intelligences.

While neuroscientists have sometimes been uncertain how to treat Gardner's work, his theory of multiple intelligences is invaluable to educators in that "MI Theory" reminds us to design both learning experiences and assessments that play to the strengths of the various types of learners within our classroom. As Laura Erlauer (2003, p. 63) explains, "Success in learning is heightened when a student learns through his or her preferred learning style or multiple intelligence." She argues that too often schools value only the linguistic and logical–mathematical intelligences and, as a result, shortchange the students whose strengths lie in one or more of the other intelligences identified by Gardner. In an elementary school class studying energy, then, a teacher committed to planning activities and assessments that address all eight intelligences might ask students to perform the following types of activities.

> *"MI Theory" reminds us to design both learning experiences and assessments that play to the strengths of the various types of learners within our classroom.*

Write a journal entry about a memorable experience that involved mechanical energy. (*linguistic intelligence*)

Solve math problems that relate to the amount of radiant energy provided by the sun. (*logical–mathematical intelligence*)

Use the materials supplied by a teacher to build a gadget that converts mechanical energy to electrical energy. (*spatial intelligence*)

Choreograph a dance routine that represents the impact of lightning on our lives during a thunder and lightning storm. (*bodily–kinesthetic intelligence*)

Write or listen to a song or rap describing the effects of the different types of energy. (*musical intelligence*)

Interview a person whose work involves the use of mechanical or chemical energy. (*interpersonal intelligence*)

Ask each student to come up with a list of ways in which he or she might personally work to conserve energy both now and as an adult. (*intrapersonal intelligence*)

Prepare a report on an animal, such as the electric eel, that can actually produce its own energy (*naturalist intelligence*)

Each of these activities is specifically designed to address a specific type of intelligence; however, these activities also activate different areas of the brain. For example, writing a journal entry or interviewing a person whose work involves energy activates the brain's temporal lobe. Solving a math problem activates the frontal lobe. Listening to a song about energy involves the occipital lobe and building a gadget that converts energy from one form to another activates the parietal lobe. It is in this way that Gardner's work on multiple intelligences relates to a cognitive understanding of the brain's functions. More information about Gardner's theory of multiple intelligences may be found in Chapter 7.

Learning Systems Theory

Another theory through which the brain and learning may be viewed is the **learning systems theory** espoused by researchers such as neurobiologist Robert Ornstein, psychiatrist Richard Restak, clinical psychologist Daniel Goldman and education professor Barbara Given. As Given (2002, p. 4) explains, "Current knowledge [of the brain and learning] . . . has moved beyond the left/right dichotomy to a broader view of five different learning systems—emotional, social, cognitive, physical, and reflective—and their numerous often overlapping subsystems that reflect specific neurobiological brain structures and functions." A short description of each of these five different systems follows:

Emotional System: The limbic area of the brain (described earlier in this chapter) is the primary controller of a person's emotions. The emotional system determines likes, dislikes, goals, desires and reactions to different interactions and occurrences (Given, 2003). In a classroom, a student's emotional system might be activated upon receiving an upsetting note from another student in the class or a teacher's compliment for excellent work on a homework assignment.

Social System: The social system of the brain controls social interactions and social emotions (romantic, maternal, friendly, etc.) and is perhaps the least understood of the five systems. Researchers believe that the right hemisphere may be more important than the left for social interactions and that the orbito-frontal cortex may play a primary role in determining one's social judgments (Given, 2002). When students are assigned to work in groups to complete a task, the social system plays a role in influencing different students' abilities to interact respectfully with their group members, divide up the work to be done and then work effectively together to carry out this work.

Cognitive System: The cognitive system processes information received by the brain. The cognitive system may be found throughout the neocortex (the four lobes of the brain). As you may recall from the opening section of this chapter, each lobe is responsible for processing a different type of information: visual, auditory, sensory, higher order, etc. The cognitive system is activated whenever a teacher plays a song, shows a video, writes on the chalkboard or passes around an object for students to touch.

Physical System: The physical system draws information from a person's physical environment. It is situated primarily in the brain stem and cerebellum (Given, 2002). A science teacher activates a student's physical system when teaching students the steps necessary to transfer microscopic organisms from a Petri dish to a slide underneath a microscope.

Reflective System: The reflective system controls the brain's higher order thinking and problem solving. This system takes the longest of the five systems to develop. It is primarily situated in the frontal lobe of the neocortex. The reflective system is activated when a teacher asks students to draw an inference about the narrator's background in a particular short story or to apply a mathematical concept learned in class to a real life situation.

While the five learning systems—emotional, social, cognitive, physical, and reflective—are described as separate entities, they are always working together. For example, imagine a teacher instructing her students to pair up and edit each other's essays on *Romeo and Juliet.* A student's emotional system is activated if he or she is paired with a student with whom he or she has argued in the past. Perhaps he or she experiences dismay at having to work with this student once again. This student's social system is activated when the pairs of students meet to exchange essays. Perhaps the student treats his or her partner collegially despite their prior tension. The partners may nod at each other respectfully or even shake hands. A student's physical system is activated when he or she lifts up his or her desk to slide it closer to his or her partner's. As he or she then reads his or her partner's essay and considers whether the point about *Romeo and Juliet* his or her partner is trying to make is a logical one, his or her reflective system is hard at work. Here, then, one may see how the relatively simple act of pairing up students to edit each other's work invokes all five of the learning systems.

While the five learning systems— emotional, social, cognitive, physical, and reflective— are described as separate entities, they are always working together.

What is the value to us as educators of learning systems theory? Given (2002, p. 79) writes that "at any one moment, all systems simultaneously vie for attention and control." Schools and teachers tend to focus primarily on a student's cognitive and reflective learning systems as made evident by the fact that subjects such as health, physical education, art and music and positions such as guidance counselor and school psychologist are typically the first items cut during times of budget cutbacks. Research has revealed, however, that the emotional, social and physical learning systems all have the capability of overriding these more *academic* systems. For example, if a student of ours got into an upsetting argument with her mother prior to leaving for school, this student's cognitive system will be unlikely to focus on our description of the quadratic formula. Her emotional and social learning systems are taking priority in her brain. Moreover, even if she puts the argument behind her, she will be equally unlikely to utilize her reflective system to solve a quadratic equation if the argument precluded her from eating breakfast before leaving for school. In this case, her physical system takes priority over the reflective system. In short then, it seems that we as educators simply cannot afford to ignore our students' emotional, social and physical learning systems because of their impact upon our students' cognitive and reflective learning systems. If we sense that a student is distracted by some type of emotional or social issue, we may be better served to quietly send this student to speak to his or her guidance counselor rather than to keep the student in class for fear that he or she will miss out on too much content. The ability of the emotional and social learning systems to override the cognitive and reflective learning systems renders it unlikely that this distraught student will benefit from remaining in class.

Educational Strategies for Brain-Compatible Learning

Having spent the first half of this chapter describing the different components of the brain, what learning and memory look like from a cognitive perspective and the theories of multiple intelligences and learning systems, we turn now to the more practical matter of how this information informs our work as classroom teachers. We have chosen to divide the remainder of this chapter into two sections: structural strategies for brain-compatible learning and instructional strategies for brain-compatible learning. In the first section—*structural strategies*—we will discuss structures and routines based on recent advances in our understanding of the brain and learning that may be utilized in either our own classrooms or in the school as a whole to support student learning. In the second section—*instructional strategies*—we will focus on pedagogical strategies that apply new discoveries about the brain and learning to our work as teachers.

Structural Strategies for Brain-Compatible Learning

Attention Span

In the mid 1980s, research studies revealed that adult workers need five- to ten-minute breaks for every one to two hours that they work (Erlauer, 2003). In 1995, David Sousa reported in *How the Brain Learns* that school-aged children cannot pay attention to a single subject for spans longer than twenty minutes. After twenty minutes of focus on a particular topic, the brain shifts its attention to something else. In discussing this finding, Laura Erlauer (2003) observes that this insight about children's attention spans does not require teachers to completely change the class's topic of study at twenty-minute intervals, but that the type of activity or means through which the students are learning *should* shift in some way after approximately twenty minutes. In other words, a teacher who has been lecturing to his or her class would be well served to transition after fifteen or twenty minutes into an activity that allows students to reflect in writing about the information that has been conveyed or to shift into groups to carry out an activity related to this direct instruction. If we as educators don't factor our students' natural attention spans into our lesson designs, we virtually guarantee losing our students' attention over the course of a lesson.

If we as educators don't factor our students' natural attention spans into our lesson designs, we virtually guarantee losing our students' attention over the course of a lesson.

Prime Learning Periods Within a Class or Lesson

The work of neuroscientists has also given educators a deeper understanding of the way in which students' capacity for learning changes over the course of a single class period or lesson. According to research conducted in the late 1990s, the *first ten minutes* of a class or lesson is the period during which the potential for student learning is highest (Erlauer, 2003). For this reason, it is imperative that we as educators utilize activities such as activators (described in Chapter 2) to fully capitalize on these opening minutes of class. Teachers who spend those ten minutes passing back papers, taking attendance or chatting with students are wasting their students' peak period for learning.

Though the first ten minutes of class represent the period during which students are most likely to focus, comprehend and commit to long-term memory the information they are taught, a second (almost as) prime period for learning occurs during the *final ten to fif-*

teen minutes of a lesson or class (Erlauer, 2003). For this reason, activities such as summarizers (described in Chapter 2) that review the content covered during a class period may be invaluable for ensuring that this content will become part of students' long-term memory. Whether through summarizers or another type of activity, utilizing the final ten minutes of class time for review greatly increases the likelihood that students will understand and remember a lesson's content.

If the opening and closing moments of a lesson or class period represent the times during which students' potential for learning is greatest, then it should be noted that the *middle stage* of a class period typically represents the low point for student learning. Erlauer (2003) encourages teachers to recognize that such a low point exists and to try to compensate by switching from one activity to another or by getting students up and moving in the middle of the class period or lesson. Such strategies may mitigate the natural lull in attention and focus that occurs in students' brains.

Prime Learning Periods Within a School Day

Interestingly, the peak and low periods for student learning over the course of the school day follow a pattern similar to that of a single class period. In other words, students tend to be the most alert during the *first two hours* and *last two hours* of their day; on the flip side, "halfway between the time you wake up and the time you usually go to sleep is your low point in terms of energy and alertness."(Erlauer, 2003, pp. 89–90). This finding suggests that the low point of our students' day in terms of energy and alertness occurs in the afternoon *right after lunch period.* For this reason, teachers whose classes fall during this afternoon period might be well-served to utilize hands-on activities, cooperative learning activities and those that get students up and moving. These are the activities that may best combat the mid-day energy and attention lull that students experience.

It also seems worthwhile to point out here that the structure of your school's master schedule may have a significant impact on student learning. More specifically, a school that utilizes a schedule in which each class meets at the same time everyday is likely to encounter situations in which the Algebra II class that meets first period (8:00–8:56 A.M.) finishes the year far ahead of the Algebra II class that meets fifth period (1:15–2:04 P.M.). Such a school might consider shifting to a rotating master schedule in which the time of day during which each class meets rotates to ensure that Algebra II doesn't *always* meet in the morning or *always* meet in the afternoon. If a schedule change is not feasible, then it becomes all the more important for us as teachers to consciously vary our instructional techniques over the course of a class period in order to maintain our students' attention.

Nutrition

While it may be difficult for us as educators to influence our students' eating habits, these habits unquestionably affect the process of teaching and learning. Neuroscientists have determined that the foods our students eat (and do not eat) affects the functioning of their brains. As Barbara Given (2002) explains in *Teaching to the Brain's Natural Learning Systems,* "It remains clear that children require sufficient intake of protein and complex carbohydrates to function effectively, mentally, and physically." Thus, the children in our classes who arrive at school without having eaten breakfast are starting the day with a cognitive disadvantage compared to their classmates. One middle school in Boston that we know of (a school in which almost the entire student body qualifies for the federal government's Free/Reduced Lunch program) has chosen to address this issue by starting each school day with a light breakfast provided free of charge to its students. While some may criticize the use of this school's limited resources on food rather than instructional supplies, the director of this middle school recognizes that, without providing food,

> *Neuroscientists have determined that the foods our students eat (and do not eat) affects the functioning of their brains.*

a high percentage of his students would begin each school day on empty stomachs. His understanding of brain-based learning has led him to the conclusion that providing his students with breakfast supports their learning as much or more than new lab supplies or textbooks. Better that they begin classes alert and focused with older textbooks than drowsy and distracted with brand new textbooks.

While students need to eat food with protein and complex carbohydrates in order for their brains to function effectively, there are also foods they eat that negatively impact their brain's capacity for learning during the school day. As Given (2002, p. 97) explains, "Simple sugars can be devastating to learning because they create a rapid increase in insulin and a 'sugar high' that is quickly followed by an overwhelming sense of sleepiness and foggy thinking." In the previous section, we discussed the fact that the school periods that come directly after lunch and in the early afternoon represent a low-point in students' capacity for learning. Those of us whose classes fall during these times must work hard to maintain our students' attention and focus. Compounding this challenge for teachers is that the foods many of our students eat for lunch are the sugary junk foods that lead to "sleepiness" and "foggy thinking."

Is this challenge completely out of our hands? Well, yes and no. While we certainly don't have complete control over our students' eating habits, the clear link that researchers have established between what students eat and how they think suggests that it behooves us as educators to take the time to make sure that our students understand this connection as well. Ideally, such learning about health and nutrition might take the form of an extended unit or several units in a health or physical education class. But in an era when high stakes testing and budget cutbacks have led to the reduction or even outright elimination of these programs, the responsibility seems to fall on all educators to convey some important lessons about nutrition to our students. Of course, this is not necessarily a bad thing. In Chapter 5, we discussed the fact that students are more motivated and engaged learners when they feel the content that they are learning is "real." Toward this end, a math teacher teaching his or her students about fractions might ask students to find the percentage of fat in foods eaten during lunch time. This lesson serves the dual purpose of educating students about nutrition while simultaneously increasing the likelihood that they will remember the mathematical concepts they are utilizing.

It may also behoove us as educators to remind our students' parents about the importance of nutritious breakfasts and lunches as well. Much of what we now know about the link between nutrition and learning has come about in the time period since our students' parents finished their own schooling. The importance of nutritious meals for alert, focused thinking may be conveyed in a respectful and helpful manner on Parent Night. Alternatively, more and more schools are developing and utilizing "School–Home Compacts" that explicitly lay out the responsibilities of the teacher, administrator, student and caregiver for supporting a student's learning. Such a document should explicitly include nutritious meals as a responsibility that a student's caregiver must assume.

Finally, there may be some value in a school faculty or school district examining the quality of the meals provided by its own food-service provider. Many schools sell candy, cookies and ice cream during lunch as a way of raising funds to be spent in other areas. While such a strategy is understandable, this strategy may actually be counterproductive if the snacks students are purchasing at lunch are reducing their capabilities as learners for the second half of the school day. Some schools are seeking out ways to provide their students with healthy, organic food options. The Berkeley Unified School District recently initiated a partnership with the Alice Waters' Chez Panisse Foundation to "create a formal curriculum that weaves organic gardening, cooking and eating healthy lunches into the educational experience of the district's 9,000 students"(Severson, 2004, p. 1). Such a partnership represents an impressive example of a school system not only recognizing the importance of nutritious lunches to student learning but realizing that the production of these meals represents a powerful learning opportunity as well.

Emotional Wellness

In an earlier section of this chapter called "Learning Systems Theory," we discussed the fact that if the brain's emotional learning system becomes distressed, such distress may limit the ability of the brain's cognitive and reflective learning systems to function properly. In other words, if a student is concerned about an earlier interaction with a bullying classmate, he or she may be unable to focus on the day's lesson. As a result, there is an important educational reason for us as educators to pay attention to the social and emotional wellness of our students; namely, the state of these learning systems has a direct impact upon our students' cognitive and reflective learning systems. In earlier chapters of this book on classroom management (Chapter 3) and questioning practices (Chapter 5), we discussed the importance of and strategies for creating a safe, respectful classroom environment. While there is no need to repeat our discussion of those strategies here, it seems important to point out that our discussion in this chapter of the interaction between the brain's different learning systems provides a cognitive rationale for investing the time necessary to create a classroom and school environment in which students feel physically and emotionally safe. Such an environment is a prerequisite for maximizing student learning.

If the brain's emotional learning system becomes distressed, such distress may limit the ability of the brain's cognitive and reflective learning systems to function properly.

Instructional Strategies for Brain-Compatible Learning

Practice, Practice, Practice

Earlier in this chapter, we mentioned a tennis coach who used to provide his team with the following recipe for success: "Learn the rules. Play the Game. Practice! Practice! Practice!" Whether or not he knew it at the time, this advice is directly in line with what we know about brain-compatible learning. More specifically, repeated practice allows concepts, skills or ideas to become more deeply ingrained in a person's long-term memory by increasing the speed with which synapses fire along a particular neural pathway. As Marzano, Pickering and Pollock (2001, p. 67) note in *Classroom Instruction that Works*, "After four practice sessions, students will reach a competence level of 47.9% of complete mastery. It will take students twenty more practice sessions, about twenty-four times in all, to reach 80% competency." In *How People Learn*, Bransford, Brown and Cocking (1999, chap. 3, p. 4) explain that world-class chess players typically require between 50,000 and 100,000 hours of practice to achieve a ranking of master or grand master.

Practice allows concepts, skills or ideas to become more deeply ingrained in a person's long-term memory by increasing the speed with which synapses fire along a particular neural pathway.

What kind of practice is most useful? In *Accessing the General Curriculum*, Nolet and McLaughlin (2000, p. 38) note that there are two different types of practice: massed practice and distributed practice. **Massed practice** "involves longer sessions of intense practice at irregular intervals" while **distributed practice** "refers to regularly scheduled practice sessions that may be shorter and less intense." "Cramming" for a final exam by staying up until two in the morning the night before the exam would be an example of massed practice. In contrast, a high school junior who learns ten new vocabulary words each week for the six months leading up to the SAT's would be an example of distributed practice. As is probably no surprise to those of us who have utilized both methods in different situations, distributed practice is a significantly more effective strategy for transferring new information into a person's long-term memory. Distributed practice allows the dendrites of neurons along neural pathways the time to develop and grow bushier and for communication along this neural pathway to become faster and more efficient. In contrast, cramming the night before a big exam provides little opportunity for such processes to occur.

20-2-20

A strategy for teachers to consider in terms of the pacing of practice and review is the "20-2-20" rule offered by Laura Erlauer (2003) in *A Brain Compatible Classroom*. **20-2-20** means that within 20 minutes of a lesson, students explain what they have learned. Within 2 days, students review and apply this new information. And within 20 days, students reflect on what they have learned. Such a system allows for students to receive the distributed practice necessary to commit a skill or concept to their long-term memory. It should also be noted that Erlauer's suggestion that the initial review take place within twenty minutes of the original learning coincides with the research described earlier about students' peak learning times within a single class period or lesson. Because the final ten minutes of a lesson represent a peak window for student learning, following up a twenty to thirty minute lesson with a short review is an important tool for helping students commit this lesson to their long-term memory.

Higher Order Thinking

One final point about practice concerns the *type* of work that students may do to best commit a skill, concept or idea to their long-term memory. In *Classroom Instruction that Works*, Marzano, Pickering and Pollock (2001) explain that in order for students to learn a skill, concept or idea well enough to recall and apply that knowledge at a future time, they must gain a conceptual understanding of this information. In other words, our students will have a far easier time remembering and applying the Pythagorean Theorem ($A^2 + B^2 = C^2$) if we take the time necessary to help them understand how the equation is derived. Toward this end, Laura Erlauer (2003, p. 83) suggests that, "It is usually far better to cut out about two-thirds of the simple, rote practice time in exchange for the more valuable synthesis, reflection, and application time of that same new knowledge." In other words, if students are learning to identify prepositions, we should avoid giving them three pages of sentences for homework with the instruction to circle the prepositions in each sentence. Rather, we might give them one page of sentences in which to find the prepositions and then ask them to write ten sentences of their own that utilize prepositions correctly. We might also ask them to cut out an article from the daily newspaper and circle the five most interesting prepositions in the article. Through assignments like these, we are pushing students to apply the concept they are learning rather than simply to identify its use.

Classroom Environment

In *Teaching with the Brain in Mind*, Eric Jensen (1998) reports that studies have found that classrooms decorated with educational posters, student work, affirmations, etc. may have a positive impact on learning. These stimuli serve to "feed the brain." For foreign language teachers and elementary school teachers in grades K-2, simply labeling the names of all of the objects in the classroom may have a positive effect on students' reading levels (Erlauer, 2003). For other teachers, similar strategies make sense as well. Earlier in this chapter, we noted that students (and adults) are unable to focus on a single topic for more than twenty minutes. At various points in a school day, students' attention will drift. If these students shift their attention to the student work, mathematical rules and sayings decorating their classroom walls, they may learn even as they are "spacing out."

Responding to and Correcting Student Work

As we described in detail in earlier sections of this chapter, from a cognitive perspective, learning is the act of creating neural pathways in the brain and increasing the speed with which the neurons along this pathway convey information from one neuron to the next.

While we have discussed this process in terms of learning a useful skill, concept or idea, it is also possible, of course, for a student to lay down neural pathways for incorrect information. Unfortunately, such information may be difficult to "unlearn." Consider your own life. Have you ever misheard a lyric from a popular song and thus learned the song incorrectly? Even after someone explains the actual lyric to you, isn't it extremely difficult to get that incorrect lyric out of your head each time you hear the song played? Students face the same challenge if they learn a skill or concept incorrectly. For this reason, it is crucial that we as teachers assess and return assignments to our students in a timely fashion. While keeping up with grading is one of the more challenging (and often mundane) aspects of teaching, it is important that we quickly diagnose our students' misperceptions and misunderstandings in order to correct these mistakes before they grow more deeply embedded in our students' brains.

It is important that we quickly diagnose our students' misperceptions and misunderstandings in order to correct these mistakes before they grow more deeply embedded in our students' brains.

Pictures Are Worth a Thousand Words

Several years ago, a special education teacher with whom we work gave us an invaluable piece of advice for helping students to learn vocabulary. She suggested that students create flashcards with the word to be learned on one side of the index card and the definition of the word on the other side. She also suggested instructing our students to draw a small picture of something that they connected with this word's meaning on the same side of the index card as the word's definition. This practice had an unquestionably positive impact on our students' ability to learn and remember the assigned vocabulary. Though we did not know it when we first began employing this strategy, the reason behind this strategy's success was brain-based. As Bransford, Brown and Cocking (1999, p. 13) explain in *How People Learn*, "Comparisons of people's memories for words with their memories for pictures of the same objects show a superiority effect for pictures. The superiority effect of pictures is also true if words and pictures are combined during learning." Of course, this understanding of the brain and memory has implications far beyond simply memorizing vocabulary words. If we understand that our students are better able to learn and remember information when it is conveyed in pictures, we may purposely include visual aids during periods of direct instruction. For example, in discussing the route that Columbus took from England to the New World, we are well-served to take the additional few minutes necessary to pull down the map of the world in the front of our classroom and literally trace the route with a wooden pointer or pencil. Even if we don't feel it to be particularly important for students to be able to trace Columbus's route across a map, the act of combining our verbal lesson with a visual aid will better enable our students to commit the entire lesson to their long-term memory.

Utilizing Different Types of Memory

You'll recall from an earlier section of this chapter on memory that brain-based education expert Marilee Sprenger breaks down the storing of memory in the brain into the following categories:

Table 8-2

Type of Memory	*Definition*	*Section of the Brain in Which It Is Stored*
Semantic memory	Information learned from words	Hippocampus (Temporal Lobe)
Episodic memory	Memory involving locations	Hippocampus (Temporal Lobe)
Procedural memory	Processes that the body does and remembers	Cerebellum
Automatic memory	The body's conditioned responses	Cerebellum
Emotional memory	Emotional information	Amygdala

(Sprenger, 1999)

In *Learning and Memory: The Brain in Action,* Sprenger suggests a number of specific strategies for effectively utilizing the strengths of these different types of memory.

Semantic Memory

In order to utilize students' semantic memory, Sprenger (1999) suggests that teachers utilize graphic organizers, peer teaching, summarizing, role-playing, debates, outlining, timelines, practice tests and paraphrasing mnemonic devices. Each of these strategies—many of which are described in detail in other chapters of this book—involves students learning from either written or spoken words. For example, paraphrasing asks students to put information they have recently learned into their own words. Likewise, a mnemonic device is a play on words that may help a student to commit information to long-term memory. Many science teachers help their students to remember the classification system of living things by using some variation of the phrase, "**K**ing **P**hillip **C**ame **O**ver **F**or **G**reat **S**paghetti!" The first letter of each word in this sentence corresponds to the different levels of classification: **k**ingdom, **p**hylum, **c**lass, **o**rder, **f**amily, **g**enus and **s**pecies. Such a phrase utilizes students' semantic memory to help them remember the classification system of living things.

Episodic Memory

Because memory can be episodic, researchers have discovered that *where* a student learns a particular skill or concept and *where* a student is expected to apply this learning may have an impact on their ability to recall and utilize this information. More specifically, Sprenger (1999, p. 52) explains that "students who learn information in one room and take a test in another consistently under-perform. Episodic memory has an important component called 'invisible information.' Students have more trouble solving math problems in English class than they do in their math classroom. Why? The walls, desks, overheads, chalkboards and even the math teacher are covered with invisible information. The content of the room becomes part of the context of the memory." This finding has enormous implications for educators. Particularly in the current climate of high stakes testing, it is important to recognize that students will perform better on a science test if they take the test in the same room in which their learning about science has occurred.

Where a student learns a particular skill or concept and where a student is expected to apply this learning may have an impact on their ability to recall and utilize this information.

Of course, this understanding of episodic memory has applications beyond high stakes testing as well. For example, one way in which a teacher may physically signify the end of one unit and the start of the next is by changing students' seating assignments or even the entire layout of the classroom. A less dramatic change would be replacing the information on the classroom bulletin boards with content about the upcoming unit. These physical changes will help students' minds to differentiate between the previous unit and the current unit and create physical associations with the new learning that will occur. In short, helping students to connect their learning to a particular type of physical space works in much the same way as connecting student's learning to pictures, described in the preceding section.

Procedural Memory

Procedural memory involves the processes that the body does and remembers. For classroom teachers, Sprenger (1999, p. 74) suggests having "students move in some way as they learn." This movement creates 'muscle memory' that, as with pictures and episodes, leads students to associate the content they are learning with their motion at the time the learning is taking place. For example, consider asking students to stand up or move to a new seat for a mini-lesson set within a larger class period. Ask students to clap their hands if they understand your explanation of a particular idea. Integrating such procedures into classroom instruction will better enable your students to recall the learning that has taken place.

Automatic Memory

Automatic memory is just that—information that may be recalled immediately without perceptible pause for thought. Most of us as elementary school students were expected to commit the multiplication tables to automatic memory. Automatic memory tends to require large amounts of practice, developing strong associations or both. For example, one of us recalls our third grade teacher asking us every night for homework to write out the multiplication tables for a particular number six times. Others remember endlessly practicing with flashcards. Repetitive drills such as these are par for the course for committing information to automatic memory. Sprenger (1999) also suggests working to develop associations between a particular type of information and something more easily remembered. For example, the vast majority of us do not have the fifty states of the United States committed to automatic memory. And yet some of our students have learned a song in which they literally rattle off the fifty states in perfect harmony. Much as young children first learn the alphabet through song, these students have committed the fifty states to automatic memory by successfully associating these states with a tune.

Emotional Memory

Perhaps the type of memory that we as teachers make the least use of is emotional memory. Just as our students are more likely to remember information that is connected to pictures, places or movement, they are also better able to remember information linked with a particular emotion or feeling. How does this work? Imagine that we complete a unit with our first graders on the Thanksgiving holiday by actually holding a "practice" Thanksgiving meal (perhaps on the final day of school before the Thanksgiving break). Students create decorations and are responsible (with the help of their parents) for bringing in a type of food that might have been eaten at the first Thanksgiving. The excitement and pleasure that students experience while participating in such a hands-on (and tasty) activity greatly increase their ability to learn and commit to long-term memory the historical background of the Thanksgiving holiday.

Moreover, the emotion that can help students better remember a skill, concept or idea does not always have to be their own. At the conclusion of Chapter 5 of this book, we explained that students are more likely to be engaged, active learners when they recognize their teacher's passion and enthusiasm for the material they are being asked to learn. We suggested that such a display of enthusiasm piques students' interest in understanding the relevance of the particular topic or skill to their own lives. There is also a brain-based rationale for teachers' expressing their enthusiasm for a particular topic of study; namely, students are better able to commit a particular piece of information or content to their long-term memory when they can link this information to the emotions expressed by their teacher at the time of instruction. For example, in Chapter 5, we used John Donne's "A Valediction Forbidding Mourning" as an example of a poem for which higher order thinking questions might be utilized. This poem is a challenging one to understand, and, when teaching this poem to our students, we typically begin by describing our own introduction to the poem. We describe struggling to understand the poem and feeling our own frustration level mounting . . . and then, suddenly, right when we were ready to give up, an epiphany occurred and it was almost as though a light bulb turned on directly over the poem, illuminating its beauty. Such an introduction is meant not only to prepare our students for the challenging reading ahead (and to exhort them not to give up) but also to allow them to link the poem's content with the emotions described by their teacher—frustration transforming into illumination. By linking content and emotion, our students are far more likely to integrate the poem's content into their long-term memory than they would be if we simply handed out copies of the poem and began reading.

Providing Structure

In previous sections of this chapter, we examined what learning and memory look like inside the brain. You will recall that students are better able to transfer new information into long-term memory if they connect this new information to knowledge they already possess. For new information *unconnected* to previously held knowledge, one strategy described in Chapter 2 was "chunking." This is the practice of grouping individual pieces of information into larger groups. For example, in *How the Brain Learns*, David Sousa (1995) notes that it is difficult for students to commit seven random numbers to memory, but adding a dash between the third and fourth digit turns those seven numbers into a "phone number." Since this grouping of numbers is more meaningful than seven random numbers in a line, these numbers are then more easily committed to long-term memory. This strategy of chunking works because the human brain is better at encoding information into long-term memory when that information is received in an organized, categorized form rather than simply as individual, unconnected pieces of information. In various studies on the way in which experts in a particular field learn new information, researchers have discovered that "experts store information in categories rather than as separate bits of information"(Nolet & McLaughlin, 2000, p. 40).

With this understanding of learning and memory in mind, there are several strategies that teachers may employ to support their students' learning. First, teachers should utilize curricula and develop units that base students' learning around "organizing ideas" (Bransford, Brown, & Cocking, 1999). Essential questions (described in detail in Chapter 2) may be helpful in this regard. For example, a social studies unit on the Revolutionary War will better serve students if the teacher focuses the unit around two to three organizing ideas rather than simply leading students chronologically through the various battles, dates and important events. Much more useful for students is an organizing idea (in the form of an essential question) such as, "What factors led the colonists to decide that they could no longer live under British rule?" Organizing the unit around this and one to two other organizing ideas will lead students to process the information they learn about the Revolutionary War in a structured, categorized way, enabling them to more easily transfer this information to their long-term memory.

Nolet and McLaughlin (2000, pp. 40–41) touch upon a second strategy for supporting student learning when they write that "teachers may help their students employ more expert storage strategies when they are clear about the kind of information they want their students to learn and the manner in which students will be asked to use the information." By this, they mean that the type of knowledge teachers expect students to learn may be divided into three categories: declarative knowledge, procedural knowledge and conditional knowledge. **Declarative knowledge** takes the form of basic facts. **Procedural knowledge** is literally *how* to do something. And **conditional knowledge** takes the form of knowing *when* to apply a skill or concept. For example, the Pythagorean Theorem itself is an example of declarative knowledge, but understanding *how* to use this formula to find the length of the third leg of a right triangle requires procedural knowledge. Finally, recognizing the various situations *when* applying the Pythagorean Theorem will be useful requires conditional knowledge.

A second example of these different types of knowledge may be seen in a lesson for elementary school students about the use of question and exclamation marks. In this case, declarative knowledge takes the form of the definition of these two types of punctuation; namely, that question marks are used to show that someone is asking a question and that exclamation marks are used to express excitement. However, understanding *how* to use these punctuation marks requires procedural knowledge and *when* to use these punctuation marks requires conditional knowledge. Demonstrating these types of knowledge would require students to create properly punctuated interrogative and exclamatory sentences or to read a paragraph in which all punctuation marks have been removed and correctly insert question marks and exclamation marks at the appropriate intervals.

Students are better able to commit newly learned information to long-term memory when they are told at the outset of the lesson which type of knowledge they will be expected to learn and the way in which they will be expected to utilize this knowledge.

Nolet and McLaughlin (2000) suggest that students are better able to commit newly learned information to long-term memory when they are told at the outset of the lesson which type of knowledge they will be expected to learn and the way in which they will be expected to utilize this knowledge. In Chapter 2, we discussed the strategy of providing students with a unit's final assessment or project *at the start of the unit*. In Chapters 1 and 2 we discussed the importance of giving the students the mastery objectives at the outset of the learning. Here we have the cognitive explanation for why such strategies promote higher levels of learning.

Using Color

In this section, we have discussed ways in which teachers may better organize the content that they convey to students. Two other strategies that come up in the literature on brain-based education involve the use of color. First, Eric Jensen (1998) suggests in *Teaching with the Brain in Mind* that teachers may increase their students' memory retention by utilizing different colored chalk or markers to categorize information they are writing on the blackboard or flipchart paper. For example, a science teacher educating his or her students about the concept of different species might choose to write all of the examples of mammals in red marker and all of the examples of amphibians in green marker. Using these colors will better enable students to remember the examples of these two species because the information is entering their brains in a structured, categorized way. Similarly, in *Learning and Memory: The Brain in Action*, Marilee Sprenger (1999) recommends utilizing a single color of paper for all handouts related to a particular topic. For example, in one of our ninth-grade English classes, we ask students to keep grammar and literary terms sections in their notebooks. All of the handouts that go into their literary terms section are printed on light blue paper and all of the handouts for their grammar sections are printed on pink paper. In this way, we work to connect the handout we are examining with the previous handouts they have received on a related topic.

Conclusion

In this chapter, we have endeavored to take advantage of recent advances in the field of neuroscience to bring you a more thorough understanding of what is occurring in our students' brains than any previous generation of educators has ever been afforded. We have tried to balance explanations of what learning and memory look like inside the brain with pedagogical strategies used by ourselves and recommended by doctors, psychologists and scientists based on their deepening understanding of the brain and learning. We have placed this chapter in the latter half of the book, recognizing that teachers might regard chapters on behavior management, assessment and standards-based teaching with a greater sense of immediacy than a focus on the brain and learning. Having now read this chapter on the brain and learning, however, we recommend taking the time to look back over those previously read chapters. Re-read the paragraphs you have highlighted or marked as particularly helpful. Strategies that have been offered throughout this book for maintaining an orderly classroom, generating activities that allow a class full of heterogeneous students to work to their potential and using questions to strengthen students' higher order thinking skills may now be viewed through the lens of the brain and learning. We believe you will find that rereading the strategies presented throughout this book with a heightened understanding of the impact of these strategies upon the brain and learning will strengthen your ability to implement these ideas in your own classroom. As more and more research has been published on the brain and learning, we know that we have had the fascinating experience of more deeply understanding *why* and *how* various strategies we have employed for years in our classrooms actually work to support our students' learning. This deeper understanding has unquestionably increased our expertise as educators, and we hope that you feel a similar benefit to understanding the nuts and bolts of learning and the brain.

Rereading the strategies presented throughout this book with a heightened understanding of the impact of these strategies upon the brain and learning will strengthen your ability to implement these ideas in your own classroom.

References

Armstrong, T. (2000). *Multiple intelligences in the classroom*. Alexandria, VA: Association for Supervision and Curriculum Development (ASCD).

Bransford, J., Brown, A., & Cocking, R. (1999). *How people learn: Brain, mind and experience at school*. Washington, DC: National Academy Press.

Erlauer, L. (2003). *The brain-compatible classroom: Using what we know about learning to improve teaching*. Alexandria, VA: Association for Supervision and Curriculum Development (ASCD).

Gardner, H. (1983). *Frames of mind: The theory of multiple intelligences*. New York: Basic Books.

Given, B. (2002). *Teaching to the brain's natural systems*. Alexandria, VA: Association for Supervision and Curriculum Development (ASCD).

Spinks, Sarah (Writer, Director, Producer). (1999) Inside the teenage brain. [Television series episode]. In *Front line*. New York and Washington, DC: Public Broadcasting Service (PBS).

Jensen, E. (1998). *Teaching with the brain in mind*. Alexandria, VA: Association for Supervision and Curriculum Development (ASCD).

Marzano, R., Pickering, D., & Pollock, J. (2001). *Classroom instruction that works: Research-based strategies for increasing student achievement*. Alexandria, VA: Association for Supervision and Curriculum Development (ASCD).

McGeehan, J. R. (Ed.). (1999). *Transformations: Leadership for brain compatible learning*. Kent, WA: Books for Educators Inc.

Nolet, V. & McLaughlin, M. (2000). *Accessing the general curriculum.* Thousand Oaks, CA: Corwin Press.

Ornstein, R. (1997). *The right mind: Making sense of the hemispheres.* New York: Harcourt Brace.

Severson, K. (2004, July 2). Academic credit for lunch with program combining cooking, organic gardening. *The San Francisco Chronicle.*

Shaywitz, S. (2003). *Overcoming dyslexia: A new and complete science-based program for reading problems at any level.* New York: Alfred A. Knopf.

Sousa, D. (1995). *How the brain learns.* Reston, VA: National Association of Secondary School Principals.

Sprenger, M. (1999). *Learning & memory: The brain in action.* Alexandria, VA: Association for Supervision and Curriculum Development.

Wolfe, P. (2001). *Brain matters.* Alexandria, VA: Association for Supervision and Curriculum Development (ASCD).

C H A P T E R

9

Working Effectively With Parents

Strategies for Difficult Parent Conferences
Tips for Successful Curriculum Nights for Parents
Sample Newsletters and Web Sites for Parents

Objectives for the Chapter

After reading this chapter, you will be able to

a. use pro-active communication to establish positive relationships with parents
b. conference effectively with parents
c. deal effectively with aggressive parents
d. maximize the engagement of uninvolved parents in their children's education
e. conduct a successful curriculum night presentation

In recent years, educators have become extremely aware of the importance of working effectively with parents. Parents come with a wide range of needs and expectations. Some are extremely aggressive consumers of their children's education. Other parents take no part in their children's education and may at times be detrimental to it. Most fall somewhere in between.

To be successful, we must be able to work well with all types of parents. Unfortunately, few teachers receive training in their pre-service or in-service education that enables them to work effectively with parents. As a result, most of us learn how to work with parents through trial and error. As with any area for which we do not receive training, we often revert to familiar models and personal experiences for guidance on the best way to proceed. This tendency leads many of us to the explicit or implicit belief that good parenting is the way in which we parent our own children or the way in which we were parented. The reality is that effective parenting comes in many forms. It is shaped by factors such as the way the parents were parented, religious beliefs, cultural norms, number of children in the family, children's birth order, community norms, work schedule, availability of child care[1], family resources and a myriad of other factors.

Colleagues in the school who have worked successfully with parents may be one of the most effective supports for learning new strategies. Colleagues have already learned (sometimes the hard way) many of the "dos and don'ts" related to establishing and maintaining effective parent communication and relationships. In addition to knowing generic strategies for working with parents, colleagues also know the culture of the community. The family demographics in each school may often influence the level of parent involvement and consumerism.

For example, a recent research study presented at the 2002 American Sociological Association meeting (Weininger and Lareau) indicated that the education level of mothers has a direct correlation to the number of activities in which the child is involved. The study reports that "a child whose mother has at least a bachelor's degree is predicted to spend about two and a third more hours participating in organized activities (per week) than a child whose mother did not earn a degree." Schools with high parent education levels typically have a higher level of parent consumerism than other schools.

A successful colleague has worked with the school's parent population well and knows what strategies work best. He or she also knows the history of the hot button issues in the community and may help the mentor navigate around those issues. One experienced fifth-grade teacher in his first year in a district described the day before the first day of school in the following way.

> Since I was new to the school and the district, the parents were invited to meet me at a coffee the day before the students returned from summer vacation. This was a school in which the parents had a reputation for being very involved and having very high expectations for teachers. The principal was concerned parents would be coming in the last two weeks in August to check me out and interrupt my work in planning and preparing the classroom. He scheduled the coffee as a way to bring them all in at the same time and limit the disruption to my planning. The plan worked. Few parents came during the last two weeks in August and 100% of the families attended the coffee.
>
> I had taught for five years and so had practice giving presentations to parents. However, my experience had been in a district in which parent involvement was far less than in this school. I planned a brief explanation about my background and the curriculum, followed by some time for questions. I had just finished my explanation about language arts and was beginning to talk about math when a parent raised his hand and asked, "Will you be spending much time teaching multiplication and division algorithms? Our children don't know these as well as they should." I answered that I intended to begin the year assessing students' mastery of various algorithms and teaching them to the extent the assessments indicated the teaching was needed. A second parent raised her hand and said, "I disagree with

[1]An article in *Education Week* (Zehr, 2002) described a daycare center in Milwaukee that had extended its hours from 7:00 A.M. to 6:00 P.M. to new hours from 5:30 A.M. to 1:30 A.M. The hours were extended in recognition of that fact that many parents worked in service sector jobs that required them to work early morning and/or night shifts.

Mr.__. I think you need to focus on math processes and problem solving. I don't want you to spend a lot of time teaching algorithms at the start of the year." Before I could respond, a heated debate ensued between those parents who wanted more emphasis on the teaching of the algorithms and computation and those parents who wanted me to de-emphasize the algorithms so there could be greater emphasis on math processes and problem solving. For the next thirty minutes, the parents debated among themselves. The principal stopped in at this time and was able to quell the debate. Shortly thereafter, the ending time of the coffee was upon us, and the principal thanked the parents for coming and ended the coffee.

I learned afterwards that the district was entering its third year of a new mathematics curriculum. There had been considerable controversy among parents and the staff about the new curriculum. Some believed it was a very exciting move toward teaching children to be math thinkers. Others believed it lacked rigor and did not adequately teach the basics.

One may see from this example the advantage this teacher would have had if he had been briefed on the mathematics curriculum.

Strategies for Increasing Success in a Difficult Parent Conference

The following ideas for working effectively with parents are based on research about parent-to-teacher communication and relationships and the authors' years of experience as teachers and in training teachers to work effectively with parents and with parents to work effectively with teachers.

The Parent Conference

Conferencing with parents is an area in which few teachers have received training. The following list of ideas for conferencing combines the research on effective communication skills with suggestions from actual teachers and parents interviewed on the topic of parent–teacher conferences.

Step 1—Be proactive. Get all the information you can about the parent and child in preparation for the first conference about the student. A conference with the child ahead of time may often give you the information you need to be well prepared for the parent. Many teachers have begun to make contact with parents early in the year, asking parents for information about their children. Examples of this strategy include asking parents to write a letter telling the teacher about their children, sending home a questionnaire, calling the parents during the first week of school and scheduling a brief "tell me about your child" conference during the first month of school.

Step 2—Location. Choose the location and setup that provides the best atmosphere for the conference. Should the conference be in your classroom? If so, do you want the doors open or closed? Is there another location that is better, such as the guidance office, a conference room or the parents' home? Do you want to sit at a table or at your desk or should you set the chairs so there is no object between you and the parents?

Step 3—Time. Most districts have a set period of time for each parent conference, however, for those conferences you anticipate will be difficult, be sure you have scheduled enough time. In these cases, allowing an extra ten or fifteen minutes of conference time may save you a great deal of time and angst over the course of the year.

Step 4—Get the parent talking about the child. Use active listening and acknowledging responses (applying the stages of listening presented later in this chapter) to give the parent the message that you are hearing what he or she has to say. Look for "hooks" in the parent's words that you may use later to start a discussion about areas that need improvement. **Hooks** are words or statements that enable you to attribute the area of discussion to the parent's agenda even if it was on your own. For example, the parent may talk about the child's strong verbal skills. This may give you the hook you need to open the conversation you wanted to have with the parent about the student's talking out without raising his or her hand.

Step 5—Be positive. "No matter how difficult the student is in your class, and no matter how serious the problems are, always find positive things to say. Parents want to hear something good, even though their children may be struggling. It gives them the strength to deal with the areas of difficulty." (Ribas, 1991, p.)

Step 6—Give concrete examples from your observations of the child to support any statements of judgment. Samples of the student's work or specific descriptions of interactions are much more helpful to a parent's understanding than generalized comments. One second-grade teacher shared a time in which he was having difficulty getting the parents to believe their daughter was having difficulty decoding words. The teacher had a practice of periodically audiotaping all the students reading orally as a way for them to hear their own growth as readers. The students loved listening to themselves read. At one conference with these parents, the teacher played the tape of their child reading. The parents immediately recognized the decoding problems that the teacher described. No further persuasion was needed to get the parents to accept reading support for their daughter.

Step 7—Think carefully about how to phrase negative information. The difficult balance here is in trying to phrase a criticism in a way that is not only clear and honest but also limits the "bite." See the stages of listening later in this book for help in this area. As stated previously, you may find examples or a good opening statement in the parent's own words if you give them an opportunity to speak early in the conference.

Step 8—Know the child as a person. Indicate to the parent that you know—or are getting to know—his or her child as a person, not just as a student. Parents always ask themselves, "Does this teacher really know my child?"

Step 9—Check your emotions throughout the conference. Resist the **fight/flight response** when presented with a confrontation from an aggressive parent. Brain researchers tell us that when humans and other animals feel threatened, the blood rushes from other parts of the brain to the brain stem. This is an evolutionary response designed to help us fight or flee from danger. Unfortunately, this same blood is leaving the parts of our brain that foster problem solving and higher order thinking, the skills we need most at this time.

Step 10—Stall. The line, "I'll get back to you later on that question," gives you some time to think and gather more information before giving the best response.

Step 11—Attend to the feelings and emotions behind the words and behavior. (See the case study activities on the following pages.)

Step 12—If deadlocked, consider using an objective third party. The third party might be an administrator, resource room teacher or another person both you and the parent trust.

Step 13—If deadlocked, see if there is some small, workable piece you might give the parent so he or she feels successful in advocating for the child.

Step 14—Check the names of the parents. For a variety of reasons, children often have last names that are different from those of their parents.

Step 15—Disengaging from the endless conference. Some parents have so much they want to say that it is difficult to end the conference once you have completed your agenda. The first thing to ask yourself is whether you are better off taking more time than you expected now because it will pay dividends down the road. If this is a difficult child or parent and the time continues to be productive, you may want to continue the meeting. At other times, the conference may be past its productive point and you need an exit strategy that does not offend the parent. One strategy teachers have used to disengage with a parent that doesn't know when to stop is to schedule this parent at a time when there is are conferences before and after the appointment. This ensures a finite amount of time for the conference. Another strategy is to have someone call you or come to get you at a specific time. In each of these cases, it is important to let the parent know in advance how much time is available for the conference, so they are not surprised when the time has passed.

Statements such as the following signal to parents that you are near the end of the conference time and may help to end the conference.

- "We are near the end of our time, and you are making an interesting point. Let's both think some more about what has been said. Please send me a note with your additional ideas."
- "We've covered a great deal so far. Let's focus on doing what we have said thus far before moving on to other ideas."

Nonverbal behaviors by themselves or combined with closing statements may be successful. For example, moving forward in your chair to a position that indicates you are preparing to stand while also maintaining eye contact sends the message that you are interested but are out of time. Or, at an appropriate break in the conversation, thank the parent for his or her time while extending your hand to shake hands. Placing your watch on the desk at the start of the conference may be a signal to the parent that there is a finite amount of time for the conference. Doing this also makes it easier for you to monitor the time without breaking your eye contact with the parent.

Teacher's additional suggestions for conducting successful parent conferences.

Involving the Uninvolved Parent

As stated previously we must be careful about our assumptions regarding parents who are not involved in their children's education. There are many reasons why parents do not take as much of a role in their children's education as we would like or as the research tells us would be beneficial to the children. These include a long commute and/or work hours, high work stress, high family stress, abuse in the home, ill health, single parent homes, low parent education level, embarrassment, limited English, drug and alcohol use, lack of transportation, lack of child care, religious restrictions, the parent having received poor parenting and having a lack of parenting training and a number of other factors.

It is the extremely rare case that a parent doesn't care about his or her child. If we believe this, then we are left with trying to figure out what factors cause a parent not to attend conferences, return phone calls, make certain that the student comes to school or make certain that the student completes homework. Some of these factors we have little power to impact. Others we have significant power to change.

The following are ideas gathered from teachers who have successfully engaged uninvolved parents in their children's education.

1. Make a home contact early in the year with positive information about the child (e.g., phone or note). For many uninvolved parents (both as adult parents and also when they were students) the school has only contacted home when there is a problem. It is for this reason that many consciously or subconsciously avoid such contact.
2. Use the stages of listening explained later in this chapter to encourage the parent's active participation in phone calls and meetings.
3. When informing a parent about an issue, have suggestions for positive changes and be open to the parent's response and suggestions. Many of the remediation strategies that work with the majority of families may not be appropriate for this family situation for reasons they do not want to readily share (e.g., lack of parent education, problem spouse or sibling in the home, multiple jobs held by a single parent or serious family illness).
4. Show the parent any notes you take during the conference. Be open to the fact that the parent may not want you to take notes during some parts of the conference. Note-taking by the teacher is often reassuring to assertive, educated parents, however, uninvolved parents may often be worried about how the notes will be used, causing them to speak less freely. Remember, some of our recent immigrant parents come from countries in which the notes of an official (in this case the teacher) are often used to justify punishments to citizens.
5. In a timely manner, follow through on what you say you will do. Many of these parents feel they are inferior to the professionals in their lives and are acustomed to being considered low priorities by professionals. Your quick follow-up signals you value them as people and appreciate their participation in the process.
6. Be aware of cultural differences, particularly those of parents who are first generation Americans. For example, in their article "Bridging Cultures with a Parent–Teacher Conference," Quiroz, Greenfield and Altchech (1999) describe the lessons they learned working with the immigrant Latino community in the Los Angeles Public Schools. They quote one Mexican–American mother's confusion after a parent–teacher conference as follows:

    > I couldn't understand what the teacher was trying to communicate when she comments on my daughter's performance. I particularly recall two confusing comments that this teacher made: "Your daughter is very sociable" and "Your daughter is outstanding in . . . ." My tendency as a Mexican mother was to feel very happy she was sociable; after all, that was what I was fostering. However, I did not know what to do about her being "outstanding." I had tried to show my daughter not to "show off," but it seemed that is was not working.

One fifth-grade teacher we worked with described his work with a child from a Chinese immigrant family. The child worked diligently on class and homework assignments. The child was always attentive and never talked with other students when the teacher wanted their attention, however, the child never answered questions in class. When the teacher described this to the parents they seemed confused by that fact that the teacher wanted the child to answer questions and give opinions. Both the parents' school experiences and the previous school experience of their child had never included opportunities for students to answer questions or give their opinions.

In one district (Colombo, 2004), they identified a gap between the perspectives of teachers and parents regarding parent–teacher communication and parent involvement. The teachers initially were frustrated by what they perceived as the parents' lack of interest and involvement in their children's education. It was learned through parent outreach that the parents perceived their involvement as infringing on the teacher's professional domain. The district addressed this issue by developing two workshops. One workshop was for teachers, and it described the cultural perspective of the parents. The other workshop was for parents, and it described the school culture and expectations related to parents' involvement in their children's education. After participating in these workshops, both groups better understood the others and were able to bridge the gap between their cultural perspectives.

7. Check to see if you will need a translator. Many students come from homes in which the primary language is one other than English. In many recent immigrant families, the parents speak less English than their children, and this lesser fluency may keep the parents from attending the conference. If a translator will be present, let the parent know ahead of time.
8. In one district in which we worked, the third-grade teachers were struggling with trying to get the parents to work with their children at home on math facts. Most of the families were recent immigrants and both parents worked, often at two jobs. One year the teachers decided to hold parent meetings to explain to the parents how they might help their children by quizzing them just ten to fifteen minutes each afternoon or evening on the math facts. The teachers planned and executed informational meetings for parents at two different times during the day. They planned a meeting during the day for parents who worked nights and another one during the evening for parents who worked during the day. The school did significant outreach and had a high percentage of parents come to the meetings. Unfortunately, after the meetings, they found that parents had disposed of many of the handouts on their way out the door. All this work had minimal impact on changing parents' involvement in the home. Upon talking with some parents, the teachers learned that many of the parents were overwhelmed by the amount of information given in the meeting and the comprehensiveness of the handout packet. They also learned that the one time during the day when the students sat with one or both of their parents was either at breakfast or dinner time.

   Rather than giving up, the teachers used this data to plan better the next year. They again scheduled meetings for parents at two convenient times. The school again did considerable outreach that brought many parents to the meetings, however, the teachers changed the program in two ways. First, they scaled back the number of concepts they asked parents to practice with the students. Second, they put all the concepts they wanted parents to use on laminated meal place mats. They included specific facts and games the parents might play with their children at the dinner table. In the parent meeting, the teachers role-played a typical meal and how parents might incorporate math practice into the mealtime. After the parent meetings, the teachers checked the garbage but did not find one place mat thrown away! More important, the parents were using the place mats with their children and the students' skills were improving.

Stages of Listening to Increase Parent Involvement

Stage I: Conference Location

Choose the best location/setting for the conversation. The best setting is situationally determined. For example, most parents will prefer complete privacy when you are addressing areas their child needs to change or when you are informing them of difficulties their child may be experiencing. In these cases, your room with a closed door is probably the best place.

Stage II: Statements That Open the Door to a Productive Discussion

Door openers indicate that you want to have a two-way conversation about the child and don't just want to tell the parent what you know about his or her child. This impression is best achieved by asking questions that push the parent to talk about those aspects of the child's personality and experience that will be helpful for you to know. At this point, the questions should be open-ended to get the parent talking and thinking.

Some door openers include the following questions.

- What does your child tell you about school?
- What does he or she like best? What does he like the least?
- When does he or she feel successful?
- Are there times in school when he or she does not feel successful?
- Who does he or she identify as his friends?

Stage III: Use Wait Time

The parent needs time to think about your question and to formulate an answer. Some may need time to translate the question and answer because English is not their primary language. Others might be worried about not sounding "smart" and, therefore, are careful in formulating their answers.

Stage IV: Passive Listening

Passive listening is a technique used to create an environment in which the parent feels that he or she may talk freely.

- Once the parent starts talking, the most important thing to do is "bite your lip and listen." Resist the urge to break in with comments or advice too soon. It may be quicker (and more gratifying to you) to give the parent advice and comments than to wait for him or her to fully answer the question.
- Use body language that indicates your openness to hearing what the parent has to say. **Body language** includes both body position and facial expressions.

Listening carefully and using appropriate body language signals to the parent that what he or she is saying is important to you.

Stage III: Acknowledgement Responses

Eye contact, nodding, comments such as "I hear you" and "I understand" and paraphrasing the parent's statements all send the message that you are listening. Remember that acknowledging is not agreeing! There will be ample opportunity to discuss areas of disagreement at the appropriate time.

Stage IV: Active Listening

Active listening gives the speaker tangible evidence of the listener's understanding. For example, the listener labels the parent's feelings about the situation (e.g., anger, excitement, pride, frustration, fear or confusion). The listener asks clarification questions and follow-up questions to gather additional information.

Ideas about how to best help a child that are discovered by the parent are far more likely to be implemented than those you give as advice that is not requested. Harry Truman said it best; "There is no limit to what you can achieve when you don't care who gets the credit." Active listening helps to lead the parent to his or her own solutions.

Stage V: Closing the Gap Between the Teacher's and the Parent's Perceptions of Performance

Rarely does a year pass when we don't have at least one parent with whom there is a disagreement about some aspect of the child's education. In those circumstances, we identify differences between your perception and the parent's perception of the situation and generate options that sound reasonable to both of you. Ask questions that help the parent discover inconsistencies between his or her perception of the child's situation and the actual situation. You want the changes parents make to "stick." The more the parent buys into the change, the more likely he or she is to permanently change his or her practices.

- Be open to the idea that you may not be completely correct in your perception. Listen and consider the parent's rationale before making a final judgment.
- Make an internal check of your frustration/defensiveness meter. If your frustration and/or defensiveness are growing faster than the progress you are making in closing the gap between your perception and that of the parent, it might be best to end the discussion and schedule a time to get together again in the near future. This will keep you from making a non-productive statement. It will also give you time to reflect and decide whether there are other ways to word your concerns that will better enable the parent to hear and "own" those concerns.

Stage VI: Concluding the Discussion

- Generate options for next steps. Decide as specifically as possible what each person will do and the deadlines for completing each task.
- Summarize the conclusions reached in the conference.
- In situations in which we want the parent to follow up, we should set a date, time, location and tentative agenda for the follow-up discussion or any follow-up activities.

The previous framework must always be considered within the context of the individual with whom the teacher is meeting. Some parents prefer that the teacher "cut to the chase" if they believe the teacher is working up to a difficult area to discuss. Most, however, prefer that the teacher work through the stages and do appreciate the give-and-take this type of discussion provides.

Teacher's additional suggestions for involving and working with uninvolved parents.

Strategies for Difficult Parent Conferences

As mentioned earlier, few teachers ever receive pre-service or in-service training in strategies for working effectively with parents. The following case studies are from actual teachers' experiences in conferencing with aggressive parents. The cases are followed by exercises designed to help in analyzing each situation. For two reasons, it is important for teachers to study cases like this prior to being confronted with a difficult parent conference situation. The first reason is so the teacher may better understand the reasons and emotions that cause parents to be aggressive in a conference. This understanding makes such behavior easier to accept and deal with in a professional manner. We must remember that we are the professionals in the situation. Because we are the professionals, we need to hold ourselves to a high standard of behavior even if the parent is acting in an irrational manner. The second reason is to learn and practice strategies that the teacher may use during a conference with an aggressive parent.

Secondary Case Study

The student is from an upper middle-class family living in a large house in an expensive neighborhood. The father is an executive for a local company and travels extensively, being away from home for long periods of time. The mother, who is not working at the present time, has recently started to travel with dad on some business trips, leaving their two children with a babysitter–housekeeper. The oldest son has a history of being a successful student and is an excellent athlete. He is fifteen-years old and has an eleven-year-old brother. The oldest son has been acting out recently by coming late to class and not working to his potential in math (and other subject areas). His math performance in middle school and freshman year in high school were in the top quarter of his class. He consistently received grades of B+ and A– in math during those years. His first quarter grade in honors math during sophomore year was a C+, and the second quarter grade had dipped to a C–.

The parents are asked to come in to meet with the math teacher and the guidance counselor to discuss the change in performance. The information is reviewed with the parents at the conference. The mother listens for the first ten minutes while the teacher describes the student's performance. She then folds her arms and crosses her legs about five minutes into the explanation. Suddenly, she gets very angry and accuses the teacher of not telling them (the parents) soon enough about the dip in performance, not understanding her child, not motivating her child and not liking her child. She says this would not be an issue if the class were more interesting. In a fit of anger, she states that her property taxes equal half the teacher's salary and that she should be getting more from the school and the teacher for her child.

Elementary Case Study

It is November and the teacher's first conference with this particular parent. The parent is the father of one of the top three math students in his second grade class. Dad is a successful attorney in his early forties. The teacher had no indication prior to the conference that the parent had concerns. The teacher begins by explaining how the child is doing in each subject area. Father quietly sits through the language arts explanation. When the teacher begins to explain the math, the father shifts in his chair. He sits back and folds his arms. After about a minute, the father interrupts to say that Jimmy is bored in math. He states that he knows where Jimmy is in math because he does math problems with Jimmy on the weekend. Dad states further that the class is doing addition and subtraction and Jimmy has known these operations since the beginning of first grade. Dad reports that he is doing multiplication and division with Jimmy and asks the teacher to do multiplication and division with Jimmy. Dad says he doesn't want Jimmy to do any cooperative learning because Jimmy knows more math than most of the other kids in the class and he doesn't learn anything from the other kids. As dad talks, his voice gets louder, his face turns red and he speaks faster. He tells the teacher this has been a wasted year so far in math, and he won't let it continue to be a wasted year. He has heard from other parents that second graders in other schools do multiplication and division and he can't understand why his son can't do it in this class. Dad goes on to say that he is *not* the only second grade parent who feels this way and asks the teacher what she plans to do.

Activity Sheet 1

Strategies for Difficult Parent Conferences

What emotions or other factors are causing the yelling and accusing behavior?

What are some emotions the teacher is likely to be experiencing?

If you were this teacher, what would you do next?

Activity Sheet 2
Strategies for Difficult Parent Conferences

1. Share with your partner a difficult parent conference in which you participated while he or she uses stages of listening techniques.
2. The partner should fill out the activity sheet below, asking whatever questions are necessary to get as much information on the sheet as possible.

List the difficult parent behaviors evident in the conference described by your partner.

List the emotions and other factors that caused the parent behaviors.

List the strategies your partner used or might have used to better manage the conference. Remember, the strategies need not solve the problem. They only need to improve the management of this difficult situation.

Activity Sheet 3
Strategies for Difficult Parent Conferences

1. With your partner, list the situations that lead to the most difficult conferences.

2. With your partner, list strategies for diffusing difficulties.

Section 2
Tips for Successful Curriculum Nights for Parents

The following poem and author's note is reprinted with the permission of the author from the Newsletter of the Massachusetts Field Center for Teaching and Learning, *Voices,* Volume XII, November/December, 1997. The poem won first prize in the 1997–1998 Teaching Voices Writer's Contest.

Parents' Night
by Mary Burchenal

One by one the tidy classrooms across the courtyard
are going black. Parents filter out toward their cars
and headlights flicker across the windows.
But there she is at my desk, smiling out of a shapeless coat.

It isn't just the heavy Russian accent that makes it hard.
I lean my head toward what she has to say
about her daughter Sonya, with, I see now, the same shy smile—
her daughter Sonya who, too, lingers at my desk after class.

She burns a trail of smoky words: Sonya loves reading very much,
she has problem with hearing—she wants to write like Tolstoi—
she liked so much last year's English teacher—
I thank him for the rest of my life.

When she breaks off, eyes eager at my face,
I pull my head back, clearing for a smooth landing,
but the sentences I pave out about the course, about Sonya's progress
somehow crumble and fall away

Her forehead wrinkles; she veers sideways and lifts off again,
circling back over the territory, words thick and halting.
I watch but cannot follow
though I try until the halls are dark.

On the drive home the mother's words are large winged moths
that brush soft bodies against my hair
and flutter thinly at the windshield.
Suddenly I see the nonsense of my replies

"Please," she'd been saying, racing against the custodian
rattling his keys as he came, snapping off lights.
"Please," she had said, those keys jangling toward my door—
"Can you love my child?"

Author's note: I have a long way to go as far as listening is concerned. In the classroom (as elsewhere) I can become much too fascinated with what I'm saying or about to say. When a student complains, "But Mrs. Bellow's class isn't having an exam. It's unfair," it's easy to get annoyed or to come up with a very articulate and rational response about the importance of exams, instead of putting energy into understanding that the student might be saying, "I'm panicked about the exam. Help!" I wrote this poem partly, I suppose, as an apology to students and parents I haven't listened to hard enough.

Tips for Successful Curriculum Night Presentations for Parents

It has many names: *Curriculum Night, Back to School Night, Meet the Teacher Coffee* and others. It is a meeting, morning or evening, early in the school year when parents are invited to come as a group to hear the teacher explain about the classroom plans for the year. In many schools, the new generation of parents are older, busier, better educated and have become more assertive consumers of their children's education. Expectations for the quality and quantity of the information they receive at these meetings have increased dramatically. The curriculum night creates parents' first impression of their children's teacher for that year. If the end result is a parent who feels confident that the child will experience academic and emotional success, a strong foundation is laid for a positive parent–teacher relationship throughout the year. If a parent leaves the meeting doubting the child will have a successful year, this "self-fulfilling prophecy" might make for a long and contentious year between teacher and parent. For all teachers, it is the most important meeting of the year. *For teachers new to the district, it is even more important than it is for the veterans.* As the saying goes, "You don't get a second chance to make a first impression."

Few teachers chose teaching as a career because they enjoy making presentations to adults that might impact the teachers' entire work year. There are teachers who look forward to curriculum nights as an opportunity to meet parents and share with them the yearly plans, however, others dread the meeting and view the ultimate objective as *survival.* Most reactions fall somewhere in between. All teachers want the meeting to be successful and want to make a positive first impression with parents. Unfortunately, pre-service and in-service programs rarely provide teachers with help for improving the quality of their presentations. Trial and error is the primary means for acquiring these skills, and each teacher is left on his or her own to find the means to success.

The authors talked with hundreds of teachers and principals about the techniques or "tricks" teachers learned for giving successful group presentations to parents. The following are strategies and ideas collected in individual interviews and group meetings with kindergarten to high school teachers and administrators.

The following list should be viewed as a menu, not a checklist. It is designed to provide a teacher with an opportunity to pick and choose strategies and implement them at a comfortable rate. The most important prerequisite to improving success in parent presentations is to increase one's confidence level. The folowing strategies provide the tools to be successful if we implement them at a rate that allows each of us to gain a reasonable comfort level with each strategy. Otherwise, the stress of worrying about properly implementing the strategies will reduce our ability to project an image of calm and confidence at the meeting.

Have a handout or outline on the desk for parents when they arrive. The handout serves three important functions. First, much of what parents are told at curriculum night meetings will be forgotten. Written material, which parents may refer to periodically after they go home, will save the teacher from answering the same questions in the future. Second, the handout will also help the teacher keep organized and on schedule throughout the presentation. Third, and most important for those of us who have a fear of speaking to groups of adults, it will focus the parents' eye contact on the handout and reduce the number of pairs of eyes staring at the teacher throughout the presentation. Newly hired teachers should ask a friend to proofread their handouts. You are so preoccupied with other things at this time of the year that mistakes are likely and will make a bad impression on the parents.

Tell parents how (e.g., note, phone or drop-in) and when (e.g., before school, lunch time or at home) you prefer that they contact you when they have a question. Teachers often have very different preferences. Parents are usually unaware of how "their" teacher wishes to be contacted. Tell parents what you prefer and most will cooperate. Include this information in your handout. I once interviewed two teachers who taught the same grade side by side. One liked to have brief conferences with parents who showed up at the door in the morning, so she might quickly dispense with the business and avoid large numbers of afternoon and evening phone calls. The other teacher found parents who dropped in very disconcerting and preferred a note from parents asking for a call in the afternoon or evening. These were two equally experienced and successful teachers with very different preferences. If your preferred method is e-mail, be sure to have an alternative for those parents who do not have access to e-mail. Increasingly, more and more parents have access to e-mail, however, the ones who don't may be the parents with whom we need the most contact (e.g., recent immigrant who doesn't speak English, homeless, etc.)

Tell parents again about your homework policy and routines if you are not getting the type of response you need. In Chapter 3, we gave examples of homework policies and procedures that work. The chapter includes sample letters to send to parents explaining the policy. In many instances, the homework routines are successfully established well before this meeting. In those circumstances, you need not review the policy again.

Check the parent handbook or any other information parents may have received from the school or district about curriculum or procedures. It usually gives a good synopsis of the program and may save you time in preparing your remarks. More importantly, though, it will help the teacher to use consistent terminology and avoid difficult questions from parents who perceive what the teacher says as different from what was written. You may be sure that at least some of the parents have read the written description carefully.

If your school has fall conferences, have a sign-up sheet available to help deter parents from attempting to have a "short" conference about their children after your presentation. A scheduled conference date does much to quell a parent's burning need to know "How is my child doing?" My favorite example of this is a husband and wife parent couple in which the husband was an elementary principal and the wife an elementary teacher. The couple described their first parents' night as the parents. They had a combined total of twenty-five years of teaching and administration between them that included conducting innumerable parents' nights as teachers. At the end of the teacher's presentation, the school's principal announced the evening was over. The husband rose and left the room to warm up the car while his wife looked around the room and said she would be out in a minute. After ten minutes, the wife did not show and the husband went to look for her. He returned to the room to find five parents lined up trying to have a "brief" conference about their children with the teacher. The wife was third in line and smiled with embarrassment when she saw her husband. *Embarrassed yes, but she never left her place in line!*

Be organized, clear, concise and cordial. Parents will assume the way you conduct the presentation is how you teach their children's classes. This is particularly true of a newly hired teacher who does not have an established reputation in the community. This is often not the case, but a new teacher without a track record in the community will have a hard time convincing parents of that. The curriculum night is an opportunity to build the parents' confidence in your ability to be a skilled, organized and knowledgeable professional.

When parents make unrealistic suggestions, fight the urge to talk about what you *can't do*. Parents often lack the perspective of dealing with a group of over twenty children at once. This inexperience may cause them to make suggestions about classroom operation that the teacher knows are not feasible. Teachers should focus their answers on what they *can do*. Watch the next presidential press conference and you will see questions focused on what the administration is *not* doing refocused with answers about what related action *is* taking place.

Leave some time at the end of your presentation for questions (but not too much). Many parents in our schools today are accustomed to questioning the professionals in their lives. They question (and disagree with) their pediatrician, clergy person, boss and each other. Scheduling time at the end of the meeting (and informing parents early on about the schedule) avoids questions that will interrupt the flow of your presentation. If you anticipate this will lead to many questions, then have a note card for each parent. Ask parents to write their questions on the note cards as they arise during your presentation. You may then select several to answer during the time you have for questions. Those that are not answered may be addressed through a newsletter if several parents have the same question or by note, phone call or e-mail if the question is personal to the parent.

If the presentation time is insufficient to allow for answering questions, then give each parent a note card. Have the parents write their questions on the cards with the understanding that you will get back to the parents with the answers. This plan is also useful if there is a particularly hot topic that might generate controversial discussion if you open it up for questions. See the next item for more information about hot topics.

Anticipate the difficult questions and prepare responses. Take a few minutes and discuss the class with a colleague. Try to think of all the questions you hope parents *won't* ask. Some difficult questions that typically arise include

- inquiries about physically or behaviorally challenged children included in your classroom. The question may be asked in a variety of ways, but the concern behind the question is "How are you going to ensure that this child's (or children's) needs don't detract from my child's experience?"
- "How will the most able students be challenged?" In recent years, most schools have eliminated or dramatically decreased ability grouping and gifted and talented programs. This has lead to increased concern on the part of parents who perceive their children as having the ability to work above grade level.
- "What is the homework policy and what is the role of parents in the completion of homework?" Homework is increasingly an area of discussion and controversy in education and in the media. If you are a teacher who is new to the district you will want to discuss your policy for homework to be sure it is consistent with that of the school and that of the other teachers in the grade or department. See chapter 3 for more information on establishing effective homework routines.

Consult with the principal or another colleague if there are questions for which you are having trouble coming up with an answer.

Don't panic if you are confronted with a parent question or statement designed to get you into a debate. Some statements designed to deal with this situation without getting into a public confrontation follow:

- "That is a good (or interesting) question/point, and I need to think about it more. Please call me (or send in a note) and we'll set up a time to talk." Note that the onus for initiating the next communication is on the parent. Often, your acknowledgement of the point is sufficient. Later, when thinking about it at home, the parent is less likely to pursue further discussion, giving *you* the option to drop it or seek a conference.

- "I understand your point of view and know that others think similarly," then go on to a new topic. When you acknowledge that the parent is not the only one who thinks something, he or she feels validated, thereby decreasing the need to prove the point is valid with a debate. Remember, validating and agreeing are two different things. Validating a point with which you disagree and withholding your disagreement until a more appropriate time is diplomacy, not surrender.
- If you feel you must make it clear that you disagree with a statement, start by pointing out the areas of agreement. You might then say, "We obviously differ on some points and I would be happy to discuss this issue with you further at another time." You may want to leave it with this statement or, as suggested previously, invite the person to contact you to set up a time to talk.

Don't be embarrassed to practice in front of the mirror, a colleague, a friend or your spouse. A typical rehearsal time for a nationally televised thirty-minute presidential speech is from four to ten hours. And remember, this is after a team of writers has taken weeks to write the speech!

Discuss your presentation with the colleagues in your building who teach the same grade or classes. Coordinating presentations is difficult for some teachers both for personal and logistical reasons, however, like it or not, parents are bound to make comparisons. They just can't help it! Coordinating or at least sharing information with colleagues will reduce and/or prepare the teacher for the inevitable comparisons. Increasingly, mentors and the teachers they mentor and their grade-level colleagues are choosing to make joint presentations on curriculum nights to limit the amount of comparing that takes place.

In elementary (and some middle schools) teachers have the students write a letter to their parents. The letter tells the parents those things the students want the parents to be certain to see while they are visiting. Parents are encouraged to write back to their children. In cases where all but a few parents come, the teacher writes a note back to the children whose parents did not come. This of course would not be possible if the majority of parents did not come.

Teachers continue to try new and innovative methods for improving their parent presentations. Some teachers use slide shows (computer or traditional) and video presentations. Media programs are time-consuming to prepare, but, for many teachers, they are effective ways to tell and show parents what the classroom program is about. Some teachers also find that pre-recording a program enables them to say what they want to say, the way they want to say it, without the fear of making a mistake due to "stage fright." One school district has its own television studio designed so one person may record a production similar to a nightly news broadcast. Teachers are able to videotape their presentations complete with pictures of the class participating in various activities. Other visual aides may also be included. The video is played for parents on curriculum night and questions are answered at the end.

Some teachers also find that pre-recording a program enables them to say what they want to say, the way they want to say it, without the fear of making a mistake due to "stage fright."

In most schools, teachers range widely in their ability and confidence in giving presentations to parents. This is even more true among the teachers that are new to the district because they have not had time to learn the building and district culture related to parents' nights. The previous strategies are tools to help teachers increase their confidence and success and to help mentors help their parents. Most teachers find that as their skill in making these presentations increases, confidence increases, leading to improved presentations and even more confidence, and so on (Ribas, 1998).

Section 3
Sample Newsletters and Web Sites for Parents

Parent newsletters and web sites are used by many teachers to keep parents informed about the curriculum and class activities. Many teachers report that these modes of communication decrease the number of phone calls, drop-in conferences and other contacts they receive from the more assertive parents. Teachers who use these modes also report an increase in student completion of home assignments. Parents find well-written newsletters informative and comforting. It is true that newsletters or web sites will not be read in some homes and in some cases these are the homes in which they may be most valuable. For the most part, teachers and parents find newsletters or web sites to be helpful means of communication. The following are samples of classroom newsletters and classroom web sites.

Many teachers report that these modes of communication decrease the number of phone calls, drop-in conferences and other contacts they receive from the more assertive parents. Teachers who use these modes also report an increase in student completion of home assignments.

Newsletter—October 26, 2001

Dear Families,

The day of ghosts and ghouls is almost upon us! As I am sure you know from the school newsletter, Halloween garb this year will consist of simple orange and black. In an effort to embrace some of the festivity of the day, our class will be having a Halloween party from 1:45 to 2:45 on Wednesday the 31st. You are all welcome to attend, and you should be hearing from the room parents about the details.

On a more personal note, I would like to thank you all for the notes, cards and words of sympathy regarding the loss of my grandfather this past week. It has been a very difficult time and coming back to such support and kindness made an enormous difference. Again, thank you.

Best Wishes, Ms. F

Curriculum Corner

Math:

This month the children will be continuing with practicing and gaining proficiency in their math facts (includes multiplication and division). We have covered all facts up through 12 and all math facts should be practiced nightly. In addition, we will continue our study of large numbers. Looking for patterns, being able to estimate and predict math sentence solutions, and finally the addition and subtraction of large numbers (three digits) will be other components of the math program. This will lead us into our unit on place value, which will begin within the next two weeks.

Language Arts:

We have been continuing to concentrate on comprehension with short stories from our Junior Great Books. These have also given the children a chance to begin writing essays. We continue to practice using the components of a good paragraph. We are continuing to implement our Writer's Workshop process using revising (content) and editing (mechanics—punctuation, capitalization, spelling, etc.). Children have had more opportunities for free writing this month. This gives them a greater sense of ownership of their writing, which will inspire them to see those pieces through to the publishing stage.

Social Studies:

We have finished the archaeology unit and have started our study of map skills. Maps are on the way! We will also take some time during this unit to discuss our various heritages, as we look at the location of the different countries on our mini-maps.

Science:

We have begun the hands-on explorations! We started with observing our own shadows at different times of day. We then moved on to the "straws in clay" experiment. Using flashlights, students used different techniques to change the length and position of their straw shadows, they then recorded their results and made written observations and hypotheses. We will continue this unit with the study of shadows on spheres, so please keep those flashlights handy!

Fourth Grade Forum

Student Council:

Congratulations go out to our two newly elected Student Council Representatives!
Erik and Courtney were elected this week in a contest that proved (in case we weren't already certain) what an incredible group of people we have in this class. All of the candidates delivered well-written and well-spoken speeches, and each of them would have made a wonderful addition to our school council. All students handled both pre and post election time with grace and class. Needless to say, I was extraordinarily proud of each of them.

Correspondent:

One of our correspondents was Jennie, who also used her position to reach out and thank members of the community. She wrote a wonderful letter to the members of the Sample District Fire Department expressing her sadness over the events of September 11th and sharing with them her favorite things about our class. Nice work Jennie! We have received responses from both the Sample District Fire Department and the Sample District Police Department, which are hanging on our Correspondent's Row. Feel free to stop in and read them!

Other Notes

Teacher for a Day:

Well, at least an hour anyway! Now that we are off and running, I would like to offer each of you the opportunity to personally enrich this class. How is this done? Well, it is my hope to have a parent/grandparent/aunt/uncle/etc. of each of the students come in and share his/her career with us! Children need real life connections to what they are learning each day, and this is a wonderful way to help provide that. It would involve a presentation and, depending on the career, a demonstration of some kind that will help bring your job to the classroom. You would also need to come prepared to answer questions the children may have. You should plan to spend at least 30–45 minutes in the classroom. We will need to meet for about 15–20 minutes either after or before school to discuss the details and, if needed, I am willing to help you in any way I can. If you (or someone else in your child's family) are interested, please send in a note letting me know what you would like to do and when you will be available. Looking forward to having you here!

Wish List:

I have had parents ask me what we need for the classroom. In response I have put together a classroom Wish List. Thank you again to all of the families who have already given so much, you have made the transition into a new space much easier!

globes
small supply bins
old tennis balls (44 to be precise—they have made such a difference!)
books (old or new)

Book Orders:

I have sent home today two special book orders. I would like to send the order in by November 16th so the books arrive in plenty of time for the holidays! There are many wonderful books available in these catalogs, but, unfortunately, they don't count towards the free book picks available in our regular monthly order.

The "Write" Stuff

My Poem
by Kayla

John Adams School is so fun
Because I like to share with everyone.
I like doing math, reading, and social studies
And I like spending time with our first grade buddies.
We have fish and five computers
And I'm thankful for all our Martha Jones tutors.
So far we have been studying the moon
And J.T. and Hayleys's birthdays are in June.
My teacher Ms. F likes to walk in the park
And her dog Remington just has a new thing—to bark!

Ms Fowler's Class
by Jennie

Hi! I am writing an article to tell you what is going on in Ms F's class. First of all, we are voting for student council. There were a lot of really good speeches! In P.E. we are playing Ultimate Frisbee. In math we are making 1,000 books made out of blank 100 charts. We have a book report every month. We also have Weekly Spotlight every week. If you do all of your homework and bring it in on time, you get a ten-minute choice time coupon. If you bring in your Book Log every day with initials you get perfect Book Log, which also earns a ten-minute choice time coupon. In my opinion, this is the best class ever!

Fourth Grade
by Rachel

Fourth grade is terrific! Art is terrific because we get to make sculptures. Ms. K is a very nice teacher. Writing is really exciting because we get to write a story or a poem or an article for the Newsletter. During reading we get to read fiction, nonfiction, and historical fiction books. Pioneer Sisters was my favorite book so far. Recess is fun because there are lots of things to do like play with chalk, play ball, play games, or play pass with the football.

Newsletter—January 14, 200-

Science:

We are continuing our study of shadows with a unit on spheres. This gives children a more concrete example of how shadows on the surface of the earth vary depending on its position. We will be doing more with our own shadows outdoors as the unit progresses.

Dear Families,

I hope this New Year finds you all healthier and happier! I had a wonderful visit with my family and a quiet holiday. We are now back into the full swing of January and, with MCAS looming on the horizon, test preparations have begun. You will be seeing items coming home marked with a red star; these are pieces that I need the children to complete absolutely independently. This means that no matter how small the question may seem, they need to handle it alone. While this test is by no means the main focus of our school day, I want our children to have all of the tools necessary to sit down to the test fully prepared.

Thank you for your continued support and, as always, please feel free to contact me with any questions!

Best Wishes,
Ms. Fowler

A Curriculum Corner

Math:

We are on our way with "Arrays and Shares." This unit will strengthen the students' understanding of the concepts behind multiplication and division. Their strong fact base will make this unit even more meaningful. The children will be continuing with practicing and gaining proficiency in their math facts (including multiplication and division). We have covered all facts up through 12 and all math facts should be practiced nightly.

Language Arts:

We are taking the opening steps towards long compositions. Early in the year, we started working on focused paragraphs. The children will continue honing this skill and will begin to link paragraphs together, along with introductory and concluding paragraphs, to form complete compositions.

We will begin a unit on biographies. Each child will have the opportunity to study a person of his/her choice and then write a biography. This unit will take children through the research process step by step. It will also help them to understand the importance of character development in their writing.

Social Studies:

We have begun a mini-unit on Civilizations beginning with the story "Weslandia" by Paul Fleischman. The children read this story aloud and were given materials to create their own civilizations. This unit has them focusing on the basic needs of a civilization, which will reinforce what they studied in the previous unit.

Fourth Grade Forum

Student Council:

Movie Night will be on January 25th at 6:30. Tickets will be sold in advance for $2.00 and there will be refreshments for sale as well. Student Council is looking for parents to donate refreshments for this event. If you are interested, please send in a note indicating what you would be willing to make. All proceeds go directly to Martha Jones Student Council.

Other Notes

Teacher for a Day:

The children had a wonderful opportunity to get up close and personal with a member of the law enforcement community. Mr. Ortiz came in last week to share his career as a Sergeant with the Boston Police Department. He helped to dispel some of the myths about law enforcement fostered on television and in movies. Children gained a clearer understanding of the many facets of police work and how they all support the goal of safety within the community.

Thank you again to Mr. Ortiz. We are still looking for more parents to come in. Remember that the children find all careers interesting, and having parents take the time to come in means so much.

Winter Wear:

With the winter weather in full swing, I would like to encourage all families to send in a "wet weather bag." This bag should contain one pair of sneakers/shoes, one pair of socks and a pair of pants (sweatpants/leggings are fine) that can stay at school. This will ensure that none of the children spend an afternoon in wet clothes. Thank you!

Wish List:

The children have voted and demonstrated great amounts of responsibility within the classroom, so within the next few weeks we will be adopting a pair of rats for the class. They come highly recommended for classroom pets as they are very intelligent and gentle. We already have a home for them, but we will need wood shavings, a water bottle, food dishes, toys, bedding and food before we can get them. Any literature on domestic rats would also be wonderful. If any families have an objection to the animals being in the room, please do not hesitate to let me know.

Two large "body pillows" were very graciously donated by a parent. Unfortunately, they are not covered and need to be before I can put them out for the children. I am all thumbs when it comes to sewing, so I am hoping that there is a parent out there with a sewing machine and a little time to put together some covers. Thank you!

old tennis balls (20 to be precise—we're almost there!)
books (old or new)
milk/juice caps (the plastic kind that you have to pull the tab off first)

Book Responses:

The next Book Response is due on January 31st. If there are any parents interested in attending the presentation portion, please let me know. I will let you know the dates/times.

The "Write" Stuff

I sit on the beautiful shore
Watching the waves crash on each other
I feel like a rich queen
Holding shiny sea glass
That looks like jewels

by Anna Ribas

The next several pages contain an example of a letter to parents from a high school biology teacher. The letter is followed by the teacher's web site.

THE SAMPLE SCHOOL
115 Main St.
Sample, CA 01111
Phone: 403-713-5365
Fax: 403-713-5180

Science Department
August 28, 2002

Dear

Welcome to SHS Conceptual Biology. I am delighted that you will be in my class and would like to share a little about the course, the class, and what we will be doing this year.

SHS Biology is a course that will encourage you to ask questions and to reflect on your observations of the natural world. Its emphasis on thoughtful inquiry and decision making will encourage you to view biology as an approach to learning as well as an ever-changing body of scientific knowledge. You will come to understand and appreciate the major theories that help to explain the natural world and the relevance of biology to your life. The course will engage you in active learning and problem solving through hands-on and minds-on activities. For example, one of the activities will require you to work as a member of a fictitious community, the Tri-Lakes Region, to study data, do experiments, and learn about some organisms that live in the lakes. You will also examine the different factors that affect the fish population in these lakes over time.

This year there are eight different sections of this course. There are three teachers who have been working together this summer to improve the course based on information from last year's students. We are very excited by the opportunity to teach this course and have you as our student. Students who elect this college preparatory course may take it for honor or standard credit. In the first week of school you will be receiving information about the expectations for each level of the course. You will need to discuss these expectations with your parent(s)/guardian(s) and should you desire to receive honor credits, you will be given a contract that will require the signatures of your parent/guardian, your guidance counselor, and you by Friday, September 13th.

If you want to get a head start on supplies for this course, you may purchase a 1.5-inch 3-ring binder with paper and dividers and a spiral bound 3 hole-punched notebook (to be used as a lab notebook). Finally, if you wish to learn more about the course and upcoming assignments, please visit my website at http://placemark.tomsnyder.com/teachers/20719/. Click on "SHS weekly planner" to get to the SHS Weekly Planner web page for the first week of school. This web page will be updated weekly to give you your assignments and news of other upcoming events in the class.

In the meantime, enjoy the rest of your summer. See you on September 6th in room 360.

Sincerely

Susan Plati

SHS Biology Weekly Planner On Line

September 3-9, 2002

Mrs. Plati

Issue # 1-1

Welcome to SHS Biology!

An introduction to the SHS Biology Weekly Planner on Line

Welcome back to school! And welcome to the SHS Biology Weekly Planner On Line! The on-line version of the weekly planner will be issued every Saturday or Sunday preceding the upcoming school week. You will get a printed copy during the first meeting of your class each week. Your assignments, explanations of these assignments, upcoming projects, tests, quizzes, and some extra credit assignments will be present in both versions of the planner. The on-line version will also have some additional extra credit assignments ("extra credit on line") as well as some websites that may help you to learn more about the topic that we are studying in biology. If you consult your weekly planner every day it will help you to stay organized and prepare for class.

Weekly Assignments

Date Due
Assignment

Friday, 6 Sept. 02
Welcome to your first biology class. See you in room 360!

Monday, 9 Sept. 02
1. Bring in 1 1/2 inch 3 ring binder with college ruled paper and dividers. 2. Bring in a spiral bound college ruled notebook that will fit inside your binder. This will be used as your lab notebook. 3. Read handouts given out in Friday's class.

Tuesday, 10 Sept. 02
Your assignments will be posted in this section each week. Usually there will be a different section for each class. Please make sure you check the right class.

Some Information about Biology

and some specific information about the SHS course

SHS Biology is a course that will encourage you to ask questions and to reflect on your observations of the natural world. Its emphasis on thoughtful inquiry and decision making will encourage you to view biology as an approach to learning as well as an ever changing body of scientific knowledge. You will come to understand and appreciate the major theories that help to explain the natural world and the relevance of biology to your life. The course will engage you in active learning and problem solving through hands-on and minds-on activities. For example, one of the activities will require you to work as a member of a fictitious community, the Tri-Lakes Region, to study data, do experiments, and learn about some organisms that live in the lakes. You will also examine the different factors that affect the fish population in these lakes over time.

Long Term Assignments and Other Things to Plan For

Check this section regularly to find out when tests, quizzes, and other special assignments are due

Happy Birthday to You!

Birthdays will be announced in this section

Make sure you have filled out the student information sheet and turned it in so that we can celebrate your birthday. (Maybe we'll dedicate a lab to you!)

Extra Credit on Line—Acid Rain

Answer the questions below and submit answers on line for extra credit. This assignment is due on Friday September 13th. You should be able to get the answers from the class work that you will be doing during the first full week of school.

1. What is acid rain and what is its cause?

2. Why are scientists concerned about acid rain?

Biology Web Sites to Visit

The Croak Mystery—Access Excellence Web Page

Here's a chance for you to be a biological detective! This is an interactive mystery about frogs and their disappearance from a certain environment. Read all the clues and record information as you go. When you think you have solved the mystery, you can submit your answer on line and you'll get a response from the people at the web site. You may wish to work with a partner on this one. If you submit to me your solution and the response that you got from the people at the Access Excellence Web site, I'll give you extra credit for this.

URL: http://www.accessexcellence.org/croak/

Have a Great School Year!

Bring in lots of questions and be prepared to work with your classmates to learn the answers to these questions.

We'll begin the year with a case study of the "Tri-Lakes Region". You'll be students at Tri-Lakes high school and will work with your lab group to analyze data that will help you solve this problem.

Our first major Unit will be Ecology—We'll look at how organisms interact with each other and their environment. You'll build ecosystems in soda bottles to help you learn this material.

Our next unit is Evolution. We'll compare human primates to non-human primates. You'll study differences and similarities in brain structure. You'll learn about Charles Darwin and the evidence that led to his theory of evolution by natural selection. And you'll learn about the diverse forms of life that exist on earth.

You'll learn how living things reproduce and develop and how they pass on their genes to the next generation. You'll also learn how genes express themselves—what determines your blood type and hair and eye color. You'll learn how DNA (the material that comprises genes) functions in a living organism.

In the homeostasis unit you'll learn how our cells function, how our blood and lungs work, and how we regulate our temperature and control water balance.

In the energy unit, we will study how all living things get their energy. You'll learn about the chemical reactions that take place inside living cells to help utilize this energy.

You'll do lots of lab work—and your lab notebook is very important in determining your term grade.

---

email: Susan_plati@sample.usa.edu
http://placemark.bigsur.com/teachers/20719/

SHS Bio Weekly Planner-BC1 Mrs. Plati Sept. 30-Oct 7, 2002
On the web at http://placemark.tomsnyder.com/teachers/20719/

Weekly Overview. This week you will study the predator-prey interactions between goldfish and brine shrimp in Lab 4—*A jar full of Interactions*. You will learn more about population growth during a class activity in which you'll observe data on populations of bacteria and humans in Lab 5—*Potential population growth*. You'll have an 80pt "quest" on Wednesday that will cover all the work that you've done since the beginning of the year.

Date Due	***Assignment***
Monday, Sept. 30, 2002	**1. Pre-lab #4—*A jar full of interactions*** **2. Read E234-E237—*Growing, growing, grown* (back to book)** **3. Finish JE 2—Reindeer on St. Paul Island p. 323-328—** Parts A and B were begun in class. Make sure that you have answered the procedural questions for part A and completed the table and graph for part B. You must complete the analysis questions for each part. Analysis Q's 1-5 part A are on page 327. Analysis Q's 1-3 for part B are on page 328.
Wednesday, Oct. 2, 2002	**1. Answer the review questions to help you prepare for the "quest." Bring the completed questions to class. They'll be collected before you take the quest.** **2. Prepare your index card of information that you may use during the quest.** **3. 80 point "quest" on all work done since the beginning of the school year.** Labs 1, 2, 3—Effect of pH and temperature on gammarus and daphnia, pH lab, bottle ecosystem Engage p-1-13, Tri lakes packet You should know what pH is and what the pH scale means. What is an acid pH? What is a base? What are some of the sources of pollution? What is the cause of acid rain? How are gammarus and daphnia important to the ecological balance of the lake? What is Eutrophication?
Thursday, Oct. 3, 2002	1. **Read E-237-238 *Inquiring Minds***—information about population dynamics. **2. Read E-238k-241—*Endless Interactions***
Friday, Oct. 4, 2002	**1. Pre-lab #5—*Potential population growth*** **2. Write up Lab 4—*Jar full of interactions***
Monday, Oct. 7, 2002	**1. Read the lab directions for Lab 6—*Using Owl Pellets to become a food chain detective*** and bring to class. **2. Read E 136-E 141—*Food Chains, webs, and pyramids.***

Long Term Assignments and other things to plan for:

1. **Keep working on your ecology vocabulary list this week.** Each time you come across one of the words in class or in your reading, you should write the definition of the word in the space on the sheet of terms.
2. **Don't forget to visit the weekly planner on line for extra credit assignments. There will be at least one new extra credit assignment each week.**
3. **Remember that it is your responsibility to make up any work missed because of absence. Labs must be made up before the next double lab period so that the analysis can be completed and turned in on time.**

Full period text on Ecology—Friday October 18th

Lab books due for the term grade on Tuesday Oct 22nd

Honor Assignments: Must be done by all students taking this course for honor credit. (May be done for Extra Credit by any student)

Make sure that you have turned in the "croak mystery" solution and your notes that you used as you solved the mystery.

Your first newspaper article review was due last week.

Your next one will be due on Oct. 11th

Student portfolios as a means for communicating to parents

Sharing a student's portfolio during conferences is an effective way to show parents the progress their child has made over time. Parents may celebrate their child's successes and growth. As parents look at their child's work and are able to more clearly understand areas of weakness, they will be better able to support their child's learning at home. Chapter 6 describes how teachers develop portfolios with their students.

Student portfolios are also an excellent means for communicating to parents the type of work students are doing in class. It is important, however, to provide the parents with some guidance on the best way to review a portfolio. One middle school parent whose child had been keeping a portfolio all year remarked that he only knew to look at the portfolio because he was a teacher. (This parent also was a teacher and reviewer for this book.) At no point did the teacher or the child share with the parent that this excellent example of the student's work existed and that the parent should occasionally review it for information about the class's work. Some teachers are now placing signature sheets in the front of the portfolio and asking parents to review the portfolios at the end of each month and to sign the sheet to indicate that they did so.

Portfolios in the Secondary Classroom

While portfolios are used at the high school level in much the same way as described for the elementary school level, there are a few distinctions. Rather than students' creating a single large portfolio that includes material from each of their different subjects, high school students are typically asked to create a portfolio for each of their core academic subjects (one for English, one for Science, etc.). These portfolios tend to consist of the same types of student work as described for the elementary school level, but, especially in the case of term papers and other types of writing assignments, students are generally expected to include the various brainstorming activities and drafts that helped them to ultimately put together the final products. The last item that high school students typically place into a portfolio is a piece of reflective writing about the various pieces of work that they have included. Generally, such a reflection activity asks students to page through their own portfolios, looking for areas in which they may see their own progress as learners as well as areas in which they recognize a need for continued improvement. Though this assignment is generally the last piece of student work added to the portfolio, it is placed at the very front in order to provide the portfolio's reader with an overview of the work it comprises.

Effectively Using E-mail for Parent Communication

More and more school districts are now providing teachers with e-mail addresses, increasing the potential to greatly facilitate communication between us teachers and our students' parents. The use of e-mail is growing especially because so many public schools have only three or four available phone lines for their 50–100 staff members, and these phone lines are rarely located in spaces ideal for private conversations. For these reasons, e-mail may be an effective way of communicating with parents.

In our own classes, we have utilized e-mail in two different ways to facilitate parent communication. First, e-mail may be useful when working with students who have trouble completing their homework assignments on a consistent basis. The first time a student fails to complete his or her homework assignment, we might simply give the student a warning; however, if the student neglects his or her homework again, we typically place a phone call home to the students' parents. For the parents who explain to us that whenever they ask their children about homework, they invariably reply that no homework was assigned, e-mail may provide a useful solution. Either nightly or at the beginning of the week, we simply e-mail these parents the homework assignments that their children will be expected to complete for our class. In this way, the parents are clued-in about precisely what their children should be working on.

E-mail may also be useful for providing parents with weekly reports on their children's academic or behavioral performance. For a child who is either disruptive in class or not working to his or her potential, we will sometimes follow up a parent conference with an agreement to send a brief e-mail at the end of each week. The e-mail fills in this child's parents about their son or daughter's in-class behavior. Perhaps an agreement may be worked out such that the child's weekend privileges—watching TV, going out with friends or using the car—are contingent upon a positive report via e-mail from the teacher.

While both of these uses for e-mail may initially appear to be time-consuming, the beauty of e-mail is that we as teachers may make a decision about when to take the time to initiate this communication. We don't have to find an open phone line or wait for a time that is convenient for a child's parents. Moreover, with e-mail, we don't risk being drawn into a forty-five minute conversation with a child's parents. Instead, we may simply fire off an e-mail whenever we are able to find a few free minutes. If the plan we have worked out with the student's parents is working correctly, the time that we invest in e-mailing about the student's progress should result in more diligent homework completion, better in-class behavior, etc. In other words, the time we invest in e-mailing is an investment upon which we expect to see a return.

References

Burchenal, M. (1997, November/December). Parents' night. *Voices, XII(6)*.

Colombo, M. (2004, May). Family literacy nights. A community builds a bridge between teachers and culturally diverse parents. *Educational Leadership*, 48–51.

Quiroz, B., Greenfield, P., & Altchech, M. (1999, April). Bridging cultures with a parent–teacher conference. *Educational Leadership*, 68–70.

Ribas, W. (1991). *An analysis of the communication that occurs between parents and teachers.* Unpublished doctoral dissertation, Boston College, Boston, MA.

Ribas, W. (1992, November). Helping teachers communicate with parents. *Principal, 72,* 19–20.

Ribas, W. (1998, September). Tips for reaching parents. *Educational Leadership*, 83–85.

Weininger, E. & Lareau, . (2002). *Children's participation in organized activities and the gender dynamics of the "time bind."* Paper presented at the meeting of the American Sociological Association, city, state.

Zehr, M. (2002, December). Late night child care meets needs of Milwaukee families. *Education Week*, 6–7.

CHAPTER

10

Researching and Reflecting on Our Teaching to Improve Student Learning and Achievement

Objectives for the Chapter
After reading the chapter, the reader will be able to a. define teacher classroom research and/or structured self-reflection b. design a teacher classroom research study to investigate a particular classroom issue c. implement a teacher classroom research study

It is not enough that teacher's work
should be studied;
they need to study it themselves.

—*Stenhouse, 1975*

Teacher Research Across the Professional Life-Span

In this chapter, we discuss the power of teacher research and self-reflection as sources for generating knowledge and understanding in the context of the classroom for teachers across our professional life-spans. We provide a framework for conducting a research study or structured self-reflection in our own classrooms and suggest possible research topics to explore. Finally, we illustrate in depth several examples of teacher–researchers' studies and how these studies changed their teaching.

Teacher's studying our own teaching may be as simple as gathering data to actively self-reflect and improve one area of our practice. For example, we may audiotape a day of our teaching to learn how much wait time we use after each question we ask. A research study may also be as comprehensive as a formal investigation of a variety of aspects in the classroom. For such a study, it may take a full year or longer to gather data, analyze it and report on what we learned. The extent of our project will be determined by the requirements of our district, the time we have, the support we receive and the level of collegial connection that is available during the study.

Figure 10-1 highlights the important work that we do as teacher–researchers.

Figure 10-1

What Do Teacher–Researchers Do

- develop questions based on own curiosity about students' learning and teaching
- investigate questions with students systematically documenting what happens
- collect and analyze data from classes, including own observations and reflections
- examine assumptions and beliefs
- articulate theories
- discuss research with colleagues support as "critical friends" to validate findings and interpretations of data
- present findings to others
- talk to students
- give presentations (talk to teacher in room next door, go to conferences)
- write about research (school-publication) and participate in teacher research web sites, online forums and e-mail communications

Mohr, M. (2004)

Understanding the Power of Teacher Research

Teacher research is individualized, and it puts teachers in the position of accepting more responsibility for our own professional development (Wood, 1988, pp.16–17). In this spirit, research becomes more than informing; it becomes "transforming" (Freire, 1985). When we as teachers take a deeper look at our practice, question our assumptions and problematize particular situations, inquiry becomes a powerful change agent and provides ample opportunities to create learning communities that result in higher levels of student success. "Teacher research is not merely a planning process distinct from change; it is change, and as such it is difficult to implement" (Burnaford, Fischer & Hobson, 1996, p. 138).

Based on Schon's notion of "knowledge in action and reflective practice," teachers are well positioned to conduct studies of teaching and learning in the context of our classrooms (Cochran-Smith & Lytle, 1993).

> In contrast to the technical model of professionalization wherein the teacher is an increasingly sophisticated consumer of other people's knowledge, the teacher–researcher movement is based on the notion that a professional plays a participatory role in the creation and use of knowledge in the field. This relationship involves

ways of knowing about teaching in which the teacher develops theories to interpret, understand, and eventually transform the social life of schools (Cochran-Smith & Lytle, 1993, p.88).

Knowledge must be constructed by the individual. Carl Rogers (1969, p. 455) put it this way: "The only learning which significantly influences behavior is self-discovered, self-appropriated learning." Teacher research should be at the heart of educational research. The knowledge generated by teachers is of utmost importance as teachers are those on the front lines of duty. Teacher research and self-reflection are more than adopting a particular teaching technique. In teacher research, the teacher is at the forefront, and "[i]t is the teacher who is at the center of action in the classroom; it is the teacher who is trying, in real life and real time, to understand what is going on in the classroom and to make a difference" (Burnaford, Fischer & Hobson, 1996, p. 8).

It is a teacher's true challenge to discover how to best meet the learning, social and emotional needs of each and every child. A teacher must also figure out how to best teach content areas in such a way that the material becomes meaningful to students. Students need to be able to connect new information and skills into their existing schemata. As teachers conduct classroom research, we are able to more easily make connections and relationships across content areas, assign more attention to affective aspects of teaching and learning and realize the need for students to actively participate in the learning process (Burnaford, Fischer & Hobson, 1996).

For example, teacher research must include structured self-analysis of our teaching of the curriculum. Through structured self-reflection, the individual teacher constructs knowledge for himself or herself. Mohr and McLean's (1987, p. 55) following perspective further supports this notion. "All the classes I've attended (and taught), all the curriculum guides I've followed, all the lesson plans I've written, and all the texts I've read didn't mean anything to me personally until I became a teacher–researcher."

It is critical that teachers are provided with chances to construct our own professional growth opportunities through reflective practice and collaborative efforts. Teachers and students know what needs to be "fixed" or changed as they understand best the complexities inherent in the classroom. The following section describes how we may utilize this powerful form of professional development in our own classrooms.

It is critical that teachers are provided with chances to construct our own professional growth opportunities through reflective practice and collaborative efforts.

A Framework for Conducting a Study in Our Own Classrooms

The following steps are guidelines we suggest for teachers wishing to embark upon a teacher research study.

1. Beginning our study. A good time to begin a comprehensive study is at the beginning of the year, however, shorter term projects may begin at any point in the year. We might decide to work independently or with other colleagues interested in this form of professional development. We might even want to establish a teacher research team consisting of ourselves and one or more other colleagues in our school. This team might meet monthly or bi-monthly. At research team meetings, each teacher–researcher shares the work he or she has done with regard to his or her study and the others ask questions, make suggestions and offer any insights they may have. If we choose to work with other educators, it is important to select a teacher leader who guides the discussions in a direction meaningful for all participants. The teacher leader should also prepare an agenda before the meeting and make sure the group sticks to it.

2. Identify problems of interest. After we have decided either to work alone[1] or to form a research team, we are now ready to begin thinking about possible research questions to further investigate. Completing the following statements may help to identify areas of interest which we would like to further explore in our classrooms.

- I would like to improve . . .
- I am intrigued by . . .
- I am perplexed by . . .
- I would like to learn more about . . .
- I would like to change or improve . . .
- I would like to better understand . . .

Figure 10-2 illustrates research questions teachers have asked themselves.

Figure 10-2

- What is the break down of the level of the questions I ask my students among recall, comprehension and/or higher order thinking levels?
- How much wait time do I provide for students?
- During group work, how can I get my two students who never speak to contribute equally in group work?
- Does the writing workshop approach impact my students' writing and their attitude toward writing?
- Does the Problem of the Week affect my students' ability to solve open-ended mathematical problems and their attitude toward math?
- What strategies are effective in helping students develop self-reflection skills?
- Does increasing parental involvement and communication (i.e., written updates, e-mail communication, phone calls) improve homework completion?
- What impact will it have on student writing and content learning if students write for ten minutes per day in all content areas?
- What if fourth-grade students worked with first-grade students one day per week?
- How can I encourage students who never raise their hands to participate in class discussions?
- What is the impact of effective effort techniques when used with a student with low confidence?

Keep in mind that our research questions may change as we begin to collect data and find that unexpected themes and/or patterns emerge. If we have a research team, it is important to talk about how and why our questions may be changing. We might also want to discuss new and perhaps more effective ways of collecting data as research questions are modified. If we are working alone, it is important to self-reflect upon these ideas.

[1]Most teachers find working with a research team to be the most effective and fulfilling way of conducting classroom research. This is not always an option, however, but teachers can still actively conduct classroom research independently.

3. Determine effective ways of collecting data. We may want to begin data collection by observing and keeping notes. By taking notes, we are beginning to gather data about our research question. We want to keep our notes focused on students' learning and/or behaviors that are related to the questions we are investigating. For example, if we have decided to explore the question about encouraging students who never participate during group work, our first step would be to observe and keep notes about what is happening during group work situations, particularly in those groups in which students are more reserved.

We want to keep our notes focused on students' learning and/or behaviors that are related to the questions we are investigating.

It is important to take time to reflect upon our notes. As we do so, we may find certain patterns or themes emerging. For example, after observing and taking notes while students are working in groups during two different activities, we may find that the groups with one or more outspoken students tend to be the same groups that have students that do not participate. Or we may find that students do not understand how to disagree effectively. In either situation, we will want to use this information to inform our instruction. In this case, students need more modeling and practice on how to work effectively with others.

It is equally important to take time periodically to write freely about what we are observing and thinking with regard to our research questions. It is often helpful to jot down our thoughts and then later revisit what we initially wrote. Keep in mind that our notes are for ourselves, so we do not need to be overly concerned with writing *perfect* entries. It might be more efficient to write in phrases or even in bulleted points.

An example of notes that were taken by a teacher who was looking at how collaborative groups solve problems during literature circles is shown in Figure 10-3. This particular teacher asked students to identify a problem they had been experiencing. Their next task was to find a way to help solve it. The teacher's notes reveal each group's problem and solution as well as her impression of how well the group's solution solved the problem.

Figure 10-3

Group 1: Problem:	Everyone talks at the same time; Students are really excited about this part of the book, but are getting frustrated with the chaotic nature of the group; Jill is really trying to get the group to stop talking over each other, but isn't having much luck; when asked to identify the problem, they all knew exactly what it was and all students took responsibility for contributing to it; hopefully their solution will prove to be effective
Solution:	Pass around eraser and student with eraser is the only one allowed to talk; student passes if he/she has no comments very effective; this solution has particularly helped John, a more reserved student, to offer his comments more frequently
Group 2: Problem:	Students interrupt each other, particularly when they do not agree with one another; it appears that Alissa and Sam do not see eye to eye on many of the issues the group brings up; I am wondering if these two students get along outside of their discussion group; when asked to identify the problem, students had some difficulty articulating it; I am wondering if they feel Alissa and Sam are causing this problem, but do not want to

	place blame on certain group members; with my help, they were able to state the problem in general terms, that is, students are interrupting one another
Solution:	Discussion director is group leader and group members raise their hands when they have a comment; discussion director must call on student before he/she speaks-somewhat effective as some group members felt the discussion director calls on his friends first; another student suggested that the discussion director must alternate between girls and boys when calling on students; I will have to observe this group next time to see if this strategy is helpful
Group 3: Problem:	Students play with pencils, erasers, and other things that distract group members; I have also noticed that Bob and Sue tend to doodle during my whole class lessons; I am wondering if the other students in this group are exhibiting these behaviors because they see Bob and Sue doing so; such behaviors seem to be disruptive to the group and I am noticing that students are not really listening to one another; there is very little building off of each others' ideas
Solution:	Group members are only allowed to bring what they prepared to the discussion-very effective and I am already noticing students responding to each other and as a result discussions have become much richer
Group 4: Problem:	Halfway through their discussion, students become restless; One of the students in this group does have behavioral issues and it appears as though the group does not know how to handle his inappropriate comments; perhaps this group gets restless because they become frustrated when the flow of their discussion is interrupted by this student
Solution:	This group built in a 3 minute break after 15 minutes-not very effective as the group had trouble pulling it together after their break; I think I am going to have to work with this group next time they meet; it seems as though they need the guidance of an adult throughout their discussion

An example of this same teacher's free writing is found in Figure 10-4.

Figure 10-4

> I am so impressed with Scott and his group. His group is so patient with him and he has learned so much from his group. I think the way they question him and do not give up when he says he is stupid and does not know the answer is terrific. He is finally developing some confidence, and I am hearing him participate more frequently. He was so appropriate and on task when he and his group performed a reader's theater and predicted the next chapter of the book today. I have also noticed that he is becoming more responsible and is coming to literature circles much more prepared than he was previously. I truly think he feels a connection to his group and does not want to let them down, which is another powerful aspect and motivator of groupwork.

It is important to note here the differences between this teacher's notes and her free writing. Her notes were directly related to her particular research question, "How do different literature circle groups solve their problems?", and they were written as she observed her students working with one another. In contrast, her free writing was written after school and focused only on a particular student that she had noticed making significant progress. Her study was not necessarily focused on this student, but, over the course of her study, it became apparent to her that literature circles greatly influenced this student's progress.

We may want to consider the following questions from time to time. If we are working with other colleagues, these questions might be asked during our meetings.

- Why were our notes significant enough to write?
- What is the connection between our old and new notes?
- Based on the data we have collected thus far, what other means of data collection should we consider using?
- Based on the data we have collected thus far, what changes do we think we should make in our teaching?

The following are other means of gathering data. Our research question or topic will determine the most appropriate method for us to use.

- **Keeping a reflective journal.** A reflective journal should be used with all projects. This is where we record our notes as well as our free writing.
- **Examining literature on our topic from research and practice.** Doing so may shed more insight into the topic we are investigating and may provide us with different strategies to use with our students. For example, if we want to help our students develop better self-reflection skills, researching this topic may provide us with ideas to help students become more self-reflective learners.
- **Audiotaping.** Audiotaping allows us to go back and listen more carefully to what students and/or the teacher said during the recorded class period. For example, we may want to audiotape four or five classes to determine the percentage of questions that are at recall, comprehension and higher order thinking levels. We would do this with the goal of using more higher order thinking questions.
- **Videotaping.** Videotaping allows us to more closely analyze what is happening during our instruction and/or during group work. We may want to use videotaping if we are looking at students during group work and trying to help all students participate

more equally. We also may want to use videotaping if we are trying to determine how to get all students to participate more equally in whole-class discussions.

- **Interviewing students.** We may want to interview students to get a better understanding of their views on a certain topic. For example, if we are researching how the Problem of the Week in mathematics class affects students' ability to solve open-ended problems as well as their attitude toward mathematics, we may want to ask students to talk about their experiences with the Problem of the Week. Do they enjoy solving these types of problems? Why or why not? Are these open-ended problems becoming easier for them to solve over time?
- **Collecting student work.** We may want to collect student work over a set period of time and look at progress made by students, and we may want to target just a few students rather than the whole class. For example, if we are trying to help a student with low confidence by using effective effort techniques, we may want to collect his or her work in order to help determine if these techniques have been successful.
- **Drawings.** We may want to have students draw themselves during a group work situation at the beginning of our study and then again at the end, if the focus of our study is to help all students participate more equally during group work. The purpose of this method in this situation is to look at how students perceive themselves while working with others. If a student's initial drawing reflects himself or herself working off to the side, we may want to focus on this student more closely over the course of our study.
- **Checklists.** A checklist may be used if we are trying to determine the types of questions we ask. As each type of question is asked, a tally mark is used to indicate the level of the question. In this way, at the end of our lesson, it is easy for us to see what types of questions were used throughout the lesson. Note that it may be helpful to have a colleague observe and use the checklist to record the types of questions in this instance. If that is not possible or if we are not comfortable with a colleague coming into our classrooms, we may audiotape or videotape the lesson and use the checklist while we listen to the audiotape or watch the videotape. Figure 10-5 illustrates a sample checklist.

Figure 10-5

Tracking Different Types of Questioning

Place a tally mark next to the type of questioning the teacher uses each time a question is asked.

Recall:____

Total:_____

Comprehension: ______________________________________

Total : _____

Higher order: _______________________________________

Total:_____

- **Questionnaires.** We may want to use questionnaires to ask students questions about a certain topic that we are choosing as the focus for our study. For example, if we are looking at how working with first graders affects our fourth-grade students, we might want to create a questionnaire that asks them different questions about their feelings about collaborative work with a different grade. Later in this chapter, there is a sample questionnaire.

Those interested in using colleagues to gather data will want to read Chapter 11. Chapter 11 contains a number of strategies that teachers may use to effectively observe peers and gather helpful data for colleagues.

4. Analyze the data. Once we have collected our data, we are ready to begin analyzing it. Burnaford, Fischer & Hobson (1996) make the suggestions in Figure 10-6 with regard to analyzing the data. We may choose to use just a few of these steps or all of the steps depending on how much time we have for analysis.

Figure 10-6

- We gather all the data in one place and spread it out. (Dining room tables and living room floors are popular for this.) We try to determine the kind of information that appears to surface: themes, common statements, patterns of behavior and/or points of frustration. For example, if we have chosen to look at the nature of our questions, we might want to use color coding to organize the data. We may have sheets of papers on which a colleague has listed the exact wording of each question we asked (or we may have listed the questions after listening to our audiotapes). We may use either a highlighter or different colored sticker dots to indicate the types of questions used. For example, each recall question may be highlighted in yellow, each comprehension question in blue and each higher order thinking question in green. Another way to analyze the data for the same study would be to create a checklist with the different types of questions listed. While we listen to the three audiotapes we used to collect the data, we may mark the types of questions used.
- After we look through the data, we begin analysis with brainstorming sentence completions, such as *I think . . .*, *I believe . . .*, *I need . . . .* Then, we examine the data for evidence to support our responses. For example, we may want to begin with the statement, "I believe that I do not provide enough wait time for many of my students during math lessons," if we are trying to determine if we do indeed wait long enough for most students to formulate responses to questions asked during class. When we look through the data we collected, we look for data to either support our statements or to show that we actually do provide enough wait time.
- We examine our reflective journals. Do we notice any particular patterns or themes emerging? Do we tend to write more freely about a particular student or a certain aspect of our teaching? If so, we might want to collect more data about the student or the facet of our teaching. For example, we may notice that in almost every journal entry we mention the same student. Why is this student mentioned so frequently? What types of things are we saying about this student? Does this student tend to dominate whole class discussions, or does this student seldom participate? Does this student behave similarly in small groups? The reflective notes in Figure

10-4 demonstrate one teacher's focus on a particular student who had made significant progress over the course of her study.

- We look through the data for surprises or unintended learning. For example, perhaps we notice that we tend to ask girls one type of question and boys a different type of question.
- We look through the data for specific improvements and/or positive changes. For example, if we are increasing parental involvement through weekly newsletters in order to affect changes in homework completion rates, we may notice that parents are becoming more supportive of both us and the students.
- We look through the data for specific challenges or setbacks. For example, we may find that having fourth-grade students work with first graders is a negative experience for some students. Perhaps a first-grade student has behavioral issues that are frustrating the fourth grader or the first grader isn't listening when the fourth-grade student reads to her.
- We invite a teacher–researcher colleague to look at some of the data. What does he or she see? What is communicated to an informed but nonparticipating observer?
- We invite the students to look at some of the data. What do they see? How do they interpret what they see? If we videotape or audiotape our students, we share the tape with them. We ask them to write what they noticed about themselves and/or others.

5. Return to the original research question. When we meet with our research team, we may want to discuss the following questions. If we are working independently, it is important to self-reflect on some of these questions.

- Has our question been answered?
- Were our results what we expected? Why or why not?
- Who do we want to share our findings with?
- How may our results help other educators?
- How will our study lead to more effective teaching and learning?

6. Share our findings. We may want to consider sharing our findings with other teachers. Our findings might be very helpful to our colleagues. If so, there are several ways in which we may want to share what we have learned throughout our journey. We may want to share our results primarily with our research team (if we are working with one) at its meetings. We may also want to share these findings with some of our colleagues not involved in the process through a presentation or informal conversation. Perhaps we would like to write about our studies in a school-wide publication or even in a national publication. We may want to participate in teacher research web sites, online forums and e-mail communications. We should take the time to share our new understandings about teaching and learning with other educators as we have the ability to highly influence others in a meaningful way.

An In-Depth Look at Examples of Teacher–Researchers' Studies

Getting Students to Work Effectively in Groups During Reading

One fifth-grade teacher–researcher felt that her students were not working as effectively as they should be during literature circles. Because she was having difficulty determining how to better help students during group work, she felt that investigating this particular issue would help her better understand the problem, and, consequently, that she would be able to better address it with her students.

She began by recording in a reflective journal her observations of students engaged in literature circles two days per week for four weeks. She also chose to audiotape a different group each time literature circles met. In this way, she was able to review and more carefully analyze how each group interacted. She was also able to have groups listen to their conversations, helping them to better understand their group's dynamics. Finally, she asked each group to complete the form shown in Figure 10-7 each time literature circle groups met.

Figure 10-7

Names: ______________________________

Date: ______________________________

Group's Discussion Topic or Focus: ____________________

Check the appropriate box. Provide evidence where possible.

	Yes	No	Sometimes	Evidence
Everyone participates and shares in the discussion process.				
The group is supportive of its individual members.				
Group members often ask questions for clarification or elaboration.				
The group discussion stays on topic.				
The group is energetic and enthusiastic.				

What was the best thing about the way this group worked together?

What was one problem this group had?

How did you solve it?

Adapted from Saskatchewan Education, 1996

As this teacher–researcher continued her study, she began to see certain patterns emerging. For example, she noticed that many groups experienced the same problem; many students interrupted each other throughout group discussions. This problem led to frustration for many students and the frustration resulted in a negative attitude toward literature circles. As this teacher began to better understand what was happening during literature circles, she was able to effectively address the issues with her students. As the issues were addressed and the teacher helped groups develop strategies to rectify the problems, students' attitudes shifted to ones that were more positive.

Understanding Students' Learning During Literature Circles

In this study, the fourth-grade teacher wanted to better understand his students' learning during literature circles. He felt that his students' literature circle discussions were not as rich as they should be and were not lasting very long. He began his five-week study by observing students at work during literature circles and recording his observations. He also used the form shown in Figure 10-8 to more carefully look at each group's learning.

Figure 10-8

SUMMARY SHEET

People in Group:

Title of Book:

Discussion Director: Write two of the "author and you"[2] questions you asked your group and the answers that were given.

Summarizer: Give a short summary of what you read.

[2]An **"author and you" question** is one for which the reader needs to use both the information in the text and his or her own experiences to formulate a response. There can be several answers to these types of questions. Such questions promote higher order thinking and lead to rich discussions.

A **"right there"** question is one for which the reader can find the correct answer right in the text. These types of questions do not require the student to use his or her own ideas to formulate a response.

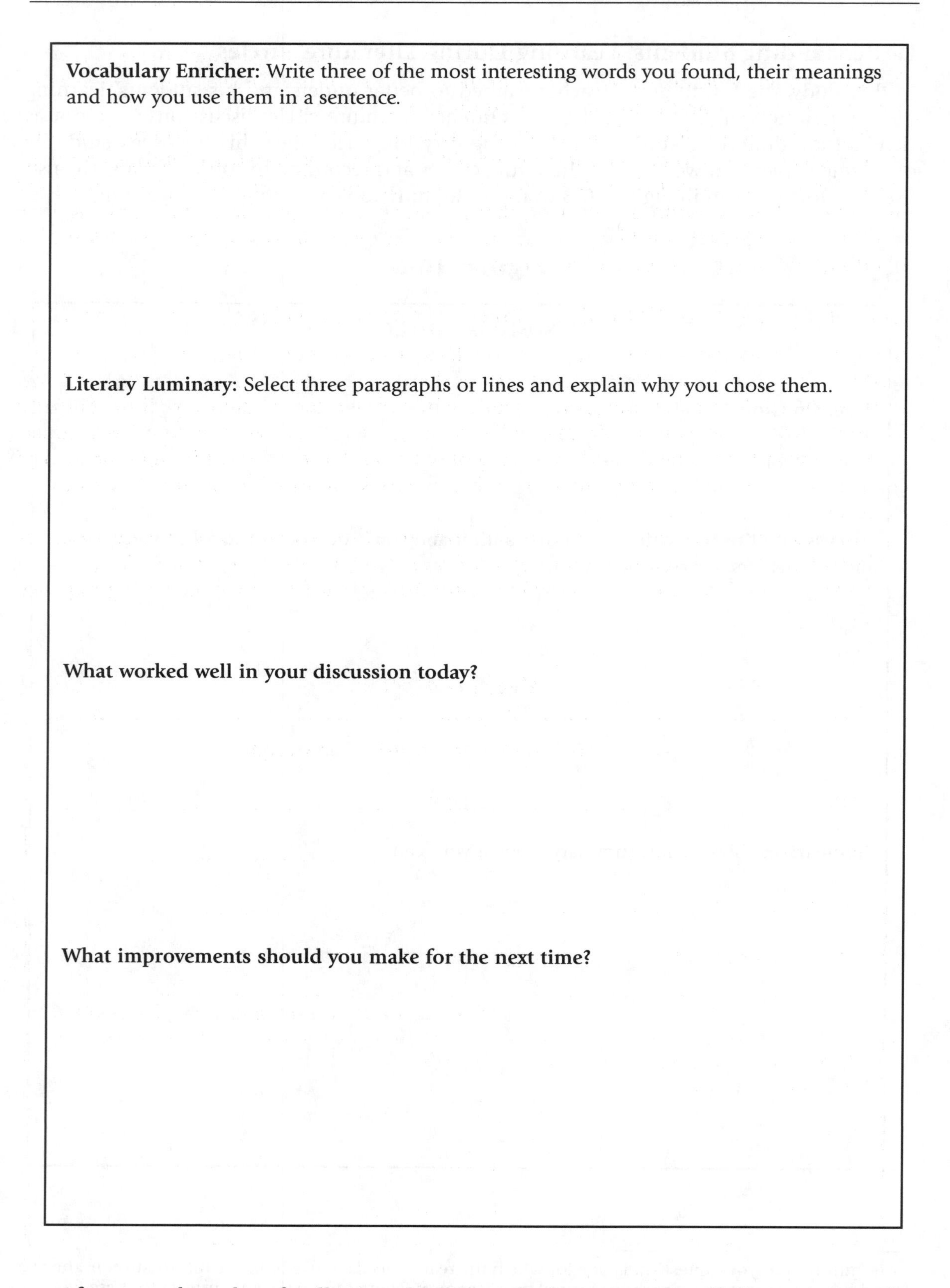
Vocabulary Enricher: Write three of the most interesting words you found, their meanings and how you use them in a sentence.

Literary Luminary: Select three paragraphs or lines and explain why you chose them.

What worked well in your discussion today?

What improvements should you make for the next time?

After several weeks of collecting data through the means described previously, the teacher concluded that many of the discussion questions that the discussion director asked were not really "author and you" questions. Instead, they were "right there" questions for which students may find the only correct answer right in the text. Such questions do not lend themselves to any sort of meaningful discussion. In addition, it also became clear to the teacher that his students were not building off of each other's ideas. Rather, they shared their required piece and then moved on to the next group participant.

As a result of this teacher's study, he was able to address the uncovered problems with the class. He spent several class lessons helping his students construct "author and you" questions which would help students have more meaningful discussions. He also taught his students how to build off of each other's ideas through modeling and practicing such skills. Consequently, his students began to have rich discussions and came to new understandings about the texts they were reading.

Getting Students to Work More Effectively in Groups During Mathematics

A high school teacher was frustrated with the lack of success her students experienced while working on problem solving in small groups. During such activities, the teacher felt that some students dominated the group's work, while others contributed very little. She also felt that many students were off task while working on such activities with others. Consequently, she felt that a better understanding of what was happening while students worked collaboratively to solve mathematical problems would inform her instruction to better meet the needs of each group.

This teacher–researcher also began her study by keeping a journal to record what she noticed about students' behavior during problem solving in small groups one day per week for six weeks. She used the form shown in Figure 10-9 to gather data about each group's experience.

Figure 10-9

Assessment Form for Problem-Solving Groups

Names:________________________________

Date:________________________________

Title of Problem:__________________________

Check the appropriate box. Provide evidence where possible.

	Yes	No	Sometimes	Evidence
The group understands what the problem is asking.				
The group formulates a plan and selects a strategy (ies).				

The group explains the plan.				
The group solves the problem, labeling the work and using visuals.				
The group clearly explains how the problem was solved, including the strategy (ies) that were used.				
Everyone participates in the problem-solving process.				

The group is supportive of its individual members.				
Group members often ask questions for clarification.				
The group discussion stays on topic.				
The group is enthusiastic.				

As this teacher's study continued, she began to realize that some of the students did not possess the necessary math skills needed to solve the particular problems. In addition, students were unsure about how to clarify misunderstandings for their group members when necessary. This lack of math skills and the lack of confidence about clarifying misunderstandings caused students to lose their focus, leading to acting-out behavior. As this teacher began to understand why students were off task, she was able to plan more appropriate tasks for her students. Over time, she noticed that all students were able to solve problems more successfully, and, as a result, their self-confidence also increased.

Getting Students to Be More Effective Mathematical Problem Solvers

In this study, a sixth-grade math teacher was having trouble getting many of her students to solve open-ended mathematical problems successfully. As a result, she chose this area of her teaching to look at more closely. She began her eight-week study by observing her students once per week while they were independently solving open-ended math problems. She recorded her observations in a journal. In addition, she collected and kept completed student work from four different students to analyze more carefully. After eight weeks of observing and collecting sample work, she began her analysis. Certain themes began to emerge as she reread her journal notes and student work. What she noticed was that many students had difficulty getting started and did not seem to choose appropriate strategies. This math teacher noted that "students read the math problem and then immediately attempted to solve the problem without what appeared to be much thought."

After reading some articles on problem solving and talking to other math educators, it became apparent to this teacher that her students needed more guidance and structure in order to solve such problems effectively. With the help of some of her colleagues, she developed the form shown in Figure 10-10 to help her students better solve problems. As a result, her students became more competent problem solvers over time.

Figure 10-10

PROBLEM-SOLVING SHEET

People in Group:____

Title of Problem:____

THOUGHT: This problem is asking us . . .

INFORMATION: The information tells us . . .

PLAN: We plan to solve the problem by . . .

SOLUTION: Show and label your steps clearly and neatly, and include a visual. Use a separate sheet of paper and attach it to this sheet.

WRITTEN EXPLANATION: Tell in order how you solved the problem, including the strategy (ies) you used. Use a separate sheet of paper and attach it to this sheet.

Better Understanding Students' Attitudes About Mathematics

The sixth-grade mathematics teacher in this study was interested in better understanding his students' perceptions with regards to collaborative mathematical problem solving. He administered the attitude questionnaire shown in Figure 10-11 at the beginning of his study and then again twelve weeks later at the end of his study. He used the results from the first time he asked students to complete the questionnaire to inform his instruction. For example, he found that many students felt that there is only one correct way to solve math problems. Such thinking led to many arguments within collaborative groups as students often felt that their strategies were the only correct ways to solve the given problems.

As the teacher began to unravel this incorrect view that many students held, he was able to help students understand that many problems may be solved by using a variety of strategies. As the students began to understand this, they also became more flexible mathematical problem solvers and more efficient collaborative problem solvers.

Figure 10-11

Pre- and Post-Study Student Attitude Questionnaire

Directions: I would like to know what you think about learning mathematics in a collaborative group. Please answer the following questions as well as you can. There are no right or wrong answers, so please just tell me what you think. For each question, circle the number under the answer that best describes how you think or feel. Circle 1 if you *strongly disagree* with the statement, 2 if you *disagree*, 3 if you are *undecided*, 4 if you *agree* or 5 if you *strongly agree.* If you have difficulty understanding any question, please ask me for help.

1. I can get along well in everyday life without using mathematics.

Strongly Disagree	Disagree	Undecided	Agree	Strongly Agree
1	2	3	4	5

2. A problem is easy to figure out, even if you've forgotten exactly how to do it.

Strongly Disagree	Disagree	Undecided	Agree	Strongly Agree
1	2	3	4	5

3. In mathematics, to know if you have the right answer, you must check with the teacher or the textbook.

Strongly Disagree	Disagree	Undecided	Agree	Strongly Agree
1	2	3	4	5

4. Many mathematics classes could be improved by using collaborative groups.

Strongly Disagree	Disagree	Undecided	Agree	Strongly Agree
1	2	3	4	5

5. There is one right way to solve most mathematics problems.

Strongly Disagree	Disagree	Undecided	Agree	Strongly Agree
1	2	3	4	5

6. It's important to learn mathematics because mathematics knowledge is useful in everyday life.

Strongly Disagree	Disagree	Undecided	Agree	Strongly Agree
1	2	3	4	5

7. There is always a rule to follow in solving a mathematics problem.

Strongly Disagree	Disagree	Undecided	Agree	Strongly Agree
1	2	3	4	5

8. There are many ways to solve mathematics problems.

Strongly Disagree	Disagree	Undecided	Agree	Strongly Agree
1	2	3	4	5

9. Working in a collaborative group is useful in all kinds of classes.

Strongly Disagree	Disagree	Undecided	Agree	Strongly Agree
1	2	3	4	5

10. Working in a collaborative group helps me to think about what I learned in class.

Strongly Disagree	Disagree	Undecided	Agree	Strongly Agree
1	2	3	4	5

11. I like to give my ideas to someone in a group to explain what I am thinking.

Strongly Disagree	Disagree	Undecided	Agree	Strongly Agree
1	2	3	4	5

12. I feel confident in my ability to clearly express my ideas when I work in a collaborative group.

Strongly Disagree	Disagree	Undecided	Agree	Strongly Agree
1	2	3	4	5

13. Expressing or explaining ideas to group members seems to be a waste of time.

Strongly Disagree	Disagree	Undecided	Agree	Strongly Agree
1	2	3	4	5

14. I never seem to be able to clearly explain my ideas when I am working in a collaborative group.

Strongly Disagree	Disagree	Undecided	Agree	Strongly Agree
1	2	3	4	5

A More Comprehensive Research Study

In this section, we provide an example of how one teacher conducted a more comprehensive one-year study in her classroom. The teacher–researcher who conducted this study in a fifth-grade classroom chose to look more closely at how collaborative learning influenced her students' understanding of both mathematical and literacy content. She collected data while her students worked together to solve open-ended mathematical problems and to discuss their reading in literature circles. As this particular teacher constructed and deconstructed the interactions of her students, she understood more deeply the complexities inherent in group work. In doing so, she was able to more clearly establish a connection between her teaching pedagogy, the content of the lessons she asked students to complete and the needs of her students. It is important to note that the teacher who conducted this study worked with a professor at a local university who made suggestions with regard to data collection procedures, made recommendations in terms of how to scaffold the learning of each group as they experienced different problems and helped her with the analysis of the data.

Data Collection Procedures

Data collection for this study was conducted from September to May of an academic year. Data collection efforts were centered around the following three areas: 1) the role of social skills in learning and understanding mathematical and literacy content; 2) strategies and techniques students use to understand concepts in these two different content areas; and 3) the impact of collaborative efforts on the learning of students with learning disabilities. Data was collected using classroom observations, focus group interviews, documents including samples of students' work and drawings, an attitude questionnaire and the reflective journal of the teacher–researcher. A rationale and a description of how each of the data sources were collected follows.

Classroom Observations and Notes

Classroom observations took place approximately one to two times per week for nine months in each of the two content areas, mathematics and literacy. The teacher recorded students' interactions, both verbal and nonverbal, in notes. These observations also included informal conversations with the students.

Audiotaping and videotaping were used to support classroom observations. Audiotaping was used during every collaborative activity that the teacher observed in order to be able to more carefully analyze what students said to each other. The teacher chose to audiotape different groups each time rather than the same group every time. It was important to transcribe each audiotape as soon as possible, as this process was time-consuming.

The teacher selected a focus group to videotape four times throughout the study—twice during a collaborative mathematical problem-solving activity and twice during literature circles. The videotapings took place at the beginning of the study and then at the end, so that the teacher was able to more carefully observe the progress the group made over the course of the study. The focus group she chose to videotape included a student with special needs. This visual of students' interactions was invaluable as it revealed both verbal and nonverbal communication among the students. Thus, the teacher was able to more carefully observe what the students said to each other, their tones of voice and the meanings students conveyed through body language, eye contact, facial expressions and their choice of seating.

Focus Group Interviews

Open-ended interviews were used to target the focus group, the same group that was videotaped. These interviews took place four times during the data collection phase of this study. The focus group worked together in mathematical collaborative activities and in literature circles. Open-ended questions were designed to assess students' perceptions and attitudes about working in groups during mathematics and literacy. The purpose of these interviews was to get a picture of the students' thinking as they were provided with an opportunity to express their viewpoints with regard to collaborative work.

Documents

Documentation of students' learning, interactions, perceptions and assumptions were captured from collected samples of student work. In the literacy groups, students completed assessment forms that evaluated each group's processes and the content that was learned. Mathematics group evaluation consisted of several self-assessment tools that focused on problem-solving processes and concept learning. Forms that might be used to collect such data may be found in Figures 10-7 through 10-11.

Attitude Questionnaire

The same attitude questionnaire was given to students two times throughout this study as both a pre- and a post-test. The questionnaire was developed by the teacher–researcher and is an adaptation from other studies. This questionnaire offered a systematic way to obtain insight into the perceptions and attitudes of the students regarding collaborative learning. The questionnaire asked students to indicate how strongly they agree or disagree (1=*strongly disagree* to 5=*strongly agree*) with a given statement on how they feel about group work during mathematics and literacy instruction. Figure 10-12 is the attitude questionnaire the teacher–researcher used in this study. This questionnaire is similar to the one used in the smaller scale study discussed earlier in this chapter, however, this more comprehensive questionnaire includes questions regarding attitudes about literacy.

Figure 10-12

Pre- and Post-Study Student Attitude Questionnaire

Directions: I would like to know what you think about learning mathematics and literacy in a collaborative group. Please answer the following questions as well as you can. There are no right or wrong answers, so please just tell me what you think. For each question, circle the number under the answer that best describes how you think or feel. Circle 1 if you *strongly disagree* with the statement, 2 if you *disagree*, 3 if you are *undecided*, 4 if you *agree* or 5 if you *strongly agree*. If you have difficulty understanding any questions, please ask me for help.

1. I can get along well in everyday life without using mathematics.

Strongly Disagree	Disagree	Undecided	Agree	Strongly Agree
1	2	3	4	5

2. A problem is easy to figure out, even if you've forgotten exactly how to do it.

Strongly Disagree	Disagree	Undecided	Agree	Strongly Agree
1	2	3	4	5

3. In mathematics, to know if you have the right answer, you must check with the teacher or the textbook.

Strongly Disagree	Disagree	Undecided	Agree	Strongly Agree
1	2	3	4	5

4. Many mathematics classes could be improved by using collaborative groups.

Strongly Disagree	Disagree	Undecided	Agree	Strongly Agree
1	2	3	4	5

5. There is one right way to solve most mathematics problems.

Strongly Disagree	Disagree	Undecided	Agree	Strongly Agree
1	2	3	4	5

6. It's important to learn mathematics because mathematics knowledge is useful in everyday life.

Strongly Disagree	Disagree	Undecided	Agree	Strongly Agree
1	2	3	4	5

7. There is always a rule to follow in solving a mathematics problem.

Strongly Disagree	Disagree	Undecided	Agree	Strongly Agree
1	2	3	4	5

8. There are many ways to solve mathematics problems.

Strongly Disagree	Disagree	Undecided	Agree	Strongly Agree
1	2	3	4	5

9. I can get along well in everyday life without knowing how to comprehend written text or a story.

Strongly Disagree	Disagree	Undecided	Agree	Strongly Agree
1	2	3	4	5

10. A story is easy to figure out on my own, even if I do not understand different parts of it.

Strongly Disagree	Disagree	Undecided	Agree	Strongly Agree
1	2	3	4	5

11. In literacy, to know if you have the right answers to questions about a story or text, you must check with the teacher.

Strongly Disagree	Disagree	Undecided	Agree	Strongly Agree
1	2	3	4	5

12. Many writing or reading classes could be improved by using collaborative groups.

Strongly Disagree	Disagree	Undecided	Agree	Strongly Agree
1	2	3	4	5

13. There is one right way to interpret a story.

Strongly Disagree	Disagree	Undecided	Agree	Strongly Agree
1	2	3	4	5

14. It is important to know how to comprehend text because understanding what you read is useful in everyday life.

Strongly Disagree	Disagree	Undecided	Agree	Strongly Agree
1	2	3	4	5

15. There are many different ways to interpret a story.

Strongly Disagree	Disagree	Undecided	Agree	Strongly Agree
1	2	3	4	5

16. There is always a rule to follow in comprehending a story.

Strongly Disagree	Disagree	Undecided	Agree	Strongly Agree
1	2	3	4	5

17. Working in a collaborative group is useful in all kinds of classes.

Strongly Disagree	Disagree	Undecided	Agree	Strongly Agree
1	2	3	4	5

18. Working in a collaborative group helps me to think about what I learned in class.

Strongly Disagree	Disagree	Undecided	Agree	Strongly Agree
1	2	3	4	5

19. I like to give my ideas to someone in a group to explain what I am thinking.

Strongly Disagree	Disagree	Undecided	Agree	Strongly Agree
1	2	3	4	5

20. I feel confident in my ability to clearly express my ideas when I work in a collaborative group.

Strongly Disagree	Disagree	Undecided	Agree	Strongly Agree
1	2	3	4	5

21. Expressing or explaining ideas to group members seems to be a waste of time.

Strongly Disagree	Disagree	Undecided	Agree	Strongly Agree
1	2	3	4	5

22. I never seem to be able to clearly explain my ideas when I am working in a collaborative group.

Strongly Disagree	Disagree	Undecided	Agree	Strongly Agree
1	2	3	4	5

Drawings

The students were also asked to produce pre- and post-study drawings as a way to depict mathematics and literacy instruction as they perceived it. The following prompts were used for the drawings: a) *Draw yourself learning in math class. Write a few sentences that describe your drawing* and b) *Draw yourself learning in reading class. Write a few sentences that describe your drawing.* These prompts were given at the onset and at the conclusion of the study to elicit students' perceptions of mathematics and literacy learning at these two different points. The decision to use drawings as a data collection source in this study was based on increasing evidence which suggests that drawings provide orderly data and reliable conclusions in qualitative studies (Fierros, Gulek, & Wheelock, 1997; Haney & Russell, 1995).

Analysis

The goal of analyzing this study was to understand how students experienced collaborative learning, how it influenced their learning in different content areas and how it impacted students with learning disabilities. The data analysis included examination of classroom observations, notes, interviews with the students, audiotapings, videotapings, samples of students' work, drawings, attitude questionnaires and the teacher–researcher's reflective journal. These analyses occurred simultaneously with data collection and data interpretation during the study. Additionally, in all phases of the research, students were given opportunities to voice their interpretations of collaborative experiences in mathematics and in literacy and to express how they perceived such events through informal conversations, planned focus group interviews, assessment tools and questionnaires.

Learning About Student Learning

As the teacher closely examined students collaborating with one another, she began to truly appreciate the power of group work. As children built off of one another's ideas, they derived greater understandings about the content that they were learning. As she watched children discuss different mathematical problems as well as literature, she was often reminded of a pinball machine as ideas bounced from one student to the next, gaining momentum and depth just as a pinball bounces from side to side when racking up points. As students became more proficient collaborators, they began to support their ideas with strong reasoning and/or evidence from the texts. In doing so, they more deeply understood what they were learning as they communicated their ideas and often tried to convince others of their value.

As time progressed, children learned that it is okay to disagree with their group members in a respectful manner. This concept was difficult for many students to accept at first as they associated disagreement with poor group work. As students began to understand this notion, however, conversations became richer as children were exposed to multiple, varying perspectives. This aspect served as a catalyst for children to provide stronger rationales for their ideas as they presented them to their groups. Students became more attuned to their own thinking and styles of learning as they were regularly exposed to the thinking and learning styles of others.

As students thought metacognitively about what they were doing, they realized how their interactions impacted their group members.

The teacher also learned that students were capable of effectively scaffolding the learning of their peers. This did not happen naturally, however, and it took a lot of modeling and practice for students to reach an advanced level of scaffolding. Reflecting about these processes was critical to students' understanding how to help others learn. As students thought metacognitively about what they were doing, they realized how their interactions impacted their group members. They began to identify behaviors that fostered greater understanding as well as those behaviors that hindered group performance. For example, one student reflected that

> I learned in my group that I shouldn't just tell someone the answer if they don't understand something. Because if I do this they won't really learn and when we have to take a test they won't know what to do and they will probably get a bad grade.

Students held each other accountable for the work that was done in collaborative groups. Groups expected all members to come to literature circles prepared for the discussion. Students were really disappointed when a group member failed to complete his or her assigned task. Such expectations motivated students to complete their responsibilities as they did not want to let their peers down. The teacher reflected on this type of peer pressure in her journal.

> I noticed that Will did not adequately prepare for literature circles for about a week. It was apparent that his group was becoming frustrated with him and had started giving him a hard time about coming unprepared. However, today he did a great job preparing and his group was very complimentary towards him. I am hoping that praise from his peers can motivate him. As students head towards adolescence, such pressure from peers will become more powerful. The thing is, when he does effectively prepare, he has so many insightful ideas that add to the richness of the discussion, and his peers recognize all that he has to offer. I will continue to monitor his participation.

Will prepared more consistently over the next several weeks, and it was evident that he derived pleasure in sharing his ideas with his group.

As the teacher observed children making decisions within their groups, she gained much knowledge about each individual student. As a result, she was able to provide the necessary support that each child needed. She also more thoughtfully grouped certain children together in such a way that learning would be maximized for all students. Several students needed encouragement in expressing themselves and their ideas, however, she realized that it was important to identify and understand the reasons for the passivity of each student. Some students lacked the confidence needed to actively participate in a group discussion. Some children lacked confidence in their social skills, while other students did not possess confidence in their academic abilities. These students needed lots of encouragement from both the teacher and peers. It was important that this encouragement focused on the task or content being studied, as students can determine the sincerity of praise. Compliments also helped these students to become more confident in their social and academic competencies.

Some students were passive during group work because they truly did not understand the content that was being discussed. It was important for the teacher to provide these students with extra support both before and during collaborative learning situations. Another reason for lack of participation was that some students were simply more soft-spoken than others and were easily intimidated. She found that these students were more expressive in groups in which a dominating student was not present. These students also needed encouragement from peers.

Many students needed additional assistance in listening to others' ideas. These children had trouble focusing, and repeatedly modeling listening was beneficial. The teacher also talked to individual students about different strategies to use to help them maintain focus. In some instances, group members assisted in helping these students by developing different reminders and techniques to redirect the students when they were off task.

The teacher also made the observation that several children had difficulty accepting other students' perspectives. These students had trouble understanding that more than one answer, response, strategy or solution could exist. She often asked groups with these students to explore and discover more than one answer, response, strategy or solution. As these children began to discover more than one way for themselves, it became easier for them to accept and value multiple perspectives.

Compromising was a concept that many children truly did not understand. Many students viewed compromising as "losing the battle." The class spent a lot of time discussing how everyone is a "winner" when all members of a group compromise. Students role-played situations in which group members compromised and instances in which students did not compromise. In doing so, the children discovered for themselves the effects of compromising. As the year progressed, necessary issues were addressed to the whole class, small groups and individual students.

Through teacher research, this educator came to powerful new understandings about herself as a teacher, her students and the impact of collaborative learning on all of her students. As a result, she was able to more prescriptively plan activities for students as well as scaffold their learning during collaborative group work in both mathematics and literacy.

Learning About Students With Special Needs

The same teacher–researcher also learned a great deal about the learning needs of students with special needs. These students particularly benefited from this study as the teacher was able to more appropriately modify assignments and make accommodations so that these children did not become frustrated and might still actively participate in the group. For example, the students with special needs were given assistance while they read and prepared for literature circles. They also listened to an audiotape as another way of conveying the meaning of the story. Before the discussion, some of the questions that had been prepared by other students were shared with these students and possible responses were discussed. Consequently, students felt more confident during literature circle discussions and were able to participate more frequently.

It also became apparent to this teacher that some of the original roles that she had implemented in literature circles needed to be modified so that all students felt as though they had a valuable contribution for the group. Eric, an ESL student with special needs, had a difficult time preparing for literature circles using any one of the roles. She thought about Eric and his many strengths, including his sophisticated ability to express his thoughts and ideas through drawing. In order to provide Eric with a meaningful way to participate in literature circles, she introduced a new role to the students—that of *illustrator.* Now Eric felt he had a valuable contribution as he drew scenes which were particularly interesting or exciting to him. He became more confident as his peers complimented him over and over on his artwork. The teacher also heard students asking Eric to make drawings for them during recess and lunchtime.

The teacher found it more difficult to integrate children with special needs in problem-solving situations. In particular, John had a language difficulty that required specific instruction on a way of thinking through problem-solving activities. The teacher did attempt to include him, however, as well as other children with similar needs, in such learning situations in the beginning of the year without properly preparing them. Unfortunately, these experiences were negative for these children as they became frustrated and discouraged. After one of these experiences, the teacher reflected in her journal,

> I feel awful as John was extremely frustrated during the problem-solving activity he was working on today. Not only did he not understand the mathematical concepts embedded in the problem, but the language was also problematic for him. I can only imagine the frustration he experienced. His group was wonderful with him, and both Michelle and Ron tried to explain the problem to him through drawings. I also unsuccessfully attempted to explain the problem to him. It was simply too difficult for him, as it was too far beyond his level of understanding. From this ex-

perience, I have learned that there are going to be times in which some children are going to be unable to participate in a particular activity because of their disabilities. It is my responsibility, however, to make sure that they still feel included and part of the classroom as they work on a related activity more appropriate for their needs.

Because some of the students with special needs were at mathematics levels that were significantly lower than those of the majority of the class, these students had never been exposed to some of the concepts that were inherent in the problem-solving activities. As a result, these students were unable to participate in the class activity at times, so they worked on problems that were more appropriate to their levels of understanding. Consequently, problem solving at levels appropriate for these students' needs allowed them to reach a level of mastery with regard to particular mathematical skills more quickly than if they had been required to continue working on problems beyond their current levels of understanding.

Although some of the content in both mathematics and literacy that was discussed during collaborative learning situations was beyond the understanding of the students with special needs, collaborative learning benefited them in that they were exposed to more complex and sophisticated ways of thinking. In addition, it was important that these children were engaged in heterogeneous groups for part of the day and that these groups were structured so that these students did feel as though they had something to offer to others.

Bibliography for Teacher–Researchers

For more information on teacher research, you may want to read one or more of the following books which have been found to be particularly helpful to K–12 teacher–researchers.

Altrichter, H., Posch, P., & Somekh, B. (1993). Teachers investigate their work: An introduction to the methods of action research. London: Routledge.

Bell, J. (1987). Doing your research project. Philadelphia: Open University Press.

Bogdan, R., & Biklen, S. (1998). Qualitative research for education: An introduction to theory and methods. Needham Heights, MA: Allyn & Bacon.

Calhoun, E. F. (1994). How to use action research in the self-renewing school. Alexandria VA: ASCD.

Cochran-Smith, M., & Lytle, S. L. (1993). Inside outside: Teacher research and knowledge. New York: Teachers College Press.

Cross, K., & Steadman, M. (1996). Classroom research: Implementing the scholarship of teaching. San Francisco: Jossey-Bass Publishers.

Glesne, C., & Peshkin, A. (1992). Becoming qualitative researchers. White Plains, NY: Longman.

Greig, A., & Taylor, J. (1999). Doing research with children. London: Sage Publications.

Hopkins, D. (1992). A teacher's guide to classroom research. Buckingham: Open University Press.

Kemmis, S., & McTaggart, R. (1988). The action research planner (3rd Ed.). Victoria, Australia: Deakin University Press.

McNiff, J., Lomax, P., & Whitehead, J. (1996). You and your action research project. NY: Routledge.

Rosnow, R., & Rosenthal, R. (1997). People studying people: Artifacts and ethics in behavioral research. New York: W.H. Freeman and Company.

Sagor, R. (1992). How to conduct collaborative action research. Alexandria, VA: ASCD.

Stake, R. (1995). The art of case study research. Thousand Oaks, CA: Sage Publications.

Conclusion

Teacher research is a powerful source for generating knowledge and understanding about students and their learning in the context of the classroom. As Dewey (1929, p. 74) put it, "Each day of teaching ought to enable a teacher to revise and better in some respects the objectives aimed at in previous work." Those who engage in such reflective inquiry, are "more intelligent, more thoughtful, more aware of what they are about" (Dewey, 1929, pp. 75–76). Most importantly, inquiry leads to teaching that promotes the highest level of student growth and achievement. These professional development opportunities in classroom research should be encouraged and supported.

Through conducting teacher research in their classrooms, teachers experience the powerful nature of inquiry as they come to new understandings about themselves as teachers and about their students. Their inquiries enable them to better understand the needs of their students, and they are able to more effectively scaffold their students' learning. Teacher research allows educators to modify lessons to more appropriately meet the needs of all students. Through such studies, teachers gain a deeper understanding of the importance of their role as teachers. As such, learning about themselves as teacher–researchers blends with learning about their students. A strong link exists between student learning and teacher learning. David Hobson (1996, p. 16) concurs with this powerful connection between students and teacher when he writes

> *Teacher research allows educators to modify lessons to more appropriately meet the needs of all students.*

> We must constantly be reminded that classroom research is not just about children; it is also very much about the teacher. Long after this year's group of students moves on to the next grade or the next teacher, you will still be there—learning about teaching and examining your practice. Your research about that process extends far beyond one class in a given year. It is about you and your profession in a much larger sense.

Experiences as a teacher–researcher provide educators with invaluable insight into the teaching and learning process. The knowledge gained from such studies will serve as a guide as these endeavors are continued in the classroom.

References

Burnaford, G., Fischer, J., & Hobson, D. (1996). *Teachers doing research: Practical possibilities.* Mahwah, New Jersey: Lawrence Erlbaum Associates.

Cochran-Smith, M., & Lytle, S. L. (1993). *Inside outside: Teacher research and knowledge.* New York: Teachers College Press.

Deane, J. (2001). *The influence of collaborative learning on students' understanding of mathematics and literacy content.* Unpublished doctoral dissertation, Boston College, MA.

Dewey, J. (1929). *Sources of a science education.* New York: Liverisht.

Fierros, E. G., Gulek, C., & Wheelock, A. (1997). *Using multiple methods of assessment to promote district level reflection about instructional improvement.* Paper presented at the annual meeting of the American Educational Research Association, Chicago, Illinois.

Freire, P. (1985). *Politics of education.* South Hadley, MA: Bergin and Garvey.

Haney, W., & Russell, M. (1995). *An investigation of two kinds of assessments: Using student drawings to illuminate the educational ecology of schools and the learning and testing of students.* Unpublished paper, Boston College, MA.

Hobson, D. (1996). Beginning with the self: Using autobiography and journal writing in teacher research. In *Teachers doing research: Practical possibilities.* Mahwah, New Jersey: Lawrence Erlbaum Associates.

Lewin, K. (1948). *Resolving social conflicts.* New York: Harper.

Mohr, M. (2004). *So, what is teacher research?* Retrieved on August 19, 2004 from http://gse.gmu.edu/research/tr/TRdefinition.shtml.

Mohr, M., & McLean, M. (1987). *Working together: A guide for teacher–researchers.* Urbana, IL: National Council of Teachers of English.

Rogers, C. (1969). *Freedom to learn.* Columbus, OH: Charles Merrill.

Stenhouse, L. (1975). *An introduction to curriculum research and development.* London: Heinemann.

Wood, P. (1988, April). *Action research: A field perspective.* Paper presentation at the Annual Meeting of the Educational Research Association, New Orleans, LA.

CHAPTER

11

Teachers Professionally Developing Teachers:

Peer-Reflection Partners, Lesson Study, Peer Coaching and Peer Observation

Objectives for the Chapter

After reading the chapter, the reader will be able to

a. give a colleague the data he or she requests about his or her teaching that will better enable a partner to reflect on and improve teaching performance
b. obtain from a colleague data that will better enable the reader to improve his or her classroom performance
c. develop a plan for analyzing and solving classroom problems with a partner or team
d. assist a colleague in developing a plan for analyzing and solving classroom problems
e. improve his or her teaching by watching a colleague teach and by reflecting on how the reader's observations may be used in his or her classroom
f. explain to a colleague the value of working with a peer-reflection partner through peer observation, coaching, lesson study and/or peer facilitation.

This chapter is designed to maximize the value of reflection on our own practice and the extent to which we all are able to learn a great deal about our practice from our colleagues. In this chapter, we will discuss an effective technique for teachers to use in working with one another to develop their teaching practice. We call this teacher team *peer-reflection partners*. Another term we use in this chapter for a similar peer professional development model is *lesson study*. Later in the chapter, we will explore more deeply some techniques for effective lesson study.

Peer-Reflection Partners

Much of what has been written previously about teachers developing their practice by working with a partner has become commonly known as peer coaching. We make a distinction between peer coaching and peer-reflection partners. People often think of the coach as an older and wiser expert teaching someone with less skill and experience the skills of effective teaching. We use the terms *peer coach* and *peer-reflection partners* to identify two different peer relationships. The first, **peer coach,** describes the relationship between an experienced mentor teacher and a novice teacher (or a less skilled teacher assigned to work with a more skilled mentor). In this case, the mentor has more experience and knowledge about the district and/or the practice of teaching and serves as a coach for the newly hired teacher. We also use the term *peer coach* when a district has a specially trained group of teachers who help teachers with their guided practice of newly learned teaching strategies. These coaches typically have received significant prior training and practice and have mastered the strategies they are coaching at a higher level than the other staff members. **Peer-reflection partners** have a different type of relationship. It is the relationship that exists between two professionals of equal status who have skill levels that enable each to learn from the other.[1]

In the first chapter, we reported the research (Feistritzer, E., 1996) that indicates that teachers find structured self-reflection to be the most effective means for building teaching competency. In Chapter 10, we looked at ways we may practice structured self-reflection to improve our teaching performance. By **structured self-reflection,** we mean the process by which we ask ourselves the following questions.

1. What data do I need to determine if the lesson went well?
2. What part of the lesson does the data indicate went well?
3. Why did that part of the lesson go well?
4. How may I use that information to further improve an area of my teaching that is not going as well?
5. What part of the lesson does the data indicate did not go as well as I would have liked?
6. Why didn't that part go well?
7. What may I do differently next time to improve the lesson?
8. Who may I go to for ideas about how to do it differently the next time?

The research supports the belief that the best person to consult, in most cases, is a trained peer-reflection partner. It indicates that reflecting on our own practices and learning from one of our colleagues are together the most effective means of professional development. The reasons for this are the following:

[1]For those who wish to learn more about mentoring, we suggest reading the book *Maximizing Teaching Success* by William Ribas, available at www.ribasassociates.com or by calling 781-551-9120.

1. Teachers know teaching. We teach every day and therefore have the most current knowledge base about what works in a classroom and what does not work. This does not mean that every teacher knows the best strategy for every classroom situation. It means that we all have an enormous storehouse of knowledge about what works and what doesn't work for us in many of the hundreds of situations we confront each day in the classroom.
2. It is easier to be honest with a colleague about the areas of performance in which we are less successful than it is to discuss them with a supervisor. Of course, this is only true if we trust that our peer-reflection partner will hold as confidential what he or she learns about our teaching. It is for this reason that we recommend that schools that use peer-reflection partners as a form of professional development have a clearly articulated confidentiality statement such as the following one.

Sample District Peer-Reflection Partner Confidentiality Statement

The issue of confidentiality in the peer-reflection relationship is as sensitive as it is important. Our district seeks to create relationships based on trust between the peer-reflection partners and expects all peer-reflection partners will observe the following confidentiality requirements.

Peer-reflection partners will not discuss their partner's performance with anyone, including school and district administrators and other teachers, *except under the following conditions.*

a. The peer-reflection partner, with the partner's knowledge, may discuss the partner's performance with appropriate administrators if, in the partner's professional judgment, the physical safety or emotional well-being of the students, either reflection partner or other members of the school community are at risk.
b. If a teacher shares his or her evaluation with the peer-reflection partner, the partner will not discuss the contents of the evaluation (including either partner's agreement or disagreement with the administrator's evaluation) with anyone.
c. The reflection partner gives his or her partner unequivocal permission to talk with a specific person.

3. Our own self-reflection is more effective when we bounce our ideas off a knowledgeable partner. The act of verbalizing the classroom problem we are grappling with to our peer-reflection partner often helps us expand on partially developed ideas or see the issue more clearly.
4. Peer-reflection partners may help us look with greater depth at a classroom issue by asking questions that expand our thinking. For example, we may be frustrated by the behavior of the *entire class.* A peer-reflection partner, through skillful and patient questioning, may help us to be more objective about the problem. Our partner's questions may help us to isolate those times when the behavior is appropriate and those times when it is not. Our partner's questions may help us identify which students are behaving appropriately, which are acting out and which students are not acting out but reinforcing the others' acting out. With this information, we will be in a much better position to put a plan in place that diminishes the problem.
5. Peer-reflection partners may give us objective data that we cannot gather ourselves, either because we are *too close to the problem* or because we cannot gather the information alone. An example of a time when a peer-reflection partner may be helpful

is when we are developing a rubric for an assignment. Giving the assignment to the students and then asking our partner to assess the student's papers based solely on the information in the rubric is an excellent way of determining whether the rubric is as specific and complete as it needs to be. If another teacher is having difficulty understanding the criteria for success, then it is very likely that students will have trouble as well. The best part about this activity is that we are putting two brains on the task of making the criteria clearer.

6. The peer-reflection partner has only one goal, helping to improve his or her partner's teaching in an area in which the partner has asked for help. Supervisors often have this goal as well, however, they are also required by law to make summative judgments about teachers' performance and, ultimately, employment decisions about the teachers they supervise. For this reason, it may be difficult for us to be truly honest about our areas of weakness, even with supervisors with whom we have excellent relationships.
7. Peer-reflection partners may observe us and give us valuable data prior to, during and/or after we have implemented an intervention. It is sometimes difficult to assess for ourselves whether something is working or not working in our classrooms. Observations by our peer-reflection partners may provide us with objective second sets of eyes. We, as the teacher being observed, usually determine which data we want our partner to collect. There are times, however, when we ask our partners to observe and gather all the data with a plan for the two of us to analyze the data together. Later in this chapter, we explain the process for observing our peer-reflection partners.
8. Research indicates that higher levels of collegial interaction in a building improve teacher morale and student performance.

Peer-Reflection Partners as a Key Component in Professional Development

Earlier in this chapter, we cited research indicating that teachers find working with colleagues to be one of the most effective means for building teaching competency. Beverly Showers and Bruce Joyce (1996, March) reported that as few as 10% of the participants who attended staff development workshops implemented what they learned. Working with peer-reflection partners may dramatically increase that percentage.

For most teachers, the reason they don't implement what they learn in a workshop or course is not because they are opposed to trying something new. Rather, they are reluctant to practice on the students with a newly learned strategy that they have not yet mastered. We only get 180 days with any group of students. It is human nature to want to give our students the teaching that we know works versus something that feels uncomfortable and less effective. Let's face it; anything we first learn to do is less comfortable and less effective than those practices we have perfected. Less effective strategies that we have perfected may be better for our students than more effective strategies that we are not yet proficient at using. The presenters have had time to practice and perfect in a classroom the new strategies they are teaching us. These strategies are more effective for them than our present strategies would be because they have already perfected theirs. When we implement a strategy for the first time, it is almost inevitable that it will not work as well as what we did before. It is easy to see why teachers who learn new strategies in a workshop either don't implement them or try them once or twice and then return to their previous strategies. At the initial stage of learning a new strategy, the older strategy with which we are proficient probably is more effective. We do the wrong thing for the right reason.

We do the wrong thing for the right reason.

In the early 80s, Baker and Showers (1984) found that adding a coaching component after the training in a new strategy resulted in much greater transfer of the learning than training alone. Working with peer-reflection partners increases the likelihood that teachers will use newly learned strategies and use them effectively. Professional development works best for teachers when the following statements are true.

1. I know I don't have to do it successfully when I'm at the guided practice and immediate mastery level of learning to use a new strategy.
2. I have someone I may talk with *safely* and in confidence about what worked and what didn't worked.
3. The person I talked with understands the complexity of the classroom and may help me self-assess and generate my own plan for using the strategy more effectively the next time.
4. I have someone who may give me ideas about how to better implement the strategy with my particular students.

When a school faculty is being introduced to new teaching strategies, the professional development that typically creates the greatest level of change contains a coaching component. Figure 11-1 shows one model for effectively creating change through professional development. You will note that the steps are very similar to those described in the introduction of this book in reference to student learning. In this model, the new strategy is taught to the teachers in a workshop or course. The teachers then have an opportunity to participate in guided practice during the coaching stage. Although administrators may be coaches, it is recommended that the coaches be peer coaches, peer-reflection partners or the consultant who taught the original workshops. When administrators coach during the guided practice stage the teachers often feel considerable anxiety that they will be downgraded in their performance evaluations. At some point, it will be important for the evaluator to assess the level of mastery, however, we recommend that this occur during the assessment stage, not the guided practice stage.

Figure 11-1

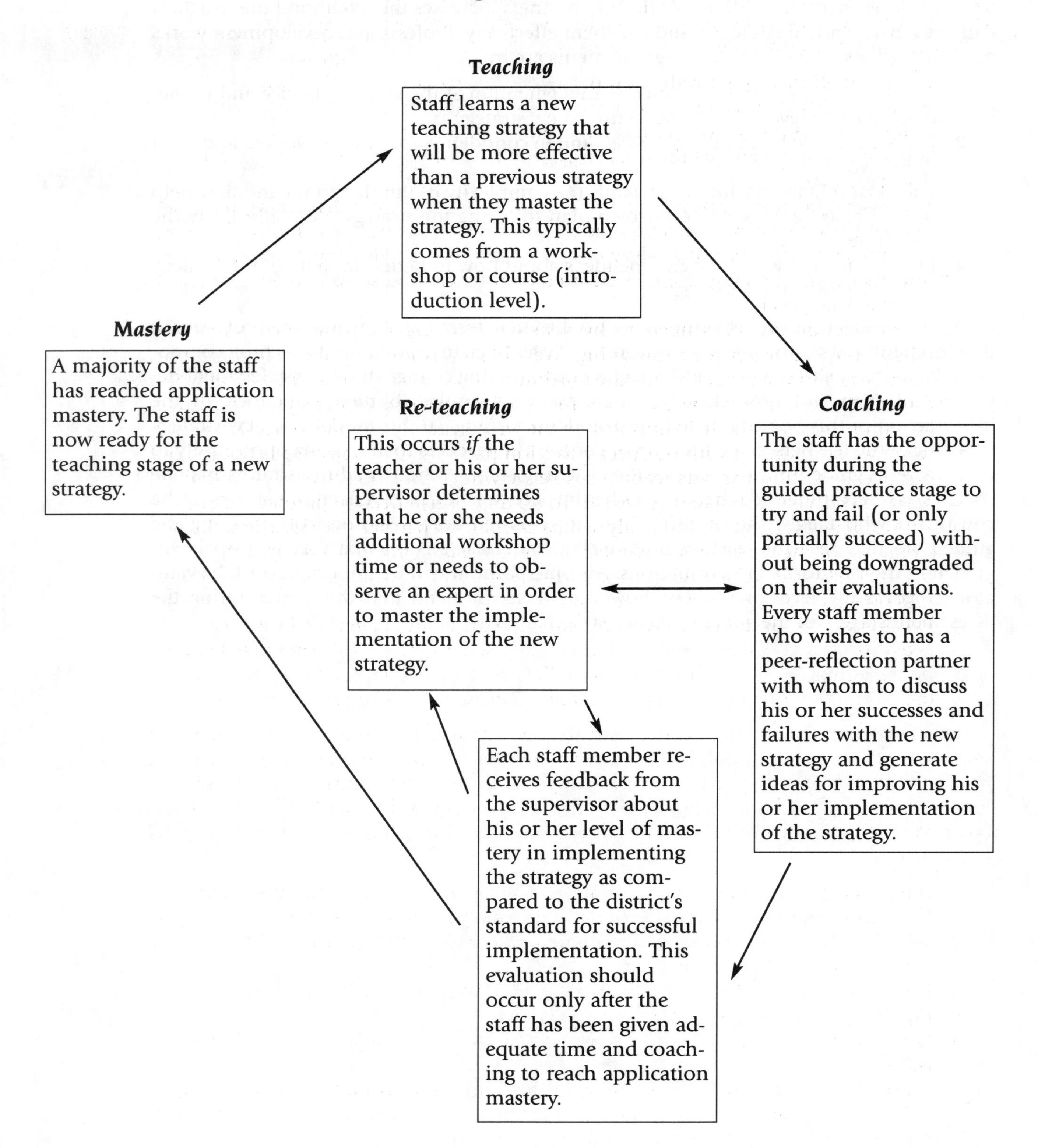
Teaching
Staff learns a new teaching strategy that will be more effective than a previous strategy when they master the strategy. This typically comes from a workshop or course (introduction level).
Coaching
The staff has the opportunity during the guided practice stage to try and fail (or only partially succeed) without being downgraded on their evaluations. Every staff member who wishes to has a peer-reflection partner with whom to discuss his or her successes and failures with the new strategy and generate ideas for improving his or her implementation of the strategy.
Each staff member receives feedback from the supervisor about his or her level of mastery in implementing the strategy as compared to the district's standard for successful implementation. This evaluation should occur only after the staff has been given adequate time and coaching to reach application mastery.
Re-teaching
This occurs if the teacher or his or her supervisor determines that he or she needs additional workshop time or needs to observe an expert in order to master the implementation of the new strategy.
Mastery
A majority of the staff has reached application mastery. The staff is now ready for the teaching stage of a new strategy.

Characteristics of Effective Peer-Reflection Partners

Effective peer-reflection partners are made, not born. There are specific skills peer-reflection partners need to assist one another with their classroom teaching.

Effective peer-reflection partners are made, not born.

1. **The most effective peer-reflection partners are successful teachers.** This doesn't mean that the teachers must have achieved awards or demonstrated an inordinate level of proficiency. It does mean that the teachers should have been evaluated as at or above the district standard.
2. **The peer-reflection partners need a common language for discussing teaching.** One of the objectives of this book is to provide teachers with a common language with which to discuss and analyze our own teaching. In this chapter, we talk about how that common language may be used by teachers to discuss and analyze teaching with one another.
3. **Peer-reflection partners need to be sensitized to the fact that there are many "right" ways to teach the same thing.** We all feel passionately about our teaching. We all teach in ways that provide the maximum success for our students. What works for us, however, may not work for another teacher given his or her style and particular group of students. It is important that we constantly remind ourselves of this when we are working with our peer-reflection partners. Our objective is not to have our peer-reflection partners teach just like we would. Our objective is to help them more effectively teach like they would. To do this, peer-reflection partners need to be able to objectively gather and analyze data about their partner's teaching and the performance of their partner's students. *This is particularly true when we gather the data through a classroom observation of our partner.* Later in this chapter, we provide examples of ways we gather and analyze data.
4. **Peer-reflection partners need to be able to conference together in a respectful, sensitive and effective manner.** As previously stated, we all feel passionately about our teaching. It is important that peer-reflection partners obtain the skills needed to discuss their partners' teaching in clear and concise yet non-threatening ways.

It is important that the second and third areas be addressed thoroughly. It is at this point that we emphasize the complexity of teaching and the estimated hundreds of decisions a teacher makes on an average day. When training teachers, we often illustrate this point with the story of the high school math class in which a student raises his hand to go to the bathroom. We talk about all the questions the teacher is asking himself or herself when the hand is first raised.

1. Is Bob the student who will be completely lost when he returns from the bathroom? If so, and I let him go, how will I catch him up and keep the rest of the class going?
2. Will Bob disrupt the other students when he comes back because he does not understand what is happening?
3. Is Bob the student who will saunter to the door, smacking his friends on the head or flipping over the pages in their notebooks?
4. Is Bob the student who will leave for twenty minutes or maybe leave school altogether?
5. Is Bob the student who will leave my room just fine but, as soon as he leaves my sight, will make faces and gestures to the students through the windows in each of the classrooms' doors between our room and the bathroom?
6. Is Bob the student who has a confidential history I know as his teacher that indicates he might vandalize the bathroom if allowed to go alone?

For the sake of making the decision easier, let's assume Bob is a student who will go straight to the bathroom, return in a timely and appropriate manner and be able to pick up the content with little difficulty. Three minutes ago, however, the teacher did not allow Sandra to go to the bathroom because her IEP indicates she might vandalize the bathroom if left unattended. None of the students have this information, so what will be their reaction if the teacher lets Bob go after saying no to Sandra?

In this scenario, the teacher is asking all these questions and making decisions based on the answers in a couple of seconds while continuing to teach mathematics concepts!

Choosing a Project

It is important that at the outset of choosing our projects we are realistic about our goals. We should endeavor to diminish the problem or increase the success. We should never aim to solve the problem. Few classroom problems can be completely eliminated. Typically the result of our plans is that the identified problems become less prevalent. Or, in the case of improving achievement, the students do better than they did prior to our interventions.

Sample Peer Coaching/Facilitation Research Projects

Example A

1. The question I need data to answer.
   The same five students answer 90% of the questions in my class. How do I get more students to answer?
2. Method of data collection
   My partner will observe my third-period class two times. I will give my partner a copy of the seating chart for the class. Each time I ask a question, my partner will put a slash on the seating chart square that represents each of the students who raises his or her hand. When I call on a student, my partner will cross the slash, creating an X. At the end of the observation, I will have accurate data on which students answer questions and which do not.
3. Method for analysis
   a. My partner and I will review the data for any likely patterns (e.g., the boys answer most of the questions, the Hispanic students answer most of the questions or the students who sit in the front of the room answer most of the questions).
   b. My partner and I will generate some suggestions for remediating the issue (e.g., using assigned seats, more wait time, calling sticks).
   c. I will implement the strategies for two weeks.
   d. My partner will come back and observe and gather data again.
   e. We will analyze the data to see if there has been a change. If so, we will discuss why the change has occurred. If not, we will discuss why it didn't occur and then try a new strategy.

Sample of a seating chart after an observation by a peer-reflection partner who is gathering data about who raised his or her hand and who was called on.

Observation 1:

White Board
Front of the Room

Door

Robert / / XX	Jamal
Maria X /	Edward
Anna X / /	

Fernando / X	William /
Cameron	Jane / / /
Catherine / / /	Mary

Irina X / /	Pedro X /
Barry /	Nicole XX
Nomar	Thomas

Theodore / /	Margarita / / /
Hamid	Tyrone
Deborah XX	

Joseph XX / / /	Jennifer
Bonita	Kimberly /
Damien	Robert /

Observation 2:

White Board
Front

Door

Tyrone /	Jamal X
Maria X /	Edward
Anna X / /	Robert X / XX /

Fernando X / /	William /
Cameron	Jane /
Catherine / X /	Mary /

Irina X	Pedro X
Barry /	Nicole X
Nomar X	

Theodore / X	Margarita / / /
Hamid	
Deborah X / /	Thomas

Joseph XX /	Jennifer
Bonita X	Kimberly /
Damien	Robert /

4. What else did you learn after studying the data from the observations?

Authors note: Examine the seating charts from observation 1 and observation 2. Answer the following questions:

1. Which students answered the most questions? What percentage of the questions did they answer? Why?
2. Which students didn't answer any questions? Why?
3. Are there any students who raised their hand but didn't get called on? Why?

Example B

1. The question I need data to answer.
2. How do I get students to take more responsibility for cleaning up and putting materials away at the end of the science laboratory periods?
3. Method of data collection
   a. My partner will observe the ending time of three science lab periods.
   b. She will keep track of the amount of time that passes from the point when I first ask students to clean up to the point when the bell rings for the end of class.
   c. She will note which students are still doing the lab after I tell them to clean up.
   d. She will note which of the students in each lab group are (or are not) doing their fair share of the cleanup.
   e. She will note what the students who are not helping are doing.
   f. She will note which of the students appear to be unaware of what they are supposed to do to clean up successfully.
   g. She will note which lab areas were clean at the end of class and which were not.
4. Method for analysis
   a. After the observations, we will meet to review the data.
   b. We will determine which students are not helping with cleanup and why they are not helping.
   c. We will create a plan for increasing those students' level of participation in the cleanup.
   d. We will see which students continue to do the lab during cleanup time and why they continue working rather than cleaning up.
   e. We will create a plan that will enable those students to begin the cleanup on time.
   f. I will implement the plan for one month.
   g. My partner will return to my classroom once again to observe and gather data.
   h. We will compare the two sets of data to determine if there has been a change. If yes, we will discuss why the change has occurred. If not, we will discuss why there wasn't any change and consider other strategies.

Example C

1. The question I need data to answer
   On most days, 25% of the students do not bring their homework in on time. How may I increase the percentage of students who bring in their homework?
2. Method for gathering data
   I will bring to our meeting two weeks of records that indicate which students bring their homework in on time and which do not.
3. Method for analysis
   a. We will categorize the students in the following way: those with all their homework completed, those missing one assignment, those missing two assignments, those missing three to five assignments, those missing more than five assignments.
   b. We will examine the students on a case-by-case basis to see what is causing each one not to bring in his or her homework.
   c. We will create a plan with the intent of reducing the percentage of students without homework to 15%.

d. We will meet again in four weeks and repeat steps a through c to determine if the behavior changed.

Example D

1. The question I need data to answer
   During times when the students are doing seatwork, how do I get them to use each other as resources rather than always needing the teacher when they get stuck?
2. Method for gathering data
   a. My partner will observe my class two times while the students are doing independent seatwork.
   b. My partner will keep track of which students need the teacher's help and what help they need.
   c. My partner will keep track of the students who get help from friends and how they do that.
3. Method for analysis
   a. We will categorize the reasons students need help into two groups. The first category is problems only the teacher may solve. The second is problems other students or other resources may solve.
   b. We will develop a plan for teaching students when they should come to the teacher, when they should go to another student and when they should access other resources.

Example E

1. The question I need data to answer
   How do I get students who master math concepts quickly to use the Problem of the Day without teacher assistance?
2. Method for gathering data
   a. My partner will observe my class two times during math.
   b. My partner will take note which students finish the seatwork and demonstrate mastery before the math period is over.
   c. My partner will note which students don't move on to the Problem of the Day and what they do instead.
   d. My partner will note which students do go to the Problem of the Day but come to the teacher for help. She will also note the reason each student came for help.
   e. My partner will note the students who start the Problem of the Day and get help from other students when they get stuck. She will note how the students go about getting that help.
3. Method for analysis
   a. We will categorize the students in the following way: those who go right to the Problem of the Day without prompting, those who go to the Problem of the Day with teacher or student prompting and those students who do not go to the Problem of the Day even with teacher or student prompting.
   b. Of the students who start to solve the Problem of the Day, which students finish alone? Which students go to another student for help when stuck? Which students come directly to the teacher when stuck? Which students give up when stuck?

c. We will examine the students on a case-by-case basis to see why some students don't ever go to the Problem of the Day. We will examine the students on a case-by-case basis to see why the students who only go to the teacher when stuck choose not to use their peers or other resources.
d. We will create a plan with the intent of reducing the number of students who don't move to the Problem of the Day, even with teacher prompting. We will create a plan with the intent of reducing the number of students who need teacher prompting to move to the Problem of the Day.
e. We will meet again in four weeks and repeat steps a through c to determine if the behavior changed.

Example F

1. The question I need data to answer
   How do I use current successful practice and research in the educational literature to increase the achievement of my African–American and Hispanic students?
2. Method for gathering data
   a. My partner and I will read the following articles:
      1. Hodgkinson, H. (2000–2001, December–January). Educational demographics: What educators should know. *Educational Leadership.*
      2. Goddard, R., Hoy, W., & Woolfolk Hoy, A. (2004, April). Collective efficacy beliefs: Theoretical developments, empirical evidence, and future directions. *Educational Researcher.*
      3. Rothstein-Fisch, C., Greenfield, M., & Trumbull, E. (1999). Bridging cultures with classroom strategies. *Educational Leadership.*
      4. Carson, B. (2004, June). A Journey from the bottom of the class to brain surgeon. *ASCD Education Update, 46*(4).
   b. We will each make a list of the following:
      1. The statements in the articles we found particularly interesting and helpful in our efforts to close the achievement gap in our classrooms.
      2. Any questions we each have related to the articles.
      3. A list of strategies for implementing the concepts learned from the article in our classrooms.
   c. We will meet and share each of our lists and answer the questions we have generated. We will each choose a strategy (or strategies) to try in our classrooms.
3. Method for analysis
   a. We will write a reflection on the strategies we tried. The reflection will include what went well and why and/or what did not go well and why?
   b. We will meet to share our reflections with one another.
   c. We will generate a list of next steps we will take to improve the achievement of our African–American and Hispanic students.

Lesson Study

Lesson study is a form of professional development that has been used in Japan for many years. In her book, *Lesson Study: A Handbook of Teacher-Led Instructional Change,* Catherine Lewis (2002, p. 1) tells us that lesson study is used throughout Japan as a primary means of professional development.

Lesson study is a process in which a team of teachers work together to perfect the planning and teaching of a lesson. It begins with one teacher's choosing a lesson that will be studied by the group. The team assists that teacher in planning the lesson or the teacher plans the lesson alone. Before the lesson is taught, the team reviews the lesson and the teacher makes any modifications the team believes will increase the success of the lesson. The team then decides which data will be helpful to gather during the lesson for analysis of its level of success in the study session that follows. Each member of the team is then assigned specific data to gather. For example, one team member may list the questions the teacher asks during the class. Another team member may track who raises his or her hand (similar to the seating plan model shown previously). A third team member may write down the names of the students who answer the questions and the answers they give.

After the lesson, the teachers analyze the data together. The data tells them which percentage of the questions were asked at recall, comprehension and higher order thinking levels. Which questions worked best in formatively assessing the students' mastery of the concepts? Which students, if any, dominated the discussion? Which students, if any, did not participate adequately? Which students seemed to master the information and skills noted in the mastery objectives and which did not?[2]

This data is then used in two ways. First, to modify the lesson for improved teaching in the future. Second, to modify the planning of upcoming lessons to make them more successful in the future.

The lesson study process is then repeated with another teacher in the team as the focus. It is important to note that the same agreement on confidentiality used for peer reflection should be used in lesson study. Those interested in learning more about lesson study may visit the web site http://www.tc.columbia.edu/lessonstudy.

The following is a typical differentiated instruction lesson. The following are the questions a lesson study group chose to examine. The teacher who designed the lesson is looking for information that will help ensure that the lesson has the right balance of whole class work, guided group work and independent work and is not only challenging but also not overwhelming for students.

Lesson study partner 1: I will track the level of on-task behavior of the class by indicating on the seating chart the beginning and ending time for any student who is exhibiting off-task behavior.

Lesson study partner 2: When the students move into their differentiated groups, I will observe the independent work of the groups at mastery to determine which students were sufficiently challenged, which students were not sufficiently challenged and which students were overwhelmed by the assigned task.

[2]See Chapter 1 for information about the process of planning lessons for mastery.

Differentiating Instruction Lesson: Language Arts Grades 2 or 3

1. **What do I want the students to know and be able to do by the end of the lesson (my mastery objectives)?**
   By the end of the lesson, students will be able to correctly give the definition of a simile and write at least three similes which describe themselves; I'm as_____ as a _____and I'm as_______ as a _____.(modeled after *Quick as a Cricket* by Audrey Wood.

2. **How will I formatively and summatively assess the students' level of mastery of these concepts?**
   a. **How will I pre-assess the students' level of knowledge? (*If you are not planning to do a mini-lesson, go directly to differentiating, which is question 3b after this pre-assessment*).**
      I will write the word *simile* on the white board. Each student will be instructed to write the word *simile* on his or her white board and to write a definition for the word *simile.* Students will hold up their white boards. I will then call on three students with correct definitions to share. I will also model similes that adhere to the *Webster's Student Dictionary* definition of *simile,* "a comparison using like or as."

   b. **How will I formatively assess after the mini-lesson to determine each student's level of mastery?**
      - I will be able to monitor their progress using the colored cups.
      - I will be able to monitor the rate at which students are moving to mastery based on their white board work. During independent work time, I will circulate around the room with the class list on a clipboard and observe the students working. I will write *i* (introductory), *g* (guided practice), *im* (immediate mastery) or *ap* (application mastery) next to each student's name.

3. **The sequence of events of the lesson**
   a. **What information and skills will I teach during the whole-class mini-lesson?**
      - I will read aloud *Quick as a Cricket* by Audrey Wood two times. This is a story which contains twenty-two captivating similes. The students will be instructed to listen for similes during the first reading. Then the students will be instructed to recall similes orally after the second reading. The purpose is for students to see and hear similes in a vividly illustrated book.
      - I will then ask students to write at least three similes about themselves on a worksheet, using this model from *Quick as a Cricket:* "I'm as quick as a cricket and I'm as slow as a snail and I'm as small as an ant." Each student has a copy of this model on his or her worksheet.
      - Students will work on the similes using their colored cups to signal that they need assistance. Only those students who have completed all three similes may give help. No student may help more than two students. Students who finish early will be instructed to write more similes using the back of the worksheet. *Quick as a Cricket* contains twenty-two similes, so students may challenge themselves to write as many as twenty-two similes.

b. **After the mini-lesson, what activity will I use with the students who are at introductory level?**
These students will come to the table area with the guided practice students for more direct teaching of the definition and more experience with similes.
What activity will I use with the students who are at introductory level?
At the table area, these students will choose two similes from *Quick as a Cricket* and write them on a white board underlining the word *as*. The students and I will then read *Quick as a Cricket* aloud and in unison. We will then make a list on chart paper of the similes that are in the book.

c. **What activity will I use with the students who are at guided practice level?**
These students will come to the table area with the introductory students for more direct teaching of the definition and more experience with similes. Then I will ask the guided practice students to guide me through some examples of similes.

d. **What activity will I use with the students who are at immediate mastery level?**
These students will write three more similes and check their work with another student at this level. If there are any errors, they will write the similes together correctly. If their similes are correct, they will move on to writing more similes. They may then illustrate their favorite similes. For further challenge, they may define *metaphor* (using a dictionary) and, using the same format, write metaphors to describe themselves.

e. **What activity will I use with the students who are at the immediate application mastery level?**
These students will write six similes and move on to the following extension: define *metaphor* and *cliche* (using a dictionary) and, using the same format, write metaphors to describe themselves (using no cliches). As an option, these students may illustrate one metaphor.

5. **What other person may assist me in planning this lesson?**
I will consult with the librarian and/or literacy specialist to see if there are additional copies of *Quick as a Cricket* by Audrey Wood as well as other picture books which contain examples of similes and metaphors.

I need dipsticking cups, worksheets, white boards, dry erase markers, the class list, a clipboard, student dictionaries, drawing paper, markers and *Quick as a Cricket* by Audrey Wood.

This lesson was developed by Deborah Mercer of the Brookline, MA, Public Schools.

Developing Thought-Provoking Lesson Study Questions

One of the best resources we may use for developing thought-provoking questions to study teaching is to convert teaching performance standards for our district into lesson study questions. For example, Appendix A contains the California Department of Education's California Standards for the Teaching Profession. In the following section, we have converted the Standard for Assessing Student Learning into potential lesson study questions.

How may I review and revise learning goals for each of my students in an effective and time-efficient manner?

Do the learning goals for my lesson reflect the key subject area concepts, skills and applications?

What other assessments may I use to determine what students know and are able to do?

Do the assessments I use reliably and validly assess what they are intended to assess?

Do the grades I give students accurately reflect what they know and are able to do?

How may I use standardized tests and other diagnostic tools to better understand the learning progress of my students?

How may I teach students to better assess their own work?

How may I better use classroom assessments to guide my planning?

How may I better communicate the results of classroom assessments to my students and their families?

Gathering Data Through Classroom Observation

There are two types of classroom observations. The first is a focused observation. During a **focused observation,** the observer is gathering very specific types of data. Focused observations may be about one or a few specifically identified areas of performance. In focused observations, the specific data to be collected is identified before the observation begins. The focused observation noted in the research examples in the peer-reflection partners section of this chapter are focused on one area for performance. The focused observation noted in the lesson study example is focused on several areas of performance.

The second type of observation is a comprehensive observation. **Comprehensive observations** gather data on the totality of the lesson. The observer gathers all the data that is available without discriminating as to what is important data and what is not. The subsequent analysis of the data leads to the identification of the areas of performance that were evident and those that were lacking in the teaching of the lesson. Most of the observations completed by teacher evaluators are comprehensive observations. Teacher coaches sometimes do focused observations and sometimes do comprehensive observations. A coach's observation would be focused if the intent of the observation is to gather data on one or a small number of areas of performance. A coach might conduct a comprehensive observation if he or she were assisting in a teacher's guided practice of a newly implemented mathematics curriculum. In this instance, the coach is trying to determine all the areas the teacher has mastered and all the areas that need reteaching or coaching.

Mentor teachers are another group that sometimes conducts comprehensive observations and at other times conducts focused observations. A teacher who is mentoring another teacher fresh out of college might complete a *comprehensive* observation early in the year to determine the new teacher's areas of strength and those areas that are most in need of remediation. The mentor and the new teacher may then jointly decide on which areas they will address first. Subsequent observations would then be *focused* on the areas identified.

Gathering Data Prior to the Observation

The primary objective when observing a peer-reflection partner or observing during lesson study is to gather data that will be helpful to the teacher in analyzing the classroom issue the teacher is trying to address. To do this best, the observer needs to have sufficient background information to observe with depth. We obtain this background data through a pre-observation conference. In that conference, the teacher gives the observer data such as that noted in the following questions. Observers find it helpful to have the teacher answer the questions and give the answers to the observing partner(s) prior to the pre-observation conference. This gives each teacher the opportunity to think about the information prior to the pre-observation conference and enables the observer(s) to ask questions during the pre-conference that add to his or her information and perspective prior to the observation. You will note that these questions are similar to those presented in Chapter one and are designed to promote mastery thinking about our teaching.

The following is information a third-grade teacher gave to her lesson study team prior to the pre-observation conference about an upcoming science lesson.

1. **What do you want the students to know and be able to do by the end of the lesson (your goals and/or mastery objectives)?**
   By the end of the unit, the students will be able to
   a. work with a partner to build a three-dimensional structure that is at least three feet tall
   b. maximize the stability of their structures using triangle braces
   c. explain verbally and in writing how they built their structures
   d. explain verbally and in writing how they used triangles to increase the stability of their structures
   e. describe various types of structures (e.g., bridges, houses, garages, office buildings, dams)
   f. work with a partner in way that ensures that the work is equally divided
   g. work with a partner in a way that ensures that both partners know the same information
   h. resolve differences with their partners equitably and amicably
   i. work with a partner in a way that does not disturb the other students in the class

2. **How will you formatively and summatively assess the extent to which the students have mastered the objectives?**
   a. I will ask students to define *stability.*
   b. I will ask students to show how to add a triangle to a structure to increase its stability.
   c. I will observe the students while they are adding triangles to their pentagon structures to increase the structure's stability.

3. **Describe the sequence of events in the lesson?**
   a. With the class sitting in a circle, I will activate the students' knowledge about structures which was taught in the previous class.

b. I will use a teacher-made exemplar to demonstrate how one may make a pentagon figure more stable using triangle supports.
c. I will ask questions that will lead the students to an understanding of how they may use triangle supports to increase the stability of their pentagon structures.
d. I will ask questions to check student understanding.
e. Students will work with a partner using straws and connectors to increase the stability of their pentagon structures.

4. **What is the classroom problem you wish to address?**
I have been frustrated by the number of students who leave the circle area not remembering what they are supposed to do when they get with their partners or groups. In some cases, as many as a third of the students need me to remind them of the instructions. What can I do to get students to remember the directions and begin to work independently after they leave the circle?

5. **What data will be most helpful to you?**
a. Write down the questions I ask to check student understanding.
b. Keep track of how many seconds I give students to process the question before I choose someone to answer it.[3]
c. Write down the names of the students who answer the questions and what they say.
d. Keep track of which students are listening during the explanation and which students are not.
e. Note what the students are doing who are not listening.
f. After I send them off to work in pairs, note which students are able to work independently and which students need my help to get started.
g. Of the students who need help, note which part of the assignment they do not understand.
h. Note how much time I spend with each pair of students who need help.

Taking Notes During the Observation

Following the pre-observation conference comes the observation. It is important that we take copious notes during the observation. The objective of a focused observation is to gather all the data that will be helpful in assessing the area(s) of performance identified for study while the objective of a comprehensive observation is to gather as much raw data as possible. It is the data that will be most helpful to our partner in addressing the identified classroom issue. *At this stage in the process, we should resist the temptation to make judgments or recommendations.* We should only be focused on getting the data. There are three important reasons why we avoid the judgments.

It is the data that will be most helpful to our partner in addressing the identified classroom issue.

1. Teaching is a very complicated activity that involves literally hundreds of decisions in the course of a day. We cannot make good judgments until we understand the reasons the teacher chose to say or do what we observed in the lesson. Since we cannot interrupt the lesson every minute to ask the teacher why he or she chose a specific strategy, we need to wait until the post-conference to ask our questions.
2. The knowledge that is most helpful is the data that will enable our partner to discover his or her own answers. The best solutions to classroom problems are those that a teacher develops through thoughtful reflection and discussion about the data an observer has gathered.

[3]For more information on *wait time* and its impact on student learning see Chapter 5.

3. If we pause to analyze what we are observing in order to make judgments during the observation, we miss much of the data that occurs during that time we are analyzing and making the judgment.

When observing, we should bring a pad and paper or a laptop computer on which to write notes. We should divide the paper into two columns as in the following example. In the right column, we should note what the students say, what the teacher says and what we refer to as "stage directions." **Stage directions** are all the data that is not spoken. They include the arrangement of the classroom furniture, information on a black or white board, wall displays, the location of the students and the location of the teacher. In the left column, we should write the time, any questions we want to ask the teacher after the observation and any notes or reminders to ourselves that we want to remember after the observation. Some note-takers prefer to put the stage directions in the left column as well. We see that as a matter of personal preference and either is correct.

We track the time because it may be useful to the teacher to know at what point a specific incident occurred in a lesson or to know how long it took to complete a certain part of the lesson. In the following notes, we see that the time used to give the explanation before the students transitioned to partner work was approximately four minutes. When we are doing the teaching, we often lose track of the time. It is hard to gauge how long each part of the lesson took to teach. Keeping track of the time is also helpful in determining the time on task of certain students. We suggest that the observer note the time at least every five minutes and more frequently during transitions.

We write down our questions and personal notes so we don't forget them. A class moves very quickly and there is so much to note that a thought we have in the first three minutes of the class is typically long forgotten five minutes later.

Videotaping

It takes a great deal of practice to get comprehensive notes. It is for this reason that some peer-reflection partners and lesson study teams choose to videotape rather than take handwritten notes. The advantage to videotaping is that you can get everything the teacher says. The disadvantage to videotaping is that the camera often does not clearly pick up the students' comments. The camera is also limited in what can be seen as it is following the teacher. It misses those things our human peripheral vision can observe, such as what the students who are not next to the teacher are doing, the displays on the walls and other important data. It also takes good equipment and practice to videotape a classroom in a way that yields the maximum amount of information.

The ideal situation for peer partners is to have a third party videotape while the partner takes two-column notes. With lesson study teams, it is often possible to have one team member videotape while the others take notes. When we make our training videos, we use a camera person experienced in classroom videotaping while one of us takes notes of the data that is not picked up by the camera. Using a camera person is probably not an option for most peer-reflection partners, therefore focused note-taking is the best alternative.

The following sample is a script of the first four minutes of the lesson that corresponds to the previous pre-observation conference information. It resulted from a single note-taker and a second person videotaping the lesson. Following the script is a rubric that shows the stages of development that notetakers pass through in building their competence to take copious literal notes. The rubric is followed by three sets of notes taken of the same classroom by notetakers at different levels of development.

3RD GRADE	SCIENCE: STRUCTURES
	The students are seated in a circle. Some are seated on the floor and others are seated in chairs. The teacher is seated in the circle on a chair. Written on a poster on the wall is the definition for stability. 20 students
1:10	Teacher: What I wanted to start with was, last week, we'd started with the word stable. Can you see that this shape is not stable? Does anyone remember the definition that we gave of stability? We did it with a structure, what was it? *Wait time< 1 second*
	Student: We said that squares aren't as stable as triangles.
Cody answers at least 25% of the questions. Does he always answer most of the questions?	Teacher: Okay, we're going to get to that, and that's a good point. Remember the test for stability? If you were to push it, it needed to come back to its original position. And certainly with this, if that's the original position, if we were to push it, did that return to its original shape? *Wait time< 1 second*
	Students: No.
	Teacher: So that's why we say this is not stable. Now, one thing we did yesterday was we took a triangle and a square, and we added washers to it. Can somebody raise their hand and share what we learned from that, so that Chris will know what we did yesterday? *Wait time< 1 second*
	Sam: We said that the square wasn't as stable as a triangle.
	Teacher: Yes, and we said it wasn't as strong or stable. And how many washers did the square hold? *Wait time< 1 second*
	Cody: 23
	Sarah: Yes, I can see that you're looking up there, and we did record it up there. And of course, how many washers did the triangle hold, everybody? *Wait time< 1 second*
	Students: 110.
What would happen if you waited three to five seconds after answering a question before you called on a student to answer?	Teacher: Yes, so one of the things we learned yesterday was the triangle was really a strong shape. All right, let's see what Emma's done. She took a pentagon, pent meaning 5, this is a 5-sided shape that wasn't very stable, and look at the straws that Emma has added to this, okay. Now let's do some stability tests on this. We're pushing in, and is it returning to its original shape? *Wait time< 1 second*
	Students: Yes.
	Teacher: So she's added some straws to make it more stable. Do we see some shapes in here? What shapes do you see? *Wait time< 1 second*
	Sam: A triangle.
	Teacher: Yes, we see our triangles, and of course, what did we learn about triangles? Triangles are strong. Now, we do have another shape down here. Now do you think maybe if you were going to add a straw, where would you add your next straw to make this just a little bit more stable? Do you have an idea? *Wait time< 1 second*
	Student: The bottom.
1:14 How many of the students	Teacher: Yes, and in fact, if you did that, we'll just use this straw as a demonstration. If she added one here, what is the shape you would see? *Wait time< 1 second* The triangle, right? So today,

understood the concept of using triangles to increase stability before you sent them back to stabilize their pentagons?	what we're going to do is, you're going to keep building with your shapes, your structures, building up, and I want you to think about the using the information we learned about triangles. Think about how to make things more stable, and keep building up.
	The students move to different parts of the room with their partners. They all know their partners and get in their partners quickly. The materials are all set out at each of the ten locations.
1:17	*At this point four of the groups have their hands raised looking for help. Six of the groups appear to be working. Sam and Cody's groups are working. The teacher moves to the first group….*

Rubric to Assess the Development of Your Note-Taking Skills

Novice	*Emerging*	*Proficient*
Your notes contain sporadic words and short statements that do not make sense to you when you go back and read them 24 hours after the observation.	Your notes are becoming more comprehensive and complete. They make some sense to you when you go back and read them 24 hours later. You still have some questions about the notes based on insufficient note-taking.	When you start your observation write-up (after the post-conference) your notes make sense to you and you have adequate data to support your claims.
You experience very high frustration because you either write notes and miss what is happening or you watch what is happening and miss some notes.	You experience high to moderate frustration because you either write and miss some of what is happening or watch what is happening and miss some notes.	You experience a small and decreasing amount of frustration caused by your either writing and missing what is happening or watching what is happening and missing some notes.
Your notes are primarily observer narrative. The quotes are limited to single words or short phrases that don't make sense when you go back and read them 24 hours later.	Your notes include most of the quotes from the teacher in a form that makes sense when you go back and read them 24 hours later. Observer narrative is less than 40% of the notes. Notes contain some student quotes. Your notes begin to note the arrangement of the room and the displays on the walls.	Your notes include most of the important quotes from the teacher and the students. Your observer narrative is reduced to brief *stage directions* such as a description of the teacher's location in the classroom. You have noted the arrangement of the room and most of the displays on the walls.
After analyzing the notes, you correctly label some claims with terms from common language. You do not have sufficient evidence to support all of the claims you have made.	After analyzing your notes 50% of the notes are labeled correctly with terms from the educational research and practice. The rest of the notes are labeled correctly with common language. You have sufficient evidence to support most of the claims you have made. Some of your claims are still too broad and need greater specificity of the components of the claim.	After analyzing your notes 80% or more of the notes are labeled correctly with specific terms from educational research and practice. For example, if it's momentum the label should tell the teacher whether it is provisioning, a filler, subdividing, managing intrusions, etc. You have sufficient evidence to support all of your claims.

Your notes do not contain time notations.	Your notes contain time notations at least every 10 minutes.	Your notes contain time notations at least every 5 minutes and at critical times (e.g., the beginning and the end of transitions, the time it takes to get the learning started at the beginning of the class).
After your initial analysis, there are at least 2 non-judgmental questions to ask the teacher at the post-conference. Immediately after the observation, more than three judgments are in the labels or notes.	After your initial analysis, there are at least 4 non-judgmental questions to ask the teacher at the post-conference. Immediately after the observation, three or fewer judgments are in the labels or the notes.	After your initial analysis, there are more than 4 non-judgmental questions to ask the teacher during the post-conference. Immediately after the observation, no judgments are in the labels or the notes.
Your labels and the teacher's answers to the post-conference questions are in the same color as your original notes.	Your labels are in the same color but the teacher's answers to the post-conference questions and other data are in a second color.	Your labels are in a second color and the information from pre-conference, post-conference and other sources of data are in a third color (or on another sheet)
Your data and labels primarily address classroom management, routines and/or teacher preparation.	Your data and labels primarily address classroom management, routines, teacher preparation and the teacher and student activities.	Your data and labels address classroom management, classroom routines, teacher preparation, the teacher and student activities, the class objectives (as stated by the teacher during the observation or one of the conferences), evidence of assessment of student learning as it relates to the classroom objectives, the teacher's beliefs related to the students' ability to meet those objectives and evidence of other important contributions to student achievement.

The following are three sets of notes from a *comprehensive observation* taken by observers at varying stages in their note-taking development. You will notice that, in the places where the notetaker missed a part of the dialogue, he or she placed three dots to indicate that some information was missing. The note-taking process is typically quite frustrating for the novice, however, as you get more practice, you will see the quality of your notes improve. The following are some tricks notetakers use to get the most comprehensive notes.

1. Avoid analysis while observing. Analysis takes up intellectual time and energy that you need to devote to getting the most accurate notes.
2. Use lulls in the lesson, such as quiet student work time, to fill in the missing notes. Your brain works faster than your hand and you often have more data still in your brain than you have down on paper.
3. Don't be afraid to get up and move to be able to hear or see something that is taking place in a part of the room that is away from you.
4. Arrive five minutes early and take down information such as the arrangement of the furniture and the wall and blackboard displays.
5. If you are gathering data about questioning practice or student behavior, bring a seating plan of the classroom with the students' names already written into each seat area.
6. Stay in the class for five or ten minutes after the lesson is over and fill in the information that is in your head but is not yet on the paper.
7. Give your partner a copy of your notes so that he or she may fill in any information you missed but that he or she remembers.

Novice to emerging	Sixth grade
Believe strongly Think creatively Posted student work on three bulletin boards Terrarium Colorful room	
9:27	Students enter and go directly to their seats.
9:30 What are they writing in the notebooks at the start of the class	Students are seated quietly while T waits quietly at the front of the room T Who is coming tomorrow ..... After today's class you will have questions to ask Teacher reviews written agenda on the easel in the front. T take out last night's homework please ... T What is the first think you have to do tomorrow S

Check to see what is on the chart paper.	T good for you.. T… S. T… S.. T Are you noticing a patter here. …. As students answer T writes something on the chart paper. T…… S…. T in you demons list you have just the worked…. ….. T What are the two assignment s we have for … Good T What are we doing next? S choral KWL Let's refresh our memories on what we did yesterday. S.. After we did… S T Why are we doing this? …… T we are building background on Why are we building background. Who is coming to-morrow? S choral ……
	T………… S…. T…. S chorally: four years T good for you What are the dates for WWII S 1939 to … T…. S…. T… S… T who was president during WWI S Franklin Roosevelt T.. S…
9:40	T: What made the depression. What was going on in our country that caused the great depression. S the stock market crashed T exactly S… T… S…

	T… S… T what was going on in Germany at that tme that they elected Aldolph Hitler. S….. T Exactly T What else do you remember …. S… T that was all part of a plan that we call what..It begins with H S the holocaust T.. S…. T….
9:43	T You are going to fill out your KWL chart right now. …. S….. T…. T what does KWL stand for everybody? S Choral T you will have about five minutes to fill inytour KWL chart….. Studdents work quietly at their desks comleting the KWL charts T most of you know this.This is just to refresh you memory. Teacher circulates around the room giving assistance where needed. Student raises his hand and T gives assigstance. T tomorrow when ? is her you will … T Now you have the information you need to start to develop what S the questions. Teacher has individually assisted five students. **Is there a beak in the video before the questioning**
	T who was a perpetrator in WWII? S… T Who was a bystander in WWII S… T.. S..
9:48	T What is nationalism/ S… T key word her is extreme Sasks a questions You are correct. You are just doing the k on the chart.
9:49	Claps hands to get attendtion

Emerging to Proficient	sixth grade
Think creatively Posted student work on three bulletin boards Terrarium Go back and read what is on the walls Colorful room	***The desks are arranged in tables.***
9:27	Students enter and go directly to their seats.
9:30 What are they writing in the notebooks at the start of the class Agenda Find Demons HW check Review WWII Background KWL … … Check to see what is on the chart paper.	Students enter and are seated quietly while T waits quietly at the front of the room Students are writing in a notebook. Teacher circulates around the room and checks student work. T Who is coming tomorrow? S Jack Lowenstein T and where is he coming from S.. T Good for you. T Let's go over the homework T prepare two thoughtful questions. Prepare the questions for who? S.. T… S… T After today's classs you will have questions to ask S.. T Question about the homework? Are you sure? Teacher reviews written agenda on the easel in the front. T take out last night's homework pelase … T What is the first thing you have to do tomorrow S .. T good for you.. T… S… T… S..

	T Are you noticing a pattern here. .... As students answer T writes something on the chart paper. T...... S.... T in your demons list you have just the worked.... T on your demons list I want you to put contract w/... ..... T What are the two assignment s we have for ... S.. T Good T What are we doing next? S choral KWL T Let's refresh our memories on what we did yesterday. What did we do yesterday, Jennifer S.. T so you wrote you facts on big blue index cards. After we did... What did we do after that? S T Right, we wrote our facts on the ... paper T Why are we doing this? Jack S... T Right. we are building background on T Why are we building background. Who is coming to-morrow? S choral ......Jack Lowenstein
	T............ S.... T Let's see what we can remember from yesterday S T No, I will ask the questions and your provide the an-swers S chorally four years T good for you What are the dates for WWII S 1939 to1945 T Right 1939 to1945 S.... T... S... T who was president during WWI Jillian S Franklin Roosevelt T..Excellent, what year was he elected president S...
9:40	T What made the depression. What was going on in our country that caused the great depression. S the stock market crashed T exactly S...

	T… S… T Who was elected to office in Germany in 1933 S Adolph Hitler T Why did the German people elect Adolph Hitler S The wanted him to help them with their depression. T.. S.. T what was going on in Germany at that tme that they elected Aldolph Hitler. S….. T Exactly, They were having a depression too T What else do you remember …. S… T What other facts can we remember from yesterday's conversation S T correct, He had a lot of people killed. T that was all part of a plan that we call what..It begins with H S the holocaust T.. S…. T….
9:43	T You are going to fill out your KWL chart right now. …. S….. T…. T what does KWL stand for everybody? S Choral T you will have about five minutes to fill inytour KWL chart….. Studdents work quietly at their desks comleting the KWL charts T most of you know this.This is just to refresh you memory. Teacher circulates around the room giving assistance where needed. Student raises his hand and T gives assigstance. T tomorrow when ? is her you will … T Now you have the information you need to start to develop what S the questions. Teacher has individually assisted five students. **Is there a beak in the video before the questioning**
Words Kill Believe Strongly Think Creatively Write passionately	T who was a perpetrator in WWII? S… T Who was a bystander in WWII? S… T…

9:48	T What is nationalism/ S… T key word her is extreme S asks a questions You are correct. You are just doing the k on the chart.
9:49	Claps hands to get attention

Proficient	sixth grade
Never doubt that a small group of committed thoughtful citizens can change the world Posted student work on three bulletin boards Terrarium Go back and read what is on the walls Colorful room	***The desks are arranged in tables of 4 students.***
9:27	Students enter and go directly to their seats.
9:30 Whata are they writing in the notebooks at the start of the class? Agenda Find Demons HW check Review WWII Background KWL In Lamb prepare 2 thoughtful questions for …	Students enter and are seated quietly while T waits quietly at the front of the room Students are writing in a notebook. Teacher circulates around the room and checks student work. T Who is coming tomorrow? S Jack Lowenstein T and where is he coming from S ….. T Good for you. T Let's go over the homework . to make sure everyone understands the first bullet. T prepare two thoughtful questions. Prepare the questions for who? S.. T…What is Thurday nights homework? S… T After today's classs you will have questions to ask S T Question about the homework? Are you sure?

	Teacher reviews written agenda on the easel in the front. T take out last night's homework please ... T What is the first thing you have to do tomorrow S T good for you.. T... S. T... S.. T Are you noticing a pattern here. .... As students answer T writes something on the chart paper. T What is the first thing we have to do S syllabicate T in your demons list you have just the worked.... T what is the demon in surround S double r T on your demons list I want you to put contract w/... ... T What is the demon in teacher S ea T right, the demon is the ea T What is the demon in tear S... T What are the two assignment s we have for ... S.. T Good T Next terrible David syllabicate first T What is the Demon S double r T... S... T What are out two assignments with the demon lists S... T What are we doing next? S choral KWL T Let's refresh our memories on what we did yesterday. What did we do yesterday, Jennifer S.. T so you wrote you facts on big blue index cards. After we did... What did we do after that? S

	T Right, we wrote our facts on the white paper T Why are we doing this? Jack Jack we need to build background T Right. we are building background on T Why are we building background. Who is coming to-morrow? S choral ......Jack Lowenstein
9:37	T he is going to discuss causes of WWI and WWII. S.... T Let's see what we can remember from yesterday T all right three hands raised over there S T No, I will ask the questions and your provide the an-swers. What are the .. for WWI T how long did that take S chorally four years T good for you T What are the dates for WWII S 1939 to1945 T Right 1939 to1945 S.... T... S... T who was president during WWII Jillian S Franklin Roosevelt T..Excellent, what year was he elected president S 1932
9:40	T Excellent and what was going on in 1932 S the great deprssion T Who was elected to office in Germany in 1933 S Adolph Hitler T Why did the German people elect Adolph Hitler S The wanted him to help them with their depression. T What made the depression. What was going on in our country that caused the great depression. S the stock market crashed T exactly S... T...What year did the stock market crash. Look it is right up there S... T actually it was 1929 T.. S.. T what was going on in Germany at that tme that they elected Aldolph Hitler. S..... T Exactly, They were having a depression too T What else do you remember ....

	S… T What other facts can we remember from yesterday's conversation S T correct, He had a lot of people killed. T that was all part of a plan that we call what..It begins with H S the holocaust T..it was all part of the holocaust. You guys did really well. What Stacey S…. T…. S… T good for you S T..
9:43	T You are going to fill out your KWL chart right now. Title it. I will put the title on the board. I bet you can almost figure out for yourself what it is going to be. …. S….. T I want you to have as complete a K as you can. T what does KWL stand for everybody? S Choral T you will have about five minutes to fill inytour KWL chart….. Students work quietly at their desks comleting the KWL charts T most of you know this.This is just to refresh you memory. T today you are just filling out the K Teacher circulates around the room giving assistance where needed. Student raises his hand and T gives assigstance. T tomorrow when ? is here you will fill out the W and L T Now you have the information you need to start to develop what S the questions. Teacher has individually assisted five students. ***T now you have some factual information. You need to what*** S ask the questions T right, you need to ask the questions
9:47 Words Kill Believe Strongly Think Creatively Write passionately	T who was a perpetrator in WWII? S Italy T Italy was a perpetrator, Japan was a perpetrator T Who was a bystander in WWII? S America T We were a bystander until when S Pearl harbor

	T We talked a bit about the definition of holocaust. What is the definition S Choral response ....
9:48	T What is nationalism/ S... T key word her is extreme S asks a questions You are correct. You are just doing the k on the chart. T do you have everything you need on your KWL S... T no, you are absolutely right you are just doing the K
9:49	Claps hands to get attention

Analyzing Your Notes Prior to the Post-Conference

The next stage of the process is to analyze our notes in preparation for the post-conference. As mentioned previously, it is good to have our partner fill in any missed data prior to our analysis. During the analysis, we read through our notes with the objective of identifying the data that will address the issue and specific question our partner raised in the pre-observation conference. We also want to write down any questions we want to ask our partner in the post-conference.

The Post-Conference

Asking good questions during post-observation discussions may be much more helpful to our partner than giving advice or making judgments. We should seek to ask thought-provoking questions rather than judgmental questions. For example, a focused observer of a high school social studies class was examining the teacher's concern that the answers students gave during question and answer times were one- or two-word answers. He wanted the students to give more thoughtful and comprehensive answers. The data indicated that the teacher asked eleven recall questions, five comprehension questions and one higher order thinking question.[4] If the observer started the post-conference with a judgmental question he might have asked the following: "You only asked one higher order thinking question? Why didn't you ask more?"

A more thought-provoking way to ask the question would be the following:

> "My notes show you asked the following questions and they received the following answers from students (show the teacher the observer's literal notes). Which of your questions resulted in the level of thinking you were looking to get from the students? Which questions resulted in inadequate answers?"

With this type of questioning, a teacher may make an in-depth analysis of his or her own practice and generate solutions for improvement. The observer may also learn more about the thinking behind the teacher's classroom decisions. For example, the teacher might conclude that he or she needs to ask more higher order thinking questions. Or, he or she might conclude that the recall questions asked at the beginning of the lesson were needed for the students to have the foundation information needed to answer the com-

[4] For more information on the types of questions read Chapter 5.

prehension and higher order thinking questions asked later in the lesson. The actual conclusion might be that the questions asked in this lesson were correct but that, in the next lesson, the teacher should quickly activate the learning from the previous class and move right into asking higher order thinking questions.

If the best course of action were the latter, then asking the judgment question may have denied the teacher data that was truly needed to improve his instruction.

Conclusion

For the reasons discussed earlier, teachers are the best people to help teachers become more effective practitioners. Thoughtfully planned peer-facilitated professional development improves teaching practice and increases collegiality. The result is high student achievement and higher levels of teacher morale.

Appendix A: California Standards for the Teaching Profession

STANDARD FOR ASSESSING STUDENT LEARNING

Teachers establish and clearly communicate learning goals for all students. Teachers collect information about student performance from a variety of sources. Teachers involve all students in assessing their own learning. Teachers use information from a variety of ongoing assessments to plan and adjust learning opportunities that promote academic achievement and personal growth for all students. Teachers exchange information about student learning with students, families, and support personnel in ways that improve understanding and encourage further academic progress.

Key Element: Establishing and communicating learning goals for all students.

As teachers develop, they may ask, "How do I . . ." or "Why do I . . ."

- use subject matter standards from district, state, and other sources to guide how I establish learning goals for each student?
- involve all students and families in establishing goals for learning?
- review and revise learning goals with every student over time?
- ensure that student learning goals reflect the key subject matter concepts, skills, and applications?
- ensure that goals for learning are appropriate to my students' development, language acquisition, or other special needs?
- ensure that my grading system reflects goals for student learning?
- work with other educators to establish learning goals and assessment tools that promote student learning?

Key Element: Collecting and using multiple sources of information to assess student learning.

As teachers develop, they may ask, "How do I . . ." or "Why do I . . ."

- use a variety of assessments to determine what students know and are able to do?
- select, design, and use assessment tools appropriate to what is being assessed?
- know that the assessment tools I use are matched to and support my goals for student learning?
- collect, select, and reflect upon evidence of student learning?
- work with families to gather information about all students and their learning?
- ensure that my grades are based on multiple sources of information?
- assess my students to support learning goals, district standards, and family expectations?
- use standardized tests, diagnostic tools, and developmental assessments to understand student progress?
- use a range of assessment strategies to implement and monitor individualized student learning goals (including IEP goals)?

Key Element: Involving and guiding all students in assessing their own learning.

As teachers develop, they may ask, "How do I . ." or "Why do I . . ."

- make assessment integral to the learning process?
- model assessment strategies for all students?
- develop and use tools and guidelines that help all students assess their own work?
- help all students to build their skills in self-reflection?
- provide opportunities for all students to engage in peer discussion of their work?
- help all students to understand and monitor their own learning goals?
- provide opportunities for all students to demonstrate and reflect on their learning inside and outside of the classroom?

Key Element: Using the results of assessments to guide instruction.

As teachers develop, they may ask, 'How do I . . ." or "Why do I . . ."

- use assessment to guide my planning?
- use informal assessments of student learning to adjust instruction while teaching?
- use assessment data to plan more effective ways of teaching subject matter concepts and processes?
- use assessment information to determine when and how to revisit content that has been taught?
- use assessment data to meet students' individual needs?
- use assessment results to plan instruction to support students' individual educational plans (IEP)?

Key Element: Communicating with students, families, and other audiences about student progress.

As teachers develop, they may ask, 'How do I . . ." or "Why do I . . ."

- provide all students with information about their progress as they engage in learning activities?
- provide opportunities for all students to share their progress with others?
- communicate learning goals to all students and their families?
- initiate and maintain regular contact with families and resource providers about student progress?
- communicate the results of assessments with my students and their families?
- involve families as partners in the assessment process.

References

Baker, R.G., & Showers, B. (1984, month). *The effects of a coaching strategy on teacher's transfer of training to classroom practice: A six-month follow-up study.* Paper presented at the annual meeting of the American Educational Research Association, New Orleans, LA.

California Department of Education and the California Commission on Teacher Credentialing, (1997, January). *California standards for the teaching profession.*

Feistritzer, E. (1996, p. 23). *Profiles of teachers in the U. S.* National Center of Education Information Report.

Joyce, B., & Showers, B. (1980). Improving in-service training: The messages of research. *Educational Leadership, 37*(5), 379–385.

Joyce, B., & Showers, B. (1996, March). The Evolution of Peer Coaching. *Educational Leadership.*

Lewis, C. (2002). *Lesson study: A handbook of teacher-led instructional change.* Philadelphia, PA: Research for Better Schools Inc.